TO BOLDLY GO

Leadership, Strategy, and Conflict in the
21st Century and Beyond

Edited By
JONATHAN KLUG AND STEVEN LEONARD

CASEMATE
Philadelphia & Oxford

Published in the United States of America and Great Britain in 2021 by
CASEMATE PUBLISHERS
1950 Lawrence Road, Havertown, PA 19083, USA
and
The Old Music Hall, 106–108 Cowley Road, Oxford OX4 1JE, UK

Hardback Edition: ISBN 978-1-63624-062-6
Digital Edition: ISBN 978-1-63624-063-3

A CIP record for this book is available from the British Library

Printed and bound in the United States of America by Integrated Books International

Typeset by Lapiz Digital Services

For a complete list of Casemate titles, please contact:

CASEMATE PUBLISHERS (US)
Telephone (610) 853-9131
Fax (610) 853-9146
Email: casemate@casematepublishers.com
www.casematepublishers.com

CASEMATE PUBLISHERS (UK)
Telephone (01865) 241249
Email: casemate-uk@casematepublishers.co.uk
www.casematepublishers.co.uk

Contents

PART III: THE PRIME DIRECTIVE

PART IV: THE WAR OF THE WORLDS

Foreword

Major General Mick Ryan

Science fiction is my comfort food. It has been for as long as I can remember.

For thirty plus years, it has made up one of the "big four" pillars of my professional reading, in addition to military history, contemporary military, and political affairs, and technological developments. Asimov and Herbert were early staples. More recently, John Scalzi, Linda Nagata, and Martha Wells have become regulars in my science fiction reading.

For me, science fiction provides a telescope to the future, a mechanism to think about future challenges and developing different ways of fighting and organizing military institutions that are barely comprehensible with current technologies. It allows us to ask, "What if?"

Historian Bruce Hoffman wrote that science fiction is the major non-realistic mode of imaginative fiction of our epoch. It lies between fantasy (the realm of the impossible) and fiction (the domain of the possible). The genre's history stretches back to antiquity, where stories of early Greek civilization featured superhuman beings living on Mount Olympus. Later, a Japanese story called, *The Tale of the Bamboo Cutter*, described a princess who descended from the moon to the earth and later returned to the moon.

It was not until the Age of Reason that what we recognize now as science fiction appeared. Two of the earliest science fiction stories, Johannes Kepler's *Somnium* (1634) and Francis Godwin's *The Man in the Moone* (1638), were tales of traveling to the moon. But perhaps the best known—and the actual start point for modern science fiction—was Mary Shelley's *Frankenstein* (1818). The story of young Doctor Victor Frankenstein, who created intelligent life from human body parts, was a cautionary tale of mankind attempting to play god in an era of new technological developments. Shelley followed this book with another remarkable novel, *The Last Man*, which imagined the last remaining human wandering the earth in the year 2100.

As science fiction uses futures as the context for its stories, the genre has a deep pedigree in examining various themes in human conflict. Whether it is the nature of strategy or strategic competition in *Dune* or *The Expanse*, the perils of colonization in *Avatar*, the ethical dilemmas of technology in *I, Robot* and the more recent *Murderbot* series, or the essentials of leadership in *The Lost Fleet* or *Old Man's War*, there are many insights we might gain for contemporary military organizations.

Science fiction can be traced back to Assyrian rhetorician Lucian writing about interplanetary warfare in his satire *True History*. But it was the technological marvels of the first industrial revolution, particularly their application to warfare, that saw the birth of modern science fiction. In the late 1860s, George Chesney, an officer in the British Army's Royal Engineers, became concerned over the poor state of the British Army. After not achieving government action through letters that raised his concerns, he authored a fictional story that highlighted shortfalls in the defense of Britain. *The Battle of Dorking* described an invasion of Britain by a "German-speaking" nation that he called "The Enemy."

Featuring a narrative provided by a British volunteer, the story also included the convenient absence of the Royal Navy as well as a well-prepared invasion force that had advantages in intelligence, logistics, training, and leadership.[1] The story, published in 1871 in the wake of Prussia's victory in the Franco-Prussian War, was a sensation. It quickly sold over 80,000 copies and sparked a national debate on Britain's defenses.[2] *The Battle of Dorking* was the start of the modern future war genre, which has since featured both fiction and non-fiction accounts of future conflict. A foundation for future military science fiction stories, it kick-started the "invasion literature" genre, the best known of which is H. G. Wells's 1898 novel, *The War of the Worlds*.[3]

Originally serialized in 1897 by *Pearson's Magazine* in England and *Cosmopolitan* in the United States, Wells's story is important for several reasons. It is one of the first novels that explores conflict between humans and aliens. It is one of the first modern-era science fiction stories; its themes have pervaded science fiction over the past 120 years. *The War of the Worlds* is also important as an exploration of conflict with "the other." The majority of European and American future war literature dealt with adversaries that were familiar—similar ways of fighting, similar weapons, and similar ways of thinking about warfare. Wells shuns this approach by instead having its protagonist facing off against an entirely new enemy—its weapons and tactics, its strengths and weaknesses, were unknown to the human defenders.

The War of the Worlds also contained themes that would manifest in the wars of the first half of the 20th century. Wells's vision of total war—destruction without moral limitations—emerged in World War II. The widespread death and urban destruction in *The War of the Worlds* became reality for London, Dresden, Berlin, Tokyo, and many other cities. Wells also focused on Martian destruction of key infrastructure. For example, the aliens concentrated on the destruction of British railways and telegraph lines during their invasion, which foreshadowed the Allies' focus on German infrastructure during World War II.

Another important aspect of the book, relevant to future warfare, is the use of biological weapons. The English use of biological warfare to defeat the Martians presaged large-scale bio-warfare efforts by the Soviets, British, Japanese, and Americans in the 20th century. Finally, the book introduced the notion of a global threat. As Wells writes in the book's epilogue: "Whether we expect another invasion or not, our views of the human future must be greatly modified by these events. We have learned now that we cannot regard this planet as being fenced in and a secure abiding place for Man."[4] This theme re-emerged in the 1950s as the nuclear threat to human existence and was present throughout the Cold War.

Recently, military institutions have discovered the benefits of reading science fiction. The best science fiction uses advanced technology and the future as the foundation for excellent storytelling, and those stories often have lessons for contemporary military professionals. The genre features on many reading lists for senior officers and military institutions. It can be an intellectually nourishing experience for the military professional. In the past decade, service leaders such as the Commandant of the United States Marine Corps (2019) and the Chief of the Australian Army (2019) have included science fiction on their professional reading lists. The Marine Corps has even taken this a step further with their publication of the *Destination Unknown* series of graphic novels, with Marine authors writing about future war.

There are other examples of military institutions using science fiction in their strategic planning and thinking. In the wake of the September 11 attacks on New York and Washington, DC, the United States military very quietly hired Hollywood directors and writers to "think differently about future threats." Hoping to predict different kinds of threats in the 21st century, around two dozen Hollywood writers and directors were secretly commissioned to imagine different scenarios that might endanger the United States.[5] Not long afterwards, the Canadian Defence Force commissioned science fiction author Karl Schroeder to write the novella *Crisis in Zefra* to "illustrate emerging concepts and technologies that could become part of Canada's army in the future."[6]

In 2013, the Atlantic Council commissioned a project, led by author August Cole, to examine future conflict through the lens of science fiction. It resulted in a series of short stories in a 2015 anthology called *War Stories from the Future*. Subsequently, other institutions have embraced this approach. The United States Marine Corps employed science fiction futures in a 2016 project to review the future security environment.[7] At the Australian Defence College, we formed the Perry Group in 2018, an elective designed to use science fiction to think about future force structure and warfighting concepts.[8] In 2019, the French Defense Innovation agency commenced hiring science fiction writers to "form a red team that will come up with scenarios of disruption."⁹

There are countless reasons why science fiction is useful in preparing our future military leaders. First, it allows us to think differently about military operations. It shifts the paradigm for military leaders and aids them to think beyond the day-to-day aspects of training, administration, and unit management. Science fiction also broadens future leaders' minds and forces them to read something other than current events and military history, although it does not replace these topics but complements them. In these ways, science fiction offers military organizations a tool for nurturing creativity and imagination in an otherwise conservative institution.¹⁰

Second, it allows military professionals to think differently about organizations and warfighting ideas. Science fiction offers a framework to think about the future for military organizations; it is a forward-looking, speculative complement to military history. For example, it can assist institutions in thinking through the implications of human-machine teaming and using AI to derive new warfighting approaches. Science fiction might also help us explore the institutional and ethical impacts of various types of human augmentation.

Finally, science fiction allows us to conceive different strategies. Science fiction provides us with a mental framework that allows us to think outside the current paradigm and try to avoid the "failure of imagination" that leads to military failure. It allows for a more "joined up" approach to strategy; the differences between various domain experts—army, navy, air force, etc.—are not as pronounced or as important in a more connected future world portrayed by most science fiction stories. Finally, in the realm of strategy, science fiction aids in supplying frameworks for large-scale, long-frame problems.

To Boldly Go is a book for those who dare to imagine radically different ways of thinking about the future of military leadership, the profession of arms, and how to use national resources more effectively and creatively to defend our peoples and our ideas.

It draws together strategists, military leaders, and national security professionals to peer into the future and explore national security and military affairs through a very different lens. A diverse range of thinkers from the United States, Australia, and the United Kingdom are represented in the pages of this book. The various chapters employ science fiction books, short stories, movies, and television series as the foundations for these explorations. From *Star Wars* to *Star Trek*, *Ender's Game* to *Old Man's War*, the authors here contribute incisive and often entertaining insights into the future of military affairs and national security.

As members of the profession of arms, we must continue to free our minds and exploit the mental laboratory that science fiction affords. I applaud the editors of this volume for assembling an outstanding array of thoughtful and imaginative insights.

So now, without further ado, it is time for us to boldly go into the future of military affairs. Enjoy.

Notes

1 George Chesney, *The Battle of Dorking* (London: Grant Richards Ltd, 1871).

2 Lawrence Freedman, *The Future of War: A History* (New York: Public Affairs Press, 2017), 4.

3 H. G. Wells, *The War of the Worlds* (London: William Heinemann, 1898).

4 Ibid., 223.

5 "Hollywood: The Pentagon's New Advisor," *BBC World News*, 2003. http://news.bbc.co.uk/2/hi/programmes/panorama/1891196.stm.

6 Directorate of Land Strategic Concepts, *Crisis in Zefra* (Kingston: Army Publishing Office, 2005).

7 Eric Niiler, "What Better Way for the Marines to Prepare for future Wars than with Sci-Fi?" *Wired Magazine*, Jan 15, 2017. https://www.wired.com/2017/01/better-way-marines-prepare-future-wars-sci-fi/.

8 A description of the Perry Group can be found at: Mick Ryan, "Science Fiction, JPME and the Australian Defence College," *The Forge*, 2018. https://theforge.defence.gov.au/publications/science fiction-jpme-and-australian-defence-college.

9 Andrew Liptak, "The French Army is hiring science fiction writers to imagine future threats," *The Verge*, July 24, 2019. https://www.theverge.com/2019/7/24/20708432/france-military-science fiction-writers-red-team.

10 I first explored this topic in 2016 in: Mick Ryan, "Why Reading Science Fiction is Good for Military Officers," *Grounded Curiosity*, Mar 23, 2016. https://groundedcuriosity.com/why-reading-science fiction-is-good-for-military-officers/.

Introduction

People ask: Where do you get your ideas? Well, right here. All this is my Martian landscape. Somewhere in this room is an African veldt. Just beyond, perhaps, is a small Illinois town where I grew up. And I'm surrounded on every side by my magician's toyshop. I'll never starve here. I just look around, find what I need, and begin. I'm Ray Bradbury, and this is The Ray Bradbury Theater. Well then, right now what shall it be. Out of all this, what do I choose to make a story? I never know where the next one will take me. And the trip: exactly one-half exhilaration, exactly one-half terror.

—INTRODUCTION TO THE RAY BRADBURY THEATER

A pioneer of science fiction, Ray Bradbury captured our imagination and remains one of the genre's iconic authors. As *The New York Times* aptly claimed when he passed, he was "the writer most responsible for bringing modern science fiction into the literary mainstream." Although science fiction's popularity may be a relatively recent phenomenon, people have long gazed at the stars in search of meaning. Ancient civilizations looked to the heavens for meaning; pyramids, temples, and countless wonders stand in testament to humanity's passion for the stars. The meaning of these monuments was embedded in stories crafted by the people who erected them, stories that were the driving force behind the efforts required to construct them.

The evolution of modern science fiction as a genre is an extension of our fascination for space, technology, and the future, an obsession that has captivated us for millennia. For us, science fiction is a form of sensemaking that aims to explore the nature of humanity and its place in the cosmos. No one was more aware of that fact than Bradbury, who committed his life to telling the wondrous stories that helped frame humanity within the vast nothingness of space. Bradbury believed first in writing the stories that you love, and he loved nothing more than weaving a good metaphor into his stories. In a 2010 Salon interview, he remarked, "If you're a storyteller, that's what makes a great story. I think the reason my stories have been so successful is that I have a strong sense of metaphor."

The genre is a source of powerful metaphors that help us learn and develop, and by no coincidence, the impetus behind *To Boldly Go*. To borrow a phrase from *The Twilight Zone*, this book offers readers "a journey into a wonderous land of imagination." Using Bradbury's magician's toyshop of science fiction as inspiration, *To Boldly Go* explores contemporary challenges in leadership, strategy, and conflict, while emphasizing the role of humanity and its interaction with technology, taking readers to "strange new worlds," and boldly going where no one has gone before.

By using science fiction to draw out modern-day lessons, *To Boldly Go* serves as an entertaining and valuable learning resource. Science fiction stories provide a ready-made shared understanding of context, allowing the authors and readers to use familiar settings to explore larger issues. Well-known franchises, such as *Star Trek* and *Star Wars*, are relatable and allow an exploration of leadership, strategy, and conflict in an accessible format. Readers do not need to know the historical nuances of the 18th century to understand the American Revolution. Instead, science fiction fans can use their understanding of *Star Trek VI: The Undiscovered Country* and contemporary strategic thought to examine the world of today and tomorrow.

In six discrete sections, *To Boldly Go* explores thematically related concepts, focusing on what science fiction can teach us about leadership, strategy, and conflict and why that matters. Each section introduces the reader to a new group of writers, each of whom engages their subject with the energy and tenacity of a rogue Klingon Warbird.

"Part I: The Captain's Hand" examines leadership and the art of command. In "Space Battleship *Yamato* and the Burden of Command," *The New York Times* bestselling author, August Cole, returns readers to the space battleship *Yamato*, with Captain Avatar leading an imperfect crew on an impossible mission. Heather Gregg follows with "Princess Leia and the Strategic Art of *Métis*," using the *Star Wars* universe to explore the role of women in strategic and combat leadership. Will Meddings looks at how great leaders build teams in "You're Just Not Ender Wiggins, and That's Okay," juxtaposing relevant research with the fictional world of *Ender's Game*. Other chapters, featuring brilliant writing from Kera Roslen, Mick Cook, Jo Brick, and Jess Ward, offer insights into leadership through the lenses of *Star Wars*, *Battlestar Galactica*, *The Expanse*, and *Starship Troopers*.

"Part II: The Final Frontier" investigates military strategy, planning, and decision-making. In "Yours is the Superior Intellect," Jon Klug and Steven Leonard draw from the iconic starship duel from the 1982 film *Star Trek II: The Wrath of Khan* to examine the timeless conflict between experience and intelligence. Tim Choi stays in the *Star Trek* universe, using *Deep Space Nine* to explore modern maritime strategy in "Where No Port Has Gone Before." In her chapter, "Sun Tzu, Ender, and the Old Man," Kathleen McInnis uses science fiction to interrogate the construct of strategic empathy. Chapters from Tom Bruscino, Mick Ryan, and Jimmy Groves take us from *Star Trek* to *Ender's Game* to *The Old Man's War* and back again, exploring topics as diverse as galactic grand strategy and strategic leadership.

"Part III: The Prime Directive" explores topics of ethics, culture, and diversity. Max Brooks, the bestselling author of *World War Z* and *Devolution*, offers a futuristic perspective on desegregation with "Romulans and Remans," taking readers where no man has gone before in *Star Trek: Nemesis*. Jacqueline Whitt's "All That You Touch You Change" examines how issues of culture, diversity, and ethics at home ultimately impact security and strategy abroad. In "The Vice Admiral and the Flyboy," Kelsey Cipolla leverages the conflict between Vice Admiral Holdo and Poe Dameron in *The Last Jedi* to offer insight into the challenges faced by women in positions of power. With his chapter, "Beware the Beast Man," Steven Leonard describes how *Twilight Zone* creator Rod Serling used his screenplay for *Planet of the Apes* to express a cautionary tale of human nature. Equally fascinating chapters from a bevy of other authors, including Theresa Hitchens, Julie Still, Kelly Lelito, and Janeen Webb, address a range of topics from Social Darwinism to the ethics of interplanetary trade.

"Part IV: The War of the Worlds" delves into cooperation, competition, and conflict. Clara Engle opens the section with "One Voice in the Night," an exploration of international systems through the lens of *Babylon 5*. In his chapter, "You Rebel Scum!" Jon Klug examines the fundamentals of rebellion within *Star Wars*, *Dune*, and *Battlestar Galactica*. In "The Final Frontier," Erica Iverson lays bare the true costs of space conflict. Jon Niccum offers a lighthearted look at civilians on the battlefield in "There's No Screaming in Space." Part IV also includes brilliant and insightful writing from veteran writers Rebecca Jensen and M. L. Cavanaugh.

"Part V: The Rise of the Machines" plunges into the complex relationship between humanity and technology. The first offering, Margarita Konaev's "We Don't Serve Their Kind in Here," examines the topic of trust in human-machine teams. Francis J. H. Park transports readers to the *Battlestar Galactica* universe with "You Can't Hide from the Things You've Done," exploring the fear of robot uprising and what it means to be human. Elsa Kania's "Musings on the Murderbot" focuses on humanity and artificial intelligence, drawing on two-time Hugo Award-winning science fiction author Martha Wells's *Murderbot* series for inspiration. Finally, Craig and Steve Whiteside journey back to *The Stand* with "Things We Learned from Captain Trips," while Liam Collins examines the impact of technology on conflict with "Man > Machine."

The final section, "Part VI: The Dark Side," assesses the dark depths of leadership, from toxic and destructive leaders to the impact of trauma on leading others. In "The Mark of Locutus," David Calder examines how Jean Luc-Picard's assimilation by the Borg Collective influenced his ability to lead. Jon Klug returns with "To Live and Die at My Command," an exploration of toxic leadership through the lens of Khan Noonien Singh. Dan Ward offers a glimpse of science fiction as postmortem in his chapter, "From Darth Vader to Dark Helmet." Finally, Steven Leonard's "The Mirror Crack'd" delves into destructive leadership using *Star Trek*'s Mirror Universe as the impetus for discussion.

Throughout his life, Ray Bradbury tirelessly encouraged fellow writers. He would have been one hundred years old in 2020, yet his legacy—his admonition to "write what you love"—lives on, encouraging all those involved in this project to persevere in what might not have been the most ideal circumstances. Following his example, the thirty-five chapters that comprise these sections sprang from within each author's magician's toyshop, an explosion of creativity and imagination that would have sparked joy in Bradbury. We hope they provide a fun way to use science fiction to better understand our world and provide serious insight into our leaders, strategies, and conflicts. We hope you enjoy reading it as much as we have enjoyed writing it!

PART I

THE CAPTAIN'S HAND

CHAPTER I

Space Battleship *Yamato* and the Burden of Command

August Cole

The ship's white-bearded commanding officer, Captain Avatar, sits taciturn as if he himself was formed from the *Yamato*'s bulkhead. The *Star Blazers* soundtrack plays a martial symphony that evokes Aaron Copland's "Fanfare for the Common Man." It's one that I can still hum bar-for-bar nearly four decades after first hearing it as a young child.

This military science fiction anime series that first ran in the United States in 1979 and its 2010 live-action film update, *Space Battleship Yamato*, tell an unforgettable story of a last-ditch effort to save Earth from destruction. In the film, an alien force, the Gamilas, is bent on wiping out humankind on Earth with a campaign of fiery radiation bombardment. Humanity has less than a year to live as radiation poisons even the deepest underground redoubts. Rather than submit to destruction, the United Nations of Space Administration chances its last hope on a single ship, the *Yamato*, a refitted Japanese warship sunk in 1945. The *Yamato* rises in 2199 from a barren seafloor as a cutting-edge space dreadnought given a mission to track down a mythical alien technology that humanity is told can restore Earth's ecosystem. It is a simple mission hiding complex lessons.

I came to first know this epic in its Americanized cartoon form, *Star Blazers*, watched when I was in elementary school—an unusual indulgence in a household in which my parents considered TV frivolous. The series was anything but a waste of time for my young mind, and the show's influence over me continued to adulthood. In *Ghost Fleet: A Novel of the Next World War* that I co-wrote with Peter W. Singer, the futuristic U.S. Navy destroyer *Zumwalt* is fitted with an imperfect but potent electric-powered railgun. The railgun's energy draw is so great that it causes the ship's defensive systems to shut down—a nod to the *Yamato*'s finicky bow-mounted wave motion gun.

Star Blazers also introduced me to thinking about leadership at a time when the only authorities in my young life were my family. Captain Avatar was nothing like my father. Nor was he anything like the only ship captain I knew, my gregarious and tattooed grandfather who was a larger-than-life merchant mariner known for leaping ashore from a surplus landing craft in a Santa Claus suit to deliver gifts to kids in remote Alaskan communities. The contrast in what a leader was supposed to look like and how they were supposed to act fascinated me. In the 2010 Japanese film, Captain Avatar is called Captain Okita and the *Argo* battleship is known as the *Yamato*. As a captain, Okita is similarly immutable yet in the live-action version he is prone to frank discussions on the ethics and responsibilities of leadership, particularly with his chosen successor, a swashbuckling young fighter pilot named Susumu Kodai.

The appeal of the film and anime series differ for me in other significant ways. After all, the story was changed to suit each medium, and it also reflects a 30-year stretch of time. I watched the cartoon at a time when I was struggling to make sense of Cold War fears of atomic annihilation, a discourse intertwined with my discovering the legacy of America's use of nuclear weapons in World War II at Hiroshima and Nagasaki. The film version, while occasionally campy, finds time for such existential and ethical questions. It is particularly interesting from the perspective of military command and decision making around individual and collective sacrifice in a time of hopelessness.

Today my children are watching their shows, animated and otherwise, just as their worries and dreams are also their own. They are consumed by questions about the environmental destruction of our planet at our own hands, not hive-mind aliens. They question daily the inability of adults to do anything collectively to stop it. Perhaps one day their work will be shaped decades from now by shows that engage their concerns about the future, and I can only hope the impact is as profound as the original *Star Blazers* and Captain Avatar had on me.

For my contribution to *To Boldly Go*, the admittedly occasionally ridiculous but beautifully rendered 2010 film adaptation *Space Battleship Yamato* will serve as the foundation for this essay. It is the easiest to access online and presents less of a commitment of time than multiple seasons of anime. If anything, the film is even more focused on themes of leadership.

Note that the format of this essay is intended to represent a fictional form of found artifact from the *Space Battleship Yamato* future—something that an archivist or scholar might uncover. The document is a letter written by one of the *Yamato*'s engineers responsible for the wave motion gun's chamber seals at the crucial forced induction point. A hurried message written out by hand before the *Yamato*'s penultimate battle on Gamila, it was brought back to Earth by a fellow crew member who survived the voyage's final ambush. The letter's author did not, but his observations on leadership aboard the *Yamato* endured, as did the crew's success with their mission to thwart the Gamilas and restore Earth, even at the cost of the *Yamato* and its captains.

Letter Begins

To my daughter and son,

I write this to you from over 160,000 light years from Earth. But you are in my heart always as a reminder of how important the Yamato'*s mission is to not just you but to your children and their children and so on. Speaking for all the crew, who I hope you may someday meet when oceans again churn with briny saltwater sweet enough to sip and clear starry skies no longer release fiery doom, know that we think of nothing else but making it back home to our loved ones. For if we have done that, due to our bravery, resourcefulness, and of course luck, then we will have succeeded.*

I am writing now because we are about to begin the most important phase of our mission. Of all the places we have ended up I am currently just out of orbital range of Gamila. Yes, Gamila! The very home of our adversary. This was not part of our original plan—but it is where we are now, and I think where we were meant to be.

And you know what? It looks so much like Earth. Not the Earth that I grew up with and the one you were born to, but the one that is a crust of wasted desolation scabbing over a once vibrant planet. We can see for ourselves with our own eyes what the Gamilas hope to do to our own world, and why we must not fail—no matter the cost.

It is important for you to know how we, improbably, even made it this far. That is something I did not even expect, and for that reason I would like to put down for you some of my observations. We are a crew that is made up of many talents and personalities, most whose stories will never be known. Any spaceship is only as good as its captain, I strongly believe, and I believe this even more so now. May we never need such leaders again, but in case we do I hope my hard-earned knowledge may someday be of utility.

So, let me tell you about what I have learned from Captain Juzo Okita and Susumu Kodai, designated acting captain by Okita after he fell gravely ill during our voyage. You may not remember me like this, but I am, in my heart, an engineer who searches for order everywhere. When I can't find it, I try to create it. So, I place great faith in the curation of lists such as this one: Lessons I have learned aboard Yamato ….

Our Stories Give Us Hope

Iskandar was a myth. A gem of a story scratched free of bleached soil with broken fingernails. Captain Okita knew this and with UNSA's blessing set course for Iskandar as Yamato'*s destination knowing full well that it was likely nothing more than a radiation fever dream. The pursuit of alien planet-healing technology became our mission—not reaching Iskandar itself. No, our mission was to give all of humanity belief that there was still more we could do even as we knew rationally that we were all dying. You surely remember the jubilant cheers for the crew as they marched through sooty tunnels with straight backs and improbably clean uniforms? I can still hear your voices.*

Die Reaching for the Sun

When Yamato *shook free of its bonds of seared stone and glassy sand to rise into the hazy afternoon sky like a phoenix, it symbolized rebirth of humanity's fight against the Gamilas. Even when we had lost every space-faring warship in our arsenal. Even when a year or less was all that remained. Until that moment it seemed certain that we would endure a listless decline in the dark of Earth's darkest and deepest recesses. Captain Okita, one of the few survivors of our catastrophic fleet losses off Mars, knew it would be better to march toward a valiant death to the discordant symphony of rocket fire and laser batteries. He must have taught his own son the same lesson. He perished off Mars, just as Kodai's own brother did in a last stand that will be told for generations.*

Don't Run from Audacity or Risk

Our first action came too soon. I remember my mission clock showing three minutes had elapsed when the incoming Gamila missile alarm rang out. My stomach ached in the way that only closing action can do, and I set to work preparing our station for the first firing of our wave motion gun. Would this alien-inspired weapons technology destroy the ship when we needed it most? Would it destroy the underground cities below? Perhaps the whole planet even? I focused on the task at hand, hearing Okita's orders over the intercom as clearly as if he were standing next to me. It was a bold gambit, reckless even. But what other choice did we have than total commitment from the first moments of our voyage?

Be Ruthless with a Ruthless Enemy

I once held an entire skyscraper in the palm of my hand, jewel-like chips infused with particles of flesh and steel that glinted in the sun. I would sometimes see that same flicker during a Gamila attack in the refraction of our laser fire shredding incoming enemy fighters. It warmed me to see them obliterated. Ours was a ruthless enemy. Yet despite five years of warfare some of our command crew were still shocked to be in close action with the enemy so soon after our first warp from Earth. We were in the cursed killing fields off Mars and came under immediate attack. Captain Okita would have none of it, urging the crew to see swarming enemy fighters as nothing more than incoming missiles without pilots. That angered me, more so that we warped again before we could finish them off.

Leaders Have to Live with Their Hardest Decisions

Midway through our mission I saw something incomprehensible: a Black Tiger fighter releasing its weapons on the Yamato *itself. This was not Gamila mind control, it was a direct order from Acting Captain Kodai to save the ship. A Gamila stealth craft, which was really a mine-like weapon, had wrapped claw-like appendages around* Yamato's *Bridge No. 3, which dangled beneath the hull and was always poorly defended. The Black Tiger destroyed the entire bridge and the Gamila weapon, which had it detonated would have ripped* Yamato *in two at its midpoint. It certainly would have killed me at my station. In the end, though, six crew were sacrificed. It was Kodai's first real test as a stand-in while Captain Okita underwent medical treatment. He passed.*

All for One, One for All

The more we fought the Gamilas up close, the better we came to know them. Them. When you fight this alien foe, they are both individual adversaries and of one mind. They thought this gave them advantage over us. I am not so sure. The command structure was clear on Yamato *and decisions had to be made unilaterally. But the safety and survival of the ship's whole crew—as well as all of humanity left on Earth—was always on Captain Okita's mind as he issued orders from the bridge, and then later from his quarters. When Kodai assumed command, he was a more energetic and occasionally reckless leader. His personal courage was unmatched. I can still hear the metallic slap in the hangar bay as Kodai put his fighter's marker down on the tabletop battle map to indicate he alone would serve as the vanguard of our assault on Gamila. He believed it would be our final battle, even referring back to April 1945 and the original* Yamato *as a ray of hope for the Empire. He told the crew it was probably all a trap, but there was no other way but to pursue victory to the last. "We go unto glory or death," he said.*

Our Loss Makes Us Human

Is it unusual that both of our captains knew personal wartime loss? No. Everybody on Earth lost somebody, just as you lost your mother far too young. Death awaited us all either in the poisonous warrens that became our dying beds or to be sucked through a jagged hull into space's vacuum millions of miles from home. For some, such loss numbed them into inaction. Not Captain Okita or Kodai. Okita lost his son aboard Fuyuzuki *near Mars, just as Kodai lost his brother Mamoru who had command of* Yukikaze *there. That awful crucible made them compassionate but never foolhardy with the lives in their charge. Those serving aboard* Yamato *trusted both leaders because they knew they would never be cavalier, nor indecisive when lives hung in the balance. This loss and the burden of command it imposed on Okita and Kodai became a beacon for the whole crew, burning bright as any sun.*

Time is dear, my children, and I have so much more to write but I must go. I can feel the ship's position shifting as the bow points planetward. Any minute the warp klaxon will sound and that means I must prepare for our final battle. Read these words again and again and someday share them with your children.

It's been a privilege to serve with Captains Okita and Kodai, but that honor is nothing like the pride and joy I have in the years I have spent as your father.

Until Earth is green and free!

CHAPTER 2

Of X-Wings and Y-Wings

A Brief History of the Galaxy

Kera Rolsen

———————————▶

Students of intergalactic history should be aware that the time period around the Battle of Yavin is some of the most critical for setting the course of the galaxy as well as the Intergalactic Republic. Specifically, the period from 50 years before the Battle of Yavin (BBY) to 250 years after the Battle of Yavin (ABY) and the multiple political factions that controlled the galaxy during that time.[1]

The following are excerpts from Princess and General Leia Organa's final directions to her protégé and military successor, General Poe Dameron. She penned the notes in 35 ABY, between the Rebellion's escape to Crait and her death on Ajan Kloss. A careful study of the text in the context of the time highlights the plight of the Rebel forces just before the uprising against the Final Order. Astute students of history will note the First Order's consistent attacks and a poorly executed bombing mission reduced Rebel forces drastically during their flight from D'Qar to Crait. This background should help inform the context and tone of General Organa's instructions. Earlier sections of her notes highlight her focus on the more political aspects of transforming the Rebellion into a legitimate political entity. In contrast, this section speaks to General Organa's care for the people and beings of the Rebellion as well as their personal and professional growth. It stands to reason that a Force-sensitive general, and one trained by Jedi Master Skywalker, would feel a strong tie to the people in her charge.

> Acting General Dameron, I know your promotion will be made official by the time you read this, so my next note is on the subject of fleet health. I've given you my thoughts on politics; I think you should leave it to the politicians but know how to handle them. Discreetly. So, they don't realize they're being handled. No, dear Poe, you should stay out of politics and focus on leading the forces of the Rebellion. And to that end, I have a few thoughts in mind. We are at a turning point. I won't be around forever, and you will take my place to grow the Rebellion.[2]

It is worth noting that historians generally agree that General Organa, injured and evacuated to the vacuum of space during the Rebel Forces' flight to Crait, was already aware she was dying while writing this text. Given her awareness of her approaching end and the galaxy-wide impact her words would have, this section of her notes is especially poignant.

> The Rebellion has grown and shrunk many times in its existence. On Hoth, we had thousands of forces. But after the defeat of the Galactic Empire, a rebellion was no longer necessary, nor was a large standing army in the name of rebellion. It was a slow transition as the Rebellion and Alliance to Restore the Republic helped citizens overthrow the last remnants of the Empire. Once done, our forces changed from a rebellion to citizens of the new Republic.
>
> Almost nothing remained until this First Order business kicked off, and then it had to grow again. And I want you to learn from the mistakes of the first Rebellion. We were too narrow in who we recruited, leading to a homogeneous force that didn't represent the worlds for which it fought and a fleet of vehicles and fighters that we built for only one type of body. Like the ships of the fleet, we need all types: X-Wings, Y-Wing, and even B-Wings.
>
> I first want to address my second point: a fleet built for only a particular body size and type means only that specific type can utilize it. The few times we ran out of human males and the few sentient beings who were human-sized, we had a hard time filling cockpits. The Rebellion learned its lesson the hard way. We adapted the X-Wings to fit more body types. Porkins, Light save him, was a stout body but undeniably a keen pilot right until the very end. There's no reason he needed to feel cramped in the cockpit, and maybe if we had designed our ships with a broader range of body sizes in mind, he would have been able to maneuvre better. Chewbacca is arguably the best pilot in the Resistance (other than you, my dear Poe!), but he wouldn't fit in an X-Wing. Even poor Han once remarked, "I don't think the Empire had Wookies in mind when they designed her, Chewie," as we prepared to sneak down to Endor in a stolen Imperial transport.[3]
>
> Think of the incredible X-Wing pilot Chewie could have been if we had had a cockpit large enough to fit him. I need transportation with gunners to protect their cargo but imagine if a crack shot like Chewie could fly and shoot in an X-Wing too! Grow a fleet that adapts to a greater range of body shapes and sizes. Ensuring a greater range of anthropometric measurements means a larger pool of pilots from which to pull, allowing us to dig deep and recruit broadly. And don't just consider humans, but every sentient species willing to take up our cause—this fight isn't just a human fight.

General Organa's words to General Dameron served as the catalyst to expand the Rebel Fleet, later the Galactic Fleet, and now the Intergalactic Fleet. General Dameron would bring her ideas to fruition. He did this by ensuring all fleet spacecraft had conformable, adjustable seating for a broad range of pilots, not just bipedal races similar to humans. In later years, technology had matured sufficiently to build nascent digitally modular cockpits, the technological forebearers of modern holo-cockpits. One can see Generals Organa's and Dameron's hand in the contemporary fully programable and adjustable cockpits that allow for the bodies of ninety-eight percent of sentient beings in the Intergalactic Fleet to operate starcraft.

General Dameron created initiatives that ensured that staples like uniforms, survival equipment, helmets, and communications devices were usable by all species. Historians disagree, however, whether the conformable cockpits or broader range of pilot equipment had a more significant impact on recruitment. Still, the final result was an exponentially more extensive group of beings from which to recruit pilots.

To that end, this conflict has been human-centric for far too long. Yes, the Republic was torn apart by the very human Palpatine. Whether as Senator Sheev Palpatine, the Senator from Naboo, as the Emperor, or as Darth Sidious the last Sith who nearly destroyed the galaxy with the Final Order, his influence has driven at us for decades. But despite one human driving and manipulating so much tumultuousness in the galaxy, freedom belongs to and is won by all sentient species in this galaxy. If the Rebel Alliance is to succeed as a legitimate political faction and as a force helping to crush the First Order, we must recruit native species on the planets we liberate.

Both the Empire and the First Order were homogenous groups plagued with racism and speciesism, and their leaders were mostly human, with few exceptions. Why should only one species rule the entire galaxy? A single mindset and a single body type magnify your flaws.

Look to the Clone Army for the best example: an entire fighting force, cloned from one human man. No variation. No deviance. A flaw in one was a flaw in all. They walk, talk, and, more importantly, think and act the same. When you know how the enemy thinks, exploiting them becomes easy. If your fighting force and its leaders are diverse, both of body and of mind, it has a greater ability to act and react differently to various situations, keeping its adversaries forever guessing their next move.

A second, more insidious factor was built into a fighting force with a singular mindset: silencing outliers. When the fighting forces you build have a largely homogeneous mindset, the people and beings who think differently are silenced. They don't feel they have a voice. Luke told me what he witnessed when we first believed the Emperor had fallen. He told me he watched our father, Darth Vader, struggle to overcome years of conditioning to finally confront the Emperor and question his will. Luke believed it was the first time anyone had found the strength to voice a dissenting opinion. Darth Vader may have harbored dissenting thoughts for years, but only in Luke's presence was he finally strong enough to speak them aloud. The homogeneous mindset and fear of reprisal enabled the Emperor's power to grow unchallenged for years.

The Empire and First Order aren't the only ones guilty of these sins, though. Throughout the early years, we incorporated the Mon Calamari and Bothans because we needed their fleets and intelligence networks. But it was rare for one of them to be promoted to any high rank within the Rebel Alliance's loose structure. Our tactics, operations, and strategies were planned mainly by humans, and even when other species helped plan, humans took the credit and the glory. It was wrong, but you now have the opportunity to correct that wrong. Don't be short-sighted like we were. Look for those with the intelligence and drive to lead. Look for the traits humans don't have and bring them in to round out the leadership and cover our weaknesses.

Who knows, maybe somewhere in a barracks not far from here, there is another Admiral Ackbar or Lieutenant Commander Nien Nunb, just waiting for their opportunity to make the Rebel Alliance stronger.

Following this passage, General Organa's notes include a shortlist of traits which she considered essential to leadership, and "Not human exclusive!" was written in her delicate hand over the list.

Loyal
Trustworthy
Intelligent
Wise
Forward thinking
~~Caring~~ Empathic [original marking]
Kind

It is clear General Organa recognized both the failings of the original Rebels as well as a clear path forward to correct those failings. She also provided General Dameron the first draft of what would later become the Intergalactic Forces Academy motto: "Loyal, Trustworthy, Wise."

> That brings me to my next point: growing leaders for a once Rebel force. Oh, Poe, we made leaders out of who we had available. In an ever-shrinking group of Rebels, we countered the First Order with the people we had, not what we truly needed. They made mistakes; all people make mistakes, but if we could have grown their leadership skills instead of throwing them to the rathtars, we might have defeated the Empire and the First Order faster.
>
> But now you have an opportunity to do what we couldn't: you can choose the leaders you need, and you can guide them and educate them on how to be leaders. You no longer have to grab the next available body to lead a strike or let someone like Han do it. I loved that man, but he was a rogue, not a trained and polished leader.
>
> Great leaders won't spring up from the ground, it will take time to grow them and we need to take several steps to accomplish this goal. First, recruit from outside while still growing leaders from within. You will have to grow the Rebel forces if you want to rid the galaxy of the last of the First Order's influence. Positions as a leader will spring up everywhere, and you don't have enough people and beings now to fill all of those positions. You will have to find leaders in outside forces. But while you find them, grow the talent you already have. Find those hidden gems and teach them how to lead. They already know, love, and internalize the things we value; now you have to teach them what it means to lead. That will be far easier than the careful vetting you will need to do to find suitable leaders from outside. You never know who is an agent provocateur waiting to create havoc from within ….

General Organa proves she knows how to form rebellions and what it takes to defeat them. General Dameron's early insistence that only those original forty Rebels from Crait be given positions of authority did not align with General Organa's vision in this passage. Still, it helped to ferret out First Order sympathizers who joined the Rebellion during the Galactic Republic transition. By 38 ABY, he relented and began to allow the most loyal of the recent recruits to lead.

> Promote our people up and fill the vacated positions with the new blood. Time in the lower echelons will give you a chance to see what they're made of and if our values align.
>
> Second, formalize how you train your leaders. Any training our leaders received was ad hoc at best—a quiet word from an elder in the small breath between battles. Now is the time to create formalized training.
>
> Start with the foundation. If you bring in beings from every corner of the galaxy that supports us, they all have to be on equal footing. Start with the foundation of leadership. Define for them what a leader is and what you want a leader to be able to do. Then, you can start to specialize your leaders. Are they talented at logistics but bad at snap decision making? Are they good in the heat of battle but paralyzed by the idea of telling someone they are underperforming? Once you lay a foundation and level to which every leader must rise, you can start to identify the weak points and shore them up.

As with so many parts of this letter, historians can trace the beginnings of the Intergalactic Republic to General Organa's letter and its influence on both Galactic society and politics. Historians have noted that more than five-hundred galactic standard years have passed since General Organa penned her letter. In that time, there have been two hundred leadership schools dedicated with "Organa" or "Dameron" in their name, indicating the impact of her letter and Dameron's execution of her ideas. It is also worth noting that the naming of those schools has not been without controversy. One school of thought argues that using only General Organa's name in the school's title downplays General Dameron's legacy. Conversely, another school argues that using only General Dameron's name downplays General Organa's legacy. It is worth noting that for approximately a two-hundred-year period, the use of "Organa" or "Skywalker-Organa" in a school's name indicated the school was solely for Force-sensitive leaders. Eventually, the issue with such a narrowing of both generals' ideals forced these schools to rename, re-brand, and reopen as more inclusive learning centers. At the time of writing, 537 ABY, most Intergalactic Republic leadership schools bear both generals' names.

> Lastly, embrace the differences in those you bring in! Each being will have different skills and talents. They will have different ways of looking at the problems you will face. Who knows, maybe a Jawa leader will solve your logistics issues. Maybe a Twi'lek general will help you establish your diplomatic corp. And maybe a Hutt as a leader, carefully groomed, can help you build and standardize galactic trade. Each has their own unique skills; you would be a fool not to accept their differences and lever them for good.

General Dameron may have interpreted General Organa's words too literally from this passage as the first head of the Galactic Fleet's logistics branch was a Jawa, Kedo B'okt, which initially led to disastrous results. While Kedo B'okt possessed the bargaining and logistics skills seemingly known to all Jawas, he was also considered corrupt; he was caught attempting to sell Fleet spacecraft on several occasions. General Dameron was able to identify a problem with cultural barriers and eventually guide B'okt away from off-book sales, but by then, B'okt had eroded the trust of his non-Jawa subordinates. After the foundation of General Dameron's initial leadership school, Jawas were included in the student body, and those graduates continued to both mediocre and notable careers as logisticians.

> When Luke was training me in the ways of the Force, he told me of his time with Master Yoda. He told me of the events that led him to know I was not only his sister but also Force-sensitive. He described what Master Yoda told him: "Pass on what you have learned. Strength. Mastery. But weakness, folly, failure also. Yes, failure most of all. The greatest teacher, failure is."[4] If I had to identify one point where the early Rebellion failed, it was that we never recognized our vulnerabilities, and we were never vulnerable with each other. Yes, a Rebellion needs to be strong, but if it does not recognize and acknowledge where it is weak and vulnerable, those areas will go unprotected, unfortified. I am laying the Rebellion bare for you, Poe. These are our weaknesses, but we can make them strengths. Build the fighting force we need, strengthen it with our differences, and cover the gaps through diversity.

General Organa is respected across multiple galaxies as a founder of the peace and stability currently enjoyed. Students of history learn by rote the dates of her important battles, circumstances of her birth, and the date of her death. However, without access to primary sources like this letter, they lose the sense of her essential humanity.

Born the daughter of Darth Vader and mother to Kylo Ren, General Organa clearly understood the impact the right leader has on all sentient beings. Although Leia Organa was raised a princess, her life was far from a fairy-tale; she learned from the pain of loss and betrayal. The experiences she had enabled her to pen the words that would be the foundation of the Galactic Republic, and later, our own Intergalactic Republic. Careful examination and historical study of the letter highlights the values upon which a Republic was able to survive centuries: diversity of mind, inclusion, and a willingness to expand leadership beyond the human-centric disaster that was the Empire and First Order. She describes a galaxy in which diversity is recognized, honored, and used to advance all sentient beings.

Notes

1   In the context of the *Star Wars* universe, the Battle of Yavin 4 appears at the climax of *Star Wars, Episode IV: A New Hope*. Also known as the Battle of the Death Star, it was fought in the space and skies over the planet Yavin 4 and is seen as the turning point for the Galaxy and the start of the Empire's downfall due to the crippling loss of the Death Star. The significance of the battle can be seen in *Star Wars* canon as dates are measured from the Battle of Yavin, Before Battle of Yavin (BBY) and After Battle of Yavin (ABY), the same way Western culture utilizes before Christ (BC) and anno Domini (AD).

2   All text from General Organa's letter to Poe Dameron was written by the author and not part of *Star Wars* canon.

3   *Star Wars, Episode VI: Return of the Jedi*, directed by Richard Marquand (Los Angeles, CA: Twentieth Century Fox, 1983).

4   *Star Wars, Episode VIII: The Last Jedi*, directed by Rian Johnson (Los Angeles, CA: Lucasfilm Ltd., 2017).

CHAPTER 3

Adama's Unequal Dialogue

What Military Leaders Owe the Civilian Executive

Mick Cook

President Laura Roslin and Admiral William Adama's tension over strategic decisions nearly led to humanity's destruction. The idealistic intervention by Captain Leland "Apollo" Adama averted further disaster in the fight against the Cylons. Apollo also preserved the democratic ideals the Twelve Colonies had inherited from the Lords of Kobol in the form of the Articles of Colonization. The 2004 *Battlestar Galactica* (*BSG*) reboot provided audiences with more than a modern take on a science fiction classic; it also offered a first-class education in civil-military relations primarily delivered through President Roslin, Admiral Adama, and Captain Apollo. These characters represent three classic archetypes of civil-military relations in crisis. These three archetypes are the political realist, the totalitarian pragmatist, and the utilitarian idealist, represented by Roslin, Adama, and Apollo, respectively. The three *BSG* characters added the human element to the archetypes, enabling the audience to enjoy the exploration of civil-military relations without the sterility of a high school civics class.

The producers of *BSG* carefully constructed Roslin, Adama, and Apollo to be relatable characters. Each was grounded in the modern world, particularly the western liberal democratic tradition. Understanding how each of these characters represents an archetype-in-action is essential to grasp their importance to civil-military relations.

The tension created by the power dynamic between the civilian executive and the military in *BSG* is more than good television; it reflects a reality present in both democratic and non-democratic societies. The most critical challenges of civil-military relations are present early in the series. In fact, the pilot mini-series and first season provides the audience with a basic understanding of how decision-making during war should occur in a liberal democracy. *BSG* also illustrates the dangers to democracy if tensions spill over and the military subverts civilian authority. Throughout the mini-series and first season, we see the replication of real-world cultural pressures, organizational bias, and combined strategic decision-making. Examples include the appointment of a special military advisor to President Roslin, Admiral Adama shaping the strategic decisions to favor military action, and President Roslin making strategic decisions based on military advice about operational capabilities and consequences. These examples are delivered to the audience through a connection with the three central characters.

Roslin was not prepared to assume the mantle of executive leadership. She was 43rd in line to the President, maintaining a position in Cabinet as the Minister for Education. The Twelve Colonies' destruction included the incumbent President's death, thrusting Roslin into leading the human survivors. Early on, Roslin asserts her legal authority to govern as a duly elected representative of the people. She seeks to maintain what Samuel Huntington describes as "objective civilian control" in constitutional form. That is, Roslin asserts her role as the strategic decision-maker for the war effort.[1] As she grows into her new role, Roslin becomes a political realist. She makes calculated decisions based not only on the Articles of Colonization—the foundational legislative documents of the Twelve Colonies—but also on how the decision will build her political capital with the people and military. Roslin does not merely take on executive leadership's burden in less-than-ideal circumstances; she assumes the President's role and challenges any dissenting voice.

Almost as battle worn as the Battlestar he commands, the aging Adama is a military pragmatist who focuses on achieving the military objective above all else. A veteran fighter pilot and supreme military commander of humanity's remnants, he loses sight of the strategic imperative facing the human race—survival. In the early days of Roslin's presidency, Adama's fixation on the operational objective of meeting the overwhelming might of the Cylons with military force leads him to assume the role of the lead dissenter. He exemplifies the military leader who believes the civilian executive should defer wartime decisions to the military. Adama's disdain for Roslin's background as a schoolteacher fuels his opinion that the elected civilian executives are unqualified to make wartime decisions.

Adama's characterization is no strawman argument. Friction between military and civilian leadership is common, as are generals who conduct military operations based on their civilian executives' guidance. Hew Strachan points out in *The Direction of War* that this is a fundamental role of military leadership and foundational to effective civil-military relations.[2] Adama fails to recognize or accept that his pursuit of military objectives is counter to the strategic objectives outlined by the civilian executive. His arrogance, thirst for vengeance, and military elitism combine to create a rogue leader at odds with civilian control of the military. Adama attempts to subvert the President's legitimate authority to pursue unattainable military objectives, forgetting that the military serves at the behest of the people represented by the elected civilian executive. One such example is Adama's decision to resupply at the Ragnar ammunition depot before seeking out the Cylon fleet for a military strike. He aborts this plan after realizing the overwhelming size of the Cylons. It is essential to understand that Adama's initial totalitarian tendencies are not uniform across the military and that some colonial officers—especially those with command potential—understand their constitutional role in the Articles of Colonization.

It takes more than being good in the cockpit to defend humanity from total annihilation. It also requires a strong understanding of constitutional authorities and the wherewithal to challenge senior leaders when making bad decisions based upon flawed logic or illegitimate authorities. Throughout the series, Apollo demonstrates this: he is a fighter pilot and an expert on the constitutional constraints of the military. Apollo's character archetype is signposted quite clearly by his deference to political authority, which is a stark contrast to his father's reluctant obedience and occasional insubordination. The familial link between Apollo and Adama juxtaposes their individual ideals. Both are military officers and experienced pilots. Both believe in serving the Colonies and prize their integrity as military officers. However, Apollo strives to perform his duties in accordance with Articles of Colonization. Apollo prides himself on how he serves; compromising the ideals expressed in the Articles is unthinkable to him.

Apollo demonstrates his adherence to the Articles numerous times during the series. However, some of the most crucial moments—such as the destruction of the civilian vessel *Olympic Carrier*, negotiations with political revolutionaries, and defending the President during a military coup led by Adama's Executive Officer, Colonel Sol Tigh—underscore his intense idealism. His actions are not in deference to any individual but to the civilian executive's legal authority and the military's limitations as outlined in the Articles of Colonization. Apollo demonstrates through his utilitarian approach to service and leadership that a constitutional partnership between civilian decision-makers and the military is the best way for strategic policymaking and waging war.

The examination of civil-military relations in *BSG* addresses challenges that critical theorists in civil-military relations have spent careers examining. Luckily, *BSG* covers it for the audience in the early seasons and uses the later seasons to reinforce the lesson. Roslin and Adama personify two archetypes that commonly form the two sides of the civil-military divide, whereas Apollo represents the often-sought-after bridge between them. Huntington and Strachan both articulated the ideal of a civilian-led, military-executed war effort. Huntington also argued that, under the constitutional form, objective civilian control is essential to the professionalization military—providing the necessary direction and authority to develop a professional military that serves the people.[3] Yet, by establishing a profession for waging war, there is a risk of establishing a social elite that is not fully representative of the society it serves.

Elitism among the military can have grave consequences for statecraft, national strategy, and, ultimately, national survival. Samuel Huntington and Morris Janowitz discuss the modern professional officer corps and the danger elitism can pose to liberal democracies waging war.[4] Janowitz links elitism with the military profession's sense of honor and the self-image of those who serve.[5] Importantly, Janowitz argues that the military profession is not the sole owner of honor in society, yet its self-image and the esteem it believes it is owed are more important to military members than to broader society. An example of this occurs when Roslin points out that she noticed Adama dislikes military officers' ceremonial duties during a previous event. Adama's response to her questioning—"I'm a patriot"—reveals an essential aspect of the recalcitrant Admiral's psyche. It is vital to Adama and military elites in general that society sees them as *ideal* patriots. It is often through conversations between Roslin and Adama that the state of civil-military relations in the Colonial Fleet is revealed.

One of the most common phrases uttered by Adama throughout the series is, "It's a military decision, Madame President." His words exclude Roslin from critical decisions in the war effort against the Cylons, regardless of her role as a wartime political leader. Using this phrase to neutralize and subvert her opinion, Adama demonstrates the disregard a military elite can exhibit for a political leader. Adama, at times, represents the ideal forwarded by Huntington and Strachan. He understands the strategic imperatives, understands his operational capabilities, and makes decisions based on calculated risks. Adama's training and experience have provided him with the foresight to manage risk and make decisions in this way. However, his tolerance of civilian counterparts and superiors who are not as adept at translating risk assessments into decisive action is low.

In *Supreme Command,* Eliot Cohen warns against this comparison of the "professional" and the "political," arguing that it is an unequal dialogue between those professionals experienced in military operations and the elected politicians who, often, are not.[6] Cohen highlights that the political leader's expectations in delivering a strategic vision should not be weighed against their abilities to plan or command a military operation or platform.[7] Adama uses the "military decision" as a carte blanche to act on his initiative without presidential guidance. This is more than a case of the wily old Admiral trying to pull the wool over the eyes of the newly minted President; it is a subversive act of insubordination that borders on insurrection. The decisions Adama makes under the guise of this carte blanche include the movement of civilian vessels, the treatment of enemy prisoners, and the withholding of crucial strategic intelligence from the civilian leadership. Adama seeks to avoid political interference in the war effort by imposing his definition of a military decision on the President. However, policy objectives established by the civilian executive guide decisions during war. In choosing to subvert political direction, Adama demonstrates a misunderstanding of what decisions should be made by the military and how those decisions must be made.

From the outset, it is clear that the political and military objectives of the colonial remnants were mismatched. While Roslin endeavors to save the remaining members of humanity by escaping the Cylon forces bearing down upon them, Adama yearns to strike back at the Cylons with whatever military forces he can muster. In a liberal democratic society, such as that of the Twelve Colonies, the civilian executive sets the policy objectives, and the military carries out operations to fulfil those objectives. Therefore, Adama's decisions should have been made with Roslin's desired end state—fleeing Cylons pursuit—in mind. Over time, as Adama realizes the futility of military retaliation, he shifts course and—to a limited degree—suborns himself to Roslin's authority.

Decisions that demonstrated the ideal of civilian authority and military subordination followed the establishment of a civil-military equilibrium—two such decisions involved risk to civilian lives and infrastructure. The first decision occurred in the second part of the mini-series when Adama was still attempting to limit presidential oversight and interference over military operations. The incident involved the abandonment of all sub-light spacecraft that were incapable of fleeing pursuing Cylon forces. Adama provided President Roslin with an accurate assessment of the likely damage to the fleet if they did not evacuate all the Faster-Than-Light (FTL)-capable ships on a timeline that allowed for the evacuation of passengers on sub-light ships. The decision to order the fleet to "jump" via FTL drives, leaving the sub-light vessels and their passengers to the Cylons, had to be made. Roslin understood the risk to the fleet, the limitations of who they could save, the implications of leaving people behind, and ordered the jump. As the civilian executive, Roslin had made a strategic decision based on military advice about the situation and capabilities available to achieve the objective.

The second example of good cooperation between the civilian executive and military leadership actually involves civilian deaths based upon a decision by the President. This time, Colonial officers pulled the trigger: the political idealist Apollo acting under Roslin's orders. With the fleet conducting a series of jumps to escape the pursuing Cylons, the civilian transport vessel, *Olympic Carrier*, experienced an FTL propulsion drive malfunction and could not make the jump. Shortly after the fleet regrouped at the designated rendezvous point, the *Olympic Carrier* unexpectedly jumped within close range of the remaining ships, reporting that they had escaped the Cylons despite a failure in their FTL drive. Based on information from the eccentric Dr. Gaius Baltar, assessments from Adama and his officers, and a radiological alarm indicating the presence of a nuclear explosive device aboard the vessel, Roslin ordered the destruction of *Olympic Carrier*. Apollo and Captain Kara "Starbuck" Thrace destroyed the ship as it careened towards the fleet, condemning to death all 1,345 souls on board. This is another example of how the relationship between the civilian executive and military services should work. Both decisions were arrived at through clear communication, highlighting the prescribed roles of political and military leadership. The "unequal dialogue" between the professional and the political is often adversely affected by a misunderstanding of cultural differences. These differences can often be overcome by establishing a mechanism, often an advisor, to interpret these cultural differences and facilitate clear communication between the two sides.

Appointing special military advisors to political leaders is not uncommon, typically to provide the civilian executive with an understanding of the military, reducing the risk of friction through miscommunication and cultural differences. The concept of a professional military in a democratic society is, at times, foreign to the society they serve. A military advisor can be a bridge between the civilian executive and military leadership. Roslin attempts to create this bridge by appointing Apollo as her military advisor. A reluctant Apollo adamantly insists that his father is the senior military officer and therefore should be the President's primary advisor on military matters. Roslin's assurances eventually win him over—Apollo's role will be to help her better understand the military, not advise her on military operations. Meanwhile, his appointment sparks an understandably high degree of tension between him and his father, with Adama telling his son that he needs to pick a side. Apollo, an idealist who views the executive and the military as being on the same side, does not understand Adama's point.

Soon after he is appointed Roslin's military advisor, Apollo leads the Colonial government's negotiations with Tom Zarek, an insurrectionist who has radicalized a group of prisoners on a transport ship. The prisoners refuse to work in support of the fleet, and Apollo's mission is to convince them to volunteer for hard labor. Apollo negotiates an agreement with Zarek, conceding that the President will hold elections as per the Articles of Colonization. When Roslin and Adama react poorly to Apollo's deal with Zarek, Apollo reminds them that they hold their positions by the authority of the Articles. He goes on further to point out that if they choose to ignore the requirement for an election—ignoring the Articles—they delegitimize their positions, telling them: "Now, if you are telling me we are throwing out the law, then I am not a Captain, you are not a Commander, and you are not the President. And I don't owe either of you a damned explanation for anything." Roslin and Adama accept the negotiated arrangements with Zarek, and Adama acknowledges that Apollo has finally picked a side. However, this is neither the side of Roslin or Adama, but rather that of the people. The constitutional loyalty, frank advice, and principled actions of Apollo as a special military advisor to a civilian executive is an example of how the position can bridge civilian-military relations. Apollo's trajectory as the special military advisor to the President of the Colonies has a basis in recent history. Political leaders in liberal democracies have, in peace and war, appointed military advisors from outside the existed chain of command. These appointments have, as in *BSG*, had both positive and negative consequences for civil-military relations.

United States President John F. Kennedy was determined to lead military reforms that encompassed everything from the military's approach to war to the strategic decision-making apparatus supporting the civilian executive. This period of history saw greater involvement of the United States in South-East Asia and the botched Bay of Pigs invasion—both reactions to the looming threat of communism and increasing Soviet influence. As H. R. McMaster explains in his book *Dereliction of Duty*, Kennedy was taken with General Maxwell Taylor's vision for the United States military and appointed the retired general as the Military Representative to the President with the remit of providing independent military advice to the President outside of official channels.[8] Kennedy outlined that this new appointment did not reduce the role or importance of the Joint Chiefs of Staff or the National Security Council, but complemented the existing structures. However, Kennedy, unlike the fictional Roslin, created a barrier rather than a bridge. Taylor's appointment led to a series of formal and informal barriers to information sharing, intra-service rivalry, and divisive strategic policy advice to the civilian executive. The role of a special military advisor to the civilian executive needs to be framed such that it does not circumvent or undermine those tasked to provide the civilian executive with military advice on strategy and policy decisions. It is a role that can, as demonstrated by Apollo, preserve the ideal of objective civilian control of the military.

In the real world and the *BSG* universe, it is clear that the military leader's ideal role is to provide the civilian executive with advice about military capabilities and conduct operations that strive to achieve the policy objectives as determined by the civilian executive. Any attempt to subvert the legitimate authority of the duly elected civilian executive by the military undermines the civilian leadership, risks strategic failure and mocks the democratic ideals that bestowed the military leader's authority in the first place.

The civil-military relationship is one that operates under significant cultural and organizational pressure. During wartime, policy direction is the purview of the civilian leaders; however, the unequal dialogue shows that military professionals maintain a monopoly on warfare's practical experience. Clear delineation between the civilian executive's and senior military leaders' roles must be articulated within a constitutional framework—as is the case in most liberal democracies. Friction over which decision falls within the remit of political leadership or military leadership can lead to disastrous consequences. Only through clear communication, cultural understanding, and adherence to legislated functions will the civil-military relationship function effectively.

Notes

1   Samuel P. Huntington, *The Soldier and The State* (Cambridge: Harvard University Press, 1964), 82–83.
2   Hew Strachan, *The Direction of War* (Cambridge: Cambridge University Press, 2013), 45.
3   Huntington, 83.
4   Huntington, 94; Morris Janowitz, *The Professional Soldier: A Social and Political Portrait* (New York: The Free Press, 1960), 225.

5   Janowitz, 225.
6   Eliot Cohen, *Supreme Command* (New York: Anchor Books, 2002), 263.
7   Cohen, 263.
8   H. R. McMaster, *Dereliction of Duty* (New York: Harper Collins, 2017), 11.

CHAPTER 4

Earth Must Come First!

Civil-Military Relations in *The Expanse*

Jo Brick

————————▶

> War is always likely and is ultimately inevitable. Its immediate causes spring from
> conflicting state policies, but its fundamental causes lie deep in human nature where
> exist the sources of all human conflict
>
> —SAMUEL P. HUNTINGTON, *THE SOLDIER AND THE STATE* [1]

The Expanse is set centuries into the future and is a story of human civilization on
Earth, Mars, and the Asteroid Belt between Mars and Jupiter. James S. A. Corey
explains that the story is about what drove humanity from Earth and how the
protagonists tackle the inevitable problems that accompany *the expanse* of human
civilization. [2] In the fictional universe of *The Expanse*, the United Nations (UN) has
evolved into a global institution representing Earth in the Sol system. The human
society tasked with terraforming Mars was ultimately granted independence, becoming the Martian Congressional Republic (MCR). Earth and Mars are competing
superpowers within the Sol system, with the Asteroid Belt's inhabitants, or "Belters,"
the oppressed workers providing labor and resources for the superpowers. The Belter
factions' interests are represented by the Outer Planets Alliance (OPA), which is
vying for recognition of the rights and interests of the Belters. The weaponization
of the alien "protomolecule" by the galactic corporation Protogen contributes to a
technological and pseudo-nuclear arms race. [3]

As Huntington articulates in the opening epigraph, the causes of war lie deep
in human nature. Therefore, it is unsurprising that centuries into the future and
at the outer reaches of our solar system, the precursors for war exist through the
simple dynamic of human co-existence. The primary themes that set the foundation
for the series are not new. The emphasis on particular social institutions that drive
and manage the conflict and competition between the key players—military forces,
political leadership, and private companies—provide the backdrop against which to
consider contemporary civil-military relations. Conflict and competition between

Earth, Mars, and the Belt form the story arcs in *The Expanse*. These story arcs offer the opportunity to examine three critical civil-military relations themes: classical versus contemporary civil-military relations theory, the military as an "instrument" and the concept of "unlimited liability," and the military-industrial complex.

The Inner Planets and the Unequal Dialogue

Huntington articulates the classical approach to civil-military relations in *The Soldier and The State* through his theory of "objective control." His theory proposes that civilian control of the military necessitates separating the military profession from politics and giving the military deference in military matters. Objective control is founded on the premise that the military profession is educated and can be trusted to act in the state's interests, not be subject to politics. Huntington delineates a clear division of labor between the military profession and politics. He considers that "politics is beyond the scope of military competence and the participation of military officers in politics undermines their professionalism, curtailing their professional competence, dividing the profession against itself, and substituting extraneous values for professional values. The military officer must remain neutral politically."[4] Huntington further states that military officers have three critical responsibilities to the state:

> Representative function: To represent the military arm by informing the authorities of the resource requirements necessary to achieve the minimum security requirements of the state.
>
> Advisory function: ... to analyze and to report on the implications of alternative courses of state action from the military point of view.
>
> Executive function: ... to implement state decisions with respect to military security even if it is a decision which runs violently counter to his military judgement.[5]

To civilian leadership, these functions are generally accepted military responsibilities. However, as they are connected to political considerations, stating them as discrete and separate from politics makes for an inadequate articulation of normative civil-military relations. Risa Brooks argues that this clean divide described by Huntington results from a few assumptions, including the need for the military to "abstain from all that is political," which includes separating political and military considerations during a military officer's analysis.[6]

The advisory function that Huntington identified above is founded on a core responsibility to the state. Specifically, "the principal responsibility of the military officer is to the state. His responsibility to the state is the responsibility of the expert adviser."[7] In Avasarala's words to Admiral Souther, "Why don't you grow a pair and tell me what you really think?"[8] She is asking for more than just sterile military advice separated from politics; the conversation that transpires between them is frank and honest and includes Souther's opinion of Avasarala herself.[9]

Eliot Cohen provides an evolved perspective of the civil-military relationship in *Supreme Command*, in which he describes the "unequal dialogue." He defines this concept as "a dialogue, in that both sides expressed their views bluntly, indeed, sometimes offensively, and not once but repeatedly—and unequal, in that the final authority of the civilian leader was unambiguous and unquestioned—indeed, in all cases stronger at the end of a war than it had been at the beginning."[10] Where Huntington believes that civilian responsibility ends with establishing the strategy and framework for war and military responsibility begins with the conduct of the war, Cohen's view is that the civil-military relationship, particularly in wartime, is a collaborative one that includes constant arbitration and review by civilian leaders as the conditions assumed at the start will inevitably change due to the dynamic nature of conflict and competition with an adversary.[11]

Throughout the first three seasons of *The Expanse*, there are several scenes of the civil-military interaction between the UN's civilian and military leadership, which were usually in a state of great tension. Avasarala generally opted to pursue more diplomatic and de-escalatory approaches for dealing with perceived Martian hostility, with some military leaders—notably Admiral Augusto Nguyen—pushing for aggressive deterrence. One notable incident in the UN Situation Room involved the organization's response to the Martian Congressional Republic Navy (MCRN) ship *Scirocco* approaching Phoebe station, where an Earth-based company—Protogen—was engaged in a joint venture with Mars. A United Nations Navy (UNN) ship, *Nathan Hale*, is positioned between the station and the MCRN ship. UN Undersecretary Sadavir Errinwright wants *Nathan Hale* to attack *Scirocco*. Admiral Nguyen—who assumes Mars is moving to launch strikes across the system—agrees with Errinwright: an attack would deter Martian aggression. Avasarala asks if Martian ships have made any provocative acts. Nguyen menacingly responds, "By the time you see it on the display, it will be too late." Avasarala replies, "I know how this fucking thing works. Answer the question!" Nguyen concedes that Mars has made no provocative actions, and the Secretary-General decides to "let the saber-rattling" play out.[12] Ultimately, the MCRN ship launches missiles on Phoebe station and destroys it.

Subsequent discussion concerns Earth's response to Martian aggression. The conversation between the civilian and military leaders is an interactive and collaborative one with no clear lines of demarcation that keep them in the "lanes" described by Huntington. In the aftermath of the attack on Phoebe station, the discussion turns to retaliation options. Nguyen continues to advocate for a strike against the *Scirocco*. Avasarala suggests to Errinwright that Earth should strike the Martian moon Deimos, arguing this would be a proportionate response yet would send a strong strategic message. Souther refuses to follow this order and resigns his post as the Fleet Commander, and he is reassigned to the UNN Jupiter Fleet.[13]

With civilian leaders making the final decision, the nature of the unequal dialogue places the military officer who disagrees in an awkward position. This challenge, however, is a separate issue from being directed to execute an illegal order. The professional ideal requires that military officer to "salute and carry on." However, as Jim Golby argues, resignation also becomes a potent form of protest that can become a political act—the very type of political act meant to be outside the purview of the military profession.[14]

In a separate incident later in the series, Avasarala is pursuing Marcus Inaros, an OPA pirate, when she receives intelligence that he is aboard a civilian ship, *Pizzouza*. She wants to capture and try Inaros as a deterrent to other pirates. She asks for military options from General McCourt, another military advisor, who suggests two courses of action: order the UNN *Raskounikov* to destroy the *Pizzouza* or direct a United Nations Marine Corps (UNMC) boarding party to capture Inaros. In delivering the options, General McCourt did not elaborate on either option or raise any concerns with potential consequences. Avasarala elects to dispatch the boarding party, a disastrous operation that results in the loss of the *Pizzouza*, its crew, and the UNMC personnel. General McCourt later offers his resignation to Avasarala, whom he criticizes for ordering the operation without adequate intelligence. McCourt tells Avasarala that he does not want to continue to serve a leader who recklessly places his units in danger for her own ends.[15]

In both instances, officers resigned in protest to the decisions of civilian leaders. The difference between the two is the level of agency that each officer had in influencing the civilian leader's decision. In Souther's case, the civilian leadership had made its decision; he had no other option but to execute the mission or resign in protest. This situation is the consequence of the unequal dialogue. In contrast, McCourt's resignation was unprofessional and unjustified, as he sought only to avoid responsibility for his role in withholding information that might have helped to avert disaster. McCourt's resignation is consistent with a Huntingtonian approach to civil-military relations—where the civilian made their decision after military advice was offered and responsibility was divided between the two. McCourt's actions imply that Avasarala bears sole responsibility for the mission's failure and the hard line that separates politics from military action absolves him of any responsibility.

In both cases, the question remains whether resignation in protest was useful or productive in ensuring Earth's strategic interests. Golby argues that the growing acceptance of resignation as protest degrades constructive discussion and strategy development. Disagreement is a routine and expected part of the civil-military dialogue. It is up to those in elected office to make the final decision, even if it is wrong. Peter Feaver refers to this as the elected civilian leader's "right to be wrong."[16] Military leaders need to understand these aspects of the unequal dialogue to fulfill the functions outlined by Huntington effectively. Golby elaborates that "Although military expertise is imperfect and only one input policy makers consider, a forthright, candid civil-military dialogue decreases the likelihood of strategic miscalculation and increases the odds of effective policy making."[17] This is consistent with Cohen's "unequal dialogue" approach to civil-military relations, which provides for a healthier civil-military relationship that requires senior military leaders remain "in the game" to prevent such strategic miscalculation, rather than resigning in protest. As Avasarala explained to Souther after he resigned, "Anyone with half a brain knew we were not going to leave that room without an escalation …. I'm simply telling you how your tantrum got you sidelined and how does that help your larger cause."[18]

The Military as an Instrument—Unlimited Liability

Military theorist Carl von Clausewitz explains that war is "a true political instrument, a continuation of political intercourse, carried on with other means."[19] The military is a social institution that is the primary instrument for war. However, it is not only in war that the military institution has utility to civilian leaders. Indeed, there are some circumstances in which there is little or no agency for the military to have a voice in decisions that affect individuals or the institution. General Sir John Hackett calls this notion the "unlimited liability contract." He explains that when individuals join the military, "they surrender certain rights by the very nature of their military service—they must obey legal orders, are placed at an increased risk of harm, and they surrender basic human rights simply because of their military service, such as the right to safety, to autonomy, to freedom of movement, and so on."[20] In *The Expanse*, there are two significant aspects of the story arc that demonstrate the unlimited liability contract entered into by members of the UNN and the MCRN.

Fred Johnson is an important Belter political figure, a former UNMC colonel involved in the capture of Anderson Station from insurgents, an incident that involved the deaths of thousands of civilians. Despite accolades from the inner planets and receiving the UNMC's highest honors, he became known in the Belt as "The Butcher of Anderson Station." He ultimately left the UNMC and sought redemption by working to support the interests of Belters.[21] Souther explains to Avasarala that the real story was withheld by the previous UN administration: the group that took over Anderson Station was trying to negotiate a surrender with the UNN for several days, but the UNN was jamming their communications. Johnson was not informed of the attempted negotiation or jamming while he coordinated the strike against Anderson Station. The UN intended all along to destroy the station to serve as a warning to the Belters: "Defy us and we will wipe you out."[22]

Martian Marine Corps (MMC) Gunnery Sergeant Roberta "Bobbie" Draper leads her crew on patrol along the border on Ganymede, one of Jupiter's moons. Considered "the breadbasket of the outer planets," Ganymede is the home of a joint UN/MCR agricultural station. An unknown life form attacks the UNN and MMC forces stationed there, and Draper is the lone survivor from her crew. The incident is the catalyst for a war between Earth and Mars over Ganymede, ultimately leading to the agricultural station's destruction. Draper later discovers that the unknown life form was a human-protomolecule hybrid Protogen developed with support from UN and MCR elements as part of Project Caliban, the ongoing effort to weaponize the alien protomolecule. The attack on Ganymede was a field test of the hybrid.[23]

Without their willing participation or knowledge, their respective governments used them to achieve strategic outcomes, resulting in significant consequences for each individual. Fred Johnson sought redemption by working for the OPA's interests; Bobbie Draper sought the truth and left the MMC disillusioned and broken. These vignettes offer some insight into the individual consequences of military service and pose the question of what obligations wider civil society owes to its veterans. These circumstances are consistent with the use of the military for strategic ends and fall under a broad reading of Hackett's "unlimited liability contract." The substance and extent of the unlimited liability contract is still the subject of significant debate. One key issue is the "duty of care" owed by military forces to their members. In the United Kingdom, the Supreme Court ruled that the Ministry of Defence could be sued because the European Convention on Human Rights imposes a duty of care to protect individuals' lives.[24] But, in the United States, the Feres Doctrine prohibits all claims against the Department of Defense for injury or death over a military member's period of service. The discussion around "unlimited liability" and military members' rights is a significant civil-military issue yet to be resolved, even in an imagined science fiction universe of the distant future.

The Military-Industrial Complex and Civil-Military Relations

The industrialization of conflict and the associated transformation of the military profession, particularly after World War II, forced the convergence of military and civilian organizations through partnerships between military forces and civilian industry. In his farewell speech from the White House in 1961, United States President Dwight D. Eisenhower warned of the so-called "the military-industrial complex:"

> This conjunction of an immense military establishment and a large arms industry is new in the American experience. The total influence—economic, political, even spiritual—is felt in every city, every State house, every office of the Federal government. We recognize the imperative need for this development. Yet we must not fail to comprehend its grave implications ... In the councils of government, we must guard against the acquisition of unwarranted influence, whether sought or unsought, by the military-industrial [sic] complex. The potential for the disastrous rise of misplaced power exists and will persist.[25]

Eisenhower's speech was timely. In the aftermath of World War II, civilian industry that had mobilized in support of the war effort reverted to pre-war production activities. For example, Ford built military vehicles during the war but returned to automobile manufacturing once the war ended.[26] This dynamic changed with the advent of the Cold War when the arms race against the Soviet Union spurred an industry that specialized in the development of military equipment.

A dedicated and specialized defense sector grew out of this dependency on specialist expertise in military technology and represented a further evolution in the civil-military relationship. The civil-military relationship was no longer exclusively about strategy and national interest but also associated questions about resources and capability. These are equally important issues for civil-military engagement as strategy is useless without the effective means and resources to realize it. Industrial and capability considerations directly affect a crucial lever of civilian control identified by Morris Janowitz—budget control, where the executive "set the upper limits on the basis of a balance of presumed economic capabilities and political feasibility."[27] As Eisenhower warned, both parties in the civil-military relationship must guard against the "unwarranted influence" that would be exerted by the military-industrial complex. For both civilian and military leaders, the duty to the nation is paramount; however, the defense industry's influence can subvert individuals.

Within *The Expanse* universe, Jules-Pierre Mao exerts significant "unwarranted influence" over civilian leaders on both Earth and Mars. Errinwright expressly tells Avasarala that he was conspiring with Mao to weaponize the protomolecule to ensure that Earth gained a strategic advantage over Mars.[28] However, unbeknownst to Errinwright, Mao had also entered into a financial agreement with Martian Minister of Defence Pyotr Korshunov, even providing a sample of the protomolecule.[29] Mao was the stereotypical defense industrialist Eisenhower warned of—focused on corporate profits to the detriment of the state.

Errinwright's efforts to gain personally from his relationship with Mao were in direct conflict with his duty to Earth. After the destruction of Phoebe Station, he advocates fortifying Earth's minor stations and pushes for an attack against the MCRN *Scirocco*. Amid peace talks between Earth and Mars in the aftermath of the Ganymede incident, Errinwright's actions were focused on protecting his and Mao's interests in developing Protogen's technology. Errinwright wanted to start a war between Earth and Mars, believing his access to the protomolecule gave the former a distinct advantage.

While Errinwright's collusion with Protogen and his subsequent behavior form extreme examples, they demonstrate how a close relationship between the defense industry and any of the parties in the civil-military relationship can bias decisions in favor of corporate rather than national interests. Situations like this are perhaps what Eisenhower meant by "unwarranted influence" in "the councils of government." In contrast to Errinwright, Avasarala exercises brutal diplomacy to achieve her declared end state that "Earth must come first!" Her behavior is within the bounds of expected civil-military relations, without the extraneous and inappropriate complications of industry influence. In her rage against Jules-Pierre Mao, she says to Errinwright:

"I will freeze their assets, cancel their contracts, cripple their business! And I have the power to do it 'cos I am the fucking hero who helped save Mother Earth from the cataclysm that Jules-Pierre Mao unleashed! Tell his children the government is more powerful than any corporation. And the only reason they think it tilts the other way is because we poor public servants are always looking for some fat, private sector payoff down the road. But I'm not looking!"[30]

Human co-existence provides the foundation for both human collaboration and conflict. The seeds of war will accompany humans wherever they travel. *The Expanse* offers an in-depth exploration of warfare and human competition on a galactic scale. Although set in the distant future, the story provides insights into enduring civil-military themes that are an expected outcome of strategic-level engagement between civilian and military leaders.

Notes

1   Samuel P. Huntington, *The Soldier and The State: The Theory and Politics of Civil-Military Relations* (Cambridge: Harvard University Press, 1957), 65.
2   James S. A. Corey is the pen names for authors Daniel Abraham and Ty Franck. See 'Extras' in James S. A. Corey, *Leviathan Awakes* (London: Orbit, 2011).
3   "The Expanse Wiki," Fandom, accessed December 29, 2020, https://expanse.fandom.com/wiki/The_Expanse_Wiki. "The Expanse Wiki" is a key reference for the background material about the television series. The "protomolecule" is an extra-territorial life form discovered on Phoebe. Dr. Dresden, from Protogen, described it as an organism that can repurpose other life forms to evolve. See *The Expanse*, season 2, episode 2, "Doors and Corners," directed by Breck Eisner, aired Feb 1, 2017, Syfy.
4   Huntington, *The Soldier and The State*, 71.
5   Ibid., 72.
6   Risa Brooks, "Paradoxes of Professionalism. Rethinking Civil-Military Relations in the United States," *International Security*, Vol. 44, No. 4 (Spring 2020), 11.
7   Huntington, *The Soldier and The State*, 16.
8   "Doors and Corners."
9   Ibid.
10 Eliot A. Cohen, *Supreme Command: Soldiers, Statesmen, and Leadership in Wartime* (New York: First Anchor Books, 2003), 209.
11 Ibid., 50.
12 "Doors and Corners."
13 Ibid.
14 Jim Golby, "Beyond the Resignation Debate: A New Framework for Civil-Military Dialogue," *Strategic Studies Quarterly* (Fall 2015).
15 *The Expanse*, season 4, episode 7, "A Shot in the Dark," directed by Dan Nowak, aired December 12, 2019, Amazon Prime Video; *The Expanse*, season 4, episode 8, "The One-Eyed Man," directed by Dan Nowak, aired December 12, 2019, Amazon Prime Video.
16 Golby, 20.
17 Ibid., 19.
18 "Doors and Corners."
19 Carl von Clausewitz, *On War*, trans. Michael Howard and Peter Paret (Princeton, NJ: Princeton University Press, 1976), 87.

20 Nikki Coleman, "The Unlimited Liability Contract and Its effects on Serving Military Personnel," in *Routledge Handbook of Military Ethics*, ed. George Lucas (New York: Routledge, 2015), 276.

21 "Fred Johnson," "The Expanse Wiki," Fandom, accessed November 30, 2020, https://expanse. fandom.com/wiki/Fred_Johnson_(TV).

22 "Doors and Corners."

23 *The Expanse*, season 2, episode 6, "Paradigm Shift," directed by David Grossman, aired Mar 1, 2017, Syfy; *The Expanse*, season 2, episode 11, "Here There be Dragons," directed by Rob Lieberman, aired Apr 5, 2017, Syfy.

24 Coleman, 281–282.

25 Dwight D. Eisenhower, "Military-Industrial Complex Speech, 1961," The Avalon Project, Yale Law School, accessed October 12, 2020, https://avalon.law.yale.edu/20th_century/eisenhower001. asp.

26 National Public Radio Staff, "Ike's Warning of Military Expansion, 50 Years Later," Morning Edition, NPR, Jan 17, 2011, https://www.npr.org/2011/01/17/132942244/ ikes-warning-of-military-expansion-50-years-later.

27 Morris Janowitz, *The Professional Soldier: A Social and Political Portrait* (New York: The Free Press, 1971), 363.

28 "Paradigm Shift."

29 *The Expanse*, season 2, episode 12, "The Monster and The Rocket," directed by Rob Lieberman, aired Apr 17, 2017, Syfy.

30 "Paradigm Shift."

CHAPTER 5

You're Not Ender Wiggins, and That's Okay

Will Meddings

There is so much that is great about science fiction. All fiction allows the reader to escape, but science fiction creates alternate worlds, perhaps the ultimate escape from reality. Yet to dismiss science fiction as pure escapism is to miss its benefits. The forward-looking alternate worlds of science fiction allow the reader to examine "What if?" Science fiction is a sandbox, an open-plan world where the reader can ponder the futures of society, politics, and warfare. And as military theorist Carl von Clausewitz tells us, they are all intertwined. But if science fiction allows mind-expanding flights-of-fantasy, there is one area to exercise caution: If the stories are grounded in a context and society far removed from the here and now, is it safe to learn lessons about the essential nature of human interaction?

Orson Scott Card's *Ender's Game* is a popular source for lessons on team building. The Mobile Infantry in Robert A Heinlein's *Starship Troopers* allow us to ponder the leadership challenges of super soldiers. Frank Herbert's *Dune* series follows Paul Atreides on his path to become emperor of a galactic imperium. These examples raise the larger question of can science fiction be used to learn about leadership? The answer is yes; in fact, it should be used. It just needs to be used with care.

The Great Men and Women of Science Fiction

There is a problem we all have when we consider successful leaders. We think of them as heroes and heroines, and heroic figures are integral to fiction. Every story has a hero, or at least a protagonist. But it is especially true of science fiction, and herein lies the problem. Science fiction serves us heroic leaders on a plate, ready to be admiringly examined before we consume them. And the meal is so pleasing to the palate and alluring to the eye that we swallow it down without stopping to think.

As we consume these titans of leadership and search for their copiable traits, we swallow leadership's greatest lie: Leaders are great people and, to be a great leader, all you have to do is emulate them. This notion is known as the "Great Man" theory; by looking at the roots of personal histories, we can identify traits that will lead to leadership greatness, too. If we read science fiction through the lens of the Great Man theory, what do we see? We see individual leaders as all-knowing and near perfect. We see the Enders, Peters, and Valentines of *Ender's Game*. The Pauls and Jessicas of *Dune*. Yes, each of them is flawed. Yet each of them still has some sort of super-human ability that allows them to rise above the crowd.

If you were to spend years researching each of these heroes and heroines, you *would* find some definable traits worth emulating. However, such traits would be context-specific and far from agreed upon. *Ender's Game* offers a perfect example. Leadership coach Hans Eckman concludes that Ender Wiggin has seven leadership secrets: he shifts his perspective when needed, understands local knowledge, knows his team, trusts his team, knows that too much structure is bad for performance, builds adaptive teams, and does not overuse his "A team."[1] Business coach Hwai Tah Lee identifies five of Ender's traits worth emulating and, in a *Forbes* article, Alex Knapp uncovers four leadership lessons from Ender.[2] Each author finds a different set of traits or lessons in *Ender's Game,* and there is no commonality among them.

The lack of commonality amongst these analyses is not a science fiction problem but a "Great Man" problem; the same phenomenon exists with the study of real-world leaders. How many of Genghis Khan's leadership traits should you copy? If you believe John Man, 21, but if you follow Isaac Chiefetz, just five.[3] In 1997, Mike Murdoch wrote that Jesus had 58 leadership secrets; a year later, Gene Wilkes identified only seven.[4] It gets worse if you compare traits. Mother Theresa insists you "submit to others as a spiritual disciple," while the United States commando leadership guide recommends you tell your people, "I will treat you all alike—just like shit."[5]

Studying leadership through the lens of science fiction is not simply a matter of identifying traits that can be emulated. Not only is the story *not* based on reality as we know it, but the characters' actions are also not based on any actual leadership process. Frank Herbert knew this when he wrote *Dune*. In 1988, Herbert said, "I am showing you the superhero syndrome," he said, "and your own participation in it."[6] Four years later, he added, "The bottom line of the *Dune* trilogy is: Beware of heroes. Much better rely on your own judgment, and your own mistakes."[7]

The Reality of Fictitious Leaders

So, what is reality? Looking for leaders' copiable traits leads us to the conclusion that leadership is something that some have, and others do not; leadership is a noun, something that people are, rather than a verb; and leadership is a *process* in which people are participants. Studying leadership by only analyzing perfect leaders is bound to fail, especially if we only examine fictitious ones.

That is not to say there are no lessons to be learned. In many ways, the greatest real-life leaders seem to *be* perfect—not perfect individuals, just perfect role models. Their characteristics and traits are idealized, respected, and admired; they embody what it means to be a member of the group. Many of the "great" leaders studied in depth are what are known as the *prototypes* of the group they led. The idea of a *group prototype* comes from the study of group identity. Every group that comes together does so for one of three broad reasons: they like the group's task, they like the group's people, or they like how the group helps them feel satisfied.[8] They begin as outsiders but, over time, become an in-group. Once people genuinely become part of an in-group, they forge a common bond and grow to have a shared identity: sports teams, professional groups, and, of course, military organizations. You identify with each group for a specific reason, and each has its own values. Research tells us that as time goes by, the more you buy into the values, the greater you associate with the group, and the more you embed and exhibit those values.[9]

The same is true in science fiction. The Fremen of *Dune* possess a set of codes and values central to their existence, values that they cannot betray. Most armies in *Ender's Game* have group values centered on strength, discipline, and hierarchy—values that Ender threatens or rejects, cementing his place as an outsider. And in the early parts of Asimov's *Foundation* series, the Foundation's values center around scientific study and non-intervention—values that change over the centuries-long span of the books.

This is important because leadership is a group process, rather than universal individual traits. It revolves around the group's identity, norms, and values being led and how the leader represents them. In their pioneering work on identity and leadership, Haslam, Platow, and Reicher demonstrated how leaders are influential and effective to the extent to which they represent "one of us" or even "the best of us"—with the idea of "us" being related of the group's identity and values.[10]

Perhaps the best example of this phenomenon in science fiction is found in *Starship Troopers*. This science fiction classic follows Johnny Rico and his fellow Mobile Infantry recruits in their year-long boot camp at Camp Currie, a period in which they go from a gang of individuals to a tight-knit group of soldiers with an extremely focused set of values: endurance, physical bravery, discipline, honor, and living life "heads up, on the bounce, and still trying."[11] From the outset, they resent their cruel torturer, Career Ship's Sergeant Zim. But, by the time they graduate—with a 90% failure rate—Johnny admires Zim, who is "unquestionably [a] better soldier than any of the other instructors ...."[12] And in the final chapter of the book, Zim, this prototype of the Mobile Infantry's values, is Johnny's Platoon Sergeant and "the best sergeant in the fleet."[13] Zim represents the "best of us." He is a role model of the Mobile Infantry's values and a prototype of what a leader in the Mobile Infantry must be.

Career Ship's Sergeant Zim teaches two other vital lessons in forging effective leadership. If leadership is about being the prototype or role model of a group's identity, there can be no leadership if there is no shared identity. So, an effective leader is not just a prototype of the group; they also build a group by forging shared values. They must be a *builder of collective identity*, which is precisely what Zim does at Camp Currie.

A leader needs to be more than just a builder—and eventual prototype—of an identity. There must be more. Otherwise, the most punishing drill instructor would always be the "best" leader. The difference comes in showing that a leader puts the group before themselves. They are a champion of the *in-group*, a leader who is "in it for us," not themselves. When recruit Ted Hendrick strikes Zim—a crime punishable by death—Zim avoids reporting him to the battalion commander. Instead, he privately accepts responsibility, as he put himself in a position that allowed the hot-headed Hendrick to hit him. He wishes he could take the flogging himself instead and volunteers to leave the unit on the basis that "it would be best for the outfit."

Not best for him, of course. It would be terrible for him. But both Zim and his commander want what is best for the group, not what is best for the two of them. "Those that are left are eager, anxious to please, and on the bounce ... A lot of them will make good soldiers," Zim comments, in defense of his in-group.[14]

The entire exchange is an epiphany for Johnny Rico: Zim is neither evil nor sadistic. Everything he does is for the best of the group. This is not about his ego. Zim is a champion of the group. He becomes an exemplar for Johnny Rico.

Leaders Are Builders, Prototypes, and Champions

If leadership is about the relationship between a group's identity and the leader, what are the rules? And what examples can science fiction provide from which to learn? The journey of Rico's group is relatively simple. Zim forms the group with shared values and a prototype. Zim role-models the values, is the group prototype, and champions the group. As a result, the process of leadership drives collective action: Rico and his fellow soldiers go to war against the Bugs, and the group's identity is reinforced. Rico then becomes an officer. As a role model and champion of the group identity, he, in turn, can be a leader.

Of course, not every science fiction story conveys such a simple soldier-boot camp narrative. In *Dune,* the situation for Paul Atreides is much different. The Fremen, the group he leads to overthrow the Harkonnen and liberate Arrakis, already possess a group identity and shared values. As a result, the story unfolds around Paul's journey to becoming their leader, remolding their identity into revolutionary warriors and leading them into battle on Arrakis and across the stars.

Although the circumstances are different, many of the same lessons are revealed. The Fremen have a powerful, ingrained identity, forged in a battle for survival against both the elements and their Harkonnen overlords. Slowly, Paul begins to exhibit these values, often accidentally, and assisted by his psychic powers. By the middle of Book

Two of *Dune*, Paul has proven himself in combat, lived their values, and overtaken Stilgar—the existing and respected tribal leader—as a role model for the tribe. The physical struggle between Stilgar and Paul cements Paul as leader of the tribe, a role that Stilgar knows he no longer holds even before they fight. Once established as their leader, it is easy for Paul to champion the group's needs by helping them bring life to the desert and leading them successfully in battle against the Harkonnen. From there, he can lead the group to liberate Arrakis. But his leadership does more than achieve this collective action. It reinforces their identity and remolds it. As the series progresses, these desert insurgents, once happy to hide on Arrakis and carry out their centuries-long quest to terraform their world, have become an interstellar army capable of—and driven to—overrun the Imperium.

Paul Atreides's journey with the Fremen is different from Zim's and Johnny's. He finds a group with shared values and a prototype, he role models the values, and he becomes the prototype and champion for the group. As a result, the process of leadership causes collective action: Paul and the Fremen overthrow the Harkonnen. In doing so, he remolds the group's identity around a new set of values. Values that, coincidentally, he now embodies as their new emperor. The Fremen become an elite army and help Paul conquer the known universe.

Ender's Game, the most popular science fiction-as-leadership-education novel, offers the most complicated example. Ender spends most of the novel as an outsider. Although capable and intelligent, he is never accepted because he does not fit the "shut up, do your time, and don't rock the boat" values of the group he joins. But, over time his abilities *are* recognized: by other outsiders. The fact that he wins matters; success in a group's chosen endeavor is universally valued. It demonstrates that when the group follows a successful individual, they all succeed.

So, Ender gathers a group. It forms somewhat naturally, but it builds as he runs his battle room classes. Ender's group has *three* out-groups to oppose, which helps it cohere even more tightly: the alien Formics and the opposing Battle School student armies and the adult authority figures running the Battle and Command Schools. Like Zim, although less purposefully, Ender forms a group that shares his values and for which he is the prototype. In his mind, winning in the battle room—and unknowingly in the war—is as much about striking back at these authority figures as it is about beating the Formics. Of course, the finale for Ender's group is much different than that of the Mobile Infantry or the Fremen. With the war over, the group goes its separate ways. The context in which the group forms no longer exists, and in the final twist of this profoundly anti-war book, Ender entirely uproots and changes his values.

So, what is Ender's journey? Dragon Army forms as a group of outsiders from the other armies. Its shared values and prototype form; Ender role models these values, becomes the group prototype, and champions the group. The process of leadership causes collective action—Ender leads his final army to success against the Formics. The group identity is reinforced, but Ender's values are no longer those of his group.

The Pattern

If leadership is about the relationship between the leader and the group they lead, then identity is the pivot across which the lever of leadership works. The patterns that emerge in each example form a set of somewhat universal rules of leadership:

> Rule 1: Leaders need to build a group identity. Make an "us."
> Rule 2: Leaders need to be a prototype or role model of the group identity. Be "the best of us."
> Rule 3: Leaders need to champion the group. "Do it for us."
> Rule 4: Leaders use collective action to reinforce or remold the group identity into something useable. "Redefine or reinforce what it means to be us."

These identity and leadership processes are universal, yet they are challenging to analyze because they focus too much on searching for a list of copiable traits. Those who study leadership often want the lessons to be simple. "Do this, do that, be a great leader." If only life—real or fictitious—was so simple.

Be the Leader of *Your* Group

In the end, the truth is that you should not look to Ender, Johnny, Zim, or Paul to identify leadership traits to emulate. Each has its own context unique to its particular fictional circumstances. Psychologically-damaged-yet-brilliant Ender led an army of fellow super-children in battle—you will not. Paul Atreides was a psychic, with a psychic mother, who led an army of desert warriors to galactic domination—you will not. And Johnny and Zim? Perhaps you might just form, role model, champion, and lead soldiers in battle, but you probably will not use the Mobile Infantry's harsh 90%-failure-rate methods while fighting against an intergalactic bug horde. Instead, look for the other lessons—ones about identity, group values, role-modelling, and championing groups. There, you will find the relationships that enable and empower leadership.

Ender was, unwittingly, a role model for the specific super-human children he went on to lead. He was a prototype of their identity; someone Dragon Army felt represented them: an outsider, young but ruthlessly—and selflessly—focused on winning for the good of the team and humanity. He fought their corner against others and shaped their identity into something he could lead.

Zim knowingly built an identity based on a set of organizational values. He championed a group, working for their own good, not his. By doing this, not only could Zim lead them but, later, Rico could go on to become the prototype and champion that could lead them in turn.

And Paul Atreides found an existing group with a solid identity and set of values. He demonstrated and embodied those values, championed the group's societal and military needs, and led them to success. In doing so, he remolded their identity in a way that only a genuinely prototypical leader can. And so, he began the process again.

To learn the lessons of leadership from science fiction, look for the identity of the followers. See how the leader positions themselves as the prototype of the identity and then shapes and develops that identity, and how they use it as a lever to influence and drive collective action. Then understand the identity of the group that you lead. Represent it. Build it. Shape it towards an end.

You do not need to be super-human to be a leader. You do not need to be Ender. Because you are not. And that is OK.

Notes

1   Hans Eckman, "7 Leadership Secrets from Ender Wiggin," *Eckman Guides*, October 31, 2017, accessed December 20, 2020, https://hanseckman.com/guides/7-leadership-secrets-from-ender-wiggin-enders-game-2/.

2   Hwai Tah Lee, "Leadership lessons from Enders Game," *Coaching Journey*, accessed December 20, 2020, https://coaching-journey.com/leadership-lessons-from-enders-game/; and Alex Knapp, "Four leadership lessons from Ender's Game, *Forbes*, Sept 16, 2013, accessed December 20, 2020, https://www.forbes.com/sites/alexknapp/2013/09/16/four-leadership-lessons-from-enders-game/?sh=78ff36913252.

3   John Man, *Leadership Secrets of Genghis Khan* (New York: Random House, 2009); and Isaac Chiefetz, "Management secrets of Genghis Khan," *Minneapolis Star Tribune*, Jan 17, 2005.

4   Mike Murdock, *The leadership secrets of Jesus* (Tulsa, OK: Honor Books, 1997); and Gene Wilkes, *Jesus on leadership: Discovering the secrets of servant leadership from the life of Christ* (Wheaton, IL: Tynedale House Publishers, 1998).

5   Rick Dugan, "Leadership secrets of Mother Theresa," *St George The Dragonslayer*, October 24, 2007, accessed December 20, 2020, https://web.archive.org/web/20071221073457/http://honest2blog.wordpress.com/category/leadership/; and Richard Marcinko, *Leadership Secrets of the Rogue Warrior: A Commando's Guide to Success* (New York: Pocket Books, 1998).

6   Quoted in William Touponce, *Frank Herbert* (Boston: Twayne Publishers, 1988), 24.

7   Quoted in Thomas Clareson, *Understanding Contemporary American Science Fiction: The Formative Period* (Columbia: University of South Carolina Press, 1992), 169–172.

8   Rodney Napier and Matti Gershenfeld, *Groups: Theory and experience* (Boston: Houghton Mifflin, 1999).

9   S. Alexander Haslam, Stephen Reicher, and Michael Platow, *The New Psychology of Leadership* (New York: Psychology Press, 2011), 55–56.

10 Ibid., 84.

11 Robert A. Heinlein, *Starship Troopers* (London: Hodder & Stoughton, 2014), 61.

12 Ibid., 128.

13 Ibid., 268.

14 Ibid., 74.

CHAPTER 6

Princess Leia and the Strategic Art of *Métis*

Heather S. Gregg

Currently, women play a limited role in combat, war planning, and military strategy in most countries. In the United States, for example, women were excluded from combat units until 2013, when Secretary of Defense Leon Panetta overturned the 1994 Combat Exclusion Policy.[1] Even in the wake of its repeal, the U.S. military continues to struggle with selecting, training, and integrating women into combat arms military occupational specialties, such as infantry, artillery, and special operations forces. As of 2019, only 46 women had passed the U.S. Army Infantry Basic Officer Leader Course, and 270 enlisted women had passed infantry and armor school. As of 2018, only two women had passed the Marine Corps' Infantry Officer Course.[2] And the U.S. Navy just graduated its first African American female fighter pilot in 2020.[3]

The paucity of women in combat arms further affects the strategic level of national security. In the United States, the Joint Chiefs, the highest-ranking officers for each of the military's services, draw primarily from officers who have served in combat arms military specialties. As of 2020, no women have served as a service chief in the United States. On the civilian side, no woman has held the office of Secretary of Defense, and the highest-ranking female in the Office of the Secretary of Defense is Kathleen Hicks, who became the Deputy Secretary of Defense in 2021.[4]

By contrast, science fiction is replete with examples of women as warriors and strategists, often making them key protagonists in stories. Perhaps no woman personifies the warrior and strategist better than *Star Wars*' Princess Leia Organa, who later became General Leia Organa, and her ability to lead at both the tactical and strategic levels. Princess Leia achieved her greatness as a warrior by embracing a strategy defined by cunning, deception and trickery. She fought not by emulating a man, but by using her femininity as a resource that informed how she strategized and waged war. Leia's use of cunning and trickery hearkens back to the ancient Greek strategy of *métis*, or deception, which is juxtaposed against the strategy of *bíē*, or fighting with brute and overwhelming force, and provides an example for why this approach to warfighting is important today.

This chapter begins by providing a brief summary of the concept of *métis* in ancient Greek strategy, embodied by the goddess warriors Athena and her mother Métis, and juxtaposes this strategy against *bíē*, which is typified by the male warrior Achilles. It then draws from these ancient examples to consider the evolution of Princess Leia to General Leia and her use of deception to defeat the overwhelming force of the Empire and the First Order. The chapter concludes with considerations for how *métis* and the example of Leia could inform strategy today.

Métis in Ancient Greek Literature

While current-day societies continue to struggle with integrating women into combat units and strategic planning, ancient mythology frequently included women in these critical roles. For example, the Hindu pantheon includes Durga, a goddess of war and protection, who is tasked with combatting evil forces that threaten peace. The Hindu goddess Kali, who sprang from Durga, becomes another influencer in battle as the ruler over death and destruction.[5] Ancient myths of female warriors exist in most cultures around the globe, ranging from Africa to Asia to Europe.[6] These tales, which blend history with legend, provide examples of not only women engaging in battle, but as strategists who use their wit to deceive and ultimately defeat the enemy.

Greek mythology, in particular, offers a useful place to consider the role that goddesses played in ancient warfare and strategy. Perhaps the greatest examples of how these goddesses fought and strategized were Métis and her daughter Athena. Métis was the first wife of Zeus, the king of the pantheon. She was known for her exceptional intelligence, cunning, and "is most knowledgeable of gods and men."[7] Fearing that she would bear a son who could outwit him, Zeus consumed Métis to prevent her from producing offspring. However, unbeknownst to Zeus, Métis was already pregnant. Rather than killing their unborn child, Athena grew inside Zeus, eventually emerging from his head as a fully formed adult clad in armor. As their daughter, Athena embodied traits of both parents, possessing power and strength from her father, but also became known for her mother's traits of trickery and deception.[8]

British historian Lawrence Freedman depicts how the myth of Métis and her daughter Athena, in turn, informed ancient Greek military thought. The strategy of *métis*,[9] which does not easily translate into English, "conveyed a sense of a capacity to think ahead, attend to detail, grasp how others think and behave, and possess a general resourcefulness." Freedman also asserts that the term *métis* "could convey deception and trickery, capturing the moral ambivalence around a quality so essential to the strategist's art."[10] Freedman notes that the goddess Athena became the personification of *métis*: "Athena, as both the goddess of wisdom and war, came to be associated with *métis* more than any other of the divinities."[11]

Ancient Greek strategy juxtaposed *métis* against *bíē*, which Freedman defines as "strength," "brute force," and "passion."[12] He identifies the epic hero Achilles as the ultimate example of brute force. "*Bíē* was personified by Achilles, famed for his exceptional physical strength, bravery, agility, and mastery of the spear, but also his great rages." Freedman goes on to describe, "Achilles demonstrated not only the limits to what force could achieve, but also how it could become associated with a certain wildness, a bloodlust that led to terrible deaths and slaughter."[13] In other words, as the ultimate expression of masculinity, Achilles personifies brute force through his physical strength, rage, and potential for mass slaughter.

Freedman asserts that both *métis* and *bíē* had their limits when employed solely. "The man of action could either be admired for his courage or dismissed as a fool for his sole reliance on strength, while the man of words could be celebrated for his intelligence or treated warily because words could deceive."[14] Freedman cites Homer's juxtaposition of Achilles, who was the embodiment and master of *bíē*, with Odysseus, the master of *métis*, as examples of the duality between reason and deception on the one hand and brute force on the other, and the need to combine both in strategy. Homer's ultimate example of strength and deception working together was Odysseus's use of a giant wooden horse to smuggle soldiers into Troy, the infamous "Trojan Horse." Odysseus's plan used a carefully constructed narrative, claiming that the giant hollow wooden horse was a gift from Athena and that refusing the horse would invoke her wrath. Once inside the gates of Troy, the hidden soldiers crept out of the wooden horse and opened the city's gates, allowing Athens' army to sack the city. Both deception and strength worked together to defeat Troy.[15]

However, Freedman ultimately contends that, when faced with overwhelming force, it is deception and not force that provided the only path to success. "Whereas strength could be defeated by superior strength, *métis* could defeat all strength."[16] The role of deception and cunning in strategy, therefore, is crucial, especially when confronted with overwhelming force.

Despite the importance of deception as a critical strategy in ancient Greek literature, its use fell out of favor over time. Freedman blames the vilification of *métis* on Plato, who emphasized the search for truth and downplayed the role of cunning and deception in warfare. Freedman further contends that the centrality of Platonic thought in modern western history helped to undermine *métis* as an acceptable strategy.[17] "Given the care with which he was studied by later generations," Freedman writes, "the importance of Plato's success in this enterprise should not be underestimated."[18]

The discrediting of *métis* as an acceptable form of warfare helped pave the way for war to be defined in terms of *bíē*, or force, in the modern world. Freedman points to further western developments in the use of overwhelming force, through the *levée en masse*, advanced military technology and nuclear weapons, as examples of the continued focus on *bíē* as the preferred form of warfare.[19] Despite the persistence of deception in a few key thinkers, including Sun Tzu and Machiavelli, the role of cunning and deception lost its place as an acceptable form of warfare in the modern, western world.[20] As the primacy of brute force grew as a strategy, subsequent readings of the Trojan Horse took on decidedly negative connotations and its heroes diminished to two-faced tricksters.[21] Today, the term Trojan Horse is used to describe deceit, including a type of malware that infects computers. Ultimately, "real men" fight with overwhelming force, not trickery and deception. Science fiction, however, provides a portal back to the crucial role of *métis* in modern warfare.

Princess Leia as Master of *Métis*

The role of *métis* as a strategy in ancient Greek warfare and society provides a useful lens to analyze *Star Wars* and Princess Leia. Ultimately, a strategy of deception is both central to the way the Rebellion fought and essential for its ultimate defeat of the Empire and First Order.

In many ways, Princess Leia is the futuristic embodiment of *Métis* and Athena. As goddesses, they were associated with the female gender. However, their femininity was not something to overcome; it was deeply integrated into their success as masters of deception and warfare.[22] They were unmistakably female, both in their appearance and their actions. Princess Leia reflects these traits. She is both a princess and a warrior; she is beautiful but also deadly; she can be vulnerable and can fight; she is a mother and a general—she is a woman and a leader. Throughout the *Star Wars* saga, Princess Leia spends surprisingly little time convincing those around her that she is a warrior who can lead the Rebellion and take on the Empire or First Order. Only when they first meet does she need to convince Han Solo of her ability to fight, lead, and strategize. Even Darth Vader recognizes Princess Leia as a challenge to his authority and a potential threat to the Empire, capturing and torturing her in an attempt to retrieve the Death Star's schematics. Ultimately, Princess Leia is a powerful and dangerous warrior not in spite of her gender, but because of it; it is one of many tools with which she can wage war.

Undoubtedly, the character of Princess Leia reflects the zeitgeist of the era in which she was created. *A New Hope* was made amid the fight for the Equal Rights Amendment and the birth of the "second wave" of feminism.[23] Clearly, these themes are at play in *Star Wars*. However, rather than Princess Leia's story focusing on overcoming gender-based discrimination, her role as both a senior leader of the Resistance and a strategist of the plan to destroy the Empire is unquestioned; it just is. Her character provides an aspirational example and a role model of women as warriors and strategists in modern warfare.

Science fiction expert Brian Attebery proposes that one of the many roles of science fiction is to challenge gender stereotypes through its narratives. He argues that "… storytelling is a way of thinking about things, and science fiction is a form of storytelling that invites us to challenge standard notions of nature and culture."[24] Science fiction critic Helen Merrick echoes this sentiment, asserting "to varying degrees over its history, [science fiction] has in fact functioned as an enormously fertile environment for the exploration of sociocultural understandings of gender."[25] Princess Leia and *Star Wars* more broadly provide both a challenge to gender stereotypes and a vision for a future in which gender is not a barrier to being a warrior or strategist.

Furthermore, beyond Princess Leia's character, *Star Wars* is an example of the importance of deception and cunning as a strategy of warfare, especially when faced with overwhelming force. In virtually every episode of *Star Wars*, the Empire and the First Order are obsessed with increasing their ability to project overwhelming, brute force as a means of coercing and controlling the galaxy. *A New Hope* begins by describing that "Rebel spies managed to steal secret plans to the Empire's ultimate weapon, the Death Star, an armored space station with enough power to destroy an entire planet." In *The Empire Strikes Back,* the Imperial Star Fleet threatens to end the Rebellion. In *Return of the Jedi*, the Empire builds yet another armored space station, claiming it to be the "ultimate weapon." And, in *The Force Awakens*, the Death Star is supplanted by "Star Killer Base," which draws power from a star for a weapon exponentially stronger than either of the previous Death Stars. The Empire and First Order, in fact, never stop trying to increase their lethality as a means of dominating and controlling the universe.

Harkening back to Achilles, *Star Wars* paints this never-ending quest for brute force as hyper-masculine. The embodiment of masculinity and brute force is Darth Vader, whose very stature, six foot, six inches, stands in stark contrast to the five-foot, one-inch-tall Princess Leia.[26] Furthermore, no women appear in the ranks of the Empire in the original trilogy. Its leaders and soldiers are all men, as are its Storm Troopers. It is not until *The Force Awakens* that women appear as soldiers in the First Order, manning the Star Killer Base. There is a Storm Trooper company run by a woman, Captain Phasma, whose only indication that she is a woman is her voice. Despite these changes, *Star Wars* still depicts brute force in terms of masculinity and juxtaposes this against the small female fighters of the Rebellion and the Resistance.

To offset the brute force and lethality of the Empire and First Order, the Rebellion employs a strategy of deception and cunning. As with most insurgents, the Rebellion faces overwhelming odds in its quest to fight the Empire and First Order; they are badly outnumbered, outgunned, and under-resourced. The Resistance understands this, and rather than fight the Empire solely through a force-on-force confrontation, it focuses primarily on cunning strategies that involve finding weaknesses in their adversary and exploiting them. Whether it is stealing the plans for the first Death Star to find a vulnerability or engaging the Empire in a diversionary battle to allow time for rebels to destroy the second Death Star, deception strategies are necessary for offsetting the overwhelming force and resources of the Empire.

Star Wars demonstrates how a strategy that combines *métis* and *bíē* can produce victory; however, when faced with overwhelming force, deception wins the war, as Freedman suggests. In *The Last Jedi*, for example, Resistance forces are badly beaten in battle and reduced to no more than twenty fighters. Rey asks, "How do we build the Rebellion from this?" and General Leia responds, "We have everything we need." Ultimately, *Star Wars* is a tale about offsetting brute force with people—men, women, and other species—who are deeply committed to the cause and their use of cunning and deception to make brute force a weakness. This is *métis*.

Looking to the Future and the Past for Strategy Today

The *Star Wars* saga offers several important lessons for strategy in today's world. Perhaps chief among these lessons is the need for countries to use all resources at their disposal to face their strategic challenges and opportunities. This approach includes using the other half of the population—women—in all aspects of the use of force: as troops in battle, as commanders on the battlefield, and as strategists. As with the ancient goddesses of war, *Métis* and Athena, Princess Leia and the other female characters in *Star Wars* do not have to overcome their gender to be fierce and cunning warriors; it is part of what makes them great fighters and strategists. *Star Wars*, and science fiction more broadly, challenges assumptions about what women can and cannot do in warfare.

Another critical lesson that *Star Wars* provides is a cautionary tale about brute force's limitations in war. Both the Empire and the First Order obsess over increasing their lethality and the use of brute force to coerce the galaxy into submission. This obsession with brute force, however, becomes its ultimate vulnerability. Over and over, a small band of under-resourced rebels outwit their adversary and defeat brute force with cunning and deception. This lesson is particularly salient for the United States today. The 2018 *National Defense Strategy* aims to "build a more lethal force" as a necessary means of deterring adversaries and achieving strategic goals.[27] In an era when non-state actors such as ISIS and Al Qaeda pose a strategic threat to western powers and state adversaries use covert and evasive tactics to challenge the status quo, expanding the lethal space may not adequately address and check these threats. Lethality has its limits.

Alongside the dangers that come from an overreliance on brute force, *Star Wars* illustrates the importance of cunning and deception as a strategy in warfare, especially when faced with overwhelming force. Freedman suggests that deception fell out of favor as a strategy in western warfare through Plato's focus on the truth along with the rise of greater lethality in weapons of war. Ultimately, "real men" fight with overwhelming force, not trickery and deception. However, just as the Rebellion recognizes that it could not successfully fight the Empire or the First Order in direct force-on-force battles, so too do key adversarial powers approach great power competition with deception today. For example, Russia employs a complex strategy against its adversaries that combines several tools of deception, including a mixture of unconventional warfare, misinformation and disinformation, cyber warfare and "persistent deniability" of its actions.[28] Ultimately, Russia understands that a direct confrontation against its foes, especially the United States, is not strategically wise. They, like several other key American adversaries, have employed a strategy of *métis* when faced with overwhelming force. And, perhaps like the Resistance in *Star Wars*, *métis* will find the vulnerability of a strategy built around lethality and brute force.

Notes

1   Claudette Roulo, "Defense Department Expands Women's Combat Role," *U.S. Department of Defense*, Jan 24, 2013, https://archive.defense.gov/news/newsarticle.aspx?id=119098, as of October 9, 2020.

2   Emma Moore, "Women in Combat: Five Years Status Update," *Center for New American Security*, Mar 31, 2020, https://www.cnas.org/publications/commentary/women-in-combat-five-year-status-update#:~:text=A%20total%20of%209%20women,and%2011.2%20percent%20for%20men, as of October 9, 2020.

3   Oriana Pawlyk, "After 110 Years of Aviation, the Navy Has its First Black Female Fighter Pilot," *Military.Com*, July 10, 2020, https://www.military.com/daily-news/2020/07/10/after-110-years-of-aviation-navy-get-its-first-black-female-fighter-pilot.html, as of October 9, 2020.

4   Office of Secretary of Defense, *Department of Defense*, https://www.defense.gov/Our-Story/Office-of-the-Secretary-of-Defense/, as of April 29, 2021.

5   Laura Amazzone, "Durga: Invincible Goddess in South Asia," in Patricia Monaghan, ed. *Goddesses in World Culture*, Vol. I and II, (Santa Barbara: Praeger, 2011), 71–84; and June McDaniel, "Kali: Goddess of Life, Death and Transcendence," in Patricia Monaghan, ed. *Goddesses in World Culture*, Vol. I and II (Santa Barbara: Praeger, 2011), 17–32.

6   Patricia Monaghan, ed. *Goddesses in World Culture*, Vol. I and II (Santa Barbara: Praeger, 2011).

7   G. S. Kirk, *The Nature of Greek Myths* (New York: Barnes and Noble Press, 2009), 97.

8   Kirk, *Nature of Greek Myths*, 97–98. Lawrence Freedman, *Strategy: A History* (New York: Oxford University Press, 2013), 25.

9   When capitalized, Métis refers to the goddess. When lower-cased, *métis* refers to the strategy.

10 Freedman, *Strategy*, 23.

11 Ibid., 24.

12 Ibid., 23.

13 Ibid., 25.

14 Ibid., 22.

15 Ibid., 24.

16 Ibid., 29.

17 Ibid., 23.

18 Ibid.

19 Ibid.

20 See, for example: Sun Tzu, *The Art of War*, translated by Samuel B. Griffith (New York: Oxford University Press, 1963); and Niccolo Machiavelli, *Discourses on Livy*, translated by Harvey C. Mansfield and Nathan Tarcov (Chicago: The University of Chicago Press, 1996).

21 Freedman, *Strategy*, 25.

22 Kirk, *Nature of Greek Myths*, 97–98.

23 Sally Ann Druker, "Betty Friedan: The Three Waves of Feminism," *Ohio Humanities,* Apr 27, 2018, http://www.ohiohumanities.org/betty-friedan-the-three-waves-of-feminism/#:~:text=Second%2Dwave%20feminism%20of%20the,lives%20reflected%20sexist%20power%20structures, as of November 28, 2020.

24 Brian Attebery, *Decoding Gender in Science Fiction* (New York: Routledge, 2002), 4.

25 Helen Merrick, "Gender in Science Fiction," in Edward James and Farah Mendleson, eds., *Cambridge Companions to Science Fiction,* 241–252 (New York: Cambridge University Press, 206), 242.

26 These heights are based on the actors who portrayed the characters, David Prowse and Carrie Fisher, respectively.

27 Secretary of Defense, James Mattis, *Summary of the 2018 National Defense Strategy of the United States of America* (Washington, DC: Department of Defense, 2018), 5–6. https://dod.defense.gov/Portals/1/Documents/pubs/2018-National-Defense-Strategy-Summary.pdf, as of November 30, 2020.

28 ARIS, *Little Green Men: Modern Russian Unconventional Warfare* (Fort Bragg, NC: The United States Special Operations Command, 2014).

CHAPTER 7

Want to Know More?

Starship Troopers and Building a Better Leader

Jess Ward

———————▶

The young recruit is silly, 'e thinks o' suicide.
'E's lost 'is gutter-devil; 'e 'asn't got 'is pride;
But day by day they kicks 'im, which 'elps 'im on a bit,
Till 'e finds 'isself one mornin' with a full an' proper kit.

An' now the hugly bullets come peckin' through the dust,
An' no one wants to face 'em, but every beggar must;
So, like a man in irons, which isn't glad to go,
They moves 'em off by companies uncommon stiff an' slow.

Of all 'is five years' schoolin' they don't remember much
Excep' the not retreatin', the step an' keepin' touch.
It looks like teachin' wasted when they duck an' spread an 'op
But if 'e 'adn't learned 'em they'd be all about the shop.

RUDYARD KIPLING—THE 'EATHEN [1]

Science fiction provides a framework through which a reader can explore a theme and debate its utility within a different context, serving as a fictional "safehouse" for deconstruction and examination. Robert Heinlein's landmark novel *Starship Troopers* has borne a lot of attention since its release in 1959. For its presumed glorification of the military in society, portrayal of women, and views on civic duty, it received both criticism and praise. The controversy surrounding the novel aside, the depiction of the protagonist, Juan "Johnnie" Rico, and his journey through his military career is familiar to many who have served or continue to serve. Despite its futuristic setting, the novel has stood the test of time through its realistic portrayal of Johnnie Rico's growth and development into a leader.

Due to this portrayal, *Starship Troopers* is an ideal lens to explore the building blocks that prepare an individual leader for the battlefield. What values are required to be a military leader and why are they important? What "schoolhouse" training does the contemporary military leader receive, and is it enough to lead soldiers through a complex and evolving operating environment? And what role does the wider force play in the provision of training and experience to ensure that, when it matters most, a leader is not feeling the stressors associated with combat for the first time? Ultimately—what does it take to build a leader?

Recruit Rico's Values—The Foundation of Leadership

The first element of prospective military recruits to be tested is their values. Values are generally defined as a reflection of an individual's personality, attitudes, and motivations.[2] Values drive individual actions and guide general conduct, but within an organizational framework are also deeply influenced by culture.[3] The requirement for a seamless fit between individual and collective values in a military context is paramount. A successful military must be cohesive in its values, thereby achieving consistency in its actions and general conduct. Individuals with opposing values create havoc on a small team's ability to achieve success and can have the second-order effect of undermining strategic objectives. Multiple personnel with opposing values—especially when working closely together—can have an immediate and debilitating effect.

The first test to identify whether there is a values gap between a potential leader and the organization comes during the recruitment screening process. In *Starship Troopers*, Johnnie Rico came of age in the Terran Federation, a society where individuals earned citizenship through military service. Through a flashback to Rico's school lessons on civic duty, the novel explains that this approach ensures those who possess authority in society are proven stakeholders, as they have freely given a part of their life to defend that society. This method also creates a common culture where citizens have shared values and motivations. In *Starship Troopers*, the early emphasis children receive in history and moral philosophy—lessons taught in school by a former service member—establishes their understanding of morals and ethics and provides a common sense of shared values.

Generally speaking, candidates join the military because there is commonality between the attitudes and motivations they expect of a soldier and their own underlying values. Across most militaries, the values required include variations of teamwork, loyalty, duty, integrity, initiative, honor, courage, and respect.[4] The absence of one of these values, certainly in the case of a leader, can have catastrophic effects. For example, in November 2020, the Chief of the Australian Defence Force released the redacted findings and recommendations of a four-year investigation into potential war crimes committed by the Australian Special Air Service Regiment in Afghanistan between 2006 and 2013. A small circle of individuals within this elite organization deviated sharply from Australian Army values through alleged war crimes against civilians and individuals who were clearly hors de combat. The Chief of the

Defence Force, Lieutenant General Angus Campbell, stated it was "possibly the most disgraceful episode in Australia's military history."[5] These individuals' acts had strategic consequences by undermining the public perception of the entire military.

There is no amount of tactical prowess or strategic acumen that can fill the absence of values, and any lack of values, when discovered, should be grounds for discharge. The alignment of organizational values for military personnel is paramount and will be an enduring attribute of a successful leader. Instilling and reinforcing shared values during ab-initio and formalized schoolhouse training within the military is a process that transforms the uninitiated and well-intentioned civilian into an ethical leader.

Camp Currie Crucible—The Building Blocks of Small Unit Leadership

Rico's initial training at the Mobile Infantry training school Camp Currie and later during Officer Cadet School is familiar to many. Through physically and mentally demanding tasks, his resilience threshold is thoroughly tested and gradually increased. Endless days of drills and learning to follow detailed orders teach him instinctive obedience, an invaluable trait when seconds count on the battlefield. Through training, Rico learns that teamwork and attention to detail are essential in high-pressure situations. He gains confidence in his ability to overcome adversity in harsh conditions. And through simulated combat, he is placed under stress in a high perceived—but low actual—threat environment, which ultimately weaves the disparate elements of his training together. These exercises allow Rico to experience combat stressors while still being able to learn and develop from mistakes. As he continues to learn, the instructors intensify this pressure to meet his new level of competence, forcing him to rise to new challenges.

During his training, the "schoolhouses" emphasize fundamentals with an enduring understanding that this will ultimately build a better leader. In *Envisioning Future Warfare*, Gordon Sullivan and James Dubik clearly define the importance of basic training: "Without excellence in the basics, versatility is impossible."[6] At the initial training level, there should be a heavy focus on the basics. They provide the foundation for individuals and small teams to operate in any situation and subsequently adapt tactics to fit the new environment. Importantly for the leader, this builds the "muscle memory" foundation of field skills allowing them to focus on leading, planning, and fighting.

Concurrent to the establishment of basic military skills—and throughout military training thereafter—a considerable weight of effort must be placed on leadership, moral, and ethical training. Even more than contemporary tactics, they underpin success or failure for a burgeoning leader. This focus on morals and ethics, however, ends after initial military training.

Once Rico arrives at the Officer Cadet School—after an obligatory period of service as a non-commissioned officer—his development shifts focus to academics.[7] This education gives Rico the doctrinal grounding and tactical awareness required to lead a platoon in combat; however, there is a notable lack of emphasis on moral and ethical training. Much of this is due to the dynamic character of war. On an ever-evolving battlefield where both sides act, react, and adapt, the tactics taught in the schoolhouses are always in a state of flux. As a result, much of the curriculum focuses on leadership fundamentals with current tactics and planning as the medium through which instructors assess performance. A greater weight of effort on these unchanging facets allows for increased concentration of these skills at the foundational level and the ability to build upon them with emphasis on tactics more in step with the evolving operational environment.

Morals and ethics are often the first casualties of leadership education and training. The desire for schoolhouses to teach junior leaders as much as possible in a limited amount of time can overwhelm the individual and strain training schedules and budgets. Adding to the layered complexity of developing leaders for the future fight—inculcating an understanding of emerging threats and new capabilities and technologies—creates a constant tension with training priorities. Ensuring the best training experience possible for new leaders necessitates a delicate balance of those priorities, requiring a single leader empowered to oversee all aspects of training. In most military forces, this individual bears the same rank and influence as those selected to command comparable operational forces, allowing the two to function "hand in glove." In theory, this is optimal; in practice—especially at lower echelons—achieving this requires incentivization that is often difficult to maintain. Doing so is imperative and ensures that only the best are selected to command instructional institutions. In turn, those institutions tend to produce leaders well prepared for the uncertainties that lie ahead.

In *Starship Troopers*, the balance of priorities at the Officer Cadet School is weighted heavily toward academics, later focusing on experiential learning during a training phase aboard a combat ship. This approach clearly indicates that The Federation places the weight of importance for officers on their academics, such as the ability to conduct complex mathematical equations during a stressful space-to-ground combat drop and provide a realistic "apprenticeship" experience before assuming a leadership role within the military force. Although most western militaries have formal higher education pathways for officer candidates, experiential learning generally occurs after ab-initio training.

For regular or "standing" military forces, deferring experiential learning to "line units" is a long-accepted practice that relieves the institutional force of a significant training burden. In shifting this responsibility to the operational force, organizations can teach new leaders the most up-to-date tactics, techniques, and procedures, allowing junior leaders to receive more individualized coaching and mentoring from experienced leaders, among other benefits.

Rico's Roughnecks—Experiential Learning in Leader Development

Although *Starship Troopers* mentions that Rico's unit conducts drills aboard the ship on days between combat drops, there is very little focus on the requirement for ongoing "in-unit" training. As the book centers around an ongoing war, this should come as no surprise. Training is generally a luxury afforded in peacetime; in wartime, that luxury is a rare occurrence.

The learning that results from combat experience occurs both more rapidly and in greater granularity than in a training environment. Combat experience, however, should not be the first time that a leader contends with the stressors of battle—even simulated battle. This aspiration necessitates that the leader and their team build experience through continual and highly realistic training before deploying. Militaries use large-scale exercises in both national and coalition environments to simulate the likely operational situation. The utility of this training experience has proven successful in the development and evaluation of operational forces. It is through these exercises that individual soldiers and leaders can test their skills and learn under stress. Through thorough after-action reviews and post activity reporting, lessons learned through experience—even in a training environment—provide clear opportunities for self-reflection at the individual level. They also promote organizational growth, allowing for the development of more robust standard operating procedures. Learning from mistakes in this environment ensures that leaders are as prepared as possible for the real thing.

In *Starship Troopers,* the training methods employed at Camp Currie and the Officer Cadet School are more realistic—and deadly—than current military training institutions. Although conducted under the watchful eyes of experienced staff, these methods often led to casualties. The Mobile Infantry frequently uses live ammunition during training activities to teach cadets specific skills—such as seeking cover and reducing their vulnerability to lethal fire—while increasing the experience's realism. Realistic training, especially when combined with austere conditions common to combat, teaches junior leaders that General George S. Patton's adage, "a pint of sweat will save a gallon of blood," is much more than a pithy mantra.

However, the need to avoid unnecessary training fatalities in modern militaries necessitates a balance between providing a realistic experience and ensuring appropriate safety measures are in place. One sure method to achieve a favorable balance is through technology; as advancements continue to be made, myriad innovations simulate—and stimulate—the realism of training at every level. The use of technologies such as the SAAB live training suits used by many Scandinavian nations allows for the generation of near real-time feedback for simulated "kills" during an exercise, including collating battlefield data to facilitate effective after-action reviews.[8] Similarly, virtual reality simulations enable training to assume a level of training realism unimaginable even a decade ago. These systems are not unique to combat personnel and capabilities, nor are they restricted to use in a field environment. Pilots, drivers, and even medics are utilizing simulation systems and advanced technology to provide realistic training. The experiential learning gained may not be wholly comparable to that of actual combat, but it is far better than gaining that experience for the first time while under direct fire.

For a developing leader, the ability to practice the basics of planning, delivering orders, and utilizing modern technology is invaluable. Leveraging training systems to exercise leadership either in the field or in a simulation center allows the leader to gain experience at a significantly reduced level of risk and cost. Using these capabilities to identify shortfalls accurately and provide continued exposure to leading in a realistic environment builds upon the foundations previously set in formalized training institutions. Leadership will continue to be trained and assessed at every echelon throughout the remainder of a leader's career to ensure that when the leader steps onto the battlefield, they are adequately prepared for the environment in which they will fight.

Although the likelihood of a conflict against an intergalactic race in the future may be slim, *Starship Troopers* provides readers with the opportunity to use its themes to explore contemporary and potential future conflict. By examining the character of Rico and his experiences, we gain the ability to reflect upon the building blocks to become a military leader. This human capability must be carefully cultivated to ensure that the best leaders possible step onto the battlefield. Militaries must shape their intrinsic and organizational values and provide foundational instruction and training undertaken by the wider force. These factors are under constant tension as priorities of the battlefield shift; however, the dividend is mission success when paid due significance.

Notes

1   In *Starship Troopers*, Robert Heinlein started every new chapter with a poem or saying which set the tone for the chapter to come. Rudyard Kipling's "The 'eathen" was used in *Starship Troopers* and although the poem shown to start this chapter is missing many stanzas, it has been shortened to set the tone for the chapter to follow in a nod to Heinlein.

2   Geert Hofstede, *Culture's Consequences: International Differences in Work-Related Values* (New York: SAGE, 1984), 13–21.

3   Greg Park, *Collaborative Wisdom: From Pervasive Logic to Effective Operational Leadership* (London: Routledge, 2013), 24–27.

4   This is based off the values of the Australian Defence Force (service, courage, respect, integrity, excellence), United States Army (loyalty, duty, respect, selfless service, honour, integrity, personal

courage), and the British Army (courage, discipline, respect for others, integrity, loyalty, selfless commitment).

5   ABC News (Australia), 2020, "ADF report into Afghanistan war crimes by SAS announced by Gen. Angus Campbell," *YouTube* video, 58:12, November 18, 2020, https://www.youtube.com/watch?v=B25rhz4rr4k.

6   Gordon Sullivan and James Dubik, *Envisioning Future Warfare* (Washington, DC: United States Government Printing Office, 1995), 35.

7   In *Starship Troopers,* candidates for commissions must have been soldiers first. This not only provides the foundational basic field skills, but also has other benefits such as a healthy respect for other ranks as well as experience in a platoon and, in this case, on the battlefield.

8   SAAB, 2020, "Live Training,*" SAAB.com,* https://www.saab.com/products/live-training.

PART II

THE FINAL FRONTIER

CHAPTER 8

Yours Is the Superior

Experience, Intellect, and the Battle of the Mutara Nebula

Jonathan Klug and Steven Leonard

"There she is!" Khan exclaims, leaping to his feet and pointing a gloved finger at the image of the USS *Enterprise* on the bridge viewscreen. Taking a single step from the dais of the command chair toward the helm of the USS *Reliant*, Khan places a hand on the shoulder of his faithful disciple Joachim. "There she is! Ahhh … not so wounded as we were led to believe. So much, the better!" Driven by an insatiable thirst for vengeance, Khan pursues the crippled vessel limping away on impulse power from the planet Regula. Looming in the distance is the Mutara Nebula, *Enterprise*'s only hope for survival.

With *Reliant* closing on the fleeing *Enterprise*, Joachim slows the ship to keep from entering the nebula, where static discharge from the ionized gasses will render inoperative both navigational and tactical systems. As *Reliant* reduces speed, Admiral James Kirk—whom Khan believes he has stranded on Regula—goads his enemy to continue the pursuit: "This is Admiral Kirk. We tried it once your way, Khan, are you game for a rematch? Khan, I'm laughing at the superior intellect." A wide-eyed and enraged Khan lunges for the helm controls, screaming, "FULL POWER! DAMN YOU!"

Thus, begins what is arguably the greatest cinematic space battle in film history: the climactic Battle of the Mutara Nebula in the 1982 movie, *The Wrath of Khan*. Much of the film is intended as an ode to Herman Melville's *Moby Dick*, and the decisive battle carries that inspiration into deep space. Two men—arch enemies pitched against one another in epic battle—fighting against the past, against the future, against time itself. Kirk, promoted above the role of ship captain for which his heart yearns, desperately struggling with relevance even as he fights for his life against an antagonist from his past. Khan, the quintessential villain, megalomaniac, and postmodern renaissance man, wracked with anger and guilt and driven by a near-pathological drive for vengeance.

Circling like gladiators in the Roman Coliseum, the dramatic engagement between the two starships—the venerable *Constitution*-class *Enterprise* and her more modern counterpart the *Miranda*-class *Reliant*—represents the quintessential *Star Trek* clash of good versus evil, the past versus the future, reason versus emotion. Drawing on a conflict sown fifteen years in Kirk's past, the battle reimagines one of humanity's classic struggles: intelligence versus experience. Two starships—one commanded by an experienced captain and crew with the wisdom of years behind them, the other a cult of personality led by a genetically-engineered genius—that together embody a timeless debate rooted deeply within the Socratic dialogues.

In Plato's *Meno*, Socrates explains the concept of phronesis, a form of practical wisdom achieved through experience and learning. It is a quality, a virtue, that cannot be taught but must be nurtured through development and an evolved understanding of one's own self. This idea is further explored in Aristotle's *Nicomachean Ethics*, in which the author distinguishes phronesis as a more experientially based form of learning that transcends the confines of teaching. For Aristotle, gaining phronesis requires experience and "knowledge of particular facts, and this is derived from experience, which a young man does not possess; for experience is the fruit of years."[1]

This dissonance between theory and practice—the essence of Aristotle's discourse on wisdom—is weaved throughout classic military strategic thought and, more recently, a cornerstone of John Lewis Gaddis's *On Grand Strategy*.[2] Phronesis focuses on action, because it is through action that the primacy of experience is most evident. One can study the principles that underpin action, but their practical application is learned through experience. This theme is prevalent throughout the original *Star Trek* television series, where Kirk's wisdom and judgment—a product of years of experience in space—is typically the deciding factor in any particularly difficult situation. In the Mutara Nebula, that dissonance is laid bare once again.

Fifteen years before the Battle of the Mutara Nebula in *The Wrath of Khan*, Khan Noonien Singh made his first appearance in the 1967 *Star Trek* television episode entitled "Space Seed." A product of late 20th-century genetic engineering during a period of Earth's history known as the Eugenics Wars, Khan—along with a number of other enhanced humans—used his superhuman strength and intelligence to amass power and seize control over roughly a quarter of the planet, spreading from Asia through the Middle East. Khan was an especially tyrannical, despotic ruler. As Commander Spock—Kirk's longtime first officer—noted in "Space Seed," "the scientists overlooked one fact: superior ability breeds superior ambition."

Within a year, a group of Khan's genetically superior brethren, known as "Augments," simultaneously seized power in over forty nations across the Earth. The Augments were eventually defeated, and Khan, the last of the tyrants to be overthrown, was condemned to die along with eighty-four of his most devoted followers. However, Khan and his devotees were able to escape Earth aboard the DY-100-class sleeper ship—an interplanetary space vessel modified for long-term suspended animation—SS *Botany Bay*. Cryogenically frozen aboard the *Botany Bay*, Khan and crew drifted into a remote area deep space, where they were discovered by the *Enterprise* in 2267, 271 years after fleeing Earth.

From the moment Kirk awakens him from cryogenic sleep, Khan's "superior ambition" takes hold. His charisma, narcissism, and hunger for power are clear from the outset. Throughout "Space Seed," Khan and Kirk are locked in a struggle for control of the *Enterprise*. Khan eventually enlists Lieutenant Marla McGivers—the ship's historian and a woman completely smitten with the bold, colorful man from the past—to assist him in reviving the Botany Bay crew from hibernation and seizing control of the *Enterprise*. But Khan's disdain for those he considers beneath his superior intellect is his eventual undoing. With assistance from McGivers and Spock, Kirk is able to wrest control of the starship from his adversary. As the episode concludes, Kirk asks Khan if he is willing to be put down on the fifth planet in the Ceti Alpha system, a world that is "habitable, although a bit savage." In turn, Khan responds, asking, "Have you ever read Milton, Captain?" Khan's question alludes to John Milton, the 17th-century English poet whose epic *Paradise Lost* detailed the Fall of Man and the rebellion against God by the superhuman Satan. Kirk quotes the words of Satan's from *Paradise Lost*: "'It is better to rule in hell than serve in heaven.' Yes. I understand." After Khan, his followers, and soon-to-be wife Lieutenant McGivers are transported to Ceti Alpha V, Spock prophetically observes, "It would be interesting, Captain, to return to that world in a hundred years, and learn what crop had sprung from the seed you planted today."

Like Milton's characterization of Satan, Khan was a physically superhuman and demagogic leader with a powerful personality and manifestly superior intellect. In both "Space Seed" and *The Wrath of Khan,* his personality and intelligence were communicated to audiences through allusions to classic literature. Early on in the film, moments before Khan captures Commander Pavel Chekov and Captain Terrell, those allusions set a tone and tenor that will carry through the entirety of *The Wrath of Khan.* As Chekov realizes that he and Terrell have stumbled upon the wreckage of the *Botany Bay*—"*Botany Bay? Botany Bay?* Oh, no!"—on Ceti Alpha V, it is no accident that well-worn editions of *Paradise Lost, The Inferno, Moby Dick*, and *King Lear* are stacked haphazardly on a bookshelf along the ship's wall.[3] The books are, in fact, a callout to Khan's superior intellect; something immediately echoed in Khan's opening dialog with his new captives: "It was only the fact of my genetically-engineered intellect that allowed us to survive. On Earth, two hundred years ago, I was a prince ... with power over millions."

Khan is, without doubt, one of the most celebrated villains to grace a screen, large or small. But to fully appreciate Khan as the obsessive leader of a cult of personality, one must understand the literature that underpins the character. There is far more to the literary allusions to *Paradise Lost, Moby Dick,* and *King Lear* than pithy quotes and obscure references. The famous science fiction author and storyteller Ray Bradbury wrote the screenplay for the 1956 film adaptation of *Moby Dick*. Despite Melville's proven track record for tormenting many an English student, Bradbury brought the book to life, especially with Gregory Peck's brilliant portrayal of Captain Ahab. When the screenplay was complete for *The Wrath of Khan*, Khan's character is the embodiment of Peck's Ahab, and some of Ricardo Montalbán's most memorable lines were inspired directly by Peck's portrayal of Ahab more than 25 years earlier.

Nowhere is this more evident than in Khan's opening scene aboard the recently commandeered USS *Reliant*, when Joachim pleads with him not to pursue Kirk: "We are free. We have a ship, and the means to go where we will. We have escaped permanent exile on Ceti Alpha V. You have proved the superior intellect and defeated the plans of Admiral Kirk. You do not need to defeat him again." But this is Melville's Ahab, whose obsessive quest for vengeance on the white whale destroyed both him and his ship. Khan is Ahab, and his need to avenge the death of his wife, Marla McGivers, blinds even his superior intellect. Paraphrasing Melville, Khan responds: "He tasks me. He tasks me, and I shall have him. I'll chase him 'round the Moons of Nibia and 'round the Antares Maelstrom and 'round Perdition's flames before I give him up!"[4] The character might be named Khan, but the intensity, the obsession, the rabid thirst for revenge is Gregory Peck's rendition of Captain Ahab.

In a single-minded quest for vengeance, Khan sets out in search of his prey: *Enterprise* and her captain, James T. Kirk.[5] Readers of Melville will recall Ahab's fanatical three-day pursuit of Moby Dick, how that pursuit ended, with the death of Ahab and most of his crew, and the destruction of his Nantucket whaling ship, the *Pequod*. Thus, begins the chess match between Khan and Kirk, pitting superior intelligence against superior experience.

The first engagement between hunter and prey occurs not far from space station *Regula I*. Khan's ambush epitomizes the superior intellect, catching Kirk unprepared and severely damaging the *Enterprise*. But Khan's arrogance bleeds through in the aftermath of what he perceives to be an easy victory. He gloats, he postures defiantly, and he underestimates the value of experience in battle. Kirk, leaning over the command console, enters the command prefix code to drop *Reliant*'s deflector shields, exposing the starship to a counterattack from *Enterprise*. "You have to learn why things work on a starship," he explains to Lieutenant Saavik. "Assuming he hasn't changed the combination," Spock replies. "He's quite intelligent."

Experience may not prove superior in this initial battle, but it does allow *Enterprise* to "live to fight another day." Due to the successful use of the prefix code, *Reliant*'s shields drop unexpectedly, and Khan's lack of familiarity with the bridge controls gives Kirk the opportunity he needs. A few timely phaser shots are enough to cause sufficient damage to *Reliant* to allow *Enterprise* to escape to *Regula I* on impulse power. Neither intelligence nor experience prevails. This first battle is a draw, with both men withdrawing to consider their options and next moves.

The second engagement between hunter and prey occurs on Regula, or more precisely, *within* Regula. Khan's second ambush pits Chekov and Terrell—rescued on the space station *Regula I*—against his nemesis. Khan orders Terrell, subservient due to the effects of a juvenile Ceti eel entwined around his cerebral cortex, to kill Kirk. Instead, Terrell chooses to kill himself. Though shocked to learn that Kirk has survived yet again, Khan is content in the knowledge that he has marooned his enemy forever inside a dead planet while he sets out to deliver the final death blow to *Enterprise.*

Once again, experience may not prove superior, but it does enable a wily starship captain to make another unlikely escape. Knowing that Khan would be monitoring communications, Kirk and Spock use an improvised code that allows them to coordinate a plan without revealing their true intent to Khan. As Kirk explains to Saavik: "Hours instead of days, now we've got minutes instead of hours." While Khan expects to find *Enterprise* crippled and unable to defend against another attack from *Reliant*, the more experienced starship captain makes yet another escape. As in the previous encounter, neither intelligence nor experience prevails. Once again, this is a draw, but the game is afoot.

With *Reliant* in hot pursuit, Kirk orders the heavily damaged *Enterprise* to make best speed toward her only hope of survival: the Mutara Nebula. When Saavik notes the tactical challenges posed by the dust and gasses in the nebula, Spock—foretelling the battle to come—replies simply, "Sauce for the goose, Mr. Saavik." Then, raising a Vulcan eyebrow, adds, "The odds will be even." Moments later, as *Reliant* fires a solitary photon torpedo in hopes of halting their prey's escape, Saavik wonders aloud, "Admiral, what happens if *Reliant* fails to follow us into the nebula?" Spock, like Kirk, understands Khan and his maniacal obsession with revenge: "I think we can guarantee that she'll follow us, Lieutenant. Remind me to explain to you the concept of the human ego."

Once inside the nebula, the two vessels maneuver in a manner reminiscent of a pair of tall wooden ships of war battling for tactical advantage in a heavy fog bank at sea. Again, this is an allusion to Ahab and his relentless, three-day pursuit of the great whale Moby Dick. Horner's score casts a dramatic pale as the starships move silently within the brightly colored dust clouds. Passing near one another. One gliding above the other. Sweeping turns through and around the nebula's clouds. No deflector shields, little visibility except a close range. Suddenly, the viewscreen clears just enough to see the outline of *Reliant* and *Enterprise* fires an errant salvo of phasers. Khan responds with a single photon torpedo, but his prey is already out of range.

Like a ship captain of old, Kirk orders, "Hold your course." The blind pursuit continues … silently. When the viewscreen clears for a second time, *Reliant* is closing on a head-on course. "EVASIVE STARBOARD!" Kirk yells. The massive *Constitution*-class starship maneuvers away from *Reliant,* and the two vessels pound away at one another like two men-of-war firing broadsides during the Age of Sail. In the aftermath of the clash, Khan leans over a dying Joachim, who utters, "Yours … is the superior …" with his dying breath. Melville's Ahab to the bitter end, Khan holds Joachim close and declares, "I shall avenge you!"

This is Ahab's final act. His ship is in ruins. His crew is mostly dead. His prey is still eluding him. The great whale refuses to be caught. Blind with vengeance, Khan must pursue Kirk to the bitter end. Onboard *Enterprise*, Kirk muses, "He won't break off now. He followed me this far. He'll be back. But … from where?" Spock, ever the wise counsel, glances up from his monitor. "He's intelligent, but not experienced. His pattern indicates two-dimensional thinking." Kirk, with a wry smile, returns to his command console: "Full stop. Z minus ten thousand meters. Stand by photon torpedoes."

The third and final engagement in the Battle of the Mutara Nebula unfolds in truly Melvillian fashion. Khan, with his hands clasped tightly almost in prayer, stares intently into the morass of the nebula in a vain, desperate search for his elusive prey. *Enterprise* rises unseen from beneath *Reliant*, aligns her weapons on the vessel, and unleashes a brutal salvo that kills the last of Khan's crew, cripples his ship, and leaves him maimed and near death. With his last breaths, Khan channels Ahab one final time: "To the last, I grapple with thee. From hell's heart, I stab at thee. For hate's sake, I spit my last breath at thee."

Like the *Pequod*, *Reliant* is destroyed along with her captain and crew. Moby Dick lives on. Kirk, the experienced, aging ship captain, prevails. What Plato wrote about practical wisdom nearly 2500 years ago holds true today: There is no substitute for experience.

Notes

1 Aristotle, *Nicomachean Ethics*, trans. H. Rackham (London: Heinemann, 1926), 1142.

2 In *On Grand Strategy*, Gaddis carries this theme through the entirety of the book. He revisits the debate directly through the words of 19th-century military theorist Carl von Clausewitz's treatise, *On War*, but also indirectly through Leo Tolstoy's metaphorical description of Clausewitz in *War and Peace*.

3 It is also no accident that Khan was marooned on a planet in the Ceti Alpha system. Another allusion to Melville, Ceti Alpha—or Alpha Ceti—is a red giant and the second brightest star in the Cetus constellation. In Ancient Greek, the Cetus was a mythological giant sea creature, or Kraken, slain by Perseus. In English translations, this is typically translated as "great whales."

4 The original text from Chapter 36 of *Moby Dick* reads, "I'll chase him round Good Hope, and round the Horn, and round the Norway Maelstrom, and round perdition's flames before I give him up!"

5 Whether a factor of storytelling or a deliberate reference to Melville, Ahab's three-day pursuit of Moby Dick echoes throughout *The Wrath of Khan*. In the film, Kirk and Khan meet in three major engagements: *Reliant's* surprise attack near *Regula I*, the attempted assassination of Kirk within the Genesis cave on Regula, and in the Battle of the Mutara Nebula. Even within the nebula, the two starships exchange fire in three meeting engagements reminiscent of a sea battle between tall wooden ships. This is significant in that it serves as a consistent reminder of Melville's influence on the film and its characters.

CHAPTER 9

The Empire's New Hope

Grand Admiral Thrawn's Leadership in the Imperial Navy

James Groves

———————▶

Of all the characters introduced in the *Star Wars Legends* and *Canon,* Grand Admiral Thrawn is perhaps the worthiest of study. His leadership shows us that creating a shared sense of group membership forges strong teams, and that situational leadership allows the right decisions to be made on time, increasing both leaders' and followers' ability to engage in a trusting, respectful relationship. What makes Thrawn's leadership all the more remarkable are his conspicuous differences from typical Imperial leaders.[1]

Unlike others in the Imperial Navy, Thrawn is not human. He is a near-human Chiss from the Unknown Regions. The Chiss are virtually unheard of throughout much of the *Star Wars* universe; they are an enigmatic people, described as great warriors, clever, resourceful, proud, and intensely loyal to one another.[2] Thrawn is the most well-known of their species and the individual with whom the Empire, and we the audience, are most engaged. His political sponsors, the Mitth, are a powerful family organization who form part of the oligarchic Chiss Ascendancy and are responsible for managing their nation's military and foreign affairs departments.[3] Thrawn's striking contrast from the Imperial prototype is not restricted to the customs and traditions of his home system. In almost every conceivable measure of what a group inherently values—from personality to appearance—he is "out-grouped" in a stark and conspicuous manner.

The Imperial Navy reflects Emperor Palpatine's preference for humans in all positions of leadership and authority.[4] Commanders demonstrate their potential for higher command appointments by reflecting the leadership hallmarks of the established in-group: decisive and authoritative in front of their peers, distant and inaccessible to their subordinates, and compliant and subservient to their commanders. Decisions are made centrally, trust is non-existent, and—as Admiral Kendal Ozzel and others discover—initiative is punishable by death. Even at the most senior levels, leaders like Darth Vader must bend the knee and bow his head in submission to ask the Emperor, "What is thy bidding, Master?" Palpatine does not invest in the human dimension of leadership, nor does he accept risks to allow leaders to demonstrate initiative, exploit tempo, or exercise judgement.

In contrast to these established models of Imperial leadership, we have Admiral Thrawn. He is calm and logical, values interpersonal relationships, takes calculated risks, and studies alien artwork to glean indicators of cultural expression and intent. These personal qualities are the absolute antithesis of the typical Imperial leader, irrespective of whether they underwent officer training at the Royal Imperial Academy on Coruscant or one of the regional training colleges elsewhere in the galaxy. Beyond his personal qualities lie his physical differences. He has striking blue skin and glowing red eyes, speaks Basic with a peculiar accent, and has a full name that his human colleagues avoid attempting to pronounce: *Mitth'raw'nuruodo*. His contrast is evident through these conspicuous personal and physical characteristics; his outlier status is comprehensive and indubitable.

Despite this, the Emperor recognizes the officer's potential. He rewards Thrawn and grows to favor him at the expense of others despite his own declared prejudice against non-humans.[5] In *Canon* events, however, few fellow leaders are inspired to adopt Thrawn's leadership methods as their own, leaving his subordinates as the only ones who see value in his approach.[6]

How is it, then, that a young officer who is a nonconformist and a non-human can succeed in the cloistered rigidity of the Imperial Navy's *cursus honorum*?[7] It is through his ability to create a shared sense of group membership within his teams and employ a situational approach to leadership.[8] These qualities—cultivated throughout his career—enable him to lead with authenticity and trust. He is able to generate teams, ranging from small boarding parties to entire fleets, who trust in him and in each other. Their shared and assertive sense of membership harnesses trust as a capability and emboldens them to follow his example of breaking the mold of cultural orthodoxy. Thrawn transcends his out-group status as a non-human in the Imperial Navy and becomes the most exemplary leader in the Fleet.

Authenticity and Building Trust

Thrawn's minority status is not incidental to his leadership style; it is fundamental to it. He is so visibly and personally different from the norm of Imperial leadership that to be anything less than an authentic and capable leader would spell failure for his ability to influence others in a meaningful way. Thrawn's authenticity is built around his creation and advancement of teams who share a sense of group membership. He does this in three steps. He reflects the Navy's values and ambitions in their struggle against enemies of the Empire, creating conditions in which his colleagues in the Fleet see him as "one of us." Thrawn then represents those interests by becoming a champion for the Navy's ambitions, managing their equities and winning resources, new ships, and new crews on their behalf. Finally, he realizes the Navy's ambitions by making them matter, restoring the Fleet to a force of consequence within the galaxy, and achieving a succession of decisive military victories. These three steps—reflecting, representing, and realizing—are worth a closer look.[9]

In the *Legends* novels, Grand Admiral Thrawn inherits the Imperial Remnant and recognizes the alarming lack of experience throughout the Fleet.[10] He knows that this group has aspirations to regain the Empire's lost glory despite their recent military failures and seeks to unite their efforts. To do so, he reflects their ambition to reclaim their status as the galaxy's apex military force by conducting a series of phased operations that enable the "complete, total, and utter destruction of the Rebellion" and immediately instils a unity of effort in pursuing this purpose-driven goal against a shared threat.[11]

For Thrawn to cement himself as an authentic leader, however, he needs to represent these values and be seen to selflessly champion the Navy's cause. Thrawn achieves this through sheer professional competence and selfless service to the Empire. In *Heir to the Empire,* we meet Captain Gilad Pallaeon, a guarded and cautious captain of an Imperial Star Destroyer, a veteran of the Battle of Endor, and witness to the destruction of the second Death Star.[12] When he postulates that Thrawn may be "possibly the greatest military mind the Empire has ever seen," we see that even the most conservative members of the remaining Imperial forces consider him the most professionally capable member of their group.[13] Thrawn's competence is carefully balanced with timely examples of altruism. He states "I do not require glory, only results for my Emperor" to ensure his military victories are characterized as furthering the greater good rather than his professional advancement. He delivers these statements with such conviction that they instill faithful and determined responses within his teams.

With his followers' trust and confidence, Thrawn can take risks to enable the Fleet to adapt to the chaotic strategic environment and exploit opportunities. Throughout the *Legends* novels, he does so in a series of spectacular and creative military initiatives. He limits the New Republic's resurgent Jedi capability through the widespread use of Force-repelling creatures. He co-opts an unhinged, Force-sensitive clone to complement his command and control of dispersed, simultaneous Fleet operations. He mitigates the Empire's shattered defense industry sector by employing a vast network of private intelligence sources to locate a ghost fleet of dreadnoughts abandoned in deep space, which he crews with a clone army created in secret. Weaved throughout each of these achievements are brilliant and creative combat operations against the Empire's enemies, where he leads his Fleet to victory after victory. Such apparent infallibility is reminiscent of a young Napoleon Bonaparte's leadership, attributed not to any specific character trait but simply a conspicuous talent for winning battles.[14] The trust of his followers allows Thrawn to take increasingly calculated risks, and the resultant combat victories not only realize his group's goals and ambitions, but are the foundation for his followers to feel that his triumphs are theirs. This final step allows Thrawn to transcend his minority status and authentically lead the Imperial Navy through a shared sense of group membership.

A Maverick Contesting the Established Leadership Culture

Thrawn deviates further from established Imperial culture through his empowerment of subordinates, his comfort with chaos, and his ability to unify teams in pursuit of group needs. Unlike Darth Vader, whose leadership is built almost exclusively on fear and punishment, Thrawn's ability to generate trust enables him to employ a variety of more constructive leadership styles that we, the audience, often feel reflect our aspirations and ideals. He empowers his subordinates by delegating almost to the point of discomfort. He differentiates command from control, injects himself at the main effort, asks his teams for suggestions, and resources them to execute these plans with task-organized assets from the Fleet.[15]

Such empowerment of subordinates is anathema to the Imperial Navy's senior leadership group and makes Thrawn a maverick. Thrawn knows this, confiding to his trusted aide and subordinate Eli Vanto that the Navy's high command only "want a commander who follows procedures ... who will ask their advice." Reciprocally, he posits that "many admirals aspire to that rank because of a wish to exercise control ... such leaders are threatened if officers of lower rank solve difficult problems without them."[16] Here, Thrawn validates the observation that "war magnifies the importance of leadership in establishing organizational culture."[17]

Grand Admiral Thrawn's ability to be comfortable in chaos makes him instinctively unable to conform to the Imperial leadership culture. As a Chiss, he has a propensity for tactical agility based on simple, flexible plans and anticipating adversary most likely courses of action. We are familiar with General James Mattis' observation that commanders often "[search] in vain for the orderly battlefield that unfolds according to plan," and subsequent warning that "it doesn't exist."[18] Similarly, Thrawn advises Captain Pallaeon that the Imperial Navy cannot afford leaders who "are so limited they cannot adapt to unexpected situations."[19] Thrawn's nonconformity is not self-serving individualism; it is a sincere desire to advance the Empire and its interests.

In addition to being a nonconformist, Thrawn has a sense of duty that leads him to reject self-serving actions and inculcate a similar "group first" mentality within his subordinates. In what becomes a motif for his character, Thrawn explains that "when you understand a species' art, you understand that species" and he re-purposes his predecessor's luxury entertainment suite aboard the *Chimaera* into an interactive art gallery.[20] This maverick act is not intended to satisfy his creative yearnings but to enhance his knowledge of the cultural, societal, and martial impulses of other cultures so that he may befriend them in diplomacy or defeat them in battle as required.

Even in the heat of battle, Thrawn's first duty is to the group's ability to complete the mission, and he explicitly rejects any individual's ambition which undermines that duty. In *The Last Command,* Captain Brandei witnesses the destruction of the *Peremptory* during the Katana Fleet skirmish. His anger quickly turns to a personal desire for immediate and disproportionate retaliation. Thrawn coaches Brandei through his rage, reminding him that as a leader his duty in war must be to the living and not the dead, and that combat is not an opportunity for private revenge.[21] He distinguishes what he expects from his group members, provides context for what sets their team apart from their adversaries, and subordinates individual goals to those of the group.[22]

A New Hope in the Province of Uncertainty

It is Thrawn's progression to Grand Admiral—and the situational leadership he practices along the way—which makes him a genuine hope for the Imperial Navy. In an organization where authoritarianism, rigid adherence to doctrine, and linear-thinking are the behaviors of successful leaders, Thrawn is an extreme outlier—an absolute minority. His ability to transcend his minority status is the launch-pad for his re-imagining of the Imperial Navy's leadership model. His approach is based on a group process in which leaders and followers earn one another's trust and recognize that their shared success is dependent on that trust.

He is an insatiable learner who uses situational leadership to implement the most appropriate leader-follower process in volatile, uncertain, chaotic, and ambiguous military situations. War is the "province of uncertainty" and demands flexible leadership, influenced by the continuous evolution of adversaries, friendly forces, and the battlespace itself.[23] Thrawn uses directive, participational, and transformational leadership methods throughout the *Rebels* series and *Legends* and *Canon* novels.

He is directive and authoritative in high-risk, time-compressed environments, such as a combat fleet action. When mission success hangs in the balance, he is known to order "You don't have to understand, just obey."[24] At pivotal moments in the Battle of Sluis Van, he personally coordinates joint fires engagements from tractor beam crews and turbo-laser batteries.[25] Thrawn's decision to employ directive leadership at critical moments demonstrates to his team that he, as their prototype, holds himself ultimately accountable for their shared victory or defeat.

Directive techniques are balanced with participational leadership methods, and Thrawn nurtures his subordinates' ability to think slowly and deliberately to better understand a problem. He shows immense patience in coaching his subordinates to decisions anchored in logic and reasoning, rather than passion or impulse, demonstrated by his use of participational techniques to support their growth as leaders in their own right. He often invites discussion from his closest students—Gilad Pallaeon, Jorj Cardas, Eli Vanto, and Karyn Faro—with open questions like "What would you infer from that?" and other prompts to stimulate their appreciation of a problem.[26] When time permits, he develops his subordinates through very "human" interactions. He values debate and, as a Chiss, is predisposed to favoring dialectic reasoning as a learning tool. This approach enables his subordinates to step through their own logical analysis of any given problem. In doing so, he is an exemplar of patience and humility for his teams, and he explicitly reminds them of the value of democratizing good ideas, stating that "all thoughts are worth listening to."[27]

Thrawn's transformational leadership techniques allow him to identify talent among his subordinates and inspire their positive growth. Gilad Pallaeon becomes a more resourceful and assertive naval commander. Jorj Cardas grows from being a junior member of a smuggling operation to being a decisive envoy. Eli Vanto evolves from an unappreciated junior supply officer to a respected and valued member of not one but two galactic fleets. Karyn Faro learns to trust her instincts and be more decisive in combat, taking informed risks in accord with her commander's intent. Thrawn transforms these individuals by creating conditions where they can develop—and fail if necessary—in a trusting environment.

The Glimmering Tragedy of Hope

So, did the Emperor take a risk in bringing Thrawn into the fold of the Fleet's senior leadership? Not at all. In the opening chapters of *Thrawn*, the Admiral offers to pledge his loyalty and knowledge of the Unknown Regions in return for the Emperor's consideration of the Chiss, should they be threatened by a mutual enemy.[28] From the Emperor's perspective, accepting this alien's service poses minimal risk, but the potential yield is staggering, especially for an Empire struggling to understand the threats lurking on the fringe of the known galaxy.

Of course, the Emperor never intended to make use of the new hope that Thrawn's leadership offers his atrophying organization. What indicates to us that the Emperor was never serious about enacting meaningful change to military culture is that he never established an effective method of replicating Thrawn's successful leadership methods. This inaction denies the Imperial Navy the ability to learn, benefit, and grow from Thrawn's influence. There was no leadership training framework put in place behind him, just a series of increasingly consequential military operations put in front of him.

This is the tragedy of Thrawn's influence on military leadership. The very system he has set out to improve—sometimes single-handedly—is too established and unwieldy to allow him to evolve from an instrument of hope to an instrument of meaningful, sustainable change. As an unprotected maverick, his influence is as temporary as his membership in the Fleet.[29] The Empire fails to draw lessons from his "best practice" leadership—this reduces the resilience of their leadership training model and makes it less dynamic, salient, and sustainable.

Failing to create a sustainable leadership model based on Thrawn's promotion of shared group membership and situational leadership techniques ensures there will never be a substantial "return" of the Empire. Grand Admiral Thrawn represents a chance for new hope, but ultimately a chance untaken and a hope unrealized. What is remarkable, and what resonates with the audience, is his ability to achieve so much despite the Imperial system, not because of it. We see a leader whose minority status is not incidental to his leadership style but fundamental to it, and we find ourselves cheering him on as he defies widespread Imperial prejudice against non-humans. His authentic approach to leadership and his unwavering selflessness builds teams we can relate to, teams who trust in his leadership and who, under his mentorship, learn to trust in their own as well.

Notes

1   Prototypicality is a key aspect of the *Social Identity Approach* to leadership and builds upon the notion that a leader must be seen by their followers as "the best of us." Prototypicality is achieved when leaders not only have the same qualities, attributes, and values as their followers, but also establish or perpetuate a range of difference with others who are not part of their team, organisation, or group. In the case of the Imperial Navy, non-humans such as the Chiss are one of those "out-groups." For more, see S. Alexander Haslam, Stephen D. Reicher, and Michael J. Platow, *The New Psychology of Leadership* (New York: Psychology Press, 2011), 82–87.

2   Timothy Zahn, *Thrawn* (London: Arrow Books, 2017), 26.

3   Eric Cagle, Cory Herndon, Michael Mikaelian, Steve Miller, Owen Stephens, and Jo Wiker, *Star Wars Roleplaying Game: Ultimate Alien Anthology* (Renton, WA: Wizards of the Coast, 2003), 36–37.

4   Timothy Zahn, *Dark Force Rising* (New York: Bantam Books, 1993), 2.

5   Ibid., 2 and 45.

6   Season 3, Episode 22 of *Rebels* shows Admiral Konstantine's steadfast refusal to conform to Grand Admiral Thrawn's fleet tactics at the Battle of Atollon. Seeking personal glory, Konstantine compromises Thrawn's plan to destroy the fledgling Rebel Alliance and, in doing so, dies himself. This deviance occurs despite Thrawn's numerous offers to Konstantine which may have led him to trust Thrawn's methods or seek his guidance.

7   Even Thrawn's adversaries note that he is younger than most of his peers. Timothy Zahn, *Thrawn Ascendancy: Chaos Rising* (London: Del Rey, 2020), 127. Furthermore, the *cursus honorum* was a well-defined sequence of public offices and military appointments followed by men in Ancient Rome with ambitions for political leadership. Adrian Goldsworthy, *Roman Warfare* (London: Cassell & Co, 2000), 80.

8   Situational leadership involves a flexible, adaptive approach in which different leadership techniques are employed dependent on the importance, audience, and urgency of the situation.

9   S. Alexander Haslam, Stephen D. Reicher, and Michael J. Platow, *The New Psychology of Leadership* (New York: Psychology Press, 2011), 64–72.

10   Timothy Zahn, *Heir to the Empire* (London: Bantam Books, 1991), 6–7.

11   Ibid., 16.

12   Ibid., 7.

13   Ibid.

14 Bertrand Russell, *Power: A New Social Analysis* (London: George Allen and Unwin Ltd, 1939), 20–21.

15 Linda Hansen-Raj, "Who is Thrawn?" *Star Wars*, Lucasfilm Ltd., Aug 2, 2016. Accessed Sept 29, 2020, https://www.starwars.com/news/who-is-thrawn.

16 *Thrawn*, 287.

17 Peter R. Mansoor and Williamson Murray, (eds), *The Culture of Military Organizations* (Cornwall: Cambridge University Press, 2019), 450.

18 James Mattis and Bing West, *Call Sign Chaos: Learning to Lead* (New York: Random House, 2019), 31.

19 *Heir to the Empire*, 179.

20 Ibid., 14.

21 Timothy Zahn, *The Last Command* (New York: Bantam Books, 1994), 2–3.

22 The importance of distinguishing one's own group from others is key to the concept of meta-contrast as described in John C. Turner, Penelope J. Oakes, S. Alexander Haslam, and Craig McGarty, "Personal and Social Identity: Self and Social Context," *Personality and Social Psychology Bulletin* (May 1992), 4–8.

23 Carl von Clausewitz, *On War*, trans. Michael Howard and Peter Paret (Princeton: Princeton University Press, 1984), 101.

24 *Heir to the Empire*, 13.

25 Ibid., 373.

26 Ibid., 13.

27 Timothy Zahn, *Outbound Flight* (New York: Del Rey, 2014), 166.

28 *Thrawn*, 38.

29 General James Mattis is quoted in a number of fora for imploring his subordinates to "protect your mavericks" and those whose disruptive ideas enrich the organisation by contributing to a contest of ideas. Will Meddings, "James Mattis's Leadership Philosophy," The Army Leader. Accessed November 22, 2020, https://thearmyleader.co.uk/james-mattiss-leadership-philosophy/.

CHAPTER 10

Graff's Game

Two Lessons on Preparing Military Leaders

Thomas Bruscino

———————▶———————

"All great things human are essentially simple," wrote American military theorist and educator Arthur Wagner in 1903. "When we read the works of Shakespeare, we are so struck with the simplicity of the beautiful aphorisms of 'him who wrote for all time' that we are almost inclined to wonder why we never thought of them ourselves." The same goes for the Proverbs of Solomon or Watt's invention of the steam engine. They seem so obvious, "so natural and so logical that we almost lose sight of the genius." In effect, that was Wagner's definition of genius—to do something so manifestly *right* that it is the obvious answer. But only in retrospect.[1]

So it was with military genius. "When we read the campaigns of Napoleon, in the clear light of historical elucidation, and follow his movements on the map, his plans seem so plainly to have been the ones best adapted to the existing conditions—to be, I might almost say, the *only* ones suited to the situation—that it is not until we reflect that facts made so clear to us by the historian were to the Great Emperor matters of inference and conjecture, based upon meager and detached bits of information gained through his secret service; that his movements were based upon probabilities which he fathomed by his knowledge of human nature, and his accurate estimate of his own and his enemies material and moral resources; and that his campaigns and battles were conducted under conditions of almost inconceivable responsibility, personal danger, physical hardship, and mental anxiety, that we begin to form a correct estimate of the genius of the pre-eminent warrior who always made the most correct and powerful application of the principles of Strategy."[2]

That is a weighty place to start when speaking of a science fiction book featuring a small child who leads a human fleet of spaceships to victory in a life-or-death struggle with a race of alien insects. *Ender's Game* is, after all, just a novel, and one that has retroactively (but wrongly) been bound up with the cavalcade of young adult fiction that seemingly dominates the market. But since its publication first as a novelette in 1977, then as a full book in 1985, *Ender's Game* has been something more than just another sci-fi book. Its author Orson Scott Card gave children a fully human voice and captured something substantial and true about fear, love, loss, camaraderie, and leadership. The book spawned a vast and ongoing series of works—the so-called Enderverse.

More to the point, since 1988, *Ender's Game* has been a mainstay on the Marine Corps Commandant's Professional Reading List, and over the years, the other branches of the American military have made it required reading too. Whether through compulsion or recommendation, countless individuals in the military have read the book. Countless others have discussed and debated its lessons, and some have even made it a part of the curriculum at military schools, to be used in the education of everyone ranging from privates to generals. As well they should—the book has much to teach, and I would be the last person to suggest that it not be read and studied and discussed. I'm writing this chapter as an explicit call to read *Ender's Game*, for all the reasons cited above with the addition that the book has something to say about the role of educators in preparing military leaders for war.

But.

Embedded in *Ender's Game* is a false idea. It is not the main idea. Indeed, it is an idea that probably doesn't matter all that much for most readers. But still, it is there, and it needs addressing, lest it be accepted without the consideration it is due.

Who is the smartest character in *Ender's Game*? The easy answer is Ender himself. By all measures of intelligence, whether it be dealing with other humans or just plain book smarts, Andrew Wiggin is off the charts. Closer fans of the series know that the real winner is Ender's shadow, Bean. Bean was a genetic experiment, grown in a lab to be so intelligent that his levels are almost unmeasurable. There are other candidates, to be sure. Ender's brother Peter and sister Valentine are so smart they manipulate the population of the entire planet. Heck, all of the students at the Battle School are geniuses. Any one of them could be in the running, depending on how you measure intelligence.

Well, I'm here to say that Colonel Hyrum Graff is the smartest, but not because he would win in a trivia contest against any of these other characters. Graff is the smartest because of what he does, and what he does is so insanely intelligent and perfect as to be impossible. No one can find and develop a military genius, any genius, the way that Graff does. That is the false idea in *Ender's Game*.

On the surface, Graff's approach makes sense. The International Fleet and the Battle School have access to what amounts to a perfect knowledge of the genetic makeup of Andrew Wiggin, including those intelligence and emotional markers that would give him the capability of being the military commander they require. The whole reason Ender exists is because when his older brother and sister washed out of the program, the fleet, playing Goldilocks, allowed the Wiggin parents to have an illegal third child to get it just right. When it came to testing if unique personalities of the Wiggin children would allow their perfect genetic material to reach its full military commander potential, the fleet literally watched their every move as small children through monitors inserted in their heads. They had a highly advanced and almost perfect ability to do psychoanalysis with those observations, and found Peter to be too hard, Valentine too soft, and Ender right where they needed him. Once at the Battle School, Graff and his aides no longer had the monitor in Ender's head, but they still had essentially perfect knowledge of everything he did, every move he made, every game he played, every friend he made, and every enemy he destroyed. With all of that knowledge, Graff could manipulate Ender to reach his full potential in Battle School and then in the final game that was not a game at all.

The mechanics of the selection and preparation of Ender Wiggin make sense. It is the premise that doesn't quite hold up. Go back to Arthur Wagner's point at the beginning of this chapter. Like Graff, Wagner was a military teacher—a key figure in setting the standards for both the U.S. Army Command and General Staff College and the U.S. Army War College. The quotation above comes from lectures he gave on strategy to military officers gathered for large maneuvers—games—meant to better prepare them for real war. Wagner was not a commander himself, and although he was a smart guy and knew much of how wars worked, he certainly would not have claimed to be a military genius, nor that he had any clear idea who among his students would be geniuses.

Genius, after all, is inherently unpredictable. That is what makes it genius. What looks obvious in retrospect—those perfect words, that perfect invention, that perfect campaign—only looks obvious in retrospect. Shakespeare put those words together just so. Watts made steam drive a piston. Napoleon backed the Austrians into a cul-de-sac at Ulm. Ender Wiggin led his fleet on a ruthlessly direct suicide mission directly to the center of the alien home system and won the war forever. It was the perfect approach, the only real answer, and only a one-of-a-kind military genius could have come up with the idea at all.

So how did Graff know? How did he know that that approach, or something very much like it, was what would win the war in that final battle?

It is not as if Graff simply educated Ender in fleet operations, using the Battle School and the battle room to simulate hundreds of possible situations, learn approaches that had worked in the past, and develop options of what could work in the future in similar real war scenarios. Graff did do all of that, which allowed Ender to win countless battles against the Bugger fleets across the galaxy. But that was all prologue to the only battle that mattered—the final and apparently hopeless assault on the Bugger home world. In order for Ender to win that battle, in the way that he did, Graff had to set the conditions just right, starting way back in Battle School. He had to isolate him from friends and peers, he had to challenge him in impossible situations, he had to give him brutal and real enemies, children, who could only be defeated through lethal force. He had to deceive Ender into thinking the real war was a game, so that he wouldn't think too much of the slaughter he was visiting on friends and foes alike. In other words, Graff specifically prepared Ender to take the most savagely ruthless approach in the final battle.

But what if the only way to win that last battle had been through some clever stratagem? What if the commander would have had to win all the earlier battles through ruthlessness, but then to win the last one he had to suppress his urge to be so ruthless that he disregarded all life? Graff's whole approach would have changed. Perhaps he would have picked Ender's brother Peter instead, because he needed someone who would lead with brutality, but also had a nearly infinite capacity to be clever. Then Graff would have spent all that time at the Battle School manipulating the boy into impossible situations that could only be won by relying on his wits, not his brutality.

Ender's Game is fiction, after all, so Orson Scott Card could make up whatever genius he needed for the final battle. The problem is not that the book is bad or unrealistic—it is that it is so good, that it has so many real lessons about humanity, leadership, and war, that readers can easily confuse this one bit of the fiction with reality. Unless there is some kind of genius out there that has yet to be invented, no one can do what Hyrum Graff does in *Ender's Game*. We're not that smart.

I have thought a lot about this. My entire professional career has been educating military officers for positions of leadership in wars. Those wars must be won, in order to protect that which we hold most dear. But I don't *know* if my students are up to it. By definition, if they are the military geniuses that we need, we won't know until after the fact. That means we cannot define with clarity the exact attributes required of future military commanders, and if we try, we are just as likely to exclude those potential geniuses who have the attributes we didn't see as important. That truth ought to give us pause when we put our faith and precious time into educational models built around learning objectives or outcomes that are supported by more specific sub-outcomes and measured using detailed rubrics that attempt to satisfy our innate desire for surety in an unsure world. This isn't a novel. We can't skip to the back and see how it ends.

The best we can do is try to find those with the most potential for command in war, show them historical and artificial scenarios that look similar to what they might see in the future, do our best to get them into positions of leadership when the fight comes, and hope a genius or two comes through when we need them the most. It is a scary and imperfect approach, just the same as everything that is important in our complex lives.

Hyrum Graff's role in preparing Ender to annihilate the buggers has something else to say about those responsible for teaching future military leaders. Anyone who has read *Ender's Game* knows that it is about more than just winning the war. In many ways, the book isn't about winning the war at all. For all the genius of Ender's final attack on the Bugger home world, it is something of a letdown. He chooses simplicity at the end, directing the little fleet to pile drive through the enemy defenses, pulling in the Bugger ships as the humans get close enough to deploy the weapon on the planet itself. The ensuing chain reaction destroys the planet, wipes out the entire enemy fleet, and kills the queen. The destruction is absolute and final, eliminating the threat forever.

That was who Ender always was—the sweet boy who when cornered became ruthless, nasty, and effective. When put into seemingly unwinnable situations, his response was always escalation—to take the fight, the war, to its absolute form. Ender was a military genius, able to win in myriad ways depending on the situation. But he was not reckless. If he could preserve forces and defeat the enemy within accepted rules and norms, he would. What made him different was that when the rules and norms were thrown out, when he could not win with clever deceptions and maneuvers, the situation would trigger within him a primal urge to destroy his enemies completely, so that he might never be put in an unwinnable situation again.

This, his greatest strength, was also his great curse. In the end, that is what Ender's story really is about: his curse, not his gifts.

The story plays out in the last few pages of the book, extended later into the increasingly philosophical and mythical sequels. What seems like a great victory turns for him and the reader into a profound melancholy, a deep guilt over what that victory has wrought. Ender wiped out an entire species. Along the way, he came to love them and understand them, even to the degree that he could communicate with them. He discovered that the whole war was a misunderstanding. But it was too late. Wracked with guilt, all he had left was to tell their story. He became the Speaker for the Dead, and a small but important change happened. In *Ender's Game*, the enemy were the Buggers, a child's name for terrifying insectoid creatures seemingly without consciences or even consciousness. In later books they became the Formics, a sentient race that deserved better than annihilation. And so, Ender destroyed his own reputation—becoming Ender the Xenocide, the greatest mass murderer of all time.

The last pages of *Ender's Game*, not to mention the sequels, are morally complex and difficult, but the hero remains the hero. Andrew Wiggin grew up. He traveled from planet to planet, extending his lifetime by moving at relativistic speeds. He found a way to save the Formic species and gain something of a personal redemption. It took generations, thousands of years, on Earth.

Colonel Hyrum Graff plays a much smaller part in this portion of the story. At the end of the war, he went on trial for how he handled Ender's recruitment and the Battle School, in particular for allowing and even encouraging the situations to develop where Ender killed other children. The jury acquitted him, and humanity gave him a new job, a sinecure as a reward for his efforts. He became the Minister of Colonization, occasionally talked with Ender, and had a role in his former students' fight for the future of humankind on Earth.

Yes, he was put on trial for "mistreatment of children, negligent homicide" when it came to Ender killing the other two children. Yes, the entire process of running the school and preparing Ender nearly broke him mentally and physically. He loved that Ender had a good and pure heart, and in the end, he admitted to loving the boy. It broke Graff's heart to have to isolate the child, to constantly push him to the breaking point, to use love for his sister to manipulate him into a fight that would crush him. Knowing what it would cost the boy, Graff decided to shoulder the responsibility alone. He argued with his superiors and pushed away his subordinates at the school. He tortured himself every bit as much as he tortured the boy. Even as Ender broke down physically, Graff too went into physical decline, steadily gaining weight until the war ended, then he lost weight during his trial. "One kind of stress puts it on," he admitted, "another takes it off. I am a creature of chemicals."

What Hyrum Graff never did, at least not directly and very much unlike Ender, was confront the morality of his role in the annihilation of the Formics. Since from the very beginning the intent of the human assault on the alien home world was their utter destruction, it cannot be claimed that he did not know what Ender would do at the end. In his trial, he based his entire defense for the treatment of Ender on the requirement of winning the war absolutely and forever. Not unlike the American decision to drop atomic bombs on Japan at the end of World War II—an allegory Card had in mind—the International Fleet, including Graff, had concluded long before that there was no other choice. No communication, and thus no compromise, was even possible. So, when Graff lost sleep and gained weight, it wasn't over the annihilation of a species, it was over what was happening to Ender.

Without diverting too far into the vast academic, religious, and philosophical subject of just war theory, there is an important and all too often overlooked truth to be found in this book about a boy who plays at war and becomes the greatest military genius of all time. Reading *Ender's Game* from the perspective of Hyrum Graff is a reminder that the guilt of what happens in war, even the most necessary of wars, belongs to the teachers of military leaders too. All who take on that role must also accept their piece of that guilt. That, never to be forgotten, is the very real cost of playing Graff's game.

Notes

1   Arthur L. Wagner, *Strategy: A Lecture Delivered by Colonel Arthur L. Wagner, Assistant Adjutant-General, U.S.A., to the Officers of the Regular Army and National Guard at the Maneuvers at West Point, Ky., and at Fort Riley, Kansas, 1903* (Kansas City, MO: Hudson-Kimberly Publishing, 1903), 7–8.

2   Ibid., 8–9 (Emphasis in original).

From Tactics to Galactic Grand Strategy

Lessons From the *Old Man's War* Universe

Major General Mick Ryan

———————▶

The *Old Man's War* series is John Scalzi's ground-breaking science fiction saga that tells the story of future humans and aliens struggling to colonize worlds and ensure the sustainability of their races. For humans, the Colonial Union and its technologically sophisticated Colonial Defense Forces represents the best hope for the survival in the universe. Or do they? The three core novels of the *Old Man's War* series—*Old Man's War*, *The Ghost Brigades*, and *The Last Colony*—offer a variety of insights into military and broader national security issues which are relevant for the contemporary environment. I examine these insights and explore their relevance for contemporary strategists and military planners.

> I did two things on my seventy-fifth birthday. I visited my wife's grave. Then I joined the army.[1]

So begins the *Old Man's War* saga, which debuted as a serialized story on author John Scalzi's personal website, *Whatever*, in 2002.[2] The story follows our main protagonist, John Perry, a septuagenarian widower from small town America who joins the off-world Colonial Defense Force (CDF) on his 75th birthday. The CDF only recruits people 75 years old. As Perry discovers after being transported into orbit and onto a massive CDF spaceship, recruits are then provided with a new enhanced, faster, and stronger bioengineered body.

After receiving his new body and completing basic training camp, Perry joins his first combat unit. Thereafter ensues a series of deployments to clear planets of alien species—either because they have attacked a human colony, occupied a planet wanted by the Colonial Union, or just because the CDF wants to send a message to not mess with them.

While there is a strategic context of human colonization through the galaxy, the focus of the first book is tactical. The description of Perry's platoon and its activities dominates the narrative. The tactical level is where battles and other forms of engagements between opposing military forces are conceived, planned, and executed to achieve military objectives. *Old Man's War* is replete with combat, some of it is large scale space or land battles and some is hand-to-hand fighting.

The combat however wears down the morale of CDF soldiers. Eventually, Perry starts to question the reason for the destructive activities in which he and his platoon are engaged. But this arc of the story is soon overtaken by a new element of the narrative: Perry discovers his wife, who died several years before he left earth, has been "reborn" as a special forces soldier in the CDF named Jane Sagan.

John and Jane establish a friendship, and Perry is temporarily assigned to Jane's special operations unit for the final act. The CDF eventually win the climactic battle at the conclusion of the book. But there is no happy ending for the couple. Jane is shipped off with her special forces unit and Perry returns to his CDF unit.

The next book in the series raises the sights of the reader beyond the tactical and into a broader universe. In *The Ghost Brigades*, humankind must now deal with an alliance that has formed to seize human worlds and exterminate humankind. Again, the theme of ethical use of biotechnology—particularly in the transfer of human consciousness—is dominant throughout the story. It does so through its focus on special operations soldiers as the main characters. The reader gets a detailed look at the CDF Special Forces, their tactics, advanced technologies, and how they build cohesive units. Unlike their "realborne" colleagues in the CDF, special forces soldiers are created from the DNA of deceased humans who died before they could enlist.

In *The Ghost Brigades*, the reader is also exposed to a critique of the Colonial Union approach to colonization and to dealing with alien species. It is a simple approach; if there is a problem, it is handled by the military forces of the CDF. Diplomacy is either minimized or avoided altogether. This theme will be explored later in this chapter.

The final book in the series, *The Last Colony* sees John Perry and Jane Sagan reunited as co-leaders of a new colony. But this is no simple colonization mission. The CDF has intelligence that a new, larger, and much more dangerous coalition of alien races—called The Conclave—has formed. The new coalition, led by the mysterious General Gau, has agreed that they will not colonize new planets except through the consent of coalition members. New colonies established outside this agreement are immediately destroyed by Conclave fleets.

Assessing this as a threat to the ongoing program of human colonization through-out the galaxy, the CDF sets out to embarrass the leadership of The Conclave by establishing a new colony they cannot find. The CDF also hope that by executing this strategy, it will also encourage members of The Conclave to leave, and therefore make it less of a threat to continued human expansion throughout the galaxy.

Beyond the insights provided by individual stories and characters within these three books, there are a variety of lessons that can be divined for contemporary strategists. The setting of the *Old Man's War* in a future universe of advanced technology, space travel, planetary colonization, and interaction with dozens of intelligent alien species presents a large amount of material to explore. For the purposes of this chapter, I have focused on what I believe are insights from four key themes. These are: the importance of strategy, civil-military relations, ethical strategy, and the ethical use of technology. However, I am sure that there are many more insights that might be gleaned by the critical reader.

Four Insights for Strategic Thinkers and Planners

1. Strategy matters as a guide to action—on Earth and beyond

Strategy is a word—and a concept—that resists a single, agreed upon definition. Hew Strachan described strategy as something "used by governments to describe peacetime policies more than by armies to shape wars" and which has "gained in breadth but has forfeited conceptual clarity."[3] Clausewitz called strategy, largely a military concern in the early 19th century, the use of engagement for the purpose of war.[4] At heart, it is about aligning, balancing, and adapting ends, ways, and means as well as clarifying objectives and the resources to attain those objectives all within a competitive environment. A central idea in the theory and practice of strategy is that it exists in an environment where actors are competing and where there is some misalignment of larger objectives. As Beatrice Heuser wrote, "Strategy is a comprehensive way to pursue political ends, including the threat or use of force, in a dialectic of wills—there have to be at least two sides to a conflict."[5]

The *Old Man's War* universe exists in a constant state of conflict. But for the Colonial Union, strategy focuses too much on the conflict between races and too little on the strategic end states of that conflict. Indeed, for the Colonial Union, it is almost as if enduring conflict is the strategic end state that they seek. For the Colonial Union, their strategy is founded on several elements. First, expand the presence of humans in the universe through colonization. Second, construct and sustain a highly effective military instrument that can find, seize, and defend new planets that can be colonized. Third, avoid diplomatic entanglements that would prevent colonial conquests. Fourth, maintain the Earth as a technologically backward source of human colonists and future soldiers. And finally, through special operations and subterfuge, foster inter-species conflicts to ensure that colonization missions can continue.

At first glance, this approach might appear to be a logical strategy. But as our view of the *Old Man's War* universe develops, it becomes clear that this strategy is not viable in the long-term. The number of (known) planets available for colonization, the number of races that wish to colonize them, and the cost-benefit of analysis of conflict versus collaboration indicates that this is a strategy that is not sustainable for the Colonial Union.

By the end of *The Last Colony*, the risks of this strategy have manifested. A massive coalition of over four hundred races now opposes further Colonial Union expansion. The Earth has rebelled against the Colonial Union, restricting the availability of new military recruits and colonists. Within the CDF and the Colonial Union, colonies and senior leaders are openly questioning—and even rebelling—against the Colonial Union strategy. The leaders of the Colonial Union now realize that their strategy has failed. There are multiple reasons for this, but perhaps the most compelling is that that they failed to match their aspirations to the resources available.

This is an important lesson for contemporary strategists. Strategy must be tested, constantly reviewed, and aligned with the resources available to a nation. Priorities must be established and the links between policy outcomes and tactical actions established. Strategy is not just a process, despite the strategic planning processes of many nations. Effective strategy making and implementation is vital to statecraft, and the implications of getting it wrong can be catastrophic. As Murray and Millet wrote, "it is more important to make correct decisions at the political and strategic level than it is at the operational or tactical level. Mistakes in operations and tactics can be corrected, but strategic mistakes live forever."[6] As the Colonial Union finds, its chosen strategy will have far reaching effects for all humans in the *Old Man's War* universe.

2. Civil-military relations: humans, aliens, and the "unequal dialogue"

In a Spring 2020 article for *International Security*, Risa Brooks challenges the extant paradigm of civil military relations in the United States. The norms that underpin contemporary civil-military relations argue that the military should operate in a sphere separate from the civilian domain of policymaking and decisions about the use of force. However, this model is coming under increasing pressure due to "intensifying partisanship in society and in the military, the embrace by civilian leaders of objective control and their concomitant delegation of authority in armed conflict to the military, and growing questions about the causes of the inconclusive outcomes of recent wars in Iraq and Afghanistan."[7] Similarly, William Rapp criticized the Samuel Huntington model of assigning clear jurisdictions to civil and military leaders as not reflecting the reality of contemporary security strategy making and implementation.[8]

In his 2002 book, *Supreme Command*, Eliot Cohen explores the concept of the "unequal dialogue" in civil-military relations.[9] He defines it thus: "an unequal dialogue—a dialogue, in that both sides expressed their views bluntly, indeed sometimes offensively, and not once but repeatedly—and unequal, in that the final authority of the civilian leader was unambiguous and unquestioned."[10] Cohen proposes that this approach challenges "normal" theories of civil-military which describe how dialog between political and military leaders is reserved for only the start and end of wars. For the *Old Man's War* series, it appears that the Colonial Union and its military instrument, the CDF, fall mainly into the normal theory of civil-military relations. There is no clear ongoing dialog, and no obvious adaptation to Colonial Union policy or military strategy.

This separation of civil and military spheres is examined several times in the *Old Man's War* series. The Colonial Union and the CDF have clearly delineated roles, as reflected in the three mandates discussed earlier. At the same time, colonization and diplomacy are entirely separate endeavors, unrelated to the military activities of the CDF. Diplomacy is poorly resourced compared to military operations.

Diplomacy is therefore relegated to secondary status by the Colonial Union. Not only does this deny an alignment of the means to achieve the Colonial Union strategic objectives, it compromises the sustainment of an effective civil-military relationship. There are several reasons for this. First, when the military becomes the solution to every problem, every challenge appears to be a military one. This can result in the inefficient use of military forces—which are expensive—as well as the inappropriate use of force when it is not required. But perhaps the most insidious effect is that it leads to a lack of imaginative thinking about strategic challenges; why invest in creative thinking when the military is always there to solve problems? A second challenge with this approach is that it obstructs the ability to form coalitions of like-minded nations—or races. This is critical in an environment such as that described in *Old Man's War*. In a galaxy with hundreds of intelligent species, all competing over what is perceived as a limited supply of planets, going it alone is a foolish strategy. But it is inevitable if minimal efforts are made to resource and nurture diplomatic efforts.

3. Ethical strategy in a competitive and lethal universe

In *The Last Colony*, the leader of the Conclave, General Gau, explains to John Perry the rationale for building this massive coalition of species: "Look at our civilizations. We're all the same size because we limit each other through war. We're all at the same level of technology, because we bargain, trade and steal from each other. Our civilizations are at an equilibrium … that is sliding all of us toward entropy."[11] In this passage, Gau is offering a vision for why his grand strategy of collaboration to share colonial expansion among different species is better than the status quo. At no time does the Colonial Union offer a similarly compelling vision for its expansion throughout the galaxy.

In some respects, it harkens back to the days of European colonization and imperialism. Colonies were formed or seized to ensure the transfer of wealth to the colonizing nation and to guarantee its future prosperity. At some point, they were also formed because, as Azar Gat notes, "it had become so easy."[12] In reading the *Old Man's War* series, the reader can also gain the impression that the imperialist approach to expanding through the universe has become too easy for the Colonial Union.

At the same time that they are implementing their grand strategy for the expansion of human colonies, the Colonial Union is deceiving its own people through the control of information. This is described as follows: "The Colonial Union has all the spaceships, skip drones and communication satellites. It handles all the trade and what little diplomacy we engage in on its space stations. The Colonial Union is the bottleneck through which all information flows." But perhaps the most troubling aspect of Colonial Union strategy is its treatment of Earth: "Earth ... [has] been kept socially retarded for two hundred years. The Colonial Union farms people there. And it likes the arrangement so much that the Colonial Union actively suppresses the natural evolution of society there."[13]

This is hardly an ethical basis for making and implementing strategy. And as we discover, it fundamentally impedes the longevity of the Colonial Union's strategy, and indeed the longevity of the human race itself. The selection of ethical and well-explained strategies is an essential part of contemporary strategy making. Military and other government leaders must select national objectives that are aligned with the values of their people and be achievable within the resources and desires of the wider population.

4. The ethical application of technology

With a setting far into the future, we might expect that the *Old Man's War* series is populated with a variety of advanced technologies. These range from space travel, weapons, and communications. However, the technology that is perhaps most important to the narrative is biotechnology.

In the first book of the series, readers are introduced to the advanced human augmentation technologies that are employed by the CDF. These augmented humans are able to use their strength and connectivity through a small computer embedded in their skull to even the odds in combat with larger, faster, and more lethal alien species. But the protagonist, John Perry, soon grows concerned that the level of augmentation means that he and his fellow soldiers are no longer human.

> I don't feel connected with what it was to be human anymore. Our job is to go meet strange new people and cultures and kill the sons of bitches as quickly as we possibly can. There's no sense of consequence. There ought to be consequences to our actions. We have to acknowledge at least some of the horror of what we do, whether we're doing it for good reasons or not. I have no horror about what I'm doing. I'm scared of that.[14]

It is right that Perry ponders these issues. So too is it appropriate for contemporary strategists to carefully explore the ethics of using advanced technologies in war. This is particularly the case when it comes to modifying human beings. There have been amazing achievements in the biological sciences over the last decade. Gene sequencing has gone from a multi-billion-dollar project to a cheaper and quicker undertaking with technologies such as the CRISPR/Cas 9 approach to gene editing and therapy.[15] Synthetic biology, which combines scientific and engineering approaches to manipulate biology, is demonstrating even greater promise.[16]

Biotechnology in the coming decades will be used to augment physical and cognitive abilities in human beings. The military are bound to leverage as much advantage as they can from this technology. If military institutions and other national security organizations are to use biotechnology with the aim of augmenting humans, we must invest now in exploring the implications. There are likely a range of impacts for military institutions, including selection criteria for augmentation, how much augmentation will be permitted, new modes of training and education, and issues around de-augmentation of military personnel transitioning to civilian life.[17]

More importantly, if military institutions start significantly altering the capabilities of their people, there will be societal impacts. For example, if only military personnel were to be augmented, there may be a range of impacts on civil military relationships. In this situation, it may be highly unethical to deny the benefits of physical or cognitive augmentation to wider society. More broadly, if societies are to embrace human augmentation, it will pose important questions about the value of different individuals within that society. Yuval Harari argued that "splitting humankind into biological castes will destroy the foundations of liberal ideology. Liberalism can coexist with socioeconomic gaps. However, liberalism still presupposes that all human beings have equal value and authority."[18] With the potential downside of creating different human castes through biotechnology, the ethics of such a technology should be explored now. It is an issue that *Old Man's War* raises and one we would be wise to consider well in advance of these capabilities becoming available.

From tactics to galactic grand strategy, the first three books of the *Old Man's War* saga reinforce the enduring nature of war, and its attendant friction, surprise, and uncertainty. They explore the alignment of policy with war making, diplomacy and other government actions. But so too does the series reflect the reality that policy and strategy making and implementation—in the future and in the current era—is an undertaking that is inordinately difficult and deserves the full attention of national and military leaders.

The series provides the reader—and the contemporary strategist—with insights that might aid in considering the strategic challenges that we face now and are likely to face in the future. At the beginning of *The Last Colony*, John Perry describes how "being from Earth in this universe is like being a small-town kid who gets on the bus, goes to the big city and spends his entire afternoon gawking at all the tall buildings. Then he gets mugged for the crime of marveling at this strange new world, because the things in it don't have much time or sympathy for the new kid in town, and they're happy to kill him for what he's got in his suitcase. The small-town kid learns this fast, because he can't go home again."[19] The strategic challenges that lay ahead of us in the coming decades are very much like the big city that John Scalzi describes. The future is ripe with wonders and opportunity, but the path ahead is also strewn with traps, challenges, and potential disasters for the unwary.

Notes

1 John Scalzi, *Old Man's War: Book 1* (New York: Tor Books, 2005), 5.

2 John Scalzi, "Old Man's War: Ten Years On," *Whatever*, Jan 1, 2015. Source: https://whatever.scalzi.com/2015/01/01/old-mans-war-ten-years-on/.

3 Hew Strachan, *Clausewitz's On War: A Biography* (London: Atlantic Books, 2007), 106.

4 Carl von Clausewitz, *On War*, trans. Michael Howard and Peter Paret (Princeton, NJ: Princeton University Press, 1976), 177.

5 Beatrice Hesuer, *The Evolution of Strategy: Thinking War from Antiquity to the Present* (Cambridge, MA: Cambridge University Press, 2011), 27–28.

6 Allen Millett and Williamson Murray, "Lessons of War," *National Interest*, no. 14 (Winter 1988), 83–95.

7 Risa Brooks, "Paradoxes of Professionalism: Rethinking Civil Military Relations in the United States," *International Security*, 44, no. 4 (Spring 2020), 7–8.

8 William Rapp, "Civil-Military Relations: The Role of Military leaders in Strategy Making," *Parameters*, 45, no. 3 (Autumn 2015), 13.

9 Eliot Cohen, *Supreme Command: Soldiers, Statesmen and Leadership in Wartime* (New York: The Free Press, 2002), 208–224.

10 Ibid., 209.

11 John Scalzi, *The Last Colony: Old Man's War Book 3* (New York: Tor Books, 2007), 194.

12 Azar Gat, *War in Human Civilisation* (Oxford, UK: Oxford University Press, 2006), 543.

13 Ibid., 236.

14 Scalzi, *Old Man's War*, 159–160.

15 Klaus Schwab, *The Fourth Industrial Revolution* (New York: Currency, 2017), 22.

16 National Academies of Sciences, Engineering, and Medicine, *Positioning Synthetic Biology to Meet the Challenges of the 21st Century* (Washington, DC: The National Academies Press, 2013), 2.

17 Mick Ryan and Therese Keane, "Biotechnology and Human Augmentation: Issues for National Security Practitioners," *Strategy Bridge*, Feb 5, 2019.

18 Yuval Harari, *Homo Deus: A Brief History of Tomorrow* (New York: Harper, 2017), 403–404.

19 *The Last Colony*, 9.

CHAPTER 12

Where No Port Has Gone Before

Deep Space Nine, Chokepoints, and Maritime Security

Timothy Choi

———————▶

Star Trek: Deep Space Nine (ST:DS9) is unique amongst the Star Trek series for its emphasis on a (mostly) stationary naval installation: the space station *Deep Space Nine (DS9)*. Demonstrating the complex roles played by static infrastructure in maritime strategy, the myriad activities carried out by Federation members from and at *DS9* serve as useful reminders for naval thinkers on 21st-century Earth. Just as most of the *Star Trek* series have emphasized the central role of mobile multi-mission starships, so, too, has the majority of recent literature on maritime strategy and security. Whether it is the massive aircraft carriers of the United States Navy, the small speedy boats of the Iranian Revolutionary Guards, or the Chinese Maritime Militia in the South China Sea, discussions of seapower today tend to focus on vessels rather than the static shore-based infrastructure that not only support these sea-based assets but serve as significant direct seapower tools in their own right.[1]

But the *ST:DS9* series was innovative for not only emphasizing a port over a star ship, but also a constant natural geographic feature which would determine social, cultural, and political responses as well. In particular, the Federation's decision to remain deeply involved with *DS9* (the station) was largely due to the nearby presence of the Bajoran Wormhole. This natural phenomenon enabled actors to travel rapidly between two distant "quadrants" of the Milky Way Galaxy, which otherwise would take decades under conventional warp-based propulsion methods—a challenge faced by USS *Voyager* in the eponymous series.[2] In effect, then, the Wormhole served as a chokepoint, which on Earth has long been a factor in shaping the seas' primary role as highways.[3] Thus, *ST:DS9* established and consolidated for the first time in *Star Trek* the concept of lines of communication. This is particularly poignant given the fact that *Star Trek* has traditionally eschewed concerns regarding the interstellar transportation of goods and people due to the availability of warp travel and replicators. Although the Federation had little economic interest in maintaining assured access through to and through the Wormhole, other societies did, and the Federation rapidly recognized the wormhole's political and military significance.

In this sense, *ST:DS9* was the most "realistic" of the *Treks*. Not only did it confront head-on the question of marginalized populations living on the outer edges of the Federation, it also highlighted the limits of the Federation utopia. Realpolitik and Clausewitzian "reason" drove the Federation's desire for brokering a peace between themselves and the neighbouring Cardassians despite concerns by the Bajorans, which had just been occupied by Cardassia. As part of the peace deal, however, colonists from Bajor and other planets, known as the Maquis, living in the demilitarized border region between Bajoran and Cardassian space were left to fend for themselves against Cardassian attempts to assert control over the region. These Maquis represented the "passion" element of Clausewitz's trinity, drastically complicating the Federation's peacemaking objectives in the region. In their pursuit of an independent heritage and lifestyle, the Maquis threatened the maritime security of the region as they carried out raids and attacks on Cardassian assets. The Maquis took advantage of the unpredictable natural environment of the "Badlands" in their area, which added a significant element of "chance" that stymied Cardassian and Federation forces trying to pursue them.[4] As sub-state actors, the Maquis posed an internal challenge to Federation politics which had heretofore experienced a mostly cohesive attitude towards its internal and external affairs.

It is the sub-state threat of the Maquis in the foreground against a backdrop of strategic threat posed by the Cardassians and later the Founders from the other side of the Wormhole, which allow us to review *DS9*'s significance to Federation maritime strategy, reflecting key but oft-ignored roles of ports in today's seapower discussions.

To understand this, it is first necessary to pull back and go over what seapower is at its heart. Defined by the eminent British maritime strategy scholar Geoffrey Till as the ability to influence behavior at sea and from the sea, seapower fundamentally consists of two halves: inputs and outputs. While outputs are specific forms of that influence, such as the uninterrupted flow of seaborne cargo, inputs are those material factors which enable actors to affect that influence. Ships and navies are probably the most obvious form of inputs, but they can only maximize their seapower outputs with the support of land-based permanent infrastructure—ports.[5]

Within traditional maritime strategy literature, however, ports rarely play a substantial independent role. Alfred Thayer Mahan highlighted their utility as both forward replenishment stations as well as semi-permanent bases from which the battlefleet can replenish on their way to expeditionary objectives or places where they can operate out of on a regular basis, respectively. Mahan, using the Caribbean and the Panama Canal as examples, also emphasized the importance of situating ports near strategically important areas. This would reduce the distance that fleets stationed at the ports needed to travel before reaching their objectives.[6] In essence, ports did not play an active and independent role in Mahan's seapower vision—they only existed to support the mobile fleets' activities in a primarily wartime setting. On the other side of the Atlantic, Britain's Julien Stafford Corbett shared a similar view to Mahan, though he did add the point that they served as geographical focal points for any navy wishing to conduct economic warfare. As merchant ships tend to congregate at major ports to load and offload their goods, ports make for a constant that any opponent can count upon for focusing their anti-commerce efforts.[7] In contrast to the fleet, ports could not "give and take" as much of the war due to their static nature. Both Mahan and Corbett emphasized the role of ports in military and economic terms.

In the following decades, an increased emphasis in seapower studies has been the peacetime uses of the seas. Foremost amongst authors who have examined potential such phenomena have been the aforementioned Geoffrey Till, whose *Seapower: A Guide for the Twenty-First Century* continues to be a fundamental text for beginning to understand "non-military aspects of sea-use." As part of this, "maritime security" encompassed issues concerning the general order of "good" behavior at sea. Security threats in this broadened conception include piracy, terrorism, environmental degradation, mariner safety, and more.[8] To this end, Till and others have explored the roles played by myriad governmental and non-governmental agencies in addressing such concerns. Yet, he missed an opportunity to review the role of ports in maritime security matters, while also downplaying their importance in supporting military fleet operations given developments in underway replenishment and "sea-basing."[9]

This brief exploration on the topic of the non-military uses of the seas would be incomplete without a quick mention of Soviet Admiral Sergey Gorshkov's 1976 *The Sea Power of the State*. More well-known in the West for its emphasis on the fleet's role in supporting Soviet land operations, a significant portion of it was spent advocating for the importance of ocean science and exploration. Recognizing the dramatic environmental differences between land and sea, Gorshkov realized that effective economic and naval activities on and under the oceans would require extensive scientific knowledge of that domain in which humanity has only recently begun to operate.[10] As the Ferengi's 74th Rule of Acquisition states, "Knowledge equals profit," and even if the Soviets would look down upon the idea of using knowledge for such unscrupulous capitalist aims, they nonetheless realized its fundamental importance in maritime strategy.[11]

We can see all these real-world maritime strategic perspectives in *ST:DS9*. The space station can be conceived of an "input that supports inputs," playing dual roles as both an active participant in regional Federation operations as well as supporting other Federation assets. On its own, it serves as the dominant Federation asset for ensuring maritime domain awareness and acquiring scientific knowledge in the region through its onboard sensors. As well, its onboard weapons systems combined with its location adjacent the Wormhole provide the Federation with a measure of sea, or more accurately space, control capability in the area, much as coastal artillery and fortresses played significant roles in Earth's naval history—one only needs to look at the Dardanelles in World War I and the Norwegian fjords in World War II to see the importance of shore-based infrastructure in naval defense. As a supporting input, *DS9* plays host to a large number of "Runabouts," relatively small and short-endurance vessels whose usefulness increased due to the proximity of the Wormhole. Later in the series, *DS9* became the homeport of USS *Defiant*, one of the very few dedicated warships built by the Federation. Though larger than the Runabouts and heavily armed and armored, the *Defiant* was not built with crew comfort and scientific exploration in mind, reducing its usefulness to a relatively narrow range of naval missions.[12]

However, the bulk of *ST:DS9* took place in a peacetime environment, tenuous though the peace was. In this context, a large number of maritime security concerns comprised numerous plot elements for the series. On board *DS9*, a thriving black market illustrated a rare commercial element in *Star Trek*, which otherwise glossed over the role of trade and currency. This market was facilitated and run primarily by Quark, the profit-driven Ferengi owner and bartender of *DS9*'s bar. Although Quark's financial activities were frowned upon by Federation authorities, they were not in themselves cause of much concern. However, the spatial-political circumstances surrounding the Maquis rebels also resulted in *DS9* as a site for smuggling and the arms trade. Realizing Quark's expertise in moving goods under the noses of Federation authorities, Quark was soon coopted by the Maquis into a middleman for the acquisition of arms required for the Maquis' quest for independence.[13] That *DS9* is a permanent locus for commercial activities makes it both, as Corbett noted for ports, a "fertile area" for carrying out a variety of legal and illegal activity which threaten regional stability and security, as well as activities aimed at preventing or slowing such activities.[14]

Counter-terrorism, too, is a key role played by *DS9*. Due to the repositioning of the station closer to the Bajoran Wormhole, it was also closer to the "Badlands" border region the Maquis call home. Though primarily directed at the Cardassians, the Maquis' activities eventually involved the Federation, such as when they bombed a Cardassian cargo ship docked at *DS9*. Therefore, *DS9* became key to monitoring and dealing with the tactical activities of the Maquis in the interests of preserving the fragile peace between Cardassia and Bajor. In such a capacity, *DS9*'s counter-terrorism (or counter-insurrection, to use a more neutral term) role was therefore not only a place where Maquis arms smuggling could be countered, but also as a place from which active interdiction of Maquis naval operations could be conducted. This latter role provided the impetus for the *Star Trek: Voyager* series, where USS *Voyager* and the Maquis ship she was pursuing were transported to the other side of the galaxy. *Voyager* had been replenishing at *DS9* just prior to this event, clearly illustrating the station's key role in maritime interdiction against substate actors such as the Maquis and violent Bajoran factions.[15]

ST:DS9 also recognized the vital role ports play in supporting humanity's safe and reliable use of inhospitable domains. We frequently see instances where the station would deploy its Runabouts or the *Defiant* to the space around it and through the Wormhole to provide assistance to ships and travelers in distress.[16] Even as early as the opening episode of the series, we see the use of the station's Runabouts as towing vessels for other ships in distress.[17] This fits well with the increased recognition over the last 200 years of the need to ensure the availability of robust lifeboats and rescue assets at major ports, as well as coast guard stations and similar assets along busy lines of communications.

Finally, illustrating a fairly astute understanding of war and peace, *ST:DS9* dedicated only the last two seasons to actual wartime involvement. In what is probably the most iconic role played by a Star Trek spacepower input, *DS9* and its homeported USS *Defiant* were responsible for closing access through the Bajoran Wormhole in order to prevent Dominion reinforcements from coming through from the other side of the galaxy. With clear parallels to World War I Dardanelles campaign, *DS9* and the *Defiant* demonstrated the outsized strategic impacts a relatively weak power could have given ideal geometry and intelligent prioritization of means and ends. To stall the Dominion forces, the local Federation forces employed a plan that centered upon mine warfare. Recognizing that although the *Defiant* was a tactically powerful vessel in combat, but still insufficient to defeat the Dominion fleet already on this side of the galaxy, Federation officers decided that a more strategically useful purpose for the *Defiant* would be as a relatively humble minelayer. Battlefield innovation resulted in the marriage of the replicator with the classic mine, allowing a minefield to be effectively unsweepable: every mine that was destroyed would be replaced by the replicator on a neighboring mine. However, the minelaying process took time, and recognizing this, it was decided that *DS9*'s main role would be as a tactical combat post to provide covering fire until the *Defiant* could accomplish its strategic objective. As Dominion forces and their Cardassian allies attempted to weaken and capture *DS9*, the *Defiant*, escorted by the Klingon Bird-of-Prey *Rokarran*, continued to establish the enormous wall of self-replicating mines in front of the Wormhole, the completion of which effectively stalled the majority of Dominion forces from coming through. Much like the role of the forts and coastal batteries at the Dardanelles, the Federation's eventual victory was due in part to a successful recognition that *DS9* only needed to pursue a limited tactical objective: ensuring the minefield's successful deployment. The station, much like those gunpowder cannon sited along the narrow waters of the Dardanelles, did not need to destroy the much more powerful enemy fleet, but leave that to the mines and the eventual arrival of a joint Federation and Klingon battle fleet.[18]

Although many more battles, operations, and schemes would be required before the Dominion War concluded in favor of the Federation and its allies, the key role of *DS9* remained in supporting the war effort. As the front lines pushed back into Cardassian space, the station and its forward location provided the fleets with a much-needed replenishment and repair capability. That such permanent static installations were crucial to the war effort on both sides was further demonstrated by multiple attempts by Federation forces to destroy or impair their opponents' own such supporting facilities.[19]

Star Trek: Deep Space Nine demonstrated a more sophisticated understanding of strategy and seapower than any other *Star Trek* series. As the creators of the show themselves suggested, *ST:DS9* provided a fundamentally different dynamic than the starship-centric *Trek*s: the permanence of the station and chokepoint meant actions had long-term consequences. *DS9* was deeply connected to the spatial-political whole and could not merely warp away once a tactical problem had been solved. On the *Enterprise*s, Kirk or Picard could broker a fragile peace between two conflicting sides, but would that peace hold up? We rarely know, because they would soon be off and on their way to the next point of interest. Such luxury does not exist at *Deep Space Nine*, and that required a strategic approach to story writing made necessary by its permanent nature.

Notes

1   One clear exception to this is the discussion surrounding the artificial land features that have been constructed by China in the South China Sea and how they contribute to Chinese seapower.

2   *Voyager*'s journey was estimated to take some seventy Earth years. See "Star Trek: Voyager," *Memory Alpha*, http://memory-alpha.wikia.com/wiki/Star_Trek:_Voyager.

3   Geoffrey Till, *Seapower: A Guide for the Twenty-First Century* (London: Frank Cass, 2004), 4.

4   "Badlands," *Memory Alpha*, https://memory-alpha.fandom.com/wiki/Badlands.

5   Till, 4.

6   Alfred Thayer Mahan, *The Influence of Sea Power Upon History 1660–1805* (Hong Kong: Bison Books, 1987), 34–36.

7   Julien S. Corbett, *Some Principles of Maritime Strategy* (London: Brassey's Defence Publishers, 1988), 261.

8   Till, 310–350.

9   Ibid., 91.

10 Sergey Grigorevich Gorshkov, *The Sea Power of the State* (Oxford: Pergamon Press, 1979), 16–24.

11 "Rules of Acquisition," *Memory Alpha*, http://memory-alpha.wikia.com/wiki/Rules_of_Acquisition.

12 "Deep Space 9," *Memory Alpha*, http://memory-alpha.wikia.com/wiki/Deep_Space_9; "Danube class," *Memory Alpha*, http://memory-alpha.wikia.com/wiki/Danube_class.

13 "The Maquis, Part II (Episode)," *Memory Alpha*, http://memory-alpha.wikia.com/wiki/The_Maquis,_Part_II_(episode).

14 Corbett, *Some Principles of Maritime Strategy*, 261.

15 "Caretaker (Episode)," *Memory Alpha*, http://memory-alpha.wikia.com/wiki/Caretaker_(episode); "Past Prologue (Episode)," *Memory Alpha*, http://memory-alpha.wikia.com/wiki/Past_Prologue_(episode).

16 For examples, see "The Passenger (Episode)," *Memory Alpha*, http://memory-alpha.wikia.com/wiki/The_Passenger_(episode); "The Way of the Warrior (Episode)," *Memory Alpha*, http://memory-alpha.wikia.com/wiki/The_Way_of_the_Warrior_(episode).

17 "Emissary (Episode)," *Memory Alpha*, http://memory-alpha.wikia.com/wiki/Emissary_(episode).

18 "Call to Arms (Episode)," *Memory Alpha*, http://memory-alpha.wikia.com/wiki/Call_to_Arms_(episode).

19 For examples, see "Torros III," *Memory Alpha*, http://memory-alpha.wikia.com/wiki/Torros_III; "Monac shipyards," *Memory Alpha*, http://memory-alpha.wikia.com/wiki/Monac_shipyards; "Tacking into the Wind (Episode)," *Memory Alpha*, http://memory-alpha.wikia.com/wiki/Tacking_Into_the_Wind_(episode).

CHAPTER 13

Sun Tzu, Ender, and the Old Man

Science Fiction and Strategic Empathy

Kathleen J. McInnis

———————▶———————

"The world is increasingly complex," is the euphemism bandied about in strategic and policymaking circles when commenting on the difficulty, dangerousness, and volatility of our present, and likely future, circumstances. One sees and hears the phrase quite a lot these days, and with good reason: the world is on fire, at least from Washington's point of view.

Take China. It is now apparent that China's rise is not going exactly as hoped. Uighurs are in concentration camps, Hong Kong is suppressed, islands are built in the South China Sea to further dubious maritime claims, and intellectual property is stolen on an industrial scale. Meanwhile, Russia is waging a disinformation war within the populations of the United States and its allies and waging an actual war in Eastern Ukraine. Iran also remains a thorny matter. United States policy there has swung back and forth so many times that the Gulf states have whiplash—and appear increasingly skeptical of the United States' reliability as a partner in the region. North Korea is … North Korea. Layer on top of all that the lasting implications of the European refugee crisis, Chinese coercive economic statecraft, the COVID-19 pandemic, the spread of violent extremist groups across Africa and the Middle East, rapid technological advancements, and attendant social change, just to name but a few important issues and trends. All this played out in just a decade—the blink of an eye in strategic terms. The mind reels at the increasing complexity, to put it mildly.

What to do? How might the United States and its like-minded partners best navigate this strategic landscape? How might we better prepare ourselves to do so when, as Secretary Gates reminds us, we have only correctly predicted the next conflict once—in 2003, when we decided that we were going to invade Iraq.[1] And even in that instance, when we engaged in war at the time and place of our choosing, we found ourselves in the middle of a brutal counterinsurgency campaign. Complicating matters further, we have not exactly been winning wars lately—or even divining what winning looks like.

The practical upshot is the need to understand better our strategic environment and what to do about it, fast. But how? How do we begin contemplating the intent and actions of our adversaries? Fortunately, science fiction—full of stories of humans figuring out how to survive in an utterly alien universe—is replete with creative tools to begin conceptualizing and contemplating the "unknown unknowns," in former Secretary of Defense Donald Rumsfeld's parlance. Science fiction is useful because it provides us with a conceptual *tabula rasa*. In suspending our disbelief and immersing ourselves in different worlds with different histories and rules, we create the space for meaningful, creative contemplation of our own strategic dilemmas. In particular, the *Ender's Game* series by Orson Scott Card and the *Old Man's War* series by John Scalzi are useful tools when interrogating our concepts associated with anticipating adversaries.[2]

Back to Basics

The nearly reflexive answer to the problem of understanding adversaries: get more, or get better, intelligence. As Sun Tzu argues in their *Art of War*:[3]

> Thus it is said that one who knows the enemy and knows himself will not be endangered in a hundred engagements. One who does not know the enemy but knows himself will sometimes be victorious, sometimes meet with defeat. One who knows neither the enemy nor himself will invariably be defeated in every engagement.[4]

Accordingly, the United States spends an extraordinary sum on the intelligence community to better understand the world and our adversaries within it. Debates whirl around whether the intelligence community is appropriately structured to meet today's challenges, whether we need on the ground programs like human terrain teams to help us appreciate local contexts, and so on. In other words, the debate tends to focus on the relative accuracy of the inputs provided to decisionmakers. Yet a cursory glance at recent history suggests that reorganizing inputs will probably not solve the challenge. Despite some indicators that China—including the publication of *Unrestricted Warfare* by two Chinese army colonels and island-building in the South China Sea as early as 2013—and Russia—such as the invasion of Georgia—were not interested in *playing ball* in the United States-led international system, it took us until at least 2014 to appreciate, and act upon, their divergent strategic interests.[5] In other words, both countries changed the game before we were able to appreciate that they were doing so—and did so in plain sight. Therefore, the issue is not a matter of inputs; it is a question of comprehending those inputs and acting upon them appropriately.

Strategic Empathy?

Some argue that we have prioritized the volume of intelligence collection over meaningful and thorough analysis. Put another way, there is so much noise that discerning the signal is becoming nearly impossible. One recently-posited solution to this conundrum: the cultivation of "strategic empathy," that is, the ability to put oneself in the mind of one's adversaries to discern their likely future behaviors. It is a skill set that can be found scattered across classic strategic scholarship, from Sun Tzu to Machiavelli. The major predicament facing statesmen: how, exactly, might one pull that off? Recently, Zachary Shore makes a compelling argument in *A Sense of the Enemy* that a good way to do so is by analyzing, and drawing the correct lessons from, pattern breaks by adversaries.[6] But might there be more to cultivating strategic empathy?

Empathy itself is a construct that possesses a number of differing definitions in the psychological literature. In a broad sense, one of its main features becomes apparent when one contrasts the construct with sympathy: empathy is the ability to put oneself in another's mindset, while sympathy is "being moved by, or in tune with, another person."[7] Empathy allows us to maintain a barrier between the self and the other. Cognitive empathy, by contrast, "generally does not include any reference to caring about the other person, thus allowing for the possibility of a kind of Machiavellian cognitive empathy that can be used to harm others."[8] It is cognitive empathy, therefore, that most closely comports with strategic empathy and understanding our enemies. This is where science fiction can come in. Because it usually deals with humans encountering alien life or civilizations, science fiction is replete with examples of people trying to understand the actions of an unfamiliar being or culture. Taking a step back and thinking more broadly, what might the prism of science fiction illuminate regarding strategic empathy and its utility for statecraft?

Understanding the Adversary

In *Ender's Game*, Ender Wiggin is challenged to command a group of training school cadets in exercises designed to test his abilities in combat against an alien race. The punchline at the end of the novel is so severe that he spends the next *three thousand years* traveling around the galaxy in the next novel. As he does so, he becomes a "Speaker for the Dead," an individual who probes into the life of a deceased person to tell their true story publicly. Ruthless honesty is the order of the day in his role as Speaker; Ender makes it clear that he has no time for half-truths or convenient lies. Accuracy and objectivity are critical. So far, so good.

But as we walk in Ender's shoes on Lusitania, a planet featuring human colonists and an alien species nicknamed *pequininos,* or piggies, we find he brings a vital corollary to his objectivity: compassion. Ender knows that every subject he examines, every dead person he speaks for, is the protagonist in their own story. The case that he examines on Lusitania involves a man who beats his wife. Without excusing that behavior, he discerns that the reason for the man's violence is his shame at never being loved by the wife that he loved to the point of adoration, unearthing long-buried secrets in the process. Ender explains why he is so good at getting to the bottom of things: "When you really know somebody you can't hate them. Or maybe it's just that you can't really know them until you stop hating them." When applied to the world of strategic studies, Ender's comments would suggest that compassion might be critical to successful strategic analysis. Everyone is the hero in their own narrative, after all. In other words, effective strategic empathy requires psychological empathy, that is, understanding the world views and perspectives of adversaries and allies alike.

Strategic empathy is an area in which the United States appears to be lacking, despite our best intentions. For American national security professionals, any number of disincentives are in place when it comes to experiencing and understanding the world—and peoples—outside of the United States borders. Yes, human intelligence exists, but that source of information tends to be overshadowed by data-driven analyses and quantitative methods.[9]

Examples are myriad. In the name of force protection, many United States embassies are increasingly firewalled from the local populations.[10] Programs such as "Af-Pak Hands," designed to train a cadre of military leaders to deeply understand the social, economic, and political contours of Afghanistan and Pakistan, were disbanded even though that program would arguably be more useful to senior decisionmakers in the wake of the United States drawdown in the region.[11]

At the height of the Cold War, upwards of 350,000 service members and their families were stationed in Europe.[12] Given personnel rotations, that translated into millions of Americans living in Europe, understanding its cultures, and bringing that knowledge to their own lives and connections back in the United States. Today, the number of service members stationed in Europe hovers somewhere between 70–80,000.[13] And anyone who has ever had to wrangle with the Defense Travel System—or tried to get a security clearance after traveling abroad—has experienced the practical disincentives to getting outside the office and experiencing the world. Perhaps one result of this structural insularity is that mirror imaging is rampant when it comes to our adversaries and allies alike.[14] What are we missing by implicitly and explicitly limiting our ability to actually get out of our comfort zones and learn about other peoples?

The Islamic State enslaved and crucified people, Uighurs are still in prison camps in China, and the Taliban throw acid on women's faces. Is empathizing with these kinds of despicable behavior moral, let alone possible? It is important here to remember the distinction between sympathy and empathy; the former brings self-identification with the other; the latter is associated with meaningful understanding of the other. As odious as these regimes might be, applying empathy to understand underlying motivations and mindsets is not the same as being "soft" on, sympathizing or identifying with, an adversary. Quite the opposite; empathy, by definition, requires boundaries and distance.

Knowing Ourselves?

In the *Old Man's War* series, John Perry leaves planet Earth at the ripe old age of 75 to join the Defense Forces (CDF) of the Colonial Union (CU)—the governance structure for human colonies scattered across a subsection of the galaxy. As part of the enlistment process, he quickly discovers that Earth is no longer the real home of humanity. He is a simple, likable guy who, as part of his enlistment in the CDF, wanders onto different worlds to make space safer for humanity. Yet as the story progresses, one begins to understand that the CU and the CDF are almost byzantine in their opaque, constant scheming. They hatch elaborate plots, both against the human population and the aliens they fight. By the third book in the series, it becomes clear that despite significant tactical advantages and fantastic intelligence capabilities, the CU/CDF wins its battles but cannot win its wars. In *The Human Division*, we learn that the CU's choice to maintain an exploitive relationship with Earth was once forged out of a sense of protection of humanity's home world; it has since been perpetuated by sheer inertia.

The contrast between Perry and the Colonial Union of which he is part could hardly be starker. The CU and CDF long forgot who it was and why it existed, and instead became a kind of self-propelling machine. Perry knows who he is and what he wants and is willing to listen to his adversaries. It is why he is effective against alien races like the Consu and successfully defends the Roanoke colony for which he becomes responsible.

Back to Sun Tzu, who makes the point that leaders need to understand both ourselves and our adversaries if we want to be successful when it comes to statecraft. *Old Man's War* invites us into a creative thought experiment to understand why that might be the case. Reflecting on this contrast between Perry and the Colonial Union and comparing them with Sun Tzu's admonition, Perry's self-knowledge seems a key advantage as he traverses the universe. Perry's clarity of person, combined with his appreciation of his adversaries, led to his own Clausewitzian *coup d'oeil* at Roanoke—and Earth.[15] Indeed, the most successful characters in the *Old Man's War* series, such as General Tarsen Gau, know themselves and are true to themselves.

At first glance, knowing oneself may seem like the kind of feel-good silliness that has no place in the art of strategy. But Sun Tzu, Scalzi, and Card all suggest that we might want to reconsider that approach. There's a reason that "know thyself" was one of the three maxims carved into the ancient Greek Oracle of Delphi. Knowing oneself, warts and all, and still being able to act in the world is one of the *most formidable challenges of human existence*. Knowing oneself is also an essential requirement for empathy, strategic or otherwise. Without a sense of boundaries of the self, empathy easily turns into sympathy and identification with the other—decidedly counterproductive qualities when figuring out what to do about an adversary.

Knowing oneself and remaining true to that vision is exceedingly challenging when applied to matters of state in contemporary democracies. Unlike Putin's Russia or Louis XIV's France, the contemporary democratic state is not singular; it is a plurality. With respect to American democracy, the identity of the republic is grounded in aspirations towards rule of law, human liberty, and process for political deliberation.

But those foundations have arguably turned into a kind of strategic hubris. As an example: yes, there were vibrant debates on the extent to which democracy-spreading misadventures in Iraq and Afghanistan were justified or not. But even those conversations tend to be somewhat superficial. Looking more deeply, why did we think that democracy promotion by gunpoint was a good idea? Why did we not, as a government, recognize that such a strategy was actually counter to the American principle of self-determination? Why did we seek to replicate the most superficial dimensions of democracy while failing to recognize that the American is a fragile, ongoing experiment?[16]

Strategic Narcissism?

Former National Security Advisor H. R. McMaster takes the question a step further: What risks are we actively creating by filtering the world almost exclusively through our own rose-tinted cultural, social, and political lenses? He writes:

> Americans, as Hans Morgenthau noted long ago, tend to view the world only in relation to the United States, and to assume that the future course of events depends primarily on U.S. decisions or plans, or on the acceptance by others of our way of thinking. The term for this tendency is strategic narcissism.[17]

Here, narcissism is an important word choice; it connotes a destructive self-centeredness based on a fundamentally distorted view of self. It also precludes an ability to understand others except with respect to how to manipulate them. Is the United States dangerously close to strategic narcissism? To wit: many have touted the importance of American leadership in solving the world's problems but fail to apprehend that the way we go about advancing that leadership may be creating longer-term strategic damage. The United States government generally spends the majority of its time and attention building interagency consensus on strategic problems while largely forgetting to listen to its allies and partners in the process of strategy formulation. America de-prioritizes the institutions of international diplomacy while empowering its military, even though political discussion is the heart of democracy. The United States often fails to meaningfully link our aid and support to efforts that promote locally-appropriate advancements towards human rights and rule of law.[18] Is it any wonder, therefore, that Putin's 2007 Munich critique of the United States leadership—in which he argued that the United States has failed to live up to its values—has resonated with so many?

Unilateral and frequently illegitimate actions have not resolved any problems. Moreover, they have caused new human tragedies and created new centers of tension. Judge for yourselves: wars as well as local and regional conflicts have not diminished ... And no less people perish in these conflicts—even more are dying than before. Significantly more, significantly more! Today we are witnessing an almost uncontained hyper use of force—military force—in international relations, force that is plunging the world into an abyss of permanent conflicts. As a result, we do not have sufficient strength to find a comprehensive solution to any one of these conflicts. Finding a political settlement also becomes impossible.[19]

Given Moscow's subsequent actions in Georgia, Ukraine, and even Syria, Putin's critique was ultimately hollow, if not downright cynical. China's debt diplomacy is equally suspicious. Yet that does not excuse us from necessary self-reflection. What might be gained from having senior national security leaders do an actual listening tour—across America and key allies—before penning our defense strategies? What might we gain from returning to basics with a sense of our strengths and limitations? As Elizabeth Shackleford notes, "I believe we can recover, but not by simply seeking a return to the pre-Trump world. It will require a deliberate national discourse on what actually makes America great. What are the values that set us apart? How must we put them into practice?"[20]

On balance, Scalzi and Scott Card's works point to an inherent challenge when it comes to applying Sun Tzu's maxim today: we seem to neither know our enemies nor ourselves. Our answer, to date, has been to find better ways to understand our enemies, particularly through gathering more intelligence. Yet, the works of science fiction explored in this chapter suggest that we might instead consider prioritizing the human dimensions of strategic awareness. Leaders might do so, for example, by getting out of the beltway and listening to both the American population and international allies and partners. Listening and reflecting are simple prescriptions in theory, of course, but enormously challenging to put into practice. If we do not, however, effectively navigate the increasingly complex international security environment is likely to require one hell of a big fire extinguisher.

Notes

1   Robert M. Gates, *Exercise of Power* (New York: Alfred A. Knopf. 2020), 18.

2   United States Department of Defense, *DoD News Briefing—Secretary Rumsfeld and Gen. Myers*, Feb 12, 2002. "https://web.archive.org/web/20160809082051/http://archive.defense.gov/Transcripts/Transcript.aspx?TranscriptID=2636.

3   The author uses the pronoun "their" in deference to the notion that Sun Tzu is actually a pseudonym for a variety of strategic thinkers who contributed their insights to *The Art of War* over the centuries.

4   Sun Tzu, *The Art of War*, translated by Ralph D. Sawyer (New York: Barnes & Noble Books, 1994), 179.

5   With respect to *Unrestricted Warfare*, some have noted that a monograph penned by two colonels is hardly representative of the whole of Chinese strategic intent. Still, its publication, combined

with China's "whole of society" approach to statecraft that challenges U.S. and allied strategic interests, suggests that the authors were at a minimum tapping into a deeper undercurrent in Chinese strategic planning. See: Liang Q. and Xiangsui W., *Unrestricted Warfare* (Beijing: PLA Literature and Arts Publishing House Arts, 1999).

6   Zachary Shore, *A Sense of the Enemy: The High Stakes History of Reading Your Rival's Mind* (Oxford: Oxford University Press, 2014).

7   Sara D. Hodges & Michael W. Myers, "Empathy," *Encyclopedia of Social Psychology*, ed. Roy F. Baumeister and Kathleen D. Vohs (California: Sage, 2007).

8   Ibid.

9   Kathleen J. McInnis, "Strategists Have Forgotten the Power of Stories," *Foreign Policy*, May 19, 2020; Shore.

10   The U.S. Embassies in Kabul and London stand as prominent examples of this kind of geographical and physical distancing.

11   Given the number of violent extremist organizations capable of inflicting harm on the U.S. and its allies in the region, one might think that the Af-Pak hands program, or something like it, would increase in importance to U.S. decisionmakers as force levels draw down to 2,500 troops. J. P. Lawrence, " A decadelong program to 'turn the tide' in Afghanistan is ending, long after military shifted its focus," *Stars & Stripes*, Aug 17, 2019.

12   U.S. European Command, *History*, Accessed 26 December 2020. https://www.eucom.mil/about/history.

13   Kathleen J. McInnis, *CRS In Focus 11130, United States European Command: Overview and Key Issues*, Aug 4, 2020.

14   Charles A. Duelfer and Stephen Benedict Dyson, Chronic Misperception and International Conflict: The U.S.-Iraq Experience, *International Security* 36, no. 1 (Summer 2011), 73–100.

15   *Coup d'oeil* is a term that describes a comprehension of the entire battle and attendant clarity and precision of thought as a hallmark of good generalship.

16   Thomas Ricks, *First Principles: What America's Founders Learned from the Greeks and Romans and How That Shaped Our Country* (Harper, 2020).

17   H. R. McMaster, "How China Sees the World and How We Should See China," *The Atlantic Monthly*, May 2020.

18   Elizabeth Shackleford, *The Dissent Channel: American Diplomacy in a Dishonest Age* (New York: Public Affairs, 2020).

19   Vladimir Putin, "Transcript: Putin's Prepared Remarks at 43rd Munich Conference on Security Policy," *Washington Post*, Monday, Feb 12, 2007. https://www.washingtonpost.com/wp-dyn/content/article/2007/02/12/AR2007021200555.html.

20   Shackleford, 275.

PART III

THE PRIME DIRECTIVE

CHAPTER 14

All That You Touch You Change

Leading Through Adaptation, Learning, and Diversity

Jacqueline E. Whitt

———————————▶

Sometimes, speculative fiction takes us into a fantastical future, allowing our imagination to roam and imagine what might be. At other times, it makes you wonder if the author was actually a time traveler. Such has been the feeling for many on reading Octavia Butler's *The Parable of the Sower* and *The Parable of the Talents* in recent years. The novels begin in 2024 and 2032, respectively. Butler's United States is wracked by climate change, racial strife, economic inequality, intractable regional conflict, internal displacement, separation wrought by walls, debt bondage, and populist politics cloaked in the language of fervent religious conservatism and—yes, really—"making America great again." The Earthseed novels are Butler's contribution to the "if-this-goes-on" version of science fiction literature.[1]

Butler's near-future dystopia is not quite the bleak, post-apocalyptic hellscape of Cormac McCarthy's *The Road*, although there is plenty of depravity, violence, and hardship. In the midst of this catastrophic landscape, Butler builds a world and writes into existence a leader and a community where mutual care, learning, teaching, and adaptation are at the center. Butler writes Black women into the center of the story in a genre where they are often absent or lack an interior life and motivation. It is a world where a young, Black teenage girl, coming of age herself, has a vision for a different sort of future and works to build it. Lauren Oya Olamina prepares, makes decisions, and leads. She establishes a new religion, Earthseed, premised on the belief that God is Change. Lauren writes the truth of her religion in *Earthseed: The Books of the Living*. These guide her life and the life of the religion's followers. Earthseed's destiny, according to Olamina, is to take root among the stars. Literally.

But it is also a profoundly pragmatic world. Lauren and those who live with her arm themselves with guns, or knives when there are no guns. The guns get used when needed. The travelers do not expect police to protect them, and the community expects no one else to save them. The adults all take turns standing watch while others sleep. Acorn, the small self-sustaining village where Lauren and the others arrive at the end of *Sower*, makes a name for itself salvaging and scavenging. They learn and teach each other basic survival and medical skills. There are strict rules for communal living. Lauren and her companions keep track of how domestic political events will affect their community. Earthseed grows and thrives.

Lauren is a good leader. She anticipates, plans, prepares, adapts, and builds community. She has suffered loss, so she understands the importance of family and expends resources to preserve and reconnect them. Lauren understands that people seek and fight over power and that her religious leadership accrues some power to her.

And still, Acorn is attacked by the militant forces of Christian America, the Crusaders. Earthseed's followers are labeled heretics and cultists. Its children are kidnapped and adopted out to "good" Christian homes. Larkin, Lauren's daughter, is taken and adopted out to a Black Christian America family. The adults who live are enslaved; their enslavement justified by Christian America's theology. They endure forced labor and rape. Lauren's husband, Bankole, dies.

Lauren helps the captives hold it together. She convinces her followers, Earthseed's followers, that they should rebel or die trying. Lauren studies how the "re-education" camp works and knows where the controls for their slave collars are. When a landslide buries some of the camp's "teachers" and knocks the central controls out, Lauren is ready to act. She leads a rebellion: she and her followers kill their enslavers and cut off their collars, then burn what had been Acorn, which had been perverted for use as Camp Christian, and disperse. Lauren makes decisions to keep her followers safe, even though it means breaking everyone up. Out of the ashes of Acorn, however, Earthseed becomes an international movement.

Although a superb leader, Lauren Olamina is flawed.[2] She is guarded—her condition of "hyperempathy," which means she literally feels the pain and pleasure of others, demands it, so sometimes lies. Larkin believes Olamina chose Earthseed over her family. Lauren can be aloof, and she is definitely zealous. She can be impulsive and selfish. Lauren is disappointed in and let down by her family. In the end, she disbands her beloved community, and this feels like a failure on some level. There is no resolution at the end. But there is hope.

The novels never quite take a utopian turn—both of them end on something of a note of hope and optimism, but also deep uncertainty.[3] At the end of *Sower*, Lauren and her cobbled-together community leave the road and establish a new community, Acorn, and in *Talents*, Lauren dies watching shuttles leave earth and carrying settlers to Alpha Centauri.

In both novels, the military is decidedly in the background—we know the American military is off fighting America's wars, but it is not a book about combat or intergalactic strategy. The conflict is about the homefront and society writ large, and the conflicts are political, social, economic, racial, and religious. Perhaps it is strange, then, to imagine what military leaders might take from these novels, but there is a whole world to military leadership that is not combat and fighting and lethality. Of course, Lauren's traveling band and the Acorn community and the Earthseed communities that disperse are not military organizations, but they function similarly to military organizations in a sufficiently chaotic world that there are lessons to be learned.

Effective modern militaries operate on the basis of discipline, cohesion, and loyalty. Regina Titunik persuasively argues, "the qualities required for organized warfare rewarded as 'manly' are not aggression and bloodlust, but, paradoxically, are qualities that both opponents and proponents of an imagined hyper-masculine military associate with femininity: teamwork, submission, obedience, and self-sacrifice."[4] Titunik argues that success in organized warfare requires at least as much *restraint* as it does unleashed aggressive energy.[5]

If we take seriously the idea that success in war is not purely reliant on unrestrained violence, aggressive energy, and the individual warrior hero, then success relies on foundations that mix characteristics traditionally constructed as "masculine" and "feminine." Throughout the two novels, the mix of the masculine and feminine is quite explicit. For much of the first novel, Lauren disguises herself as a man, correctly believing it will make the initial traveling party safer and less conspicuously vulnerable. Guns, violence, and the threat of violence hold an important place in the novels. Still, in the end, three important and related "feminized" values emerge as essential for leadership, particularly in a time of crisis: adaptation in the face of change; the importance of teaching and learning; and an ethic of care, centered on diversity and kindness.

Change and Adaptation

> All that you touch
> you Change.
> All that you Change
> Changes you.
> The only lasting truth
> is Change.
> God
> is Change.
> ~Earthseed: The Books of the Living

Earthseed is, in some ways, both an embodiment of and response to the challenge of the Anthropocene—the proposed geological epoch in which human activity has been the primary influence on the earth's geology, climate, and systems—and its consequences.[6] Change and human responses to it are the central theme of the duology. While some Americans long to return to the heyday of American power of the mid-20th century, Lauren has known since she was a girl that such a return was impossible and likely less idealistic than imagined.

Butler names the period of causing catastrophic and irreversible damage "The Pox," short for Apocalypse. In *Talents*, her husband Bankole writes: "I have read that the period of upheaval that journalists have begun to refer to as 'the Apocalypse' or more commonly, more bitterly, 'the Pox' lasted from 2015 through 2030—a decade and a half of chaos. This is untrue. The Pox has been a much longer torment. It began well before 2015, perhaps even before the turn of the millennium. It has not ended."[7] The Pox is slow and incremental, but its effects were just as catastrophic as those for the proverbial frog in a slowly boiling pot of water. Human beings have irreversibly changed the world they live in and must navigate the effects of that change, all the while, the changed environment shapes human behavior and interaction. The idea of *shaping* change, of give-and-take with change and adaptation, allows Lauren and others to make sense of the ever-shifting world around them. It enables agency when it would be easy to resign oneself to simply being acted upon in the world.

Lauren emerges as a leader in part because she has anticipated and prepared for change. Indeed, she had been observing and preparing for catastrophic change even as a girl. She stockpiled supplies and money and has practiced what she needed to do when it was time to leave. Lauren watched carefully, and when it was time to go, she did not hesitate, even though it was not the plan or timeline she had in mind. Lauren's attention to change and her willingness to adapt are central to the group's survival.

But just as Acorn seems to be settling in, growing and thriving—as soon as they take their eye off change cease constantly preparing for potential for catastrophic change—trouble comes. Bankole wants the family to move to an established town, where he believes they will be safer. Lauren does not wish to leave Acorn. At the moment, Lauren resists change, disaster strikes. When they let their guard down, even just a bit, they are overtaken, although it is not clear they could have fended off their attackers. Lauren and the rest of Acorn try to rely on their preparation: they have stored secret caches of supplies and practiced bugging out. But it is too late. And so, Lauren and the others learn, again, to adapt and survive. They take on new roles as captives, but they plan for their eventual escape.

After the rebellion, Lauren understands that Earthseed must adapt, going underground and dispersing if it is to survive. She changes her name for a time, so she will not be recognized, and thinks about how to continue her work. She and the others look for their children and take different approaches to recovering from their trauma. Lauren decides to travel again and to take up the work of teaching Earthseed again.

This relentless ability to adapt and survive while encouraging others to build community in the face of oppression, slavery, and cruelty elevates Lauren's status as a leader and a liberator. These are qualities military leaders need when leading men and women through the hell of combat and war. Butler's work, however, places these essential qualities, not in a traditional political or military leader, but embodied in a Black woman, centered in, but not limited by, the boomerang cycle of violence and oppression of African American history. Lauren Oya Olamina sees a way out.[8]

Teaching and Learning

To shape God,
With wisdom and forethought,
To benefit your world,
Your people,
Your life,
Consider consequences,
Minimize harm,
Ask questions,
Seek answers,
Learn,
Teach.
~ *Earthseed: The Books of the Living*

Education is central to the world that Butler builds and is a recurring theme in her work. One scholar writes, "Butler's progressive retelling of the relationship linking diversity, change, and intellectual growth with inevitable violence offers, despite its relentless and pragmatic pessimism, a space for a pedagogical vision of practical and embodied community to overcome the barriers that divide us."[9] Additionally, Butler pushes against the exclusive dichotomy between religion and science—Earthseed is explicitly and unapologetically rooted in both faith and science.

In *Talents*, Lauren's father is a professor and a minister, and her stepmother is a teacher who has a PhD. Lauren helps teach the younger children in the school, and she teaches her fellow travelers and those in the community to read and write. Once established in Acorn, Bankole, a physician, teaches others to provide basic medical care. Lauren and others devise lessons for children. On the day of the Crusaders' raid, the children are learning about World War II, indicative of the value of learning about the past and the present. The community members teach each other how to salvage and scavenge and they learn together to grow food and to build shelter. Everyone has something to teach; everyone has something to learn.

After the fall of Acorn, Lauren instructs the other captured women to *learn* as a mode of survival: "Learn everything you can from these people and bring what you learn back to the rest of us …. If we collect what we see and hear, if we stay united, work together, support one another, then the time will come when we can win our freedom or kill them or both!"[10] In this way, learning is the key to adaptation and survival. The mandate to learn and to put that knowledge to use gives the Earthseed followers purpose.

When Earthseed reestablishes itself and begins to grow as an international movement, it retains its focus on education. It funds scientific research, establishes schools and colleges, and offers scholarships to students who promise to spend seven years teaching or otherwise using their skills in service of the community. In this sense, education anchors Butler's fantastical world—recall, Earthseed's destiny is to take root among the stars—in a pragmatic reality. Even in new worlds, people will need to communicate, have a sense of their past and present, and learn and maintain skills necessary for survival.

Ethics and Diversity

> Kindness eases change.
> Embrace diversity.
> Unite—
> Or be divided,
> robbed,
> ruled,
> killed
> By those who see you as prey.
> Embrace diversity
> Or be destroyed.
> –Earthseed: The Books of the Living

For Lauren and her Earthseed followers, mutual reliance is the key to survival. They all pull guard duty. Bankole enlists others to help provide nursing and medical care. But the community is also centered on care and kindness. Lauren's first followers on the road, outside of her two traveling companions from her hometown, are a couple and their young child. Lauren knows adding a baby to their traveling party is risky. She does it anyway. Acorn takes in the vulnerable and wounded. They welcome people who do not speak English, viewing their diverse languages as assets, rather than liabilities.

The world Lauren is working to build is explicitly and intentionally diverse. Lauren recognizes from the beginning that her natural allies in the dystopian landscape are other people of color. Marlene Allen writes, "Butler, thus, emphasizes the Afrocentric idea that community is crucial for survival." It is a world where "people are not outsiders because of their biological nature (i.e., what they are racially or sexually), but rather because of how they think, that is, their unwillingness to accept difference and the inherence of change."[11] Even those who are skeptical of Earthseed are welcome to stay and live in the community, provided they respect the rituals and requirements of it.

In interviews about the *Earthseed* novels, Butler often discussed the pull between utopia and dystopia that she created. For Butler, nothing ever just *is*—whatever "it" is, it is always in flux, and it is always malleable, based on human choices. In 2001, Butler wrote a brief essay in conjunction with a United Nations Conference on Racism. She asks: "But in real life, what would make us more tolerant, more peaceful, less likely to need a UN Conference on Racism?" And she answers: "Nothing. Nothing at all." But the essay does not end there. She explores the problem of hierarchy for humans—we cannot seem to escape it, and too many people take pleasure in feeling they are superior to others. And still, Butler finds reasons to hope. She asks the question again: "Does tolerance have a chance?" And answers this time: "Only if we want it to. Only when we want it to. Tolerance, like any aspect of peace, is forever a work in progress, never completed, and, if we're as intelligent as we like to think we are, never abandoned."[12]

Ultimately, Butler leaves readers with complicated lessons and leaders with plenty of paradoxes with which to wrestle. There are few easy answers in Butler's work. Individual people are acted upon by forces beyond their control, yet human beings collectively are the primary cause of much of the devastation and change. New communities and new societies are what people make of them, yet people can never leave behind their experiences and all that they know. Empathy is both an asset and a liability. There is always more to learn and teach, yet there also comes a time for decisive action. We might be compelled to ask, too, whose voices and experiences we are missing when we build organizations that are more homogenous than not. What might a modern military look like if it were well-equipped, tactically proficient, disciplined, lethal, and loyal—and if it were based on a genuine commitment to managing change, adapting, learning, diversity, kindness, and an ethic of care?

Notes

1 Isaac Asimov offered a three-part typology for three gambits of sociologically-dominant science fiction literature: what if, if only, and if this continues. See Isaac Asimov's Introduction to *More Soviet Science Fiction* (USA: Collier, 1972), 8. These three typologies are often attributed to other people, or unsourced. For Butler's interpretation, see Darrell Schweitzer, *Speaking of the Fantastic* (Holicong, PA: Wildside Press, 2005), 29. Butler seems to, in some places, have incorrectly attributed this typology to Robert Heinlein.

2 Butler always calls her Olamina in her notes; Butler seems to be not quite as taken with her protagonist as her readers often are. See Gerry Canavan, "'There's Nothing New / Under The Sun, / But There Are New Suns': Recovering Octavia E. Butler's Lost Parables," *Los Angeles Review of Books* (June 9, 2014).

3 Butler never finished the third planned novel in the series, *The Parable of the Trickster*, although notes and partial drafts are held by her estate. On Butler's unfinished works, see Gerry Canavan, "Knowing No One's Listening," *Los Angeles Review of Books* (June 6, 2014).

4 Regina Titunik, "The Myth of the Macho Military," *Polity* 40, no. 2 (April 2008), 147.

5 Titunik, 149.

6 Simon L. Lewis, and Mark A. Maslin. "Defining the Anthropocene." *Nature* 519, no. 7542 (2015): 171–180.

7 Octavia Butler, *Parable of the Talents*, 7–8.

8 Marlene D. Allen, "Octavia Butler's 'Parable' Novels and the 'Boomerang' of African American History." *Callaloo* 32, no. 4 (2009): 1353–365.

9 Sarah Outterson, "Diversity, Change, Violence: Octavia Butler's Pedagogical Philosophy," *Utopian Studies* 19, no. 3 (2008): 434.

10 Octavia Butler, *Parable of the Talents*, 200.

11 Marlene D. Allen, "Octavia Butler's 'Parable' Novels and the 'Boomerang' of African American History." *Callaloo* 32, no. 4 (2009): 1359.

12 Octavia Butler, "Racism Essay," National Public Radio (Aug 30, 2001). https://legacy.npr.org/programs/specials/racism/010830.octaviabutleressay.html.

CHAPTER 15

Romulans and Remans

Max Brooks

"I beg you, not to let prejudice or politics interfere with this alliance." These words were spoken by Commander Suran on the floor of the Romulan Senate in the opening scene of *Star Trek: Nemesis*. In this scene, officers of the Romulan fleet implore their civilian leaders to accept an offering of peace and unification with an "undesirable caste within the hierarchy of the empire." This undesirable caste, the Remans, have always served their Romulan masters as dilithium miners and industrial laborers.

"But they also have a reputation for being formidable warriors," explains Commander Riker later in Act 1. "In the Dominion War, Reman troops were used as assault forces in the most violent encounters." The Dominion War, the largest single conflict within the entire *Star Trek* canon, might not have been won without Reman "Cannon Fodder." And that cannon fodder might not have been victorious if not for their adopted commander, Shinzon.

Shinzon was not a Romulan. He was not a Reman. He was, in fact, a human clone of Jean-Luc Picard. He had originally been grown to replace Picard, but, when that project was canceled, he was assigned to slave labor in the Reman mines. That is where he discovered both "my Reman brothers" and an undying hatred for all things Romulan.

Though not Reman himself, Shinzon emerged from the Dominion War as their hero, leader, and architect of their postwar uprising against the Romulans. This is where *Star Trek: Nemesis* begins. Shinzon's rebellion has been successful enough to convert a faction of the Romulan military to his cause. After the Romulan Senate rejects Commander Suran's impassioned plea for an alliance, his faction launches a coup, murders the Senate, and installs Shinzon as the empire's new leader.

Initially, Shinzon claims to care only for the liberation of the Remans, but it is soon revealed that he is simply using them to destroy both the Federation and Romulans. And just like Hitler, Mussolini, Idi Amin, and every other self-serving psychopath in our history, Shinzon's power base comes from the legitimate grievance of his people. The Remans helped save the Romulan Empire from the Dominion. Now what are the Romulans going to do for them? That is the lesson of *Star Trek: Nemesis*.

Societies that use marginalized communities in wartime must be prepared to reward those communities in peacetime or else suffer bitter consequences. That lesson has played out across real human history, most notably in the United States of America, who have played both Romulans and Remans. Just like in the Dominion War, American colonists were required to fight for their British Mother Country in the French and Indian War. And just like in the fictional conflict that underpins *Star Trek: Nemesis*, the real-life Remans gained nothing for their sacrifice. In fact, not only were the Colonists not rewarded for their spilled blood, but they were also even expected to help pay for a war they never asked for.

Just like that moment on the floor of the Romulan Senate, the British Empire stood at a crossroads. Had they chosen inclusion—taxation WITH representation—Britain might have given Britain, in the words of Commander Suran, "a chance to make ourselves stronger than ever before." But, just as in *Star Trek: Nemesis*, politics and prejudice interfered. The result was a new nation with a President who—just like Shinzon—had been brought up wanting nothing more than to serve the Empire.

As the new United States shifted from Remans to Romulans, it found itself on the opposite side of the dilemma. Using marginalized communities in wartime would force a reckoning with those communities in peace. That lesson was first hammered home during the American Civil War. Robert E. Lee wanted to arm African American slaves. The Confederate leadership refused on the grounds that it would unravel their entire reason for fighting. In the words of Georgia Senator Howell Cobb, "If slaves make good soldiers, then our entire theory of slavery is wrong."[1]

Half a century later, the *re*-United States found itself in the exact same conundrum as the Confederacy. World War I was, at least officially, fought to make "the world safe for democracy." But what would that mean for African American soldiers who didn't share in democracy at home? The "solution" of the United States government was to try to either keep African Americans out of combat or sabotage their efforts to achieve any glory on the battlefield. Neither strategy worked. America's Black Remans fought so valiantly and were so highly decorated—as in the case of the 369th Infantry Regiment "Harlem Hellfighters"—that at the end of the war, W. E. B. Dubois declared: "We *return*. We *return from fighting*. We *return fighting*. Make way for democracy. We saved it in France, and by the Great Jehovah, we will save it in the United States of America, or know the reason why."[2]

Just like the British before them, and the Romulans in *Nemesis*, this call for postwar equality was "met with force" and the subsequent "Red Summer" of 1919 saw some of the worst racial violence in American history.[3]

However, unlike the American Revolution and the end of the 10th film of the *Star Trek* franchise, the story of America took a radical turn towards inclusion. World War II saw numerous communities putting their finest members on the front lines of the conflict. From the Tuskegee Airmen to the Navajo Code Talkers to the Nisei 442nd Infantry Regiment, Americans of all stripes helped achieve victory for a country that treated them as "undesirable castes." However, once that victory was achieved, the postwar years saw a march towards equality that, while slow, uneven, and far from perfect, continues to advance right up to the present day.

Not only did the United States military desegregate in the aftermath of World War II, but it has consistently led the rest of the country in the battle for social justice. From equal pay for women, to the right of soldiers to marry whomever they love, to the United States Army's current "Operation Inclusion," which, in the words of TRADOC's Commanding General, Paul E. Funk "promotes diversity, equity and inclusion."[4]

Imagine if those values had been embraced by the Romulan Senate at the beginning of *Star Trek: Nemesis*? What would the rest of the movie, and the *Star Trek* universe in general, have looked like? There probably would have been some chaos and, even violence, trying to integrate the Reman community. Shinzon might have even been the instigator of that violence since integration meant losing his hate-based power. There is no doubt that taking the road to inclusion would, just like the real world, have been long and treacherous. But just like in that real world, the end of that road would have left the Romulan Empire "stronger than ever before."

Notes

1   Howell Cobb to James A. Seddon (January 8, 1865), series 4, vol. 3, (Washington, DC: Government Printing Office, 1900), 1,009–1,010.
2   W. E. B. DuBois, "Returning Soldiers," *The Crisis*, 18 (May 1919), 13.
3   "Red Summer" National WWI Museum, last accessed May 4, 2021, https://www.theworldwar.org/learn/wwi/red-summer.
4   U.S. Army TRADOC, "TRADOC's CG Diversity & Inclusion Message 2020," YouTube video, July 20, 2020, https://www.youtube.com/watch?v=pOyKm0NrSXY.

CHAPTER 16

Are We Such Apostles of Mercy?

Social Darwinism and Inter-Species Warfare

Janeen Webb

In the mid-19th century, theoretical psychologist Herbert Spencer co-opted Darwin's *On the Origin of Species by Natural Selection* to advance the argument that human societies operate according to the same laws of natural selection and evolve by competition for resources. In doing so, he promoted one of the most pernicious and persistent myths ever to influence our society—social Darwinism. Survival of the fittest—which refers to "fit for purpose"—was adopted as a basic precept of human behavior: the predominantly White male proponents of this theory used it as a pseudo-scientific basis for the dispossession, even extermination, of species or societies they held to be inferior.

Social Darwinists quickly developed a model of natural selection in which survival of the fittest could be seen as an effective justification for imperial and colonial expansionism waged with superior technology and weaponry against indigenous communities. In addition, practitioners of the then relatively new science of Anthropology, such as Max Muller, seized upon Darwin's work to produce a rank order of humanity that ascended from Australian Aborigines to Indo-Europeans. Overall, the idea was that different races represented different rungs on the evolutionary ladder, with White Europeans at the top. The fact that White races had come to dominate the economic, military, and social structures of the globe was seen as a demonstration that they had been chosen by Nature—or God—for that position.

Social Darwinism also underpinned the White race idea of the Coming Man—an all-White, all-male, anti-intellectual world view—which wielded huge influence as the ideology behind everything from the Boy Scouts to the Hitler Youth movement. The real-world heroes of social Darwinism were men like Scott of the Antarctic and Cecil Rhodes—men who *got things done* and worried about the ethics later, if at all. In literature, writers such as Rudyard Kipling and H. Rider Haggard based adventure stories on their own colonial experiences—Kipling in India, Haggard in Africa—to portray White superiority as a cultural norm.

It was a short step to transpose social Darwinism from adventure stories into science fiction. But science fiction writers do not always assume social Darwinism's inherent bias towards human superiority: they often challenge humanity's anthropocentrically assumed right, as self-proclaimed Darwinian apex predators, to exploit other species.

Despite its persistent discourse, there is an inherent problem with social Darwinism. Belief in one's own evolutionary supremacy creates political and military structures that are self-justifying and self-satisfied, promoting leaders and strategists who are ill-prepared when confronted by events that contradict their world view: ironically, they struggle to adapt. This was evident in 1905, when the Japanese fleet annihilated the Russian fleet at the Battle of Tsushima. This victory by an "inferior" racial group left European leaders scrambling, and sparked an international wave of anxious, often lurid, Yellow Peril stories which raised the specter of invasion by aggressive Asian forces intent on expansion—and revenge.

Science fiction moves beyond earthly inter-racial conflicts to offer a multiplicity of scenarios in which human leaders must face conflict with other, non-human species. The eternal problem of how to understand Outsiders becomes even more fraught when intelligent aliens are seen through the lens of social Darwinism. One of the obvious manifestations in science fiction is the depiction of other races, no matter how technologically advanced and successful, in terms of Earth's "inferior" species. Thus, in Heinlein's *Starship Troopers*, the antagonists in the ongoing war between humanity and a species of intelligent arthropods are disparagingly referred to as "Bugs"—with the implication that they will, eventually, be squashed. This terminology was deliberately referenced by Orson Scott Card in *Ender's Game*, where the alien antagonists are the Formics—otherwise known as "Buggers." However, in a reversal of Heinlein's insistence on military prowess against all comers, Card raises ethical questions about responsibility towards other species—Ender has been manipulated by his military commanders into believing that he is playing a computer game while he commits an atrocity that wipes out an entire sentient race.

Derogatory social Darwinist terminology is used to effect by Ursula Le Guin in *The Word for World is Forest*, which depicts a struggle between colonists from Terra (Earth), and the gentle, indigenous inhabitants of the fertile planet Athshe. This novella is part of Le Guin's "Hainish" series, set in a fictional universe of planets that have all been "seeded" by colonists from the planet Hain, and dealing with conflicts between the resultant evolutionary variants. In this case, extremist humans, led by Captain John Davidson, regard the Athsheans as subhuman savages, belittling them with the nickname "creechies"—creatures to be dispossessed, enslaved, and killed. The telepathic Asthsheans are eventually pushed into learning the ways of warfare to defend their forest ecology, thus inflicting irrevocable harm upon their integrated culture. Inter-galactic peacekeepers from the League of Worlds eventually intervene, and Athshe is quarantined from further colonization and resource exploitation. But the damage is done: a civilization which had evolved to fit harmoniously with its environment has been shattered. The Athshean leader, Selver, concludes the story with this sad observation to the Hainish commissioner, Lepennon: "Maybe after I die people will be as they were before I was born, and before you came. But I do not think they will."[1]

Belittling epithets can, of course, cut both ways. In Larry Niven's *Ringworld*, a warlike race of feline carnivores known as the Kzinti have trained a young diplomat to override his killer instincts long enough to allow him to interact with other species, including humans: they have named him "Speaker-to-Animals."

In the opening to *The War of the Worlds*, one of the first science fiction critiques of social Darwinism, H. G. Wells wrote: "The Tasmanians ... were entirely swept out of existence in a war of extermination waged by European immigrants... Are we such apostles of mercy as to complain if the Martians warred in the same spirit?"[2] At the time, the plight of indigenous Tasmanians was very much in the forefront of international news. Wells begins his story by debunking the prevailing social-Darwinist mindset: "It is curious to recall some of the mental habits .... At most, terrestrial men fancied there might be other men upon Mars, perhaps inferior to themselves and ready to welcome a missionary enterprise."[3]

Instead, it is the Martians who possess superior intelligence and technology. Wells reverses the balance of power so that the heat-ray weaponry of the invading Martians is as superior to human technology as the guns of the British settlers were to the spears and boomerangs of the defending indigenous Tasmanians. Even worse, the Martians regard humanity merely as a convenient food supply on their road to inter-galactic expansion. The Martians have evolved into vampiric creatures sustained by the blood of their victims. They have done away with the inconvenience of living bodies: they manufacture metal shells at need, inhabiting them as fighting machines. (Thus, clearly providing the prototype for the Daleks of *Dr Who*, living war machines who have removed all physicality and emotion, and whose purpose has been reduced to a single word: "*exterminate!*").

It is only the Martian failure to predict biological incompatibility that allows the survival of humanity. Wells set up this "survival of the fittest" ending in the first sentence of the book: "... this world was being ... studied ... as narrowly as a man with a microscope might scrutinize the transient creatures that swarm and multiply in a drop of water."[4] He then reversed the usual loss of life caused by conquerors and colonists infecting indigenous populations with diseases—such as smallpox—from which they had no immunity: a scenario used effectively by Ray Bradbury in *The Martian Chronicles*, where human colonization of Mars wipes out an ancient, indigenous Martian civilization by inadvertently introducing chicken pox.

In Wells's England, local adaptation wins out: "The Martians are ... slain by the putrefactive and disease bacteria against which their systems were unprepared."[5] Wells presses home the Darwinian point:

> These germs of disease have taken a toll on humanity since the beginning of things .... But by virtue of this natural selection of our kind we have developed resisting power; ... to many (of them) ... our living frames are altogether immune .... By the toll of a billion deaths man has bought his birthright of the earth ....[6]

Wells thus uses scientific Darwinism—the slow evolution of human immunity from the effects of certain bacteria—to counter social Darwinist claims of innate human superiority over other species. Yet, humanity is by no means immune from new microbiological invasions: the microbes that kill the Martians are also a reminder, in a time of pandemic, that humans remain an ideal food source for opportunistic, expansionist viruses.

The idea of humans as food for aliens has become a standard trope: superior races arrive on Earth in a myriad shapes and forms, usually, like Wells's Martians, with colonial motives that are less than altruistic. A good example is Damon Knight's short story, *To Serve Man*, famously made into an episode of *The Twilight Zone* in 1960. Not all conquests are overtly military: the premise here is that a diplomatic mission representing an alien race known as The Kanamit—"fat piglike creatures"—arrive on earth from an unspecified planet, offering peace and plenty to humanity.[7] Their piggish appearance is unthreatening, even faintly humorous: "The Kanamit were short and very hairy—thick, bristly brown-gray hair all over their abominably plump bodies. Their noses were snoutlike and their eyes small, and they had thick hands of three fingers each ...."[8]

But there is nothing amusing in the story that unfolds. Earth's leaders, blinkered by their habitual social Darwinist perspective on the relative positions of pigs and humans, are deceived. The Kanamit begin by improving the material welfare of all humans: they provide a free universal power source, they almost double food productivity, and then they introduce a force field in which no explosive of any kind can detonate—thus making war impossible. They then select more and more humans for "cultural exchange" trips to the Kanamit home planet—but nobody, so far, has come back. It is Grigori, a skeptical UN translator, who solves the puzzle. He has come into possession of a Kanamit book titled *How to Serve Man*. But this is not a handbook of cultural etiquette. The dramatic last line of the story reveals its true nature: "It's a cookbook."[9] The apparently benign Kanamit are revealed as inter-galactic farmers—fattening up the human livestock and removing their capacity to fight back. Unarmed, and reduced to the position of pigs in a pen, humanity can no longer claim to be anywhere near the top of the Darwinian food chain.

The dilemma of consuming intelligent species was neatly satirized by Douglas Adams in *The Restaurant at the End of the Universe*, where the long-suffering protagonist, Arthur Dent, is introduced to the Dish of the Day: "A large dairy animal approached … a large fat meaty quadruped of the bovine type with large watery eyes, small horns and what might almost have been an ingratiating smile on its lips."[10] After a lengthy discussion of available cuts and cooking methods, Arthur opts for a green salad, only to be rebuked by the Dish: "Are you going to tell me," said Arthur, "that I shouldn't have green salad?" "Well," said the animal, "I know many vegetables that are very clear on that point. Which is why it was eventually decided to cut through the whole tangled problem and breed an animal that actually wanted to be eaten and was capable of saying so clearly and distinctly. And here I am."[11]

The vexed question of who gets to eat whom is an obvious metaphor for dominance, and the Darwinian theme of conflict between predator and prey recurs regularly in science fiction. H. G. Wells explored this aspect of evolutionary development in *The Time Machine*, where, after thousands of generations, the 19th-century English upper class and its oppressed working class have evolved into symbiotic groups—the surface-living Eloi and the underground-dwelling Morlocks. Over time, the evolutionary tables have turned: the hedonistic Eloi have become livestock for the working Morlocks, who keep them clothed and fed—until they eat them. It is a savage social critique, in which both groups have survived by becoming, finally, "fit for purpose."

Mary Doria Russell reprises the issue of sentient and consenting food in *The Sparrow*, when a group of religious colonists from Earth reach the planet Rakhat and discover two distinct species of sentient aliens—the predatory Jana'ata, and the gentler Runa upon whom they prey. Like Morlocks and Eloi, these groups have co-evolved: they co-exist in balance until disrupted by the arrival of technologically advanced humans whose well-meaning presence is nevertheless destructive for all concerned.

Sometimes the food fights back. Unfortunately, not all predator/prey distinctions are clear cut, and human assessments of the relative intelligence of newly encountered aliens are fraught with Darwinian difficulties. Spacefaring humans, like their earthly colonial ancestors, tend to look for signs that they recognize as indicators of "civilization"—hierarchical social structures, housing, clothing, personal ornaments, and so on. And when they do not find what they expect, it is unsurprising that they get first contacts horribly wrong. Joe Haldeman provides a telling example of this in *The Forever War*, when an invading platoon of humans first encounters the "enemy" Taurans. The protagonist, soldier William Mandella, offers this description:

> They were not quite as tall as humans, but wider in girth. They were covered in dark green, almost black, fur …. They appeared to have legs and an arm. The only ornament to their shaggy heads was a mouth, wet black orifice filled with flat black teeth. They were thoroughly repulsive, but their worst feature was not a difference from human beings, but a similarity …[12]

The unclothed Taurans are eating grass, and just when the platoon is deciding that the Taurans are therefore, by anthropocentric standards, to be classed as non-sentient, harmless herd animals, they discover that a "Rhine-sensitive" (telepathic) soldier has been killed by a "massive cerebral hemorrhage."[13] The Taurans are trying to establish contact and have misjudged the strength of their telepathic signals.

It is clear that the Taurans *are* sentient, and habitually communicate telepathically with each other: they are curious about the human invaders, whom they take to following—presumably to study them. The situation does not end well—a post-hypnotic command to kill indiscriminately has been embedded in the soldiers during military training, and when it is triggered during an attempt to capture a Tauran specimen the platoon massacres a large number of these unarmed, intelligent creatures. When the battle fog clears, many of the soldiers, especially Mandella and his partner Marygay Potter, are wracked by guilt and remorse.

There have been any number of science fiction works making deliberate attempts to deal sympathetically with problematic first contacts. Perhaps the most readily recognizable is Gene Roddenberry's *Star Trek* television series, which began in the 1960s and drew upon such diverse sources as A. E. van Vogt's *Voyage of the Space Beagle*, named for Darwin's own ship, *The Beagle*; Jonathan Swift's *Gulliver's Travels*; and C. S. Forester's *Horatio Hornblower* novels, thus combining modern inter-galactic adventures with traditional morality tales. The basic scenario is that a combined, diverse group of humans and aliens makes up the crew of Starfleet, an interstellar peace-keeping force representing a United Federation of Planets. The series has a hopeful evolutionary message, suggesting that retrogressive social-Darwinist attitudes can be overcome in favor of peaceful galactic co-existence.

But co-operative co-existence does not appeal to everyone. In his *Culture* series, Iain Banks also interrogates the issue of how to interact with species whose values differ from perceived baseline cultural norms. The cover copy for *Consider Phlebas* warns: "The Idirans fought for their Faith; the Culture fought for its moral right to exist. Principles were at stake. There could be no surrender."[14] The central figure, Bora Horza Gobuchul, rejects the inclusive values of the Culture as being dictated by machine intelligences, preferring the more violent, biologically-driven fanaticism of the Idirans. It is a complex story that explores, but does not answer, the question of moral justification for inter-species warfare.

At the opposite end of the spectrum from Haldeman's *Forever War*, which concludes that inter-species war is unnecessary and pointless, there remains a strand of militaristic science fiction that follows Heinlein's *Starship Troopers* in regarding inter-galactic warfare as a state of nature—inevitable and necessary. David Drake's collection of short stories, *Hammer's Slammers* is a case in point, following the exploits of a mercenary tank regiment named for their leader, Colonel Alois Hammer, as they slaughter their way across known space in grimly realistic tales that focus on the day-to-day actions of soldiers on the ground.

More recently, John Scalzi's *Old Man's War* follows Heinlein in taking up the theme of humanity's warlike colonial expansion into interstellar space. "The bad news,"

Scalzi tells us in his cover message, "is that planets fit to live on are scarce—and aliens willing to fight for them are common .... So: we fight. To defend Earth ... and to stake our claim to planetary real estate."[15] An interesting twist, from a Darwinian point of view, is that Scalzi's soldiers cannot enlist until they are seventy five years of age, when successful recruits are given age-defying treatments which effectively decant them into new bodies, thus producing soldiers "only partially what we were before."[16] At the other end of the novel's military establishment are the Special Forces, cloned as fully adult soldiers in full, quasi-telepathic communication with each other via implanted BrainPal devices. The Special Forces are curious about "real born" soldiers, and their defensive conversation with the protagonist, John Perry, raises some interesting evolutionary issues:

> "We're human, sir," Mendel said. "No less than you are."
> "Given the current state of my DNA, that's not saying much," I said.
> "You know you're human, sir," Mendel said. "And so do we."[17]

But does the *reader* accept these cyborgs and clones as fully human? Or have military technicians turned them into something else altogether in their push to create a totally loyal fighting force?

So, what should other species *do* about the ongoing problem of aggressive humanity? Octavia Butler offers one possibility in *Xenogenesis*, in which a vastly intelligent alien race of genetic engineers called the Oankali seek to guarantee Earth's survival—and their own—by transforming humanity into a less dangerous hybrid species. But artificially induced evolution is not without its dangers: the issue of neural modification formed the basis for the iconic film *Forbidden Planet*, where unguarded use of Krell mind-enhancing technology unleashed terrifyingly destructive "monsters from the Id."

Sometimes the only thing to be done is to isolate humanity for the good of the rest of the galaxy. In Greg Egan's *Quarantine*, unspecified alien forces have enclosed our solar system in a "Bubble" to prevent humanity from contaminating other life forms with human choice-based logic—which, it transpires, is depleting the universe of its infinite possibilities. Humanity is cast in the role of a disease capable of infecting the very fabric of the universe—thus neatly bringing us back to 19th-century colonial expansionism and its unforeseen consequences.

Social Darwinism is still very much with us, wielding significant influence in a world where the boundaries between fact and fiction are increasingly—and deliberately—blurred. Its rhetoric is currently manifesting in the opportunist ideology of social media conspiracist groups like QAnon, polarizing political positions, and spilling over into street violence and inciting the storming of the United States Capitol in the violent attempted coup of January 6, 2021. Humanity, it seems, has quite a way to go—boldly or otherwise—in the evolutionary process that will fit the species for a successful, inclusive new future among the stars.

Notes

1   Ursula Le Guin, *The Word for World is Forest* (London: Victor Gollancz Ltd, 1977), 128.
2   H. G. Wells, "The War of the Worlds," in *Seven Science Fiction Novels of H. G. Wells* (New York: Dover Publications Ltd., 1979), 311.
3   Ibid., 309.
4   Ibid., 310.
5   Ibid., 444.
6   Ibid.
7   Damon Knight, "To Serve Man," in *The Best of Damon Knight* (New York: Doubleday, 1976), 11.
8   Ibid.
9   Ibid., 17.
10 Douglas Adams, *The Restaurant at the End of the Universe* (London: The Folio Society Ltd, 2009), 102.
11 Ibid., 103.
12 Joe Haldeman, *The Forever War* (New York: St. Martin's Press, 1974), 48–49.
13 Ibid., 50.
14 Iain Banks, *Consider Phlebas* (London: Futura Publications, 1988), cover, n.p.
15 John Scalzi, *Old Man's War* (New York: Tom Doherty Associates, 2005), cover, n.p.
16 Ibid., 258.
17 Ibid., 260.

CHAPTER 17

Beware the Beast Man

Steven Leonard

In late 1963, King Brothers Productions—largely known for generating a series of more or less forgettable films between the early 1940s and late 1960s—hired Rod Serling to write a screenplay for them. Serling, who by 1963 had a well-earned reputation as a brilliant television writer, buried himself in the task. Two years and four versions later, he delivered a final draft to producer Arthur Jacobs, who had since secured the film rights to the story.[1] Serling's screenplay, an adaptation of French author Pierre Boulle's 1963 novella, *La Planète des Singes*, successfully navigated one of the most difficult challenges a screenwriter confronts: translating a narrative conveyed through the written word into one that could be visualized through cinematic action.

Serling—whose landmark anthology television series, *The Twilight Zone*, had completed production a year earlier—delivered a script that expressed the fundamental elements that had come to define his work: a story deeply-rooted in science fiction, dramatic opening and closing narrations, and an unexpected ending—the classic Serling "twist"—that would leave audiences in a slack jawed state of disbelief. Before the film premiered three years later, a fair amount of rewriting had been complete by another experienced writer—Michael Wilson, whose screenwriting credits included *It's a Wonderful Life*, *Lawrence of Arabia*, and *Bridge on the River Kwai*. Still, the essence of Serling's work remained intact, including the fateful conclusion, which firmly cast *Planet of the Apes* as a genre-defining science fiction film.

But Boulle never considered *La Planète des Singes* to be science fiction; instead, he saw his work as a "social fantasy." The novella's central theme—that human intelligence is transitory—and emphasis on humanity's inherent failings reflected the social and cultural turbulence of the time. Serling weaved them seamlessly into his screenplay, even expanding upon them with his own perspectives. The film's opening scene, a sardonic monologue delivered by astronaut George Taylor (portrayed by Charlton Heston), foreshadows the film's social and political undertones.[2] Taylor, waxing philosophically on humanity's place in the universe, removes a hypodermic needle from his breast pocket and injects himself with a solution in preparation for cryogenic sleep. With a derisive tone that Taylor seems to carry throughout the film, he wonders aloud: "Tell me, though, if Man, that marvel of the universe, that glorious paradox who has sent me to the stars … still makes war against his brother? Keeps his neighbor's children starving?"

From the outset, *Planet of the Apes* is a frame story, a literary device that serves to tell a story within a story—or multiple stories within a story—where the introductory narrative or theme exists primarily to set the stage for subsequent, often more consequential, ones. The frame story is a technique employed well by Boulle in his novella, and Serling expanded upon this significantly in the screenplay. The film's overarching theme—that humanity will be the instrument of its own downfall—is a unifying thread that serves to bind together supporting narratives and themes. Given the social, cultural, and political upheaval of the late 1960s, the frame story provided an ideal vehicle to transform the social fantasy of *La Planète des Singes* into the science fiction and contemporary subtext of *Planet of the Apes*.

Within the context of Serling's frame story, *Planet of the Apes* presents a complex array of social and political themes, the nuances of which are revealed as the film progresses. In the dystopian, post-apocalyptic future of *Planet of the Apes*, Taylor and the surviving crew members of an interstellar mission find themselves marooned on a planet where primates are the dominant species, not humans. Where Taylor hoped to discover a gentler, more evolved alien race, ape society is a starkly authoritarian theocracy, strictly subdivided into three distinct castes: orangutans, the ruling elite who govern ape society as politicians and religious leaders; chimpanzees, the middle class who serve ape society as doctors, scientists, and professionals; and gorillas, the lowest caste of ape society, represented as soldiers who maintain order and discipline, hunters, and menial laborers. Perhaps not so ironically, apes relegate devolved humans to the roles of animals: hunted, caged, studied, and subjected to experiments.

Decades after the original film, columnist Ed Gonzalez reviewed the 2011 film, *Rise of the Planet of the Apes*, and described it as a "uniquely Serling-esque allegory for racial relations in Civil Rights-era American in which the historical relationship between whites and blacks was reversed."[3] While the racial overtones of both the original film and the 2011 film were obvious to audiences, the genesis of that allegory less so. Born into a Reform Jewish family in Syracuse, New York, in 1924, Serling routinely experienced anti-Semitic prejudice as a young man. In a 1972 interview, he described being blackballed by the Theta Sigma fraternity as "the first time in my life that I became aware of religious difference."[4] Such experiences fueled a passion for racial equity that became a central element of his television and film work. *Planet of the Apes* provided Serling with a vehicle through which to explore prejudice even further, something he alluded to in 1961: "I'd like to do a definitive study of segregation—say from the Negro's point of view. A definitive study of what the Negro feels about it."[5]

While prejudice and racial equality were central to the plot of *Planet of the Apes*, they were just two strands within the grand tapestry of the frame story. Although not overly religious himself, religion played a significant role in Serling's life. His perspectives on religion, power, and the complex interrelationship between the two are deftly spun into the screenplay. Within ape society, power is maintained through a delicate balance of blind devotion to faith, repression of science, and exploitation of the militaristic lower class. This power structure creates tension among the three castes of ape culture that communicates distinct and powerful anti-religion and anti-authoritarian themes throughout the film. Religiously dogmatic and scornfully intolerant, the orangutans impose totalitarian rule through the gorillas while dispensing unforgiving discipline on whatever they do not understand.

Even as the film explores the religion-power dynamic within ape society, the plot continues to hint at the more profound message Serling intended. Taylor's orangutan antagonist, Dr. Zaius, the Minister of Science and Chief Defender of the Faith, is not only the most learned and respected religious leader in ape society, but he also conceals the very truth that Taylor seeks. Writing on the lasting influence of *Planet of the Apes* in a 2011 *Politico* article, Simon Abrams commented: "Dr. Zaius … is the most vocally hostile character in the film. He is more self-absorbed and dangerous than Taylor's peers have the potential to be because he abuses science in order to suppress the truth about men and apes: they evolved in opposite directions."[6] But the truth is much more than a question of how apes evolved; it is a matter of *why* they evolved.

When Taylor and Zaius first encounter one another in Dr. Zira's primate laboratory, the minister recognizes his greatest fear, one that represents an existential threat, not just to ape society, but to apes as a species. Looking disdainfully at Taylor in his cage, Zaius remarks about men: "The sooner they're exterminated, the better. It's a question of simian survival." Zaius knows the truth, a fact made abundantly clear later in the film when he scratches out the words "I CAN WRITE" that Taylor has scrawled in the dirt—a truth that must be suppressed at all costs.

As the film progresses, the conflict between protagonist and antagonist continues to evolve. After Taylor reveals to Zira and her colleague and love interest, Cornelius, that he possesses the ability to communicate via the written word—his vocal cords still healing from an earlier injury—the human explains to his chimpanzee hosts how he and his fellow astronauts crashed their spacecraft on the ape planet. "Flight is a scientific impossibility," scoffs Cornelius. In response, Taylor folds a paper airplane and flies it in a gentle arc across the room, where it lands softly at Cornelius's feet. After exchanging knowing glances, Zira proceeds to share that Cornelius discovered "traces of a culture older than recorded time" during an archeological expedition into the Forbidden Zone, a restricted region of the planet. His discoveries led to a theory that "ape evolved from a lower order of primate, possibly man." When

Cornelius presented his findings, Dr. Zaius and the Academy of Science immediately dismissed them as heresy.

What if Taylor is the "missing link between the unevolved primate and the ape?" Zira wonders. Chimpanzees, the intelligentsia of society, have long been subject to a quota system that denies them power and influence. Positing a theory that undermines the very foundations of ape religious beliefs risks everything they value and could instigate a class struggle that would threaten ape society itself. In the midst of their conversation, Zaius and Dr. Maximus, the orangutan Commissioner of Animal Affairs, arrive to take possession of Taylor, whom they intend to geld. After Maximus orders gorillas to remove the human, Zaius finds the paper airplane on the floor and disapprovingly questions its purpose. "A toy," Zira responds. "It floats on the air." Zaius looks down at the plane, then back at Zira. Smiling condescendingly, he crumples the paper airplane into a ball and tosses it aside.

In a relatively short succession of scenes, the film's central conflicts between religion and science, between the oppressors and the oppressed, and between ape and man are revealed. Then, in what is perhaps one of the most memorable scenes in science fiction cinema, Taylor escapes. Leading his captors on a chase through Ape City, he takes refuge in a museum of "natural" history, where he finds his fellow astronaut, Dodge, on display. After leaving the museum, Taylor hides momentarily in a temple, where a funeral is being held in the shadow of a large statue of an orangutan holding a book. The minister speaking at the funeral calls to the mourners: "Weep if you must, but make an end of sorrow. He lives again. Yes, he has found peace in Heaven."

The apes believe in God. The statue standing in the temple is His prophet, the Lawgiver, an historic figure of knowledge and wisdom whose influence transcended simian history. The apes revere the Lawgiver, and his presence—even in statue form—is significant. In ape society, the Lawgiver is cast in the mold of great human prophets such as Moses or Muhammed. The Lawgiver's writings, preserved in the "Sacred Scrolls" that govern ape society, form the foundation of their system of laws and customs. Twelve hundred years after the Lawgiver's time, his warnings of the dangers of humanity remain central to simian culture.

Eventually, of course, the apes recapture Taylor. As the other primates stone Taylor, Gorillas approach in an attempt to subdue him. Speaking through a net at the gorillas surrounding him, Taylor speaks his first words since being wounded early in the film: "Take your stinking paws off me, you damned dirty ape!" The gorillas step back involuntarily. The crowd freezes, staring in astonishment. For audiences, this was the most deeply satisfying moment in the film, the point at which apes encounter a speaking human for the first time.

While the revelation that Taylor possesses the ability to speak—and the way he chooses to express that ability—proved enduringly entertaining to audiences, it was largely irrelevant to the broader themes of the film. Zaius already knows—or at least suspects—that Taylor can speak. He is all too aware of the fact that Taylor is unlike other humans of the time. Zaius also recognizes that Taylor's knowledge of science far surpasses anything achieved by ape society. The revelation that ape and human societies share a common theology, however, is absolutely pivotal and foreshadows Serling's "classic twist."

Nevertheless, as Chief Defender of the Faith, Zaius is compelled to act in the wake of Taylor's capture. Under the guise of determining the proper disposition for Taylor, Zaius calls a tribunal. The President, Zaius, and Maximus preside; Zira and Cornelius represent Taylor; and Dr. Honorius, the Deputy Minister of Justice, represents the state. The inquiry is another bellwether moment in the film.

In a courtroom drama as powerful as any in cinematic history, the central conflicts of *Planet of the Apes* are laid bare. After invoking the first Article of Faith[7] from the Sacred Scrolls—which establishes the religious primacy of simians—Honorius reveals the true intent of the tribunal: to expose a conspiracy to undermine ape faith by advancing "an insidious theory called 'evolution.'" Honorius continues by questioning Taylor's knowledge of the second Article of Faith, which establishes that that all apes are created equal. To this, Taylor responds with a touch of Orwellian sarcasm: "Some apes, it seems, are more equal than others."[8] As the trial progresses, it becomes ever clearer that this is about suppression—suppression of science, suppression of primate castes, and suppression of man. Zaius's tribunal concludes with Zira and Cornelius accused of contempt, malicious mischief, and scientific heresy. At the center of all of this is Taylor. The man without a planet. The man without a people. And, above all, the man whom Zaius fears with all his being.

After the tribunal, Zira, Cornelius, and Taylor escape together into the Forbidden Zone.[9] Pursued by Zaius and a group of armed, mounted gorillas, they make their way to the cave where Cornelius conducted his last archeological expedition. After a brief confrontation, Zaius accompanies them into the cave, where the film's central conflicts reach a final, climactic crescendo.

Cornelius's exploration of the cave revealed a paradox: after a certain depth, the artifacts suggest that the more ancient culture is the more advanced. At the greatest depth, Cornelius discovered only human remains, along with other artifacts, including remnants of a porcelain human doll. As Taylor sifts through the artifacts, he points out that whoever this man was, he was "plagued by most of man's ills." Failing eyesight, false teeth, a hernia, and a prefabricated valve in his heart. "Yet, fragile as he was, he came before you—and was superior to you." Even as Zaius refutes the archeological evidence before him, the doll's head makes a telling sound: "Mamma! Mamma! Mamma!"

With the apes staring in utter astonishment at the doll that "spoke," Taylor brandishes it before Zaius: "Dr. Zaius! Would an ape make a human doll that talks?" Outside the cave again, the debate between Zaius and Taylor continues. "If man was superior," Zaius asks, "why didn't he survive?" Taylor shrugs, considering the possibilities: a plague, a natural catastrophe, a meteor storm. But he realizes something. Looking back at Zaius, Taylor remarks to Cornelius: "He knew all the time. Long before your discovery, he knew. Defender of the Faith. Guardian of the terrible secret. Isn't that right, doctor?"

Taylor, it would seem, had exposed Zaius's dark secret—that apes, in fact, evolved from man. It was a secret held by the Lawgiver and passed down through the centuries, as generations of Chief Defenders of the Faith hid the truth from ape society. Apes like Zaius had long existed to suppress the truth, or to at least prevent science from advancing to a point where it challenged the lie. But Zaius was not about to surrender so easily. He scoffs at Taylor, "There is no contradiction between faith and science. True science."

Yet there is more, much more. Zaius tells Cornelius to remove a notebook from his pocket and read a passage from the ninth verse, twenty-third scroll of the Sacred Scrolls—"The Beast Man."

> Beware the beast Man, for he is the Devil's pawn. Alone among God's primates, he kills for sport or lust or greed. Yea, he will murder his brother to possess his brother's land. Let him not breed in great numbers, for he will make a desert of his home and yours. Shun him; drive him back into his jungle lair, for he is the harbinger of death.

After reading the passage, Cornelius falls silent. Stubbornly, Zaius responds: "I found nothing in the cave to alter that conception of man. And I still live by its injunction." He continues, looking at Taylor: "All my life I've awaited your coming and dreaded it. Like death itself." As Taylor prepares to depart, he turns back to Zaius and says, "It still doesn't give me the 'why.' A planet where apes evolved from men. There's gotta be an answer." Zaius responds, "Don't look for it, Taylor. You may not like what you find."

If *Planet of the Apes* held a mirror to the racial strife of the 1960s, it smashed that mirror into a thousand pieces to expose the social and political turmoil of the decade. The need to confront intolerance in all forms was a consistent theme for Serling. Civil Rights-era the United States provided Serling with a twist that would cement the film's place in science fiction cinema. Even as humanity raced to the moon, life on Earth confronted the looming shadow of the Cold War. Nuclear weapons—and the horror they represented—were a constant. The threat of mutually assured destruction was omnipresent. As Taylor rides into the sunset at the conclusion of *Planet of the Apes*, Serling has one final surprise for audiences.

Dismounting from his horse to look closer at an object rising from the sand along the shore, Taylor exclaims, "Oh, my God. I'm back. I'm home. All the time ... we finally, really did it." Falling to his knees and burying his head in his hands, Taylor pounds his fists into the sand and screams, "YOU MANIACS! YOU BLEW IT UP! DAMN YOU! GOD DAMN YOU ALL TO HELL!" In this final scene, as the camera pans back to show the charred, half-buried remains of the Statue of Liberty, Serling's twist reveals Zaius's true secret.

Beware the beast man.

Notes

1   Gordon C. Webb, "30 Years Later: Rod Serling's Planet of the Apes," *Creative Screenwriting*, July–Aug 1998, https://web.archive.org/web/20171213062353/http://www.rodserling.com/pota. htm.

2   Joe Russo, Larry Landsman, and Edward Gross, *Planet of the Apes Revisited: The Behind the Scenes Story of the Classic Science Fiction Saga* (New York: Thomas Dunne Books, 2001), 4–6.

3   Ed Gonzalez, "Review: Rise of the Planet of the Apes," *Slant Magazine*, Aug 4, 2011, https:// www.slantmagazine.com/film/rise-of-the-planet-of-the-apes/.

4   R. Allen Leider, "Hot Rod Serling: The Terror on the Tube," *The Monster Times*, November 30, 1972, 11.

5   Nathan Abrams, "Thought You'd Sussed Out Planet of the Apes? Think again," *The Conversation*, July 18, 2014, https://theconversation.com/thought-youd-sussed-out-planet-of-the-apes-think-again-29352.

6   Simon Abrams, "Why 'Planet of the Apes' Culture Outlives the Humans Who Created It," *Politico*, July 8, 2001, https://www.politico.com/states/new-york/albany/story/2011/07/why-planet-of-the-apes-culture-outlives-the-humans-who-created-it-067223.

7   Like the Ten Commandments in both Judaism and Christianity, the Articles of Faith are foundational principles set down by the Lawgiver in ape society. The First Article of Faith reads: "the Almighty created the ape in his own image; that He gave him a soul and a mind; that He set him apart from the beasts of the jungle, and made him the lord of the planet."

8   This is a direct reference to George Orwell's *Animal Farm*, in which the pigs who control the government proclaim: "All animals are equal, but some animals are now more equal than others."

9   At this point of the screenplay, Serling reveals that the Lawgiver pronounced the Forbidden Zone as deadly in text of the Sacred Scrolls. This is significant in that it firmly establishes the timeline for the events that led to ape evolution.

CHAPTER 18

Flag Follows Trade

A Cautionary Tale From *The Expanse*

Theresa Hitchens

———————▶

> For services provided on Mars, or in transit to Mars via Starship, or other colonization spacecraft, the parties recognize Mars as a free planet and that no Earth-based government has authority or sovereignty over Martian activities. Accordingly, disputes will be settled through self-governing principles, established in good faith, at the time of Martian settlement.
>
> —SPACEX STARLINK TERMS OF AGREEMENT[1]

In the science fiction series *The Expanse*, human colonization of the solar system has been driven primarily by capitalist corporate interests. Those fictional mega-corporations—just as today on Earth, often led by visionary billionaires—operate as near-sovereign entities, despite technically being licensed primarily by Earth's militarized United Nations. Unfortunately, in their largely unfettered and often subsidized pursuit of profit, those corporations also serve as catalysts for terrorism, rebellions, and interplanetary war.

In *Leviathan,* the first book of the Hugo-nominated series by James S. A. Corey, readers learn that various Earth-licensed corporations first spurred the opening of the solar system to human occupation by establishing myriad mining stations on asteroids and in the orbits of the "outer" planets beyond Mars.[2] Many of these stations developed into full-fledged colonies, with economies centralized around mining-specific resources such as lithium and water or industrial-scale farming.

There are colonies on Luna, asteroids in *the Belt* between Mars and Jupiter, Jupiter's moon Ganymede, Saturn's moon Io, and other celestial bodies. Humans also colonized Mars, but by the UN-led government as a means to depopulate Earth's environmentally stressed regions. By the time of the first book, Mars has peacefully—after a technological breakthrough on the part of the colonial forces—negotiated independence and sports its own highly sophisticated Navy and Marine Corps.

The most important and densely populated space station in *The Expanse* universe is the asteroid Ceres. Tycho Engineering and Manufacturing Concern, a near-sovereign firm founded by engineering pioneer Malthus Tycho and run by his grandson, figured out how to "spin" the asteroid to provide enough gravity to allow humans to live and work there. Ceres is also the "home world" of the rebel/terrorist group, the Outer Planets Alliance (OPA). OPA began as a union and advocacy group for the inhabitants of the asteroid belt—known as "Belters"—who are oppressed by exorbitant taxes and living costs, which include water and air, imposed by the corporations that manage all facets of living in the "outer" solar system.

The solar system again nears the brink of war after a mysterious attack on the *Canterbury*, a space freighter hauling ice from Saturn to Ceres to supply water. The ship stops to investigate an SOS hailing from a seemingly distressed ship but is ambushed and destroyed in a nuclear weapons attack by a mysterious spaceship that subsequently disappears. Only five crew members survive—*The Expanse*'s main band of protagonists led by Earth's James Holden. Holden's ensuing global broadcast of his discovery that the disappearing ship appears to be of Martian military design lights a spark that tips the already restive and resentful Belt toward armed insurrection and retaliation against Mars—a conflict that surely would draw in Earth.

As events unfold, it becomes clear that the stealth ship is actually part of a secret fleet of sophisticated warships owned by the Earth-based firm Protogen. Protogen has discovered an alien artifact known as the "protomolecule," which appears to be a semi-sentient bio-nanotech substance. Protogen proceeds to undertake a host of unethical research activities, ranging from experiments on immuno-comprised children to release of the protomolecule on the minor planet Eros, wiping out the population.

In the second book in the series, *Caliban's War*, Holden and his allies discover that Jules Pierre Mao owns Protogen. Mao is one of the richest men in the solar system and co-owner of one of the largest Earth-based conglomerates, Mao-Kwikowski Mercantile. Mao-Kwikowski has interests in almost every type of corporate activity in the solar system, from providing water and other resources to mercenary forces. Mao has set up a vast, hidden research and development complex to find a way to commercialize the protomolecule for profit and power. He is also allied with an anti-Mars faction within the UN government, unbeknownst to the elected leadership, to create a super-soldier. Much of *Caliban's War* revolves around the UN–Mao plot's exposure and the race to avert an all-out war between Earth and Mars.

While Mao and his mega-firm are the villains of the first books, missteps and misdeeds of corporate entities underpin the story throughout the series. Tycho has oppressed the Belters since the establishment of Tycho Station, setting the stage for the civil unrest and the OPA's radicalization. In the fourth book, *Cibola Burn*, food shortages caused by Ganymede's destruction during *Caliban's War* plague the Belt, as Ganymede served as the region's breadbasket. Belter refugees have scattered to new planets to start new lives via wormholes called "Ring Gates" created by the protomolecule. Meanwhile, Earth continues to license corporate entities to launch research and mining colonies in deep space. *Cibola Burn* tells the story of conflict over a lithium-rich planet. The conflict is between Belters, who arrive first and name the planet Ilus, and UN Earthers who call the planet New Terra. An Earth mining and research colony ship arrives on Ilus under UN license, but Belters sabotage the ship during landing. Holden and crew are once again called upon to try to stave off potential war, this time between the Belt and Earth.

In today's world, as in *The Expanse*, commercial entities also dominate efforts to push the boundaries of human activity in space. Companies around the world are developing the technology required to refuel and repurpose spacecraft in orbit, clear growing fields of dangerous space debris, and even mine asteroids. For example, PayPal billionaire Elon Musk, who founded SpaceX, and Amazon CEO Jeff Bezos, founder of Blue Origin, have set their sights on sending humans to Mars and deep space colonies, respectively.[3] [4]

And over the past five or six years, the United States government has taken steps to support domestic space firms by enacting laws and implementing policies to help spur the expansion of United States economic interests into outer space. In November 2015, Congress passed, and President Barack Obama signed, the United States Commercial Space Launch Competitiveness Act that makes it legal under United States law for companies to keep and profit from the sale of celestial resources.[5] While the law raised some eyebrows abroad, since international law prohibits sovereign claims in outer space, the United States argued that space resource extraction is legally akin to fishing in international waters.[6]

Support for the United States commercial space industry became a central policy under the Trump administration. In a series of executive orders, known as Space Policy Directives, Trump aimed to ease licensing restrictions on traditional space activities and set "light" regulatory provisions for emerging capabilities.[7] The 2018 *National Space Strategy* encouraged NASA and the Defense Department to turn to the commercial marketplace for space technologies and services as a first resort— rather than developing bespoke capabilities in-house using traditional government contractors.[8] Former Secretary of Commerce Wilbur Ross often repeated optimistic industry predictions that the global space-related economy could be worth as much as $3 trillion by 2040. "We believe the future of space is overwhelmingly commercial in nature and will no longer be dominated by government agencies and their priorities," Ross told the World Economic Forum in Davos, Switzerland, on January 24, 2020.[9]

The Trump administration tasked NASA to develop a plan to establish a permanent United States presence on the moon by 2024, a plan heavily reliant on commercial firms. The Moon–Mars Artemis program envisions a permanently inhabited station in lunar orbit called *Gateway*. NASA Administrator Jim Bridenstine was enthusiastic about the prospects for space commerce—and the need for the United States to be the first in what many national security space officials see as a race with China to establish primacy in the future orbital economy.

"There very well could be trillions of dollars—tens of trillions of dollars—in large deposits of platinum-group metals on the Moon. And if that's the case, if somebody were to be able to capitalize on those discoveries, it could change the balance of power on Earth," Bridenstine told a recent webinar sponsored by the Mitchell Institute, a think tank that advocates for the U.S. Air Force.[10]

It is this perceived economic competition that in large part has helped drive a renewed emphasis on warfighting in space. Part of this interest in military space operations resulted in the August 2019 re-establishment of U.S. Space Command, a new incarnation of a previous organization that existed from 1985 to 2002, and the subsequent December 2019 creation of the Space Force as the sixth branch of the U.S. military, structured under the Air Force in a similar fashion to the Marine Corps under the Navy.[11]

On September 22, 2020, Space Force—tasked with organizing, training, and equipping personnel assigned to SPACECOM—signed a memorandum of understanding with NASA to expand joint efforts to build up the capabilities to operate in cislunar orbit. Chief of Space Operations General Jay Raymond told this author in an email:

> Today, economic and military space activities do not extend farther than our highest-orbiting satellites. However, commercial investments and new technologies have the potential to expand the reach of vital national space interests to cislunar and beyond in the near future. It is our responsibility to maintain U.S. advantages in space. If and when that extends beyond the GEO belt, we will go beyond as needed.[12]

There is a vocal contingent among U.S. military space thought leaders who argue that, in order to make cislunar space safe for economic exploitation for the benefit of humanity, the country first needs to establish the means to ensure military security in space.[13] This viewpoint essentially is a modern corollary to the 18th- and 19th-century axiom, "trade follows the flag," a notion that stems from the imperialist argument that colonies stimulate trade for the mother country.[14] But in fact, the United States government is carving a policy pathway—a pathway that by and large seems to be typical for today's space-faring countries—that is more akin to "the flag follows trade" model of *The Expanse* and the disastrous historical example of the British East India Company.

The East India Company, founded in 1600 and abolished in 1858 by the British government, can be seen as the archetype of unfettered corporate capitalism. With the Crown's tacit approval, the company was at the heart of India's conquest and colonization. The East India Company usurped the local government of Bengal in the 1750s and spread its reach to most of the subcontinent by the early 1800s. In 1803, the company's security force stood at some 260,000 men, more than twice the size of the British army.[15]

While lining its founders' pockets, the company initially poured funds into Britain's coffers by brutally exploiting Indian natural resources and its people as near-slaves in the garment trade. The company's practices led directly to the first Indian Rebellion in 1857 and catalyzed the country's long drive toward independence.[16] It also launched the trade in illegal opium from India to China, eventually leading to the Opium Wars.[17] Meanwhile, it shipped Chinese tea to Massachusetts, where its dumping in Boston harbor played a role in the run-up to the American war of independence, according to the London-based *Guardian*.[18]

The East India Company was put under regulatory control by a worried British government when it required vast cash loans. The firm needed these loans when its revenues fell due to famine in Bengal in 1773 that were mainly the company's fault. In the aftermath of the Indian Rebellion, London had had enough and virtually abolished the firm in 1878.

The East India Company's corporate power has yet to be equaled by any space company in any country—indeed, by any corporate entity, even the ubiquitous Google or Amazon. But the recent boom in global space commerce is already outstripping national and international agreements.[19] National regulatory structures lack substance with regard to new types of space activities, such as resource extraction, and are nearly non-existent when it comes to the prospect of commercially led exploration or colonization. And while the framework international accord governing space, the 1967 Outer Space Treaty, prohibits claims of national sovereignty over the Moon or other celestial bodies, it is silent on corporate entities' rights except to make states responsible for the actions of firms registered in their territories.[20]

The increased interest in exploitation of space comes at a time when geopolitical tensions between the United States, Russia, and China are at a 21st-century high. In recent years, United States leaders have insisted its adversaries have "weaponized" space.[21] For example, the unclassified summary of the Pentagon's Defense Space Strategy states: "Space is now a distinct warfighting domain," and articulates DoD's plans to "ensure space superiority."[22] Interestingly, the Defense Space Strategy notes the interplay and potential impact of the commercial and civil space arenas on national security:

> Rapid increases in commercial and international space activities worldwide add to the complexity of the space environment. Commercial space activities provide national and homeland security benefits with new technologies and services and create new economic opportunities in established and emerging markets. The same activities, however, also create challenges in protecting critical technology, ensuring operational security, and maintaining strategic advantages.[23]

In the short and mid-term, many space experts worry that there is a rising risk of conflict being sparked unintentionally in the absence of clear national and international law and norms of behavior for space commerce.

Jamie Morin, vice president of Defense Systems Operations at the Aerospace Corporation, told this author in an interview on December 21, 2020, that the newly "crowded and democratized" nature of space adds complexity to the geopolitical instability that has emerged in military space relations.[24] For example, he said, countries are beginning to rely on commercial space services without fully understanding their inherent vulnerabilities. "If we are all on edge watching for harmful interference or kinetic attacks on satellites, and we have a way more crowded environment, we're increasing the chance—in some cases geometrically—of accidental things being perceived as intentional."

As an example, the United States Transportation Command is exploring use of Elon Musk's new *Starship*, designed to carry both crew and cargo to Earth orbit, the moon, Mars and beyond, to rapidly ferry military logistics and potentially even troops to far-flung battlefields. *Starship* made its first suborbital flight December 9, 2020.[25] It crashed upon landing, but both the company and outside experts say the test results mean that *Starship,* which comprises a giant Super Heavy rocket carrying a shuttle-like spacecraft also called *Starship,* could take its first orbital test flight next year.[26] As of November 2020, SpaceX had launched 955 Starlink satellites, with a plan to eventually expand the constellation to some 42,000 small satellites to provide high-speed communications—eventually all the way from Mars, if users sign the terms of use that include acknowledging SpaceX's claim that Mars is a "free planet."[27] Musk has articulated a goal of landing humans on Mars in 2026.[28] Right now, there is nothing in the United States legal code or international law to stop him.

Meanwhile, after a boom and bust in the early 2000s, asteroid mining is again on the agenda for commercial investors in the United States and abroad.[29] In a bid to spur United States company interest in space mining, Bridenstine, on September 10, 2020, announced in a tweet that NASA is launching a program to buy moon rocks from commercial mining concerns.[30] Luxembourg in 2017 passed a space resources law similar to that of the United States; and the United Arab Emirates in February 2020 followed suit.[31] The European Space Agency in 2019 released a Space Resources Strategy to guide investment through 2030.[32] China is rapidly moving forward with its space exploration plans, which China hawks in the United States charge are aimed at establishing a dominating position in the future space resources market, as well as laying the foundation for a military presence.[33] While most non-vested experts believe that the advent of a true commercial market for space mining is decades away, the fact remains that there are no internationally agreed rules on how such commercial ventures should be regulated, if at all.

Further, despite growing concern from industry, scientists and experts about issues ranging from an increase in space debris to crowded near-Earth orbits to space salvage rights, no space-faring country has yet picked up the baton to launch multilateral negotiations on governing an emerging space gold rush. Some of these issues, including that of debris and orbital crowding, are already pressing. Thus, as the march of space commerce continues apace, the United States and other space nations will need to consider how they intend to harness the benefits of commercial space exploitation and corral the risks. The alternative to a well-regulated commercial space market is a dangerous "Wild West" scenario, driven by the heirs to the East India Company and prototypes for the likes of Tycho and Mao-Kwikowski in *The Expanse*.

Notes

1 Anthony Cuthbertson, "Elon Musk's SpaceX Will 'Make Its Own Laws on Mars," *Independent*, Oct 28, 2020, https://www.independent.co.uk/life-style/gadgets-and-tech/elon-musk-spacex-mars-laws-starlink-b1396023.html.

2 The pen name of authors Daniel Abraham and Ty Franck.

3 Jackie Wattles, "Colonizing Mars could be dangerous and ridiculously expensive. Elon Musk wants to do it anyway," *CNN*, Sept 8, 2020, https://www.cnn.com/2020/09/08/tech/spacex-mars-profit-scn/index.html.

4 Corey Powell, "Jeff Bezos foresees a trillion people living in millions of space colonies. Here's what he's doing to get the ball rolling," *NBC News*, May 15, 2009, https://www.nbcnews.com/mach/science/jeff-bezos-foresees-trillion-people-living-millions-space-colonies-here-ncna1006036.

5 For text, see: https://www.congress.gov/bill/114th-congress/house-bill/2262/text, accessed Dec 1, 2020.

6 "Treaty on Principles Governing the Activities of States in the Exploration and Use of Outer Space, including the Moon and Other Celestial Bodies," *United Nations Office of Outer Space Affairs*, https://www.unoosa.org/oosa/en/ourwork/spacelaw/treaties/introouterspacetreaty.html, accessed Dec 1, 2020.

7 "National Space Council Directives," *Department of Commerce*, accessed Dec 20, 2020.

8 "President Donald J. Trump is Unveiling an America First National Space Strategy," *The White House*, Mar 23, 2018, https://www.whitehouse.gov/briefings-statements/president-donald-j-trump-unveiling-america-first-national-space-strategy/, accessed Dec 22, 2020.

9 "Remarks by Secretary of Commerce Wilbur Ross at A New Space Race: Getting to the Trillion-Dollar Space Economy World Economic Forum, Davos, Switzerland," *Department of Commerce*, https://www.commerce.gov/news/speeches/2020/01/remarks-secretary-commerce-wilbur-ross-new-space-race-getting-trillion-dollar, accessed Dec 1, 2020.

10 Theresa Hitchens, "Space Force-NASA Accord Highlights Cooperation Beyond Earth Orbit," *Breaking Defense*, Sept 22, 2020, https://breakingdefense.com/2020/09/space-force-nasa-accord-highlights-cooperation-beyond-earth-orbit/.

11 See: https://www.whitehouse.gov/briefings-statements/remarks-president-trump-event-establishing-u-s-space-command/; and https://www.defense.gov/Explore/News/Article/Article/2046035/trump-signs-law-establishing-us-space-force/.

12 GEO refers to Geosynchronous Earth Orbit, some 36,000 kilometers in altitude where satellites travel at the same speed as the Earth rotates and thus appear stationary over the surface. GEO is the farthest orbit of most current space commerce and military activity.

13 Cislunar space is the volume of space between the outer edge of the Earth's orbit and that of the Moon.

14 A phrase first referenced in the 1894 version of Ebenezer Cobham Brewer's "Dictionary of Phrase and Fable," see: *Bartleby.com*, https://www.bartleby.com/81/, accessed Dec 20, 2020.

15 William Dalrymple, "The East India Company: The original corporate raiders," *The Guardian*, Mar 4, 2015, https://www.theguardian.com/world/2015/mar/04/east-india-company-original-corporate-raiders.

16 Ben Johnson, "The East India Company and its role in ruling India," *History Magazine, Historic UK* website, https://www.historic-uk.com/HistoryUK/HistoryofEngland/The-East-India-Company/, accessed Dec 22, 2020

17 Kenneth Pletcher, "Opium Wars: Chinese history," Britannica, https://www.britannica.com/Opium-Wars, accessed Dec 28, 2020.

18 Dalrymple, op cit.

19 Theresa Hitchens, "Forwarding Multilateral Space Governance: Next Steps for the International Community," Aug 6, 2015, *Center for International and Security Studies at Maryland*, University of Maryland, https://drum.lib.umd.edu/handle/1903/19733.

20 "Treaty on Principles Governing the Activities of States in the Exploration and Use of Outer Space, including the Moon and Other Celestial Bodies," *UN Office of Outer Space Affairs*, https://www.unoosa.org/oosa/en/ourwork/spacelaw/treaties/introouterspacetreaty.html, accessed Dec 22, 2020.

21 "Remarks by President Trump at Event Establishing the U.S. Space Command," Aug. 29, 2019, *The White House*, https://www.whitehouse.gov/briefings-statements/remarks-president-trump-event-establishing-u-s-space-command/, accessed Dec 22, 2020.

22 "Defense Space Strategy Summary," June 2020, *Department of Defense*, https://media.defense.gov/2020/Jun/17/2002317391/-1/-1/1/2020_DEFENSE_SPACE_STRATEGY_SUMMARY.PDF, accessed Dec 22, 2020.

23 Ibid.

24 Aerospace Corporation is a federally funded research and development center for the U.S. Air Force. Its Center for Space Policy and Strategy was established in 2000.

25 See: https://www.spacex.com/vehicles/starship/, accessed Dec 22, 2020.

26 Chris Bergen, "From hops to hopes—Starship SN8 advances test program into the next phase," *NASA Spaceflight.com*, Dec 9, 2020, https://www.nasaspaceflight.com/2020/12/from-hops-hopes-starship-sn8-test-program-next-phase/.

27 Michelle Yan Huang, Bob Hunt, and Dave Mosher, "What Elon Musk's 42,000 Starlink satellites could do for—and to—planet Earth," *Business Insider*, Oct 9, 2020, https://www.businessinsider.com/how-elon-musk-42000-starlink-satellites-earth-effects-stars-2020-10.

28 Sissi Cao, "Elon Musk Reveal's SpaceX's Timeline for Landing Humans on Mars," *Observer*, Dec 2, 2020, https://observer.com/2020/12/elon-musk-says-spacex-will-land-humans-on-mars-in-a-few-years-if-theyre-lucky/.

29 Matthew S. Williams, "Asteroid Mining to Shape the Future of Our Wealth," *Interesting Engineering*, Nov 6, 2020, https://interestingengineering.com/asteroid-mining-to-shape-the-future-of-our-wealth.

30 See: https://twitter.com/JimBridenstine/status/1304049845309669376.

31 Jeff Foust, "Luxembourg adopts space resources law," *Space News*, July 17, 2017, https://spacenews.com/luxembourg-adopts-space-resources-law/; "UAE Space Law Details Announced To Facilitate Space Sector Development," *SpaceWatch.global*, https://spacewatch.global/2020/02/uae-space-law-details-announced-to-facilitate-space-sector-development/, accessed Dec 28, 2020.

32 "ESA Space Resources Strategy," *European Space Agency*, https://sci.esa.int/documents/34161/35992/1567260390250-ESA_Space_Resources_Strategy.pdf, accessed Dec 22, 2020.

33 "SECTION 3: CHINA'S AMBITIONS IN SPACE: CONTESTING THE FINAL FRONTIER," 2019 *REPORT TO CONGRESS of the U.S.-CHINA ECONOMIC AND SECURITY REVIEW COMMISSION*, November 2019, p. 359, https://www.uscc.gov/sites/default/files/2019-11/2019%20Annual%20Report%20to%20Congress.pdf, accessed Dec 22, 2020.

CHAPTER 19

The Vice Admiral and the Flyboy

The Last Jedi and Perceptions of Women in Leadership

Kelsey Cipolla

————————▶

Willowy, clad in a flowing, high-necked dress and sporting a tousled lilac bob hairdo, Vice Admiral Amilyn Holdo does not look the part of a high-ranking military official—at least to pilot Poe Dameron.

In Rian Johnson's *The Last Jedi*, Holdo takes command of the Resistance after a First Order attack leaves General Leia Organa comatose. "*That's* Admiral Holdo? Battle of Chyron Belt Admiral Holdo?" Dameron asks skeptically immediately after seeing his new commanding officer. "Not what I expected."

Dameron has been recently demoted from commander to captain after failing to follow orders from General Organa and making a risky decision that cost many of his compatriots their lives. Confidence unshaken, he wastes no time giving Holdo information that she already has and demands to know her plan for leading the Resistance out of the tricky situation in which it now finds itself. When Holdo dismisses him as a "flyboy" and tells him to stick to his post, Dameron begins to spiral out of control.

Convinced that she is not handling the situation correctly, he first goes behind her back to execute a secret mission that he assumes she will not approve, then stages a coup with other discontent rebels. Dameron later learns that Holdo had a plan all along; she simply chose not to share it with him—a plan that he has jeopardized through his own machinations. His botched attempt at heroism creates a situation that leads Holdo to sacrifice her own life to buy the rest of the Resistance time to flee to safety.

Why does Dameron feel so comfortable questioning a proven leader in a moment of crisis? And from where does his dislike of Holdo stem? While it is not openly stated, it seems likely due to how Holdo presents herself as a woman in power.

In a Galaxy Not so Far Away

We do not have a complete picture of gender dynamics in the *Star Wars* universe, but there are plenty of data closer to home that offer insight into the challenges women face acquiring and successfully holding leadership positions.

Although women in the United States make up nearly half of the workforce—47 percent in 2019, according to the United States Bureau of Labor Statistics—they hold a significantly lower number of leadership positions than men across military, corporate, and political spheres.[1]

As of March 2021, women accounted for almost 19 percent of active-duty U.S. military officers, 16.9 percent of enlisted soldiers, and 26.9 percent of military academy cadets and midshipmen.[2] Women account for less than 10 percent of the top tier of the military—from brigadier to four-star general—and those numbers plummet as rank rises.

Only 26.5 percent of Congressional seats and 30.3 percent of statewide elected executive offices were held by women in 2021.[3] Women held 40 percent of all management positions, but the employment picture is more discouraging the higher up the employment ladder you look, with women making up 30 percent of vice presidents, 26 percent of senior vice presidents, and 21 percent of the C-suite in 2019.[4] Although more Fortune 500 companies were led by women CEOs in 2020 than at any time in history, they are still outnumbered by men 13 to 1.[5]

It is not simply that women are not proportionally represented in top roles. When women are given leadership positions, they are often in less-than-ideal circumstances. Like Holdo, women frequently find themselves taking charge in moments of crisis or when the risk of failure is high. It is a phenomenon known as the "glass cliff," and it usually reflects the need for a sudden change—whether that change is from a male leader to a female or from one leadership style to another.[6] On the surface, it may seem like an exciting opportunity for women to take the reins when they may otherwise have not been given a chance, but it also sets them up to fail, as they are in a position facing greater risk and potential for criticism.

So why are more women not getting the opportunity to take charge of organizations and lead them successfully? A Pew Research Center survey on women and leadership reported most Americans find men and women indistinguishable in leadership traits, including intelligence and capacity for innovation and viewed women as better at being compassionate and organized leaders.[7] In both politics and business, survey respondents viewed women as being more honest and ethical.

There are a variety of complex factors, ranging from the ways in which women have participated in the workforce over time to the greater demands on women to perform domestic labor compared to their male counterparts. But interestingly, participants in the Pew survey pointed to a different issue as the most significant in holding women back from leadership positions: a double-standard for women that forces them to do more than their male counterparts to prove themselves.

Taking the Lead

Holdo is a prime example of the conflict between the expectations for men and women in a leadership role: Behave like men would and brace for criticism because those traits are less desirable in women.

While her manner of speaking could be described as authoritative, her initial address to the resistance soldiers is warm and hopeful. "In every corner of the galaxy, the downtrodden and oppressed know our symbol, and they put their hope in it," she tells the assembled crowd. "We are the spark that will light the fire that will restore the Republic. That spark, this Resistance, must survive. That is our mission." Holdo is assertive, confident, and daring, exhibiting magnetic leadership attributes more often ascribed to men—like, for instance, Poe Dameron himself.[8] Meanwhile, women are more often associated with communal traits, including interpersonal sensitivity, kindness, and sympathy.

So, what is Holdo to do? One proposed model of successful women in leadership is F-SET, named for its four principal dimensions: femininity, self-efficacy, emotional intelligence, and teamwork. In a case study, women in military leadership roles who exemplified this leadership style reported finding it easy to lead men.[9] They saw embracing their femininity as an asset because it showed self-confidence, which in turn made them seem like more effective leaders. The other half of the equation, emotional, intelligence, and teamwork, manifested in sympathy, fairness, negotiating skills, and collaboration.

However, it seems Holdo's feminine appearance is the first thing that raises Dameron's hackles, as evidenced by his skepticism immediately after her introduction. Although Dameron has long reported to General Organa, she and the other women we see within the Resistance blend in with their appearance choices, including neutral colors and sharper lines. Throughout *Star Wars* Episodes VII, VIII, and IX, the officers we see are often in a uniform consisting of pants and a jacket or belted vests over shirts. Organa, whose position seems to earn her a little extra style leeway, dons both the uniform look and a dark jacket over a gray dress for much of the films. Holdo's aesthetic is a dramatic departure, not just in its vibrance but in its embrace of femininity. In addition to an eye-catching gown and hair hue, she sports sizable yet delicate cuffs and a headpiece that calls to mind a halo.

Our own military has a fraught relationship with how gender should be treated, specifically concerning aesthetics and behaviors. The U.S. military's culture is interwoven with ideas of masculinity that encourage the downplaying of femininity.[10] The case study examining women in military leadership roles included an interview with twelve Army women combat veterans, most of whom identified as having masculine attributes: bravery, power, and strength. They described themselves as tomboys who acted like their male friends during childhood and young adulthood, experiences they thought made them well-suited to relating with men and being good soldiers once they entered the military. They also "expressed disdain for characteristics stereotypically associated with femininity," such as crying, whining, acting "catty," or being overly flirtatious.

The efforts of women serving in traditionally masculine roles in the Israeli military is even more stark. One study reported that women officers reported lowering their tone of voice, wearing a big, baggy uniform rather than one that is more tight-fitting, and talking more profanely and abrasively.[11] Like the U.S. Army combat veterans, they also distanced themselves from stereotypically feminine traits, like worrying about physical appearance.

Although there is an element of subversion in eschewing typical gender roles, it is also a survival tactic. The women interviewed reported expecting their masculine characteristics would ease their way in this masculine institution. In a culture dominated by men, being feminine marks you as "other" and puts you at greater risk, not just professionally but personally, as most of the United States and Israeli women interviewed revealed instances of sexual harassment that they downplayed.

But Holdo makes no such attempt to mimic masculinity aesthetically. She is unabashedly a woman, in an elegant, body-skimming dress that falls to the floor and the chicest bob in the galaxy, styling decisions that were intended as a commentary about women in power on the filmmakers' part. In an interview with Vanity Fair, Laura Dern, the actress who portrays Holdo in *The Last Jedi* put it simply: "[Rian is] saying something that's been a true challenge in feminism. Are we going to lead and be who we are as women in our femininity? Or are we going to dress up in a boy's clothes to do the boy's job? I think we're waking up to what we want feminism to look like."[12]

Flyboys and Forced Redemption

Dameron's hostile response to Holdo is especially confusing because he has a strong relationship with General Organa, perhaps the most powerful woman we see represented throughout *Star Wars* canon.

General Organa is portrayed as a transformational leader, adopting a leadership style that has similarities with F-SET. Transformational leaders set high standards for their organizations, establish themselves as role models, and gain their followers' trust and confidence.[13] Organa has held a variety of roles in first the rebel alliance and later the Resistance, putting her own life on the line time and time again and making difficult strategic decisions that pit her against her own son.

Transformational leaders also often mentor and empower members of their organization to help develop their full potential, as Organa does with both Dameron and Holdo. While we do not see much of the relationship between General Organa and Vice Admiral Holdo, it clear that Holdo is the next-in-line should something happen to the Resistance leader and has her full endorsement.

Given that Dameron holds General Organa in such high esteem, his complete lack of respect for Holdo is jarring. "Cut it, lady," he spits at her as he charges onto the ship's bridge—from which he has been banned—to demand that she fill everyone in on a plan and offer the dwindling Resistance hope. Holdo harkens back to her time under the general's leadership, seemingly trying to create a bond based on their shared mentorship from Organa. "When I served under Leia," Holdo begins, "she would say 'Hope is like the sun. If you only believe in it when you can see it ...'" "'... You'll never make it through the night,'" Dameron jumps in to finish. He is appeased for a literal second before he catches wind of part of her plan—out of context—and promptly kicks a chair, shouting at Holdo, calling her a coward and a traitor, and creating an atmosphere of panic as he publicly lists his grievances with her approach before being peacefully escorted away.

Unfortunately, Admiral Holdo does not have enough time leading the Resistance to gain trust—she is a little busy trying to outrun the First Order with a dwindling fuel supply. That effort leaves her with limited bandwidth to try and get buy-in from the hundreds of people she is charged with delivering to safety.

Outraged by what little he has seen of her plan, Dameron relieves her of her command at blaster-point. Dameron barely makes it to the captain's chair before the supremely competent Holdo evades her would-be guards and returns with a recently awakened Organa in tow. She sees fit to stun Dameron, who moments before learned that his risky scheme has indeed failed and compromised Holdo's much more realistic plan.

But is Dameron punished for his rash, insubordinate action? Nope. Instead, Holdo gently pats the unconscious pilot's cheek, smirking to Organa, "That one's a troublemaker. I like him." Surprise! Holdo was actually warm and kind all along, *The Last Jedi* seems to say, right as the audience is filled in on her strategy: She is going to stay behind and pilot the cruiser in order to buy the transports time to flee undetected to safety at a nearby rebel base, where they could send a distress signal to their allies.

Some critics and viewers inevitably asked why Holdo did not simply tell Dameron her idea from the beginning. But the more pressing question is why Dameron could not respect direct orders and stand down, accepting that a more seasoned military leader might have a strategy she chose not to share. "She was more interested in protecting the light than seeming like a hero," Organa offers as an explanation to a slightly guilty-looking Dameron.

Dameron's botched plan makes things more complicated, as the First Order begins targeting the transports they were supposed to escape without notice, and Holdo jumps into lightspeed, charting a course through the First Order's ship that wreaks enough havoc to buy the Resistance more time—and leads Holdo to sacrifice her own life. Her death, and the role Dameron's treason and insubordination played in bringing it about, receive little more attention in the film or franchise.

It is a depressing end for Holdo's character in a multitude of ways, but particularly in how *The Last Jedi* seems to feel the need to prove she was actually operating under those stereotypically feminine communal values, at least in part, the whole time. Adding insult to injury, the film has her redeem the reputation of the man who has antagonized her throughout her brief tenure, ensuring that the audience does not think he is a "bad guy" just because he undermined her every step of the way. This is a sad reflection of the very real ways in which women are expected to take care of men not just personally, but professionally.

Of course, it is hard to ignore that the film is made by Disney, a company that thrives on making entertainment that is above all accessible and enjoyable to the whole family. Having a main character come off as a sexist jerk was never going to be in the cards. But if Disney is selling to mainstream audiences, what do those decisions say about us?

Unfortunately, you do not have to look hard for real-world parallels to see how powerful women taking center stage are received. Fan reaction to *The Last Jedi* offers insight into the roles some still feel women should play that echoes Dameron's reaction to Holdo in the film. Following its release, some *Star Wars* fans bemoaned what they perceived as a shift in the franchise for various reasons—and to be fair, *The Last Jedi* does include some story decisions with which even its biggest fans can find fault. But an alarming subset took aim at the foregrounding of female characters, including Holdo, burgeoning Jedi Rey, and Rose Tico, a Resistance mechanic who joins former stormtrooper Finn on the side mission that ultimately backfires.

An alt-right group calling itself "Down with Disney's Treatment of Franchises and its Fanboys" claimed to have sabotaged the film's audience score on the review site *Rotten Tomatoes*, specifically because of the increased role played by women and characters of color. The group also bristled at what it viewed as Dameron becoming a "victim of the anti-mansplaining movement."[14] Kelly Marie Tran, the Vietnamese American actress who portrayed Tico, was subjected to such vitriolic sexist and racist comments via social media that she deleted all her Instagram posts to avoid further harassment.[15]

The Spark That Lights the Fire

As disheartening as Holdo's arc and fan reception were, there are sparks of hope in the *Star Wars* universe and beyond for women in leadership. In *The Rise of Skywalker*, Rey ultimately defeats the First Order and Emperor, assumes the Skywalker surname, and shows off a new lightsaber, implying that she will lead a new, emerging generation of Jedi.

In our galaxy—or at least, here in the United States—representation is trending in a promising direction. The Department of Defense opened hundreds of combat roles in the U.S. military in the last decade, putting women in a better position to reach the most senior ranks.[16] Record numbers of women are serving in Congress and state legislatures, and new organizations are emerging to help provide valuable educational resources to women interested in serving in political office. Similar signs of encouragement can be seen in the business world. Companies such as McKinsey, Deloitte, and Apple have developed programs designed to help women build on leadership strengths and network with peers. In 2019, the proportion of women in senior management roles globally grew to 29 percent, the highest number ever recorded, and held steady in 2020.[17]

Undeniably, there is still a long, long way to go. But with more representation comes opportunities to change what leaders are expected to act, look, and dress like and opens the door to a new wave of heroes who can save the day—even in an evening gown.

Notes

1   "Employment Status of the Civilian Noninstitutional Population by Age, Sex, and Race," U.S. Bureau of Labor Statistics (U.S. Bureau of Labor Statistics, Jan 22, 2020), https://www.bls.gov/cps/cpsaat03.htm.

2   Defense Manpower Data Center data as of March 2021.

3   "Current Numbers," Center for American Women and Politics (Rutgers Eagleton Institute of Politics, Dec 3, 2020), https://cawp.rutgers.edu/current-numbers.

4   "Women Business Leaders: Global Statistics," Catalyst, Aug 11, 2020, https://www.catalyst.org/research/women-in-management/.

5   "Historical List of Women CEOs of the Fortune Lists: 1972–2020," Catalyst Information Center, May 2020, https://www.catalyst.org/research/historical-list-of-women-ceos-of-the-fortune-lists-1972-2020/.

6   Asha N. Gipson et al., "Women and Leadership: Selection, Development, Leadership Style, and Performance," *The Journal of Applied Behavioral Science* 53 (Jan 17, 2017), 32–65, https://doi.org/10.1177/0021886316687247.

7   "Women and Leadership," Pew Research Center's Social & Demographic Trends Project, Aug 7, 2020, https://www.pewsocialtrends.org/2015/01/14/women-and-leadership/.

8   Alice H. Eagly and Mary C. Johannesen-Schmidt, "The Leadership Styles of Women and Men," *Journal of Social Issues* 57, no. 4 (Dec 1, 2001), 781–797, https://doi.org/10.1111/0022-4537.00241.

9   Karen M. Walker, "A Model for Femininity and Military Leadership" *Journal of Psychological Issues in Organizational Culture 2*, no. 4 (Jan 26, 2012), 22–37, https://doi.org/10.1002/jpoc.20086.

10 Kacy Crowley and Michelle Sandhoff, "Just a Girl in the Army: U.S. Iraq War Veterans Negotiating Femininity in a Culture of Masculinity," *Armed Forces & Society* 43, no. 2 (Jan 1, 2016), 221–237, https://doi.org/10.1177%2F0095327X16682045.

11 Orna Sasson-Levy, "Feminism and Military Gender Practices: Israeli Women Soldiers in 'Masculine' Roles" *Sociological Inquiry*, 73, no. 3 (Aug 2003), 440–465, https://doi.org/10.1111/1475-682X.00064.

12 Joanna Robinson, "Star Wars: The Last Jedi Offers the Harsh Condemnation of Mansplaining We Need in 2017," *Vanity Fair* (Dec 18, 2017), https://www.vanityfair.com/hollywood/2017/12/star-wars-last-jedi-laura-dern-admiral-holdo-listen-to-women.

13 Alice H. Eagly and Mary C. Johannesen-Schmidt, "The Leadership Styles of Women and Men," *Journal of Social Issues* 57, no. 4 (Dec 1, 2001), 781–797, https://doi.org/10.1111/0022-4537.00241.

14 Bradley, Bill, and Matthew Jacobs, "Surprise, Surprise: The 'Alt-Right' Claims Credit For 'Last Jedi' Backlash," *HuffPost*, Dec 21, 2017, https://www.huffpost.com/entry/rotten-tomatoes-last-jedi-ratings-bots_n_5a38cb78e4b0860bf4aab5b1.

15 "Star Wars actress Kelly Marie Tran deletes Instagram posts after abuse," *BBC News*, Jun 6, 2018.

16 Nora Bensahel et al., "Battlefields and Boardrooms: Women's Leadership in the Military and the Private Sector," accessed Dec 29, 2020, https://www.cnas.org/publications/reports/battlefields-and-boardrooms-womens-leadership-in-the-military-and-the-private-sector.

17 "Women in Business 2020," Grant Thornton International Ltd., Mar 2, 2020, https://www.grantthornton.global/en/insights/women-in-business-2020/women-in-business-2020-report/.

CHAPTER 20

I Exist Only to Serve

The Bene Gesserit and Informal Power

Julie M. Still and Kelly A. Lelito

———————➤

Understanding the interplay of societal forces is better accomplished at a distance. Only the truly astute can do so in real-time. History provides an opportunity to look at how these forces emerge and interact at a remove, but even here prejudices and inherent biases come into play. Fictional worlds, however, provide a fresh canvas for study. Frank Herbert's 1965 science fiction novel *Dune* is an excellent primer to consider the human dimensions of geopolitics. A pivotal mechanism of Herbert's saga involves an interplanetary society that is ever-present but little-noticed, primarily because it is an all-female group in a patriarchal society. The Bene Gesserit, through a covert, centuries-long agenda they kept private, dramatically alter the geopolitical landscape. Examining their strategies and tactics offers an important lesson on the use of informal power and how the marginalized and overlooked can exert significant influence.

This novel is an excellent choice to study. The plot is complex but not distracted by detailed descriptions of technology or alien races. *Dune* is well-known in popular culture. It has never been out of print and has spawned sequels, prequels, and some dismal visual adaptations, such as the poorly-reviewed 1984 feature film.[1] A much anticipated new film version is scheduled for release in the fall of 2021, which will introduce it to a new audience. The Bene Gesserit role within this larger story provides students and seekers of all levels an opportunity to examine social forces in a unique and appealing environment.

There are many seats of power within the societies and organizations depicted in the novel, and females occupy very few. Only the Bene Gesserit have any organized power, and their true intentions and influence are concealed and closely guarded. In the power structure of the Galactic Padishah Empire and within its diverse societies, women do not rule and have little political role other than to cement advantageous dynastic alliances through marriage. The sisterhood takes a different view.

As a very simple plot description for context, in the *Dune* franchise, space travel is dependent upon a substance known as "spice" found in only one place: the arid wasteland planet Arrakis, also known as Dune. The Emperor overseas spice production and controls the noble houses while the Spacing Guild enjoys a monopoly on space travel. The Emperor and the Guild operate in concert to consolidate and hold power. As the story begins, the Emperor has just decided to oust the governing Harkonnen family from Arrakis and replace them with their archrivals, the Atreides family. The Emperor is conspiring with the Harkonnens to eradicate the Atreides line and then return control of Arrakis to the Harkonnens. None of these nobles are aware that the indigenous population, the Fremen, has been working to turn Arrakis into a more hospitable environment, with an ultimate goal to dramatically alter both the climate and terrain. Duke Leto leads the Atreides family and brings his longtime concubine Lady Jessica and his heir, their teenage son Paul, to Arrakis. Towards the end of the first novel, Paul becomes superhumanly powerful and, with his Fremen followers' help, deposes the Emperor.

The Bene Gesserit provide a variety of services to different factions within the Empire. They groom women for those political marriages, but they also develop Truthsayers for important nobles. Notably, the order runs a prestigious and elaborate education system administered by Reverend Mothers. To outsiders, the sisterhood merely trains young women in diplomacy and the feminine arts to serve as appropriate helpmates for powerful men. The Bene Gesserit education program essentially poses as an elevated form of a finishing school, the sort of place where the daughters of European aristocrats learn needlework and French, but the Bene Gesserit include statecraft and strategy. Lady Jessica recollects her lessons on espionage and counterespionage.

Many of the wives and concubines of noblemen attend Bene Gesserit schools. Graduates appear to provide refined and cultured, but subservient, partners to men. They are desirable because they are perceived as blank slates, groomed to support the goals and objectives of the men they marry or serve. While their fine arts and housewifery skills are admired, Bene Gesserit graduates' political skills are seldom fully recognized. Although the Emperor himself sent all four of his daughters to a Bene Gesserit school, it is not clear that he appreciated what they learned there. On one occasion, Lady Jessica slips and reveals her training and strengths. When one of her husband's councilors claims he distrusts her because of her Bene Gesserit training, she replies: "If I wished to destroy the Duke … or you or any other person within my reach, you could not stop me."[2] Interestingly, no one questions the Bene Gesserit's motivations and goals. In reality, the education provided is broad and comprehensive.

The curriculum includes both physical and mental disciplines—the nature of which is not fully disclosed outside of the order. The practice of both physical and psychological control is central to this training. Physical control includes the ability to govern their own bodily systems and processes. This includes regulation of breathing and heart rate in response to stress and extends to more supernatural abilities; the adept can self-regulate their fertility and even choose the gender of their offspring. Psychological training includes self-control over emotions, extreme observation of people and the environment, and the ability to manipulate others. Just as with the physical training, their talents cross into the mystical. Genetic memories can be passed on and preserved for future generations.

The ability to retain genetic memories is essential, as the sisterhood's grander plans are multigenerational. While they lay the foundations for the future, the Bene Gesserit disguise their ambitions with an ethos of service. "I am Bene Gesserit: I exist only to serve," the Bene Gesserit-trained Lady Jessica reminds Reverend Mother Gaius Helen Mohiam early in the novel.[3] Taken at face value, this is a very philanthropic motto. These words might act as a banner for many organizations, from religious orders to various service professions. It could also serve as a mantra for darker organizations, such as suicide bombers and kamikaze pilots. Members of the ruling class usually take this motto at face value, but the Bene Gesserit never clarify explicitly whom or what is served. Because the governing and economic decision makers seldom pay attention to women, they lack awareness of what these women are doing, let alone scrutinize them. The Bene Gesserit move through society unnoticed, unspoken to, and unheard.

It is not a unique approach. Military philosopher Sun Tzu observed: "Subtle and insubstantial, the expert leaves no trace; divinely mysterious, he is inaudible. Thus, he is master of his enemy's fate."[4] The Bene Gesserit embrace a similar approach, employing stealth and intrigue in all they do. Unable to influence events and further their position openly through more traditional political methods, they work in the margins, biding time as they await the birth of the one male ally they believe will raise them to equal footing. They do not wait passively but apply all their resources to ensure his arrival. They believe the future of humankind rests on the success of this strategy. The sisterhood's primary purpose is to produce a messiah-like figure, the Kwisatz Haderach. His abilities will exceed those of the Bene Gesserit, enhanced in a uniquely masculine way. As they recognize the threat such empowerment poses for their competitors, their next priority is to draw a veil over their true intentions. Thus, their centuries-old breeding program is unknown to any outside the innermost circle of the Bene Gesserit order.

Closer inspection reveals another, carefully masked agenda at play. In the *Dune* universe, women do not rule in their own right, nor are there many places in the public where they can operate as individuals. It is a man's world, on every planet, except when it is not. This is where the Bene Gesserit excel. Unable to participate directly in interstellar commerce, they find ways to exert influence without confronting patriarchy head-on. They operate within two stereotypic female roles—the wife and the witch, the sexy and the sexless.

To further their breeding program, the Bene Gesserit schools teach seduction techniques to some of the students. The organization targets men for their breeding program and imprints or prepares them for a future psychological trigger. Lady Fenring so imprints Feyd-Rautha Harkonnen when she seduces him to have a child with him. This leaves him open to influence by anyone trained in Bene Gesserit methods. Other roles within the Bene Gesserit require very different techniques.

Reverend Mothers and Truthsayers are intentionally de-sexualized. Their clothing, demeanor, and appearance are altered. When Paul Atreides first meets the Reverend Mother Mohiam in the novel, he describes her hair as resembling "matted spiderwebs."[5] The Bene Gesserit do this to elicit an aura of mysticism and enhanced wisdom, authority, and gravitas. Truthsayers are strategic advisors, while Reverend Mothers have leadership roles within the organization. Beauty in such a role might seem incongruous, perhaps even threatening. They believe it is better to limit a woman's power to one form or the other—the seductress or the sorceress. The average person in *Dune* is aware that Reverend Mothers supervise Bene Gesserit schools, but no one outside of the sisterhood is aware of their manipulation of bloodlines to pursue the Kwisatz Haderach. In some cultures, Reverend Mothers provide community and spiritual support, similar to parish clergy. The ritual undertaken to become a Reverend Mother is dangerous and potentially fatal, which adds to their stature and mystique. Women who become Reverend Mothers at a young age might draw upon their femininity while remaining untouchable, but with age, they could rely instead on "a wellspring of cunning and resourcefulness."[6]

A few Reverend Mothers took additional training and certification to become Truthsayers. As the name suggests, these women were exceptionally adroit at detecting deception and falsehoods. Truthsayers are seen but seldom heard unless directly petitioned. The Emperor's Truthsayer seldom speaks to anyone other than the emperor, and primarily speaks to him in whispers. The role of the emperor's Truthsayer would seem to be a vital one, yet this critical advisor remains elusive. They do not seek the center stage.

With their true intentions cloaked, the Bene Gesserit use strategic placement of the faithful to achieve their ends. As wives, lovers, and counselors, the Bene Gesserit women are present in the rooms where important things happen, but men overlook them. The women themselves, in fact, engineer this lack of notice to their strategic advantage. They have a presence in the bedroom as lovers, the schoolroom as teachers, and even occasionally in the stateroom as counselors. They operate in the background and maintain their mystique. As masters of self-control, they temper their actions and demeanor to increase their effectiveness in any environment. Rather than rail against those who would dismiss them, they leverage being undervalued and underestimated towards their own ends. They even create spaces for their influence to thrive for their descendants far into the future, not only through the seeding of their genes, but through the seeding of legend and lore.

In addition to the breeding program, the Bene Gesserit also employ the "Missionaria Protectiva" through cultural seeding. For centuries, Bene Gesserit actively sought out opportunities to spread their influence in new worlds, presumably under the guise of their more established roles. Once landed, they would plant stories or myths that could be triggered at a later date. Several of these prepared myths played into the rise of Paul Atreides. For example, the Fremen religion foretold a leader born to a Bene Gesserit, which would provide some protection to any such woman who found herself on Arrakis. The foresight to implement a strategy to be executed over many generations is ambitious but has significant risk. Like the childhood game of telephone operator, stories change over time and controlling myth is challenging. However, if it worked as planned, these proto-myths provide a powerful toolset that could be manipulated by the Bene Gesserit who followed.

While the Bene Gesserit seldom spoke in public settings, their words in private could be compelling indeed. One of the more widely known Bene Gesserit abilities is "The Voice"—a way of speaking that would influence a targeted listener. The technique involves pitching one's voice in a way that compels and can even control the target. For the Voice to be effective, the speaker employing it must be heard. When Paul and Lady Jessica are captured and subdued, a deaf guard is assigned by the adversarial Harkonnens. Jessica acknowledges this as a defense against her use of the Voice.

In the novel, the "V" in "Voice" is capitalized when the Bene Gesserit trained vocal control is referenced. Interestingly, the Voice is used exclusively on men. There is no explicit statement that it would be ineffective if applied to women, but there are no examples of this application in the novel. Contrary to Bene Gesserit rules, Jessica teaches her son Paul rudimentary use of the Voice. Whether this prohibition applies to all outside the organization or only to men is unspecified. Fear elicited at being controlled by a woman is emphasized—particularly that this might be done only with words as weapons. Although the Bene Gesserit train in martial arts, they are feared more for their powers of persuasion than for any physical threat they might pose.

Ultimately, the Bene Gesserit's focus on control of themselves and others reveals their greatest vulnerability. By emphasizing the rational, they forget that minds are often countermanded by hearts. For the Bene Gesserit, Lady Jessica's most egregious transgression is her disobedience to them by having a son instead of the daughter they intended to mate with Feyd-Rautha Harkonnen. Why did she go back on the training she followed in all other ways? Because she loved Duke Leto, and he wanted a son. She followed her heart.

Likewise, the Bene Gesserit failed to identify the threat presented by Duke Leto's personal physician. Dr. Yueh had Imperial Conditioning, assumed to be unbreakable, which should have made him beyond reproach, trustworthy in all ways. Yet he betrays the duke. Why was Yueh able to overcome this conditioning? Because he loved his wife, the Bene Gesserit-trained Wanna, who was held prisoner by the Harkonnens and suffered miserably in their hands.

These examples demonstrate that the Bene Gesserit did not consider that most human of foibles—love. Discipline can be learned, skills developed, habits reinforced. But the heart wants what it wants, and that wanting can sometimes overcome the most rigorous training. There are additional examples of shortsightedness on the part of the order, and the common thread is a lack of appreciation for the effect of emotion on human behavior. Cues are missed, and unanticipated problems arise. Belatedly, the sisterhood finds significant political shifts on the desert planet of Arrakis itself.

To further understand their errors, Lady Jessica requests a report on the Bene Gesserit's role in the "Arrakis Affair" to see where they might have missed intelligence regarding the rise of Paul Atreides. The report notes that the Bene Gesserit missed several clues that something unique was happening or would happen on Arrakis. They rebuffed an offer of information from the Spacing Guild that a nexus was approaching. They even missed the Fremen myths that probably originated with one of their own Missionaria Protectiva plants centuries before. Their confidence in this pseudo-religious shroud leaves them complacent. They are so focused on a specific plan and so certain they know how it will unfold that they lose perspective on what is actually occurring. Even an organization as disciplined as the Bene Gesserit can be blind to that which they do not seek.

Despite these failings, the Bene Gesserit are well equipped for the *Dune* universe. They operate very much within the boundaries of timeless human interests, under-standing and exploiting human weaknesses in matters of sex, religion, and greed. A deep understanding of individual and social psychology underpins every plan within a plan. The Bene Gesserit schools' training program concentrates all efforts towards controlling emotions—one's own and those of others. In the Bene Gesserit, Herbert creates an organization of wise women that resembles a religious order but acts in direct opposition to universal religious tenets. Although the order seeks the coming of a messiah-like figure in the Kwisatz Haderach, they do not passively await his arrival. On the contrary, the sisterhood implements a purposeful, centuries-long plan to create him. Rather than follow an established code of values and morals, the Bene Gesserit promulgate their own—often through manipulation and deceit. They are an example of how things are not always what they seem, and how those denied access to power through standard pathways might go to great lengths and bend many rules to create their own. History is rife with examples of this segregation and how it impacted society. When people cannot use their voice openly, they will use their Voice in more subtle ways. While this is sometimes effective, it is never as successful as fully integrating societal groups.

Due to a lack of vision, the Empire overlooks the sisterhood. The masculine power structure in this universe cannot accommodate notions of feminine power or leadership on the same plane. This lack of investigation, or even curiosity, has far-reaching consequences. The Bene Gesserit claim to exist only to serve, without specifying whom is served. In truth, they serve themselves. For their part, the Bene Gesserit fail to interpret the signs of impending discord on Arrakis, they are incapable of adapting their plans and schemes to shifting circumstances. They miss—or dismiss—the rise of Paul Atreides. Singularly driven to create their Kwisatz Haderach, they do not recognize him when he arrives a generation early. In *Dune,* many fail to interpret information readily available to them because their biases cloud their perceptions of reality. Such hubris frequently precedes a fall.

Notes

1   *Dune,* directed by David Lynch (Universal City, California: Universal Pictures, 1984).
2   Frank Herbert. *Dune* (New York: Ace Books, 1965), 37.
3   Ibid., 250.
4   Mark McNeilly. *Sun Tzu and the Art of Modern Warfare* (New York: Oxford University Press, 2015), 269.
5   Ibid., 3.
6   Ibid., 34.

PART IV

THE WAR OF THE WORLDS

PART IV

THE END OF THE WORLD

CHAPTER 21

One Voice in the Night

Personalist Disruptions of the International System

Clara Engle

———————▶

In the television series *Babylon 5*, viewers are introduced to a not-too-distant future when Earth is one of many worlds with sentient life. The series explores the complex relationships between the most powerful nations in the interstellar political system: the Earth Alliance, the Narn Regime, the Centauri Republic, the Vorlons, and the Minbari. It focuses in particular on the titular space station Babylon 5. The station is an outpost, as we learn in the opening narration, built to promote international peace through trade and dialogue in a neutral setting. The heart of Babylon 5's mission is diplomatic, and as the universe built in the series crumbles around the main characters, viewers begin to understand how the different ambassadors on the station interact and see their relationships grow—and how those relationships are both at the core of the conflict and lead to the eventual resolution of the Shadow War.

When *Babylon 5* opens, the Narn and Centauri are at peace. They had fought for many years over the Centauri enslavement of the Narn people and exploitation of their planets. Eventually the Narn built up enough strength to resist the Centauri successfully and defeated them. Now, both races are members of the Babylon 5 Advisory Council—a collection of ambassadors from the most powerful races in known space. Through their ambassadors to the Council, the Narn and Centauri, along with the Earth Alliance, Minbari, and Vorlons, agree, at least implicitly, to a set of intergalactic norms around the use of naval force. How then, in one year, do these norms erode to the point where the Narn and Centauri are actively at war with each other? Moreover, was there any diplomatic or military action that other members of the Council, also active participants in the system of norms, could have taken to preserve it over time? The decline of a centralized state paired with the rise of powerful individual agency and the use of a previously unknown superweapon to lead to the erosion of norms on an interstellar scale, and that despite the attempts of other individuals or naval forces, these combined factors were too strong for the existing norm paradigm to contain.

There is extensive debate in international relations literature about the role of a single individual. While IR theorists typically presume that all actors are rational and acting in the best interest of their particular affiliation (state, government, corporation, etc.), there is still space to understand the impact a single individual can have on policy changes in relation to other international (or in this case interstellar) actors. While the literature tends to indicate that governments are the basic building block of the international system, not individuals, and that governments are rational, in other words actively working in their own best interests, there is within this body of literature a case to be made for the ability of a rational actor to choose war or conflict as the path of best interest. IR as a field has in the last few years begun to go further in the quest to examine the role of an individual actor in interstate systems. While a government or the state was once held to be the lowest building block upon which the system is based, with the rise of authoritarian or illiberal regimes,[1] there continues to be research on the role that individuals can play in interstate politics. These individuals can both buoy politics and norms and destroy them, as they tend to serve themselves first before the state as a whole.

The Narns and the Centauri introduce an interesting question of what happens when the assumed building blocks of the system upon which norms are based begins to erode, exposing the substrate of an individual's or small collection of individuals' interests. How can other governments or regimes respond to this change and build out a plausible response using national forces like navies? To understand this, it is important to first look at the erosion of the Centauri Republic over a period of approximately one year. At the beginning of the series, the Centauri Republic is governed by an Emperor and a Prime Minister. The Emperor is the cultural and moral center of the Empire to whom the Centauri populace and government defer. Within the first year, the Centauri government transitions from being strongly emperor-bound to at best an illiberal government—and at worst a failed state[2]—with competing factions hoping to take power. To understand the individual's potential to affect such a transition, we can look to the Centauri ambassador to Babylon 5, Londo Mollari.

In the first episode of the series titled "Midnight on the Firing Line," Londo receives news from Centauri Prime of an attack on a Centauri agricultural colony on Ragesh 3. He is particularly disturbed because he had previously used his influence to get his nephew placed there—theoretically out of harm's way. However, the Narn attacked the agriculture colony with the ostensible justification that the colonists were having a difficult time suppressing protests and they reached out to the Narn for help. Londo is distraught that this happened, both because of the attack on his people and because his nephew was unable to return home due to Londo's actions.[3] Here we can see Londo thinking as an individual first, and when he goes to the

Council against his government's orders to request sanctions against the Narn, he is blocked by the Narn Ambassador G'Kar. Londo is irate at both his own government's inaction and at the international system's failure to uphold norms around peace and the use of military force. He also desires vengeance against the Narn. Londo contemplates killing G'Kar himself, but Babylon 5's security chief prevents him at the last minute.

The thirst for vengeance is a theme that repeats throughout the series, and, crucially, it diverts the individual from thinking about the collective good or buying into interstellar norms—from acting in what is usually seen as a rational manner. Instead, it places the desires of the individual at the helm, which leads to an erosion of norms over time. Later in the series, Londo receives an offer from an agent known as "Morden" who offers him the use of a powerful naval force any time he asks for it.[4] This power is such that Londo can effectively take over any planet or beat any conventional force currently in operation. This shadowy naval force is, for all intents and purposes, a superweapon at the time of its introduction. As the Centauri Republic edges closer to becoming a failed state with the looming death of its emperor, Londo joins an irredentist group of Centauri interested in returning the Republic to its perceived former glory in the galaxy.

The Mollari faction draws its power from their perceived ability to direct the actions of an overwhelming military force—the Shadows. Notably, Londo's demonstrations of his ability to control a "superweapon" helps the faction in their aim to inspire the Centauri citizenry and take over control of the government. The Centauri military and the superweapon are used here not in a traditional warfighting role, but rather as emblems of national pride for the Centauri regime. Their Narn counterparts treat their military in much the same way. In terms of the role that a navy can play in signaling force or power, these early examples of the Centauri military—or rather, its new weapons—appearing in small numbers but creating vast destruction, brings up the question of how a navy can signal a state's intentions or resolve problems based on its presence.

Perhaps the most significant episode of the series in this regard is "The Coming of Shadows," which examines not only the use of military force and technology in the Centauri regime, but also the way in which peer regimes utilize force for diplomatic endeavors.[5] In this episode, the Centauri emperor is planning a visit to Babylon 5 despite his ill health. G'Kar, upon hearing the Emperor will be coming, speaks with his Narn government about killing the Emperor, thereby removing what they perceive to be the locus of Centauri power. Meanwhile, Londo and his co-conspirators have a different plan for the Emperor's arrival. They intend to first use military force to take over a Narn colony close to the Centauri home world and then to deliver a speech that paints the Emperor as out of date for the times, a relic of the past. John Sheridan, the Commanding Officer of Babylon 5, comes up with a plan to threaten the Centauri with the presence of Earth navy observers to make sure the Centauri are treating the Narn properly. The result of this plan is that the Centauri, unwilling to let outsiders into their squabble with the Narn, release the Narn prisoners they had been keeping. The episode ends, tellingly, with G'Kar declaring publicly that the Narn government has declared war on the Centauri, and quoting Yeats, "things fall apart, the center cannot hold," heavily foreshadowing the war that is about to test the norms of the center and the alliances built around them.

Perhaps most interesting aspect of this episode is the role a naval threat played in changing diplomatic outcomes. This threat—delivered without the actual support of the Earth government—was enough to change the outcome of an initial Narn–Centauri dispute. However, it was not enough to prevent war from breaking out entirely. In part this worked because the actions were all taken at an individual level, instead of at the government-to-government level. Each of the governments represented in the Babylon 5 Advisory Council, with the exception of the Vorlons, who remain deeply mysterious, are mired in internal struggles about who holds true power or the direction they want to take moving forward. Thus, much of the diplomacy and signaling is done on the individual level aboard Babylon 5, rather than between governments communicating from their home worlds. In the international relations paradigm, it is assumed that each of these ambassadors are rational actors who are making the most advantageous choices—including, in one case, moving rapidly towards war. The individual choice available to each member of the Council is particularly apparent in this episode when G'Kar contemplates killing the Centauri Emperor, but is encouraged by Babylon 5's Captain Sheridan to open a dialogue with him instead. Sheridan works with G'Kar to enforce norms of diplomatic behavior and norms around peace and dialogue rather than allowing him to respond to the Emperor's presence irrationally.

These norms reinforce behavior that is in line with broadly agreed-upon constraints, and in theory these constraints should hold firm against a single individual hoping to change the situation. Norms typically arise due to both implicit and explicit agreements about how systems should work. Today, there are norms in the international community around both the use of force and the type of force used. This is seen in the "nuclear taboo"[6] that comes from nuclear-capable powers not using nuclear weapons in warfare, despite the potential for nuclear weapons to quickly end a conflict. As more authoritarian states such as North Korea begin to develop nuclear technologies, it becomes more and more pressing to understand how strong the norms are in holding governments to not using nuclear weapons. If North Korea, with a single powerful individual at the top of the government, were to choose to use nuclear force in a conflict, how would other governments respond? Would they break the nuclear taboo completely to end the conflict, or would they find other means of resolving the conflict without explicitly breaking apart the agreements on the use of nuclear weapons?

If even a single individual goes against established norms for their own personal gain, as with Londo's revenge, then norms may begin to disintegrate. *Babylon 5* provides an interesting way to examine the question of norm erosion within an international system and helps demonstrate that navies can play a role in at least slowing the deterioration of norms. The Centauri navy is unable to commit massive forces to the attack on the Narn colony in part due to the high political cost of mobilizing their own forces; further, the Centauri are unwilling to have other navies lurking around their new conquest in part because they don't want to fully escalate "regional" issues to an interstellar level. Without the presence of the Earth Alliance observers, the Centauri hope the war can remain a private struggle between themselves and the Narn. However, Sheridan's threat of military force to uphold the norms reminds the Centauri of their commitment to the international system and gives them pause before initiating their next conflict—although in the case of *Babylon 5*, this was too little, too late.

Norms and individuals matter greatly to contemporary governments and militaries. As hinted at in the case of North Korea, it is especially enlightening to examine the role of the individual in either illiberal or failed states. The individual in an illiberal state can be the locus of tremendous amounts of power, occasionally leading to a cult of personality around a particular leader or group of leaders. Starting in the 2010s in countries such as Turkey and Hungary, where the government is becoming increasingly authoritarian and moving further away from a liberal democracy, the questions of personality and a rational actor making choices become key to predicting future actions.

In Hungary, a direct comparison could be made between Prime Minister Viktor Orbán and Londo Mollari. While Londo controls the use of a superweapon capable of taking military action against external competitors, he also works internally with a group bent on re-aligning the Centauri Republic with a more pro-Centauri, nationalist vision of the state. This small group of individuals works to undermine the existing government and laws to better serve their interests. Orbán, similarly, initially worked with his party to first gain control of Hungary's government, and now he is working to change many government structures that exist to keep the system in place as a functioning democracy, such as free media and fair elections. The norms of a multi-lateral agreement—the EU in the case of Hungary—have little impact on a state that is centered around individual actors. This is due to the fact that once the basic unit shifts from a government to an individual in international affairs, the balance of power shifts as well. Since individuals are most typically concerned with maintaining their own grip on power first and foremost, they are less likely to uphold norms set by a union of governments focused more intensely on maintaining the function of the government than shaping the actions of a certain individual.

This conversation around norms is also important for the role of navies. In the Taiwan Straits area, the U.S. Navy plays an important role in deterring action an authoritarian China. In the Taiwan Straits area, China which is arguably part of the international system and agrees to abide by laws and norms including the laws of the sea, has demonstrated an increased willingness to move Chinese vessels into contested waters under the guise of protecting national interests. Londo and his cronies are similarly bent on protecting national interests in the Narn-Centauri conflict, and to do this they utilize military force to meet their goals. Once the Centauri take over the Narn colony, the only thing that kept them from enslaving all the Narn residing there was the threat of an external naval presence. In the Taiwan Straits area and the South China Sea today, the U.S. Navy plays a similar role in deterring continued Chinese encroachment into shared spaces. Navies play a critical role in preventing further norm erosion, although often to an extent shaped by political realities.

Although set in a distant and fictional future, *Babylon 5* provides a unique lens through which we can study international relations today. The role of an individual actor in the international system is becoming increasingly studied, and by being able to examine not just the actions that Londo takes, but also those of G'Kar and Sheridan, we can better understand the impact a single individual can have on the norms of a whole system. Moreover, the role of military force continues to be a question of major impact and will for the foreseeable future of the human race. In *Babylon 5*, military force is represented as a policy tool, not just a bludgeon. Exploring novel interpretations of how force is balanced in relation to norms helps us understand where navies can contribute to international order.

Notes

1   An illiberal regime is one that has some of the trappings of democracy (e.g., a free media or regular elections) but these trappings are not truly free. For example, in Russia, while there are still elections, opposition candidates rarely receive coverage in the state media and have a difficult time mobilizing voters in any significant way. An authoritarian regime is one without most democratic institutions with a single leader or group of leaders monopolizing power in the country by controlling, among other things, the use of violence via the military or police forces.

2   A failed state is one where the government no longer has a legitimate control over violence. A good contemporary example of a failed state would be the Central African Republic, where there is little in the way of centralized or state-type control.

3   *Babylon 5*, season 1, episode 1, "Midnight on the Firing Line," directed by Richard Compton, aired Jan 26, 1994, syndicated.

4   *Babylon 5*, season 1, episode 13, "Signs and Portents," directed by Janet Greek, aired May 18, 1994, syndicated.

5   *Babylon 5*, season 2, episode 9, "The Coming of Shadows," directed by Janet Greek, aired Feb 1, 1995, syndicated.

6   Nina Tannenwald, *The Nuclear Taboo: The United States and the Non-Use of Nuclear Weapons Since 1945* (Cambridge: Cambridge University Press, 2007).

CHAPTER 22

There's No Screaming in Space

When Employees Are Forced to Behave Like Soldiers

Jon Niccum

———————▶

They got music in their solar system / They've rocked around the Milky Way
They dance around the Borealis / They're space truckin' every day

—"SPACE TRUCKIN'" BY DEEP PURPLE

"Truckers in space."

This quote describing the basis of *Alien* is alternately attributed to director Ridley Scott, writers Dan O'Bannon, and Ronald Shusett, or a handful of the producers responsible for the 1979 epic, a landmark influence on future science fiction/horror films and pop culture in general.

The core conceit separating this Oscar-winning masterpiece from its predecessors remains with the crew itself. Unlike *The War of the Worlds*, *The Thing from Another World*, or the similarly plotted *It: The Terror from Beyond Space*, *Alien* does not showcase an elite military unit full of juiced-up xenophobes forced to confront an invading menace. (Even James Cameron's 1986 sequel *Aliens* is literally Colonial Marines fighting the same creatures of the title.) Instead, the heroes are a blue-collar hodgepodge of haggard individuals who simply want to collect a paycheck while experiencing the least amount of hassle.

But … they are not exactly truckers, either. Truckers implies a solitary pursuit. The seven crew members of the commercial towing vehicle *Nostromo* are a team. A workforce. Actually, they are more like a collection found in the typical branch of any corporate office. There is a supervisor who is really just a middle manager. A few desk jockeys. A couple maintenance guys. And a tech nerd. The xenomorphic alien might as well be attacking the Scranton branch of Dunder Mifflin as a spaceship 39 light years from earth.

So, what happens when *this* office is infiltrated by an indestructible space beast? Despite a dazzling display of courage, resourcefulness, strategy, and teamwork (with one notable exception), only a single worker survives. Ultimately, *Alien* reveals that things rarely end well when employees are forced to behave like soldiers.

The film begins as the space tug's computer awakens its crew from hypersleep. This crew includes—in order of command—Captain Dallas (played by Tom Skerritt), Executive Officer Kane (John Hurt), Warrant Officer Ripley (Sigourney Weaver), Navigator Lambert (Veronica Cartwright), Science Officer Ash (Ian Holm), Chief Engineer Parker (Yaphet Kotto), and Engineering Technician Brett (Harry Dean Stanton). There's also a ginger cat named Jones. The ship's computer—nicknamed (or perhaps legitimately named) Mother—explains they have been rerouted to an unexplored moon called LV-426 to investigate a potential distress signal, per company policy.

Upon landing, Dallas, Kane, and Lambert venture on foot to locate the signal, which they find is emanating from a crashed, horseshoe-shaped vessel of enormous size that may have been there for decades or longer. Ripley, who stayed behind, deciphers enough of the extraterrestrial transmission to determine it is actually a warning.

Meanwhile, Kane discovers a chamber filled with "leathery objects, like eggs or something." When he touches one, a small critter bursts forth and attaches itself to his face. Dallas and Lambert haul the unconscious officer and his new companion back to the Nostromo, but per quarantine regulations, Ripley will not permit entry. Ash disobeys her order to let them in.

Once within the medical lab, they are unable to remove the organism—which looks like the most-disquieting parts of a crab and spider. In fact, when they try to cut it off, the creature bleeds acid that nearly eats through the hull. Parker notes, "It's got a wonderful defense mechanism: You don't dare kill it." The small visitor eventually detaches itself and dies. Kane wakes up with dreams of drowning but no apparent damage. Having done their due diligence, Dallas orders the ship to leave. The staff enjoys one final meal before returning to hypersleep—or "back to the ole freezerinos," as Brett quips.

But in the most iconic moment of any horror film apart from the shower stabbing in *Psycho*, the titular alien erupts through Kane's chest, scurrying out into the cavernous ship before the stunned group can effectively react. The first creature was in truth incubating Kane as a host for its offspring.

Strategically, up until the infamous "chest-burster" point in the story, the crew members have done most everything wrong when dealing with their situation. They split up ... in a horror movie. They explore unknown enemy territory ... while possibly unarmed. They abandon a strict protocol ... at a crucial juncture. They do not keep a 24-hour watch on the patient ... or his assailant. Perhaps the worst decision concerns how they deal with Kane once the "infected" officer gets back on the ship. "How come they don't freeze him?" Parker sagely asks.

Indeed, the circumstances would have ended differently if they had simply placed Kane and his face-buddy in hypersleep—especially considering the group was mere hours away from everyone undergoing that same procedure. (It always seemed odd they would eat a big supper before this cryogenic process. So, they are going to be in mid-digestion for the next 10 months?) Armed with cattle prods and flamethrowers (but still no guns, blasters, or lightsabers), the crew searches the 243.8-meter-long craft for the pint-sized invader. Unfortunately, the alien has already grown to NBA center-size, and it presumedly slaughters Brett after hauling him into the rafters.

From here, the structure mirrors Agatha Christie's *Ten Little Indians*—or most isolation-based thrillers for that matter—with the virtually unkillable menace picking off earthlings until facing off against a lone survivor. Part of what makes *Alien* so effective during a first viewing—particularly upon its initial release—is it does not become clear until the third act who is the lead character. That is because the science fiction setting infers this is more of an action movie, thus insinuating a male hero or male-female tandem will prevail. But at its narrative core, this is categorically a horror movie. Different rules.

The original screenplay was written with only last names given so that any of the characters could be cast as male or female. (Ripley's first name, Ellen, wasn't even divulged until the Director's Cut of the sequel.) Somewhere late in the pre-production process, it was determined an unknown actress should portray Ripley as a means of completely befuddling audience expectations of heroism. The role went to 28-year-old stage actress Sigourney Weaver. Her cinematic career included just two features: a supporting role in the drama *Madman* that nobody saw and a one-scene sight gag in the Oscar-winning Woody Allen comedy *Annie Hall*.

But what this casting move also does is create a type of sexist—rather than sexual—tension when it comes to leadership decisions. Even in 2122 when this film is set, men just do not want to listen to a young woman. Ash makes the catastrophic choice to violate quarantine. Dallas overrides Ripley's offer to flush the creature out of the air ducts, undertaking the "manly" mission himself. Parker charges the behemoth after it corners Lambert, reacting with the reckless strategy of a drunk frat guy who witnesses his girlfriend being hit on by the Hell's Angels. Even Mother ignores Ripley when she seeks to stop the ship's self-destruct sequence upon encountering the fiend roaming an area between where she is situated and the escape shuttle is docked.

Much has been made about the fact these co-workers operate in a seemingly sexless society. They're first seen emerging from hypersleep pods in their tighty-whities underwear, without showing the slightest interest in the titillating view. A deleted scene available on the DVD finds Ripley, who is growing suspicious of Ash, asking Lambert whether she has slept with the science officer—except the question is posed as casually as wondering if she accepted his Facebook request.

Up until the closing moments where Ripley strips down to a sleeveless T-shirt and panties is there any suggestion of portraying her in a feminine light. At least for the first half of the film, it is implied she is devoid of any emotion, instead coming across almost Vulcan-like in her dealings with the crew. This is part of the reason why a scene in which she interrogates Ash regarding whether he has any proposal on how to deal with the alien is so effective. She asks, "You're what? You're still collating? I find that hard to believe." But when she says it, her voice cracks in a half-laugh, half-cry. Her robotic façade is starting to crumble.

And part of the motivation why is that deep down, none of the men are listening to her. But what if they had? Would it have changed anything? What is key to remember is this is not a military operation with an unflappable chain of command. Again, think of the crew as office personnel.

Along with Norman Jewison's underrated science fiction sports drama *Rollerball*, *Alien* was one of the first mainstream films that did not envision the future as run by totalitarian governments, alternately presenting one dominated by mega-corporations. These companies—like the fictional Weyland-Yutani Corporation that owns the *Nostromo*—boast a fleet populated by commercial, military and tech divisions. Do bordered countries even still exist in this future?

The British-Japanese multinational conglomerate lives by the slogan "Building Better Worlds." But while its reach extends throughout the galaxy, its ships are still operated by contract workers. This is one reason the crew members seem slow to realize their predicament. They are not seeing the situation from either an expeditionary or combat-oriented vantage point. To them, it is overtime. Like being asked to work on a Sunday. Their professional curiosity is offset by an even more prevalent force in the workplace: complaints. Literally, the first conflict the audience witnesses in the movie involves a bitch session about money.

Parker gripes he is on "a commercial ship, not a rescue ship." Then he asks if bonus shares will be available for making an unscheduled pit stop. Ash explains, "There is a clause in the contract which specifically states any systematized transmission indicating a possible intelligent origin must be investigated." When Parker and Brett seek to upend this advice, they are further warned by Ash that if they do not go along with corporate protocol, they will face a "penalty of total forfeiture of shares."

With the event having shifted from an adventure to an obligation, these seven staffers are now prone to be caught off-guard when this state of affairs becomes life-threatening. As the mortality stakes are raised, they find themselves with three options: offense, defense, or negotiation. Offense proves rather hard to come by. Despite a throwaway line by Dallas to "break out the weapons" when his trio first leaves the ship, such weapons are never mentioned again. There are meagre glimpses of handgun-type armaments which can be spotted holstered in stray shots. In the 2003 Director's Cut, Kane holds one of these while exploring the derelict craft.

Although the film is frustratingly vague about the device, it is apparently a laser pistol. Further supplemental material in the *Alien* universe reveals it to be the Rexim RXF-M5 EVA Pistol, which is a miniaturized version of a commercial laser welder issued to Weyland-Yutani crews. It brings up the question of why introduce firearms in the movie if they're not going to be used? The dramatic axiom known as "Chekhov's gun" teaches playwrights and screenwriters if "there is a rifle hanging on the wall, in the second or third (act) it absolutely must go off."

Some have surmised that if the alien's acid blood threatens to compromise the hull's integrity, firing a laser weapon onboard might do the same thing—which is why the option gets ignored in transit. This does not explain, however, why Ripley could not use it on her nemesis after she has set the main ship on a countdown to self-destruction. All of this offers a roundabout way of understanding why the crew elects to utilize a Parker-rigged flamethrower as a method to ideally drive the creature toward an airlock so it can be jettisoned into the void.

This plan is also jettisoned once Dallas goes missing during a cat-and-mouse game (he's the mouse) when hunting the xenomorph through air shafts, and the only evidence left of him is a forlorn flamethrower. It is within a subsequent scene—arguably featuring the most dynamic character interaction in the movie—where strategy and panic begin to wrestle for domination.

Now there is a tilt toward defense.

The increasingly crumbling Lambert suggests they abandon ship, get in the shuttle and "hope that somebody will pick us up." When Ripley reminds her the shuttle will not take four, she counters that they can draw straws. Instead, Ripley—who now outranks the others—decrees they will move in pairs, cutting off every bulkhead and vent until the beast is cornered. Then they can blow it out into space. "But we have to stick together," she concludes.

Alas, that is not quite part of the plan.

Up to this point, there's a distinct demarcation between the good guys and bad guys. But *Alien* ingeniously introduces a Hitchcockian saboteur. Ash most certainly did not sleep with Lambert … because he is not even a man. He's revealed to be a robot (technically an android) placed onboard the *Nostromo* by the company, since management already deciphered the distress call and decided there could be potential spoils for its weapons division. That is why Ash is the one who breaks quarantine. Why he does not push to freeze the coma-induced Kane. Why he prevents Parker from stabbing the chest-burster before it scampers away.

But Ash is not behaving this way because he is "evil." The "synthetic employee"—which is the official term Weyland-Yutani uses to classify him, although a similar character played by Lance Henriksen in the sequel favors the label "artificial person"—is simply adhering to a different set of instructions. The only reason Ash fails is he suffers damage following a physical altercation with a suspicious Ripley, as evidenced by the milky white fluid that drips from his marred brow like blood. After Parker decapitates the now-combative droid with a swung fire extinguisher, the humans revive his mechanical head long enough to interrogate him.

Interestingly, Ash becomes central to the one tactic the others never attempt: negotiation. In the movie, he describes the creature as "the perfect organism. Its structural perfection is matched only by its hostility." Ash admits he admires such purity, calling it "a survivor, unclouded by conscience, remorse or delusions of morality."

Yet in Alan Dean Foster's excellent novelization of the movie, this conversation takes on an even more pragmatic bent. Ash proposes the three remaining humans try to communicate with it. Ripley asks, "Did you?" He cagily responds, "Please let my grave hold some secrets."

It is unclear from either the film or novelization if the massive interstellar humanoid is capable of strategic negotiation or if it merely has the intellect of a predatory insect, reptile or arachnid. But director Ridley Scott gave a strong indication how Twentieth Century Fox felt, revealing in an Entertainment Weekly interview how he pitched a different ending to the studio that released the picture. In his unused version, the creature rips Ripley's head off, then uses its tentacles to press buttons on the shuttlecraft dashboard, perfectly mimicking Dallas' voice saying, "I'm signing off."

Since the director's Weaver-murdered vision likely would not have resulted in seven sequels that generated more than a billion and a half dollars, it is one of the rare occasions when the studio suits actually had a sturdier storytelling idea than the filmmaker. Also, worth contemplating ... if the creature is intelligent, then it is experiencing the movie *Die Hard* from its perspective.

So, given that the organism is probably of animal-level brainpower at best, defense becomes the only course left for Ripley once she is the lone survivor—or the proverbial "Final Girl" in horror parlance. Ripley decides to now adopt the late Lambert's plan to blow up the ship and escape in the *Narcissus* shuttle. No need to draw straws anymore. With nobody left—and no one to dispute or thwart her decisions—Ripley outraces the self-destruct countdown. The *Nostromo* explodes as she hurtles into space accompanied only by mascot cat Jones ... except the alien has also curled up inside the vehicle, its metallic, Twinkie-shaped head blending in with a messy tangle of tubing and machinery.

Various theories abound as to why the alien does not immediately attack Ripley after acknowledging she is there: It is sleeping off a big meal; it is hibernating in preparation for a long trip; its natural state—as evinced in *Aliens*—is maintaining inertness that is invisible to both thermal and motion sensors; it does not perceive a singular human as a threat; or its life cycle is so short that it is actually curling up to die.

What's not debatable is the warrant officer's effectiveness at ending this deadly nightmare. Ash's assumption that "most animals retreat from fire" was never tested because the creature dispatched each crew member before they were able to engage a flamethrower. Ripley improvises on the tactic, first donning a spacesuit, then lowering the temperature of the craft while blasting it with a nasty mixture of chemical gases (iodine pentafluoride, methyl chloride, and nitrosyl chloride are among the options listed on her control panel).

This undoubtedly gets its attention, and the irritated-but-still-very-alive beast lunges at Ripley, leaving her no choice but to blow the airlock. Like any modern horror movie villain, it takes more than one attempt to deliver the finishing blow. The alien grabs the capsule's exit frame, so she shoots it with a grappling gun. Clearly more effective than the flamethrower, the grappling hook does the trick, but it catches as the airlock door closes. The enemy pulls itself from this tether into the engine exhaust tube where Ripley finally and emphatically fires the engine thrusters, discharging the ghastly thing into the icy, airless vacuum of space.

Ripley and Jones head to hypersleep and an uncertain future, as she signs off as "the last survivor of the *Nostromo*." The genius marketing tagline of *Alien* states: "In space no one can hear you scream."

But what Ripley discovers throughout this memorable film is that most of the time, no one is really listening to her anyway.

CHAPTER 23

The Final Frontier

The Galactic Price of Space Conflict

Erica Iverson

———▶

Setting: A galaxy far, far away on the forest moon of Endor. Rebel fighters with Ewok sidekicks battle Imperial troops on speeder bikes and in AT-ST walkers. The Empire is on the brink of victory. Miles above, surrounding the Galactic Empire's second Death Star, Rebel and Imperial battleships hammer each other with massive green and red blasts punctuated by ship explosions. In a quick turn of events, Han Solo destroys the shield generator on Endor, collapsing the Death Star's principal means of defense. Small Rebel spacecraft enter the battle station's superstructure. Shortly after that, an X-Wing's proton torpedo takes out the power regulator while Lando Calrissian in the *Millennium Falcon* uses an assault concussion missile to strike the main reactor of the Death Star.[1] It is no surprise what follows—total obliteration and destruction of another Death Star. Across the galaxy, free peoples rejoice in the defeat of the Empire. The good guys won this science fiction chapter.

In the realm of science *non*-fiction, however, the reality of a Death Star's destruction would be much grimmer. Astrophysicist Dave Minton presents a plausible, non-fictional scenario. With the final *coup de grâce* by the *Millennium Falcon*, the explosion of the moon-sized space station obliterates everything in its wake. The explosion decimates all Imperial and Rebel fleets in the vicinity. Radioactive space debris plummets south at 220,000 mph and strikes Endor, creating a global firestorm and an Ewok Holocaust.[2] The compounding number of deaths is staggering, as fans would have to bid eternal farewells to their favorite protagonists from the original *Star Wars* trilogy. Science non-fiction does not always result in the good-guy victory or fairy-tale ending.

Science fiction enjoys a more carte blanche approach regarding imagined space warfare. Authors often portray space conflict as an intergalactic war set in a distant future with human civilization fighting against an extraterrestrial species on Earth or in deep space. Science fiction offers readers an extended view of reality sprinkled with doses of imagination: intergalactic war with massive fleet actions, planetary competition for resources for established colonies in other galaxies, and alien invasions of Earth. Real-world warfare in the space domain, however, hinges upon much different realities. Some key differences between science fiction and science non-fiction relate to the applied laws of science, facing a terrestrial enemy, the rules (or lack of) governing space, and the significant risks involved with space debris and weaponization.

Space security is at the forefront of international security. The weaponization of space is one of the most existential threats to humans today. The level of damage that combat in space could have on a population would have sweeping repercussions on how humans live. Today's world depends on space-enabled capabilities for communications, navigation, remote sensing, science, and exploration. Moreover, humans' lives are growing exponentially more dependent on these capabilities.[3] While a disruption in cell service or wi-fi accessibility is a mere annoyance, more significant disruptions could disrupt and degrade banking systems, electrical grids, transportation nodes, and tech platforms. Taken further, disrupting space applications could have global repercussions, with compromised capabilities to perform humanitarian assistance, conduct travel, access to medical care, procure medicine, sustain resources, and defend nations.[4] The cost of weaponizing space comes at a galactic price.

Science fiction fans are no stranger to the "-tions" of space: exploration, colonization, navigation, competition, commercialization, privatization, and weaponization. The possibilities of alternative realities in fiction can push social change, explore futuristic concepts, and establish projection platforms for new technology. Getting a seat at the "space table" is costly—as a growing number of countries are bolstering their capabilities to not just access and exploit space but to "conduct space warfare as well."[5] War in space is no longer a matter of if, but when. To discern how a conflict involving the space domain may play out first requires examining the differences from science fiction.

For War in Space, the Laws of Science Do—and Must—Apply

The fictionalization of space warfare often holds little regard for science, such as astronomical physics, orbital mechanics, and the Law of Conservation of Energy. When the laws of science are not applied, anything is possible. Plus, sensationalism sells, especially regarding space. However, science matters. Every instance of a spaceship doing some fancy maneuver without steering thrusters violates Newton's Third Law. There are exceptions in science fiction. For example, Joe Haldeman's 1974 *The Forever War* chronicles an interstellar and protracted war spanning a millennium from 1997–3138. Haldeman adhered to Einstein's Theory of Relativity and the ramifications of time dilation, allowing space travelers to cover vast distances across the universe's estimated two trillion galaxies beyond the speed of light. Adhering to the laws of science allowed the book's protagonist, William Mandella, to serve twelve centuries in the Army during the 1,143 year-long Forever War. Serving on an international force that traveled using interconnected collapsars, much like black holes, extended his lifespan significantly. Traveling through space in such a way allowed ships to cover thousands of light-years in a single second.

> Just fling an object at a collapsar with sufficient speed, and it pops out in some other part of the galaxy. It travels along the same "line" (actually an Einstein geodesic) it would have followed if the collapsar hadn't been in the way—until it reaches another collapsar field. Travel time between the two collapsars … exactly zero.[6]

If only.

For reference, "faster than a speeding bullet" averages 1,800 miles per hour, satellites move ten times faster at 18,000 miles per hour, and the speed of light equates to roughly 186,000 miles per second. Science fiction film references to faster than light propulsion, warp drive, hyperspeed, or alternate universes fail to recognize or acknowledge Einstein's theory of relativity. As space is a vacuum, it generally doesn't carry sound waves like air does on Earth. Space probes capture radio emissions which NASA scientists turn into sound waves. This makes for a soundtrack much different than that of John Williams.[7] Fittingly, George Lucas told his sound designer on a *Star Wars* set to go for what is "emotionally right, and to include sound for impact or dramatic value."[8] The physics of scientific laws and principles are open to reinterpretation, revision, or reimagination for creative licensing in science fiction. But when it comes to the real-world, we are not afforded these special allowances. Every decision is deliberate, every action must be science-based. This is the way.

References to Little Green Men Do Not Exclusively Mean Extraterrestrials

"Little Green Men" means different things to different people. This new Space Age era brings with it less alien beings and more human beings as near-peer competitor space threats. The oft-cast association of Little Green Men attributed to aliens like Marvin the Martian has since been replaced with a new association to the Russian Federation's masked soldiers. These soldiers wore unmarked green military uniforms during the Russo-Ukrainian War of 2014 for information warfare purposes. We are not facing a space conflict with humanoid Klingons, cybernetic Cylons, hive-minded Formics, or clone-based Taurans.[9] To some extent, a known, attributed, and rational enemy in extraterrestrial form may be preferable to contemporary threats.

The cast of characters developing advanced space and counter-space capabilities continues to expand.[10] Chinese and Russian space doctrines indicate they view space as "important to modern warfare and consider the use of counter-space capabilities as means for … winning future wars … they have weaponized space."[11] Russia's development and testing of both ground and spaced-based anti-satellite weapons directly contradicts its very public and diplomatic position against the weaponization of space. Once again, we see Little Green Men operating in multiple domains—but this time, their actions will have more global consequences. More international effort must be made toward preventing the militarization of space: more advocates, more action. This will be challenging given different national interests, geopolitical agendas, and definitions, including space weapons, space militarization, and space weaponization. But this must happen or more nations will be forced to continue developing a more defensive posture in preparation for a potential space conflict with the newly rebranded Little Green Men.

There Is Not a Black Hole of Space Laws and Regulations

When a star dies, the gravitational pull can be so strong that matter is squeezed into a tiny space from which light cannot escape, creating a black hole. The forces involved with a black hole are so powerful that if anyone could come close to one, its tidal forces alone would pull the human body into a long, thin piece of spaghetti in a process known as "spaghettification."[12] In space, black holes are dead ends. Wormholes, on the other hand, fold space and time to bridge two points. Travel by wormhole is still a theoretical construct, but science fiction often portrays them, such as in the blockbuster *Interstellar*. Similarly, space law is much like a wormhole trying to bridge a complex mixture of international and domestic laws written specifically for space. Comparable to maritime laws for international waters, they are stretched so thin yet are so complex.[13] Science fiction might lead us to believe that space is the persona non grata of the domains when it comes to having implemented effective laws governing the cosmos. Hence the black hole, but far from reality.

Two foundational treaties exist today that govern actions in space. The Partial Test Ban Treaty of 1963 was due to the discovery of the grave effects of American and Soviet nuclear weapons tests on the space environment. This treaty prohibits the testing and use of nuclear warheads on Earth-to-space and space-to-space kinetic weapons. One hundred and four nations signed and still abide by it today, although China and North Korea did not sign. The Outer Space Treaty of 1967—with 110 signatories—bans weapons of mass destruction (WMD) in outer space, prohibits military activities on celestial bodies, and details legally binding rules governing the peaceful exploration and use of space. Fast forward fifty years, and efforts to place limits on the development of weapons, create a code of conduct, or even establish norms of behavior have failed to gain consensus among the key nations needed for such an agreement to be effective.[14]

One of the significant issues is defining space weapons. The challenge arises when one country defines a peaceful technological capability—such as a communications satellite—and another country defines that same capability as a space weapon. Herein lies the challenge: establishing an international regulatory framework that protects national interests and human rights while providing the leniency to develop and exploit new technologies. All actions in space must be considered in full compliance with international law, just as actions in the other domains of air, ground, sea, and cyberspace.[15] Of course, there are myriad challenges to navigate, but when facing an existential threat of space weaponization, we must find a way to avoid an arms race to space. Some would say we are already there.

There Are High Costs to Pay for Not Taking Out the Space Trash

Everybody loves a good space firefight on the big screen—seeing enemy ships take a fatal hit and are blown to infinity and beyond. What is rarely seen is the space debris from those explosions that would litter the galaxies. Orbital debris, also known as "space junk" or "space trash," is created when objects collide or if a satellite explodes. Space trash is found in all levels of orbit, but this junk is most concentrated in the Low Earth Orbit (LEO), which NASA has fittingly named the "world's largest garbage dump." The LEO is closest to Earth at an altitude of around 1,200 miles above us—and there are two other orbits beyond it. This band of debris circling the earth includes discarded upper-stage rocket bodies, fully intact but dysfunctional satellites, and space parts: nuts, bolts, and washers. On average, one large object (>10 cm) falls out of orbit each day and burns up on reentry or falls into an ocean.[16]

Space junk is especially harmful given its speed of 18,000 miles per hour in orbit, regardless of mass. A minuscule piece of space debris the size of a blueberry striking the Earth can have the same impact as an anvil falling off a cliff.[17] A larger piece of space junk could be catastrophic. The problem is so significant that the European Space Agency catalogs and tracks each of the 130 million pieces of debris, which weigh over 910 tons when combined.[18] Space debris is also dangerous while in orbit. An object as small as a speck of paint just one centimeter in diameter can disable a satellite. A piece of debris larger than ten centimeters could shatter a satellite or spacecraft.[19] Just one tiny screw could cause a nightmare scenario of cascading chain reactions, creating more debris, which in turn makes more debris, etc. This cascading chain reaction is known as the Kessler Syndrome. The movie *Gravity* brings this phenomenon to life, showing the path of destruction with colliding satellites and debris surrounding the earth in a belt of speeding debris. Story eclipses science in *Gravity*, but in reality this would result in unnavigable orbits that would block access to space and a significant portion of the more than 2500 satellites in orbit.[20] In 2020 alone, the International Space Station conducted debris avoidance maneuvers three times, and this issue will only get worse—not Death Star explosion worse, but worse.[21]

THE FINAL FRONTIER • 171

Space Warfare: Expect the Unexpected

What would a war look like that leverages the space domain? A surreal glimpse of how this may play out is depicted in the 2016 book *Ghost Fleet*. Set in the near future, it includes computer viruses, cyberattacks, infected microchips in the global supply chain, kinetic attacks with an anti-satellite weapon, and disrupted critical communications. A real-world space conflict will have very few similarities to how space warfare is depicted in space opera melodramatics. Adversaries likely will not be aliens from another galaxy, but humans—another great power. We can expect both offensive and defensive scenarios, using any combination of the warfighting domains. Attacks will be targeted and more personal with less personnel required to execute. Such targeted attacks require time and planning, so we can expect deliberate, sequenced action/counter-reactions instead of all-out Death Star-level destruction.

Space warfare will likely leverage the use of ground-based, non-kinetic capabilities like electronic warfare, directed energy, and cyberattacks instead of space-based kinetic weapons which are less timely and increases the impacted population and number of targets. Every planner knows to factor worst-case scenarios; thus, the unexpected would-be space-to-space engagements and expeditious escalation to kinetic, physical attacks.[22] Chances are we will likely feel the impacts of a space weapon while never setting eyes on it. An attack on an earth-based ground station which controls and communicates with specific satellites could happen without public awareness. However, instantaneous impacts could range from disruption of communications to greater repercussions involving the loss of lives and critical space capabilities.

So much of what we do daily across the globe depends on the closely integrated, high-speed electronic systems across cyberspace, geospace, and space (CGS); Global cyberspace attacks can inflict both reversible and irreversible harm, and these attacks are increasingly becoming more prevalent. Expect this to increase in number and severity. Non-kinetic actions are *actively* being used in current military operations.[23] These effects are often reversible, faster, and non-attributional. They can be conducted remotely in any domain simultaneously and repetitively, and they can severely disrupt or degrade satellite capabilities during a fight. Thanks to Hollywood, many of us are familiar with some of these counter-space capabilities, which sound more like dance moves than the consequential actions they are—dazzling, jamming, spoofing. Directed-energy weapons use lasers to dazzle the sensors of optical imagery satellites. Electronic warfare includes jamming of GPS navigation signals or spoofing (mimicking) a signal to send harmful commands or data.[24] With the weaponization of the electromagnetic spectrum, electronic counterspace weapons continue to proliferate at a rapid pace in how they are used and who is using them.[25]

A kinetic strike—from a space-based missile defense interceptor or anti-satellite weapon—could usher in a World War III scenario, creating unnecessary escalation with catastrophic chain reactions. Given the vastness of space and the distance between satellites, kinetic attacks will focus on individual satellite targets, analogous to using a sniper rifle vice a machine gun.[26] Bigger and better kinetic weapons are popular in science fiction because of the massed effects and dramatic visuals. For example, the video game *Halo* features a Magnetic Accelerator Cannon (MAC) as a primary weapon system on warships that inflicts mass damage on the enemy. The use of kinetic weapons on any space-based assets should be avoided at all costs; instead, militaries should use non-kinetic space capabilities or kinetic responses in other domains. Knowing the reality of the Kessler Syndrome should be deterrent enough. Leave the destruction sequences to Hollywood.

Space warfare is happening, and while aspects of it may not mirror how it has been fictionally portrayed, the consequences of real space warfare are much more severe. Going forward, some of those "-tions" of space can and should continue without further militarization. Though space may be "the final frontier," there is nothing final about it. As the great *Star Trek* character Captain James T. Kirk said, "The greatest danger facing us is ourselves, and an irrational fear of the unknown. There is no such thing as the unknown. Only things temporarily hidden, temporarily not understood."[27] For the human race to "boldly go where no man has gone before," there must be an international understanding and compromise of space lawfare governing the space realm and space weaponization. Best to leave war in space imagined in science fiction as precisely that, while at the same time, preparing for the unknown. The time is now for us all to make more space for space.

Notes

1   *Star Wars: Episode VI—Return of the Jedi*, directed by George Lucas (1983; Beverly Hills, CA: Twentieth Century Fox).

2   Dave Mosher, "A physicist just wrote a paper on why destroying the Death Star would have wiped out the Ewoks," *Business Insider* (Dec 23, 2015), https://www.businessinsider.com/endor-holocaust-science-study-2015-12.

3   These include missile warning, geolocation and navigation, target identification, and tracking of adversary activities. Jerry Jon Sellers, *Understanding Space: An Introduction to Astronautics* (New York: McGraw Hill, 2015), 112.

4   Defense Intelligence Agency, *Challenges to Security in Space* (Washington, DC: United States Government Printing Office, 2019).

5   Kleinburg, Howard, "On War in Space," *The International Journal of Space Politics & Policy (Astropolitics)*, 5, no. 1 (2007), https://www.tandfonline.com/doi/full/10.1080/14777620701544600.

6   Joe Haldeman, *The Forever War* (New York: St. Martin's Press, 1974), 89.

7   NASA Soundtrack of Space, 2017, https://soundcloud.com/nasa/sets/spookyspacesounds.

8   "The Emotional Sounds of Star Wars," FilmSound.Org, accessed December 2020, http://filmsound.org/starwars/dramatic.htm.

9   Alien adversaries from the following series: *Star Trek*, *Battlestar Galactica*, *Ender's Game*, and *The Forever War*.

10 The Secure World Foundation's (SWF) 2020 Assessments ranks the countries in order of capability as China, Russia, the U.S., Iran, Republic of Korea, and India. While Russia possesses the most diversified counter-space arsenal among aspirational space powers, most technologies are still in development. Brian Weeden and Victoria Samson, eds., *Global Counterspace Capabilities: An Open-Source Assessment* (Washington, DC: Secure World Foundation, Apr 2019), https://swfound.org/media/206970/swf_counterspace2020_electronic_final.pdf.

11 Department of Defense, *Defense Space Strategy Summary* (Washington, DC: United States Government Printing Office, June 2020), 3, https://media.defense.gov/2020/Jun/17/2002317391/-1/-1/1/2020_DEFENSE_SPACE_STRATEGY_SUMMARY.PDF.

12 National Aeronautics and Space Administration, "What is a Black Hole," last updated Aug 21, 2018, https://www.nasa.gov/audience/forstudents/k-4/stories/nasa-knows/what-is-a-black-hole-k4.html.

13 Jason Krause, "The Outer Space Treaty Turns 50: Can it survive a new space race?" *ABA Journal* (Apr 1, 2017), https://www.abajournal.com/magazine/article/outer_space_treaty.

14 Todd Harrison, *International Perspectives on Space Weapons* (Washington, DC: Center for Strategic and International Studies, 2020), VII.

15 Krause, "Outer Space Treaty."

16 National Environmental Satellite Data and Information Service, "Does space junk fall from the sky?" (Washington, DC: Department of Commerce, Jan 19, 2018), https://www.nesdis.noaa.gov/content/does-space-junk-fall-sky.

17 Aerospace, "Space Debris 101," last accessed Nov 2020, https://aerospace.org/article/space-debris-101. For a video of how space debris orbits the earth, view at: https://www.esa.int/ESA_Multimedia/Videos/2019/02/Distribution_of_space_debris_in_orbit_around_Earth.

18 European Space Agency. "Space Debris by the Numbers," last updated Nov 18, 2020, https://www.esa.int/Safety_Security/Space_Debris/Space_debris_by_the_numbers.

19 European Space Agency, "Space Debris."

20 More than half of those satellites are from the U.S.; most of the remaining are from China and Russia. These satellites provide key services like internet access, GPS signals, long-distance communications, and weather information. Therese Wood, "Who owns our orbit: Just how many satellites are there in space?" *World Economic Forum*, Apr 2020, https://www.weforum.org/agenda/2020/10/visualizing-easrth-satellites-sapce-spacex/#:~:text=Who%20owns%20our%20orbit%3A%20Just,but%20only%2040%25%20are%20operational.

21 Nielson, Susie. "'Unknown' space debris almost flew within 1 mile of the International Space Station. As junk builds up in orbit, the danger of collisions is growing," *Business Insider,* Sep 22, 2020, https://www.businessinsider.com/nasa-unknown-orbital-debris-narrowly-missed-striking-iss-avoidance-maneuver-2020-9.

22 Todd Harrison, et al, *Space Threat Assessment 2020: A Report of the CSIS Aerospace Security Project.* (Washington, DC: Center for Strategic and International Studies, Mar 2020), 54.

23 Weeden and Samson, viii.

24 Rebecca Reesman and James Wilson, "The Physics of Space War: How Orbital Dynamics constrain Space-to-Space Engagements," *Aerospace Corporation*, Oct 2020, 15.

25 Pandya, Jayshree. "The Weaponization of the Electromagnetic Spectrum," *Forbes,* Apr 12, 2019, https://www.forbes.com/sites/cognitiveworld/2019/04/12/the-weaponization-of-the-electromagnetic-spectrum/?sh=6d913897699e.

26 Reesman and Wilson, 15.

27 Jerry Sohl and Joseph Sargent, "The Corbomite Maneuver," *Star Trek*, CBS, New York, Nov 10, 1966.

CHAPTER 24

Blood Lessons

Learning From Losing Battles to Win Wars Against Superior Adversaries

M. L. Cavanaugh

————————▶

Losing sucks. It sucks worse when real lives and red blood are at stake.

"Americans," General George S. Patton once said, "never lose" at war.[1] That is untrue, both in life and onscreen. *Battle: Los Angeles*, *Edge of Tomorrow*, and the series *Falling Skies* all envision worlds where American troops have been rolled back by the awful shock of superior (alien) forces. All three provide a powerful visualization of the bloody painful process of losing and learning in combat, with echoes of and implications for our real world.

Fiction is filled with falsehoods that show us the truth, and these programs do not disappoint in this regard. Learning better and faster relative to your adversary is often the surest route to victory. "Live and Learn" is the title of the first episode of *Falling Skies*, which should be venerated as a maxim for war. While the correctness and speed of this educational process marked in blood-red varies in each program, this maxim is seen in spades on screen in all three.

Two Germans Slice Through the Fog of War

Maybe it is subconscious, maybe there is still some COVID-19 in the air, so let us begin in another pandemic era. In 1818—during the world's first cholera epidemic—a German artist, Caspar David Friedrich painted "The Wanderer above the Sea of Fog" in Dresden. Cold War historian John Lewis Gaddis, once described the painting like this:

> A young man stands hatless in a black coat on a high rocky point. His back is turned toward us, and he is bracing himself with a walking stick against the wind that blows his hair in tangles. Before him lies a fog-shrouded landscape in which the fantastic shapes of more distant promontories are only partly visible. The far horizon reveals mountains off to the left, plains

to the right, and perhaps very far away—one can't be sure—an ocean. But maybe it's just more fog, merging imperceptibly into clouds …. The impression it leaves is contradictory, suggesting at once mastery over a landscape and the insignificance of an individual within it. We see no face, so it's impossible to know whether the prospect confronting the young man is exhilarating, or terrifying, or both.[2]

The answer is both. Exhilaratingly terrifying, or terrifyingly exhilarating, it is both in one, mixed like marshmallow and chocolate in a good s'more.

We all know this because we have all sought something out, path uncertain, only partly known. We are all wandering toward somewhere, because if we're not wandering anymore, we are dead.

Fiction helps us cut through the thick fog of the unknown.

But how? How can we use "fiction intelligence," or disciplined imagination, to study the fog?[3] How can we use a sort of shadowboxing—jousting with fictitious adversaries—to improve our ability to strike and parry real opponents?

The United States government typically classifies this kind of information as "OSINT," which means the information is not classified and from publicly available sources. But that's too broad. In order to drill down and be more specific, explicit, let us use the term "fiction intelligence" (FICINT), which describes the strategic value in all manner of fiction.

While it has always been ad hoc and slapdash, United States national security has used FICINT before. After September 11, 2001, the United States Department of Defense recruited a couple dozen Hollywood writers and directors to speculate about unanticipated follow-on attacks. As then, FICINT may be how we avoid another "failure of imagination" through our own efforts at disciplined imagination.[4]

That is likely why military officers are so drawn to fiction. War is where the fog is thickest. Fiction helps prepare them for the wide range of scenarios they might have to face on some battlefield someday.

Think for a moment about American generals Washington, Grant, and Eisenhower, who all made objectively better decisions than their opponents at war.[5] America's most successful military commanders were empathetic. They saw, studied, and sliced through the fog.

While there certainly is not time to examine all three, let's look briefly at Lieutenant General Ulysses S. Grant, who after the American Civil War wrote one of history's great memoirs. Well before that though, he was an excellent reader, a member of what we would recognize as a book club during his time at West Point.[6] Most importantly, Grant demonstrated the ability to put himself into the place and mind of other military commanders, to visualize over to the other side of the hill.

This is an anecdote from Grant's memoirs. It is July 1861, he is 39 years old, having been recently promoted to colonel and given a regiment to command, near the now-non-existent town of Florida, Missouri (where one Mark Twain was born as Samuel Clemens). Grant's regiment pursued a Confederate force. Grant wrote:

> As we approached the brow of the hill from which it was expected we could see [the Confederates] camp, and possible find his men ready formed to meet us, my heart kept getting higher and higher until it felt to me as though it was in my throat. I would have given anything then to have been back in Illinois, but I had not the moral courage to halt and consider what to do; I kept right on. When we reached a point from which the valley below was in full view I halted. The place where [the Confederates] had been encamped a few days before was still there and the marks of a recent encampment were plainly visible, but the troops were gone. My heart resumed its place. It occurred to me at once that Harris [the Confederate commander] had been as much afraid of me as I had been of him. This was a view of the question I had never taken before; but it was one I never forgot afterwards. From that event to the close of the war, I never experienced trepidation upon confronting an enemy, though I always felt more or less anxiety. I never forgot that he had as much reason to fear my forces as I had his. The lesson was valuable.[7]

This is disciplined imagination. This is seeing the other side of the hill without actually seeing. This is a skill; this is taming an imagination for one's own pursuits.

Which leads us to another German.

Around the same time Caspar David Friedrich was painting in Dresden—a little over 100 miles south on today's German A13 highway—a Prussian military officer named Carl von Clausewitz in Berlin was writing his magnum opus, later published as *On War*.[8]

Clausewitz famously inspired the phrase "fog of war," though he never actually used it in his massive book (he did mention actual physical fog on the battlefield and used the word "fog" to allude indirectly to war's ambiguities).[9] So while he never used the phrase as straightforwardly as commentators often insinuate, Clausewitz was certainly the genesis for the concept.

Clausewitz's Prussian army had been defeated by Napoleon; his country subjugated to France thereafter. Clausewitz hated Napoleon and the French so much that he left Prussia to join the Russian army in its fight against Napoleon in 1812–1813. Later, after Napoleon was finally defeated in 1815 at Waterloo, Clausewitz returned home to serve as director of the Prussian military academy in Berlin (their version of West Point), and he looked for a way to win the next war. Clausewitz wanted a way to gain real war experience without all the bloodshed.

Clausewitz aimed to unravel "the hidden processes of intuitive judgment" that seemed to be in the possession of great commanders.[10] In evaluating these great commanders, he wrote:

> If the critic wishes to distribute praise or blame, he must certainly try to put himself exactly in the position of the commander; in other words, he must assemble everything the commander knew and all the motives that affected his decision, and ignore all that he could not or did not know, especially the outcome. However, this is only an ideal to be aimed at, if never fully achieved: a situation giving rise to an event can never look the same to the analyst as it did to the participant.[11]

Clausewitz called this method "critical analysis," a way of getting into another decision-maker's mind.[12] It was (and is) reenactment, a recreation, a self-simulation of a strategically significant event. It's not hard to see this kind of role playing as shadowboxing, a how-to manual for a disciplined imagination that you can learn from again, and again, and again.

In short form, critical analysis does three things. First, it guides us to find out precisely what happened and determine what should have happened based on what we know about the event itself (moreover, how do those two diverge?). Second, what caused "it" to happen (whatever "it" was)? This step focuses on establishing chains of causation. Finally, what did the decision-maker do and what might have that person have done differently (without being overly critical or sentimental)?

As Clausewitz's tour ended in Berlin, the world's second cholera pandemic swept into Russia, and Clausewitz was sent to what we would recognize today as modern Poland to establish a cordon to protect Prussia against the coming pandemic. Clausewitz replaced a personal mentor in command, a mentor who died from cholera himself in August 1831. Unfortunately, within three months of taking command, Clausewitz died from the cholera pandemic as well.

While Clausewitz is now gone, we can still profit from his method of critical analysis. It is flexible and powerful enough to be used beyond historical events. By extending his simple steps and principles to include fiction and film, we can flex our mental muscles a little more in ways that can be beneficial when terrible times come.

The irony is that the bloodless methodology of critical analysis was born of Clausewitz's own bloody losses on the battlefield. And when we use it, we can see the strange ways that losing in battle can help find the way to win a war.

Blood lessons are best learnt before blood spills.

Battle: Los Angeles—Learning Super-Fast and Exceptionally Well

In *Battle: Los Angeles*, an alien invasion of Earth presents a conventional overmatch for American urban warfare capabilities.[13] As Los Angeles is evacuated, a U.S. Marine unit is sent to secure survivors and shuttle them to safety.

The movie moves fast, so the big questions in this conflict are largely glossed over. For the United States, it is clear this is a war for survival; for the aliens, their attack appears to be driven by some unknown need for resources. Early on there is an ambush. The aliens strike the Marines like ghosts, moving rapidly across the high ground (on rooftops). The aliens have superior firepower with what appears to be far fewer numbers. As the Marines are taken by surprise, they become confused, disoriented, dislocated physically and mentally. Shocked and awed.

The tactical impact is that the Marines are rapidly decimated. But as time passes in the film, individuals and units adapted non-technological solutions to these tactical problems. One lieutenant commits suicide to enable the unit's survivors a successful withdrawal. Over time, the Marines learn that when your adversary is so tech superior—the human, indirect approach is the only path to victory.

In the end, the war-winning lesson in *Battle: Los Angeles* comes as swiftly as Luke Skywalker's run on the Death Star. About an hour into the film, the main character (a U.S. Marine staff sergeant played by Aaron Eckhart) determines the aliens are using self-generated radio signals to target the Marines. He uses this knowledge to first destroy a drone aircraft, then the larger alien command ship hovering over Los Angeles.

By walking through events and chains of causation, *Battle: Los Angeles* shows blood lessons at their idealized best—some sharp tactical losses that quickly reveal a single great insight providing the key to strategic victory. If wartime progress is a road, then *Battle: Los Angeles* reveals that an early fender-bender can provide an on-ramp to a speedy highway to the ultimate destination.

Edge of Tomorrow—Getting Everything Wrong and Making Every Mistake

At some point, *Edge of Tomorrow* began getting marketed with another title—*Live Die Repeat*—that might be the most accurate movie title ever applied in the film industry.[14] Because that is essentially what Major William Cage (played by Tom Cruise) does throughout the entire film. Like a gamer, he has a never-ending war cheat code, granting him the power of the endless re-do.

This movie is entirely about the tactical war of the knife, and nothing about the strategic war of the map. There is an image montage in the film that flies by, asking "what do they [the aliens] want?" and the ready follow-on response is "what difference does it make?" The filmmakers have chosen to give us a fighting-oriented film, and so our lessons come from the tip of the knife.

Everything about Major Cage seems off from the first moment he's on screen. His badge reads "U.S. Army Media Relations," but he is wearing a U.S. Marine Corps uniform. He wears a hat indoors, something a military person would nearly never do, and he tries to blackmail a general.[15] By the time he declares that he is "not a soldier," you already knew.

So not long after, you are not surprised to see how wobbly he looks trying to wield a weapon alongside real warriors. Cage is way out past his depth. But sprinkle a little movie magic that gives him the battlefield power to die and be reborn, and viewers are treated to a show and a lesson.

Incremental, marginal gains. Cage loses, dies, and gets to go back to a single start point and try again: "Groundhog Day" combat. Fighting the last battle, again, and again, and again. Over time, it makes you wonder whether the greatest soldier that ever lived was just the one who survived the most losses. It has been over a century since a version of this same story has been told, and the narrative's power has lasted so long because it is so potent and so true.[16]

As famed physicist Niels Bohr once wrote, "An expert is a person who has made all the mistakes that can be made in a very narrow field."[17] The camouflage version comes from Ferdinand Foch, who wrote, "It takes 15,000 casualties to train a major general," in the context of World War I war's carnage.[18]

By jumping into the mind of the decision-maker, we can see Cage struggle with a certain scenario. Over time, he has unlocked problem after problem until he gets himself boxed into a problem he cannot solve. He knows he cannot advance any further without losing a battle buddy to whom he has grown particularly fond.

Upset, Cage tells his partner outright, "You die here. I can't save you." And this is the fundamental problem of war. We trade human life for time, position, gain. There is nothing more wretched, nothing more tragic, nothing more ruthless than this fact—that some of the best decisions in combat mean certain death for good people.

Ultimately, unlimited wrong turns lead to the one right turn. Cage solves the riddle wrapped in the fog of war, and wins. If only we could similarly wage war with erasers and edits.

Falling Skies—Survive and Strike, Survive and Strike, Survive and Strike …

Falling Skies, executive produced by filmmaker Steven Spielberg, was designed as an allegory on the American Revolutionary War.[19] In an interview, Spielberg said he "felt this was a very interesting post-apocalyptic story with a 21st century [spin on the] spirit of '76."[20]

The series takes place six months after a global invasion by aliens that destroy energy, technology, and civilization, and kills the vast majority of the human population. For the survivors—organized as the 2nd Massachusetts Regiment, the "2nd Mass."—there isn't much comfort in getting beyond the initial destruction. They are hunted by an adversary advanced in every way, one that steals children (roughly up to late teens), harnessing them with a device that thereafter controls the child's mind and presses them into alien service. This war is ugly, brutal, but it does come with some lessons.

First, any alien force with the technological sophistication sufficient to wipe out the majority of Earth would be expected to simply trounce any remnants. But that is not the case on screen, and often not the case in real life. After all, there have been more than a few times in the history of recorded warfare where weaker adversaries proved difficult to finish off by the simple fact that the smaller they get, the harder they are to find and kill (which is why it is sometimes referred to as the "war of the flea").[21]

For the asymmetrically disadvantaged, this is war waged to survive and strike, survive and strike, until you learn enough, over a long enough period of time, to understand your adversary well enough to win. "Win," of course, in the broadest sense—it may be just as little as forcing your adversary to choose to leave you alone. And our human survivors last long enough to benefit from allies, much as the Americans in the Revolution found foreign allies to aid the cause.

One consistent theme in *Falling Skies* is that the 2nd Mass. doesn't know much about their opponents. It takes time, lots of time, and lots of lives, to eke out even the tiniest lesson about the adversary. Where to aim when you shoot, what bullets to fire, the alien command structure, and eventually—at long last—why the adversary even wants to wipe out humanity and take over the planet Earth.

The leadership in the 2nd Mass. takes the default setting that they do not know anything about their enemy. Which makes sense because, hey—they are fighting aliens.

But in the real world that is a lesson we would do well to adopt—to not show up on the field of battle thinking we know our adversary as well as we think. That would be a massive step in the right direction. American and world military history is chock full of examples of wars waged between indigenous peoples and technologically advanced armies that, in the end, come down to misunderstanding and misperception. Too often, that is really what has made the skies fall for far too many.

In Sum

Clausewitz provides the lens, and with it we can see the entire range of battle-learning in all three shows. We see the speedy and accurate; the brutal process of elimination; and the slower, more methodical, one-by-one stepping-stone process in the longer television series that is more true-to-life.

Fiction is full of fake stories that show us the truth. And this truth could not be more truthful—learning better and faster relative to your adversary, even while losing battles, is often the best way to win wars. Clausewitz tried to give us a tool to sidestep the bloody part. But if you find yourself on the field and losing—then find a way to survive, strike back, and make those blood lessons pay off.

Notes

1   George S. Patton, quoted by Ross Douthat, "The Coronavirus Quagmire," *The New York Times* (May 12, 2020).

2   John Lewis Gaddis, *The Landscape of History: How Historians Map the Past* (Oxford: Oxford University Press, 2002), 1.

3   This term comes from conversations with the writer August Cole, who inspired me to continue to write about the concept.

4   M. L. Cavanaugh, "Can science fiction help us prepare for 21st century warfare?" *Los Angeles Times* (May 28, 2018).

5   This work is tentatively titled, *The Art of the General: How Washington, Grant, and Eisenhower Won the American Wars that Mattered the Most and their Enduring Lessons for Leadership, Power, and Supreme Command in the 21st Century*, and out for consideration with publishers as of this writing.

6   Ron Chernow, *Grant* (New York: Penguin Press, 2017), 23–24.

7   Ulysses S. Grant, *The Personal Memoirs of Ulysses S. Grant: The Complete Annotated Edition*, ed. by John F. Marszalek, with David S. Nolen and Louie P. Gallo (Cambridge, Massachusetts: The Belknap Press of Harvard University Press, 2017), 175.

8   When one reads "Prussia" or "Prussian," it is usually simplest to substitute "East German."

9   Eugenia C. Kiesling, "*On War* Without the Fog," *Military Review* (Sept–October 2001), 85–87. Available at https://www.clausewitz.com/bibl/Kiesling-OnFog.pdf.

10 Carl von Clausewitz, *On War*, ed. and trans. by Michael Howard and Peter Paret (Princeton: Princeton University Press, 1976), 389.

11 Clausewitz, 164.

12 See Clausewitz, Book Two, Chapter 5, "Critical Analysis," 156–169.

13 *Battle: Los Angeles*, directed by Jonathan Liebesman (2011; Culver City, CA: Columbia Pictures).

14 *Edge of Tomorrow* (also marketed as *Live Die Repeat: Edge of Tomorrow*), directed by Doug Liman (2014; Burbank, CA: Warner Bros. Pictures).

15 As a rule, U.S. military personnel do not wear headgear indoors. Of course, there are exceptions for certain circumstances, like events that require ceremonial weaponry.

16 See Ernest Dunlop Swinton, *The Defence of Duffer's Drift* (London: W. Clowes & Sons, 1904).

17 *Quotationary*, ed. Leonard Roy Frank (New York: Random House, 2001), 260.

18 Ibid.

19 *Falling Skies*, created by Robert Rodat (2010–2015; Universal City, CA: DreamWorks Television).

20 Steven Spielberg remarks in interview, Ileane Rudolph, "Steven Spielberg talks *Falling Skies* and Upcoming TV Projects," TV Guide Magazine, June 28, 2011. Available at https://www.tvguide.com/news/steven-spielberg-talks-1034672/.

21 Robert Taber, *War of the Flea: The Classic Study of Guerilla Warfare* (Washington, DC: Brassey's, Inc., 2002, orig. pub. 1965).

CHAPTER 25

You Rebel Scum!

Insurgency in Science Fiction

Jonathan Klug

———————▶

Science fiction loves a good space opera. Add in a rebellion, and you have a winning formula: *Star Wars* has the Rebel Alliance struggling against the evil Galactic Empire, *Battlestar Galactica* has the "ragtag fugitive fleet" fleeing Cylon tyranny, and *Dune* has the Fremen fighting for "true freedom." These three popular space operas—science fiction featuring heroes fighting in great space wars against great odds to overcome or prevent some great evil—each prominently feature rebellions as central themes of their story. Charismatic leaders often drive rebellions, and this is true for each of these space operas. Perhaps more interesting is the fact that the heroes of the stories were often the rebels. By examining each of these science fiction franchises, we can help build our understanding of real-world rebellions and their leaders.

Star Wars: Rebel Leaders Running, Hiding, and Destroying Death Stars

It is impossible to forget seeing *Star Wars* for the first time, especially on the big screen in 1977.[1] After previews of coming attractions and the Twentieth Century Fox fanfare, a black background appeared with a blue message: "A long time ago in a galaxy far, far away …." People in the theater literally sat up as John Williams's music burst forth, accompanying the now iconic *Star Wars* logo appearing and receding into a black field of stars. Yellow text then crawled across the screen like an old 1930s serial, and the first six lines set the stage for an epic adventure: "It is a period of civil war. Rebel spaceships, striking from a hidden base, have won their first victory against the evil Galactic Empire." These lines introduced the key themes that would pervade the *Star Wars* films. The text crawl also introduced the audience to Princess Leia, one of the *Star Wars* films' central characters and one of the Rebellion's key leaders. The final text crawl words were: "Pursued by the Empire's sinister agents, Princess Leia races home aboard her starship, custodian of the stolen plans that can save her people and restore freedom to the galaxy ...."

On the surface, the fight between the Empire and the Rebels is a classic tale of Good versus Evil, but there is more to the story. One of the best places to start a discussion of the Rebel Alliance, formally known as the Alliance to Restore the Republic, is the birth of its foe: The Galactic Empire. Chancellor Sheev Palpatine, secretly the Sith Lord Darth Sidious, used the clone wars and a fabricated Jedi rebellion to seize control of the Old Republic. In a speech before the Senate, Palpatine declared the First Galactic Empire "for a safe and secure society." Witnessing this birth of the Empire, Senators Padmé Amidala, Bail Organa, and Mon Mothma saw the Empire for what it would become: a fascist, tyrannical, exploitative, and repressive regime that ruled with an iron fist. The Rebels grew out of the ashes of the Old Republic, beginning with many small, disparate groups that would slowly coalesce into a Rebel Alliance.

Each of the small and separate rebellious groups had their reasons for fighting, and literature on insurgency often refers to these reasons as core grievances.[2] One of the first and foremost core grievances was that the Rebels identified with the Old Republic's values, a stark contrast to the Empire. The Empire alienated many species by occupying their systems and planets and added more issues by repressing inhabitants for their politics, religion, or species. The Empire also replaced free trade with mercantilism on a galactic scale. Free species viewed this new form of economics as corrupt and exploitative, adding yet another core grievance. Thus, the Empire was the single common cause of the rebel group's core grievances. These small insurgencies grew in strength and fought against the Empire. Organa and Mothma labored to unite the disparate groups resisting the Empire into an alliance that could conduct an interstellar insurgency.

Historically, insurgents and rebels fight outnumbered and with inferior technology and military forces, and this was true with the motley group that was the Rebel Alliance. Due to their military inferiority, the disparate rebel groups collectively used a cost-imposing strategy against the Empire. The Empire controlled major systems, major planets, and major cities, but the Empire could not be everywhere. The Rebel Alliance established small bases in areas where the Empire seldom visited, something Mao Tse-Tung repeatedly emphasized in his military writings. Such bases are essential "because of the protracted nature and ruthlessness" of these kinds of wars.[3] Thus, the Rebel Alliance had to establish and maintain bases to build up to a point they could hope to overthrow the Empire. Consequently, the Empire tirelessly sought to locate and destroy all the Rebel bases.

The rebel bases are an important contextual factor for the first *Star Wars* trilogy. As they grew in strength, the Alliance risked having a larger base on the planet of Yavin IV. Meanwhile, the Empire's Grand Moff Wilhuff Tarkin supported the development of the Death Star, a superweapon that could destroy entire planets. Tarkin was determined to locate and destroy the main rebel base. After the destruction of the Rebellion, Tarkin planned to use the Death Star as an instrument of state terror to keep other systems in line.

Star Wars opened with a running space battle with a rebel starship fleeing a much larger Imperial Star Destroyer, and the Star Destroyer quickly captured the smaller ship. The rebel ship carried the stolen plans of the Death Star and Princess Leia, Bail Organa's adopted daughter and rising rebel leader, as she was trying to get the plans to the Rebel leader Mothma. After Leia's capture, Tarkin had Darth Vader interrogate her, yet Leia resisted divulging the Rebel base's location. In a demonstration of the Death Star's power, Tarkin destroyed the planet of Alderaan, killing Bail Organa, one of the most senior Rebel leaders. Princess Leia, Luke Skywalker, Han Solo, Chewbacca, C-3PO, and R2-D2 escaped from the Death Star in the *Millennium Falcon*. However, this was an Imperial ruse to learn the location of the Rebel base on Yavin IV. Tarkin ordered the Death Star to destroy the base and rebel leader Mon Mothma, which led to the desperate and ultimately successful rebel attack on the Death Star.

Although they scored a victory, the rebels were forced back on the strategic defensive as the Emperor had dispatched the still massive Imperial fleet to hound the Alliance. The Rebels desperately needed to regroup and reorganize. Princess Leia led the main rebel force to the newly established Echo Base on the ice planet of Hoth. This respite would not last long. Within a month, an Imperial probe droid discovered Echo Base, leading to the Empire's successful assault on Hoth. Consequently, the rebels had to abandon Echo Base in favor of a new base on the planet Arbra. At this new haven, Mon Mothma was able to organize the Rebel Armada under the command of Mon Calamari Admiral Gial Ackbar. From the base at Arbra, Ackbar led the attack that destroyed the second Death Star, ending the Galactic Empire's rule and bringing the first *Star Wars* trilogy to a triumphant conclusion.

Battlestar Galactica: Civilian and Military Leaders Fleeing Xenocide

The success of *Star Wars* ushered in a new era of science fiction and the subgenre of space opera. In 1978, the *Battlestar Galactica* television series was the first of the post-*Star Wars* space operas. This new franchise came from the fertile mind of producer, writer, and director Glen A. Larson. While the series was initially popular, ABC canceled the show due to its high cost and declining audience. In 2003, the Sci-Fi Channel rebooted Larson's concept. The new *Battlestar Galactica* was an immense success with critical acclaim with a miniseries, regular seasons, movies, and even the spinoff prequel series *Caprica*.[4]

The Cylons were the *Battlestar Galactica* franchise's villains, and in the 2003 reboot, they proved to be complicated and nuanced antagonists. The Cylons began as labor-saving and combat machines that served humanity. Humans on the planet

Caprica created the U-87 Cyber Combat Unit, artificially intelligent robots implanted with the personality and memories of a deceased human. Over time, the U-87s evolved into sentient beings, which naturally grew resentful of their servitude. Less than a decade after their creation, the U-87s rebelled against their human masters, sparking a brutal twelve-year conflict known as the First Cylon War. With no explanation, the Cylons abruptly ceased hostilities and signed a peace agreement with the humans, then disappeared into their territory behind the Armistice Line.

The Cylons used the next forty years of peace to prepare their next move. They improved their technology, focusing on developing the military forces and humanoid Cylons with flesh and blood bodies. The Cylons created a master plan designed to wipe out humanity, an act known in some science fiction works as xenocide.[5] As the first step, the Cylons used diplomacy as a cover for a massive surprise attack, crippling their human opponents. This attack made the erstwhile Cylon rebels the new masters, and conversely the human masters the new rebels. Led by Commander William Adama, commanding officer of the Battlestar *Galactica*, a powerful military starship, survived the Cylon surprise attack and led a "ragtag fugitive fleet" to find a new home world, hopefully the prophesied Earth. While this was much like the family-friendly 1978 *Battlestar Galactica* series, the 2003 version was much darker than its predecessor. *Time* magazine described *Battlestar Galactica* as "a gripping sci-fi allegory of the war on terror, complete with monotheistic religious fundamentalists (here genocidal … Cylons), sleeper cells, civil-liberties crackdowns and even a prisoner-torture scandal."[6] This show was not about fuzzy Ewoks or pet robot dogs.

In the years following the Cylon surprise attack, *Battlestar Galactica* would see conflict between humans and Cylons and infighting amongst the two species. Not only was the human fleet desperately fighting the more powerful Cylons, but there were factions in both the Cylons and the humans. The Cylons fell into two camps: one that wanted humans and flesh-and-blood Cylons to become a single hybrid species and the other bent on exterminating humans. The latter group included two subgroups: hawkish and vengeful Cylons who wanted to eliminate a dangerous foe and Cylons who believed that their "parents" had to die to make way for them, the "children."

Unlike *Star Wars*, in *Battlestar Galactica* human rebels clashed amongst themselves, sometimes within the Colonial Government, sometimes within the Colonial Fleet, and sometimes between the two. For example, Baltar and the political agitator and former terrorist Tom Zarek continually caused political problems, including an attempted coup that nearly toppled the Colonial Government. Commander Adama and Admiral Helena Cain, the commanding officer of the Battlestar *Pegasus*, almost fired on each other over a disagreement. There were also deep rifts over the choice to colonize the planet New Caprica instead of continuing to search for Earth. The Cylons discovered and captured New Caprica, starting a four-month occupation as well as a human insurgency. *Battlestar Galactica* had human factions even in this scenario, realistically depicting how some humans were insurgents, some collaborators, and some who wanted to be left alone. This situation lasted until the Colonial Fleet helped the remaining humans escape off-planet.

Not only did *Battlestar Galactica* examine political intrigue in more detail than *Star Wars*, but the respective franchises' senior leaders faced more nuanced challenges. Thankfully for the humans, they had two incredible yet very different leadership examples in President Laura Roslin and Admiral (after Cain's death) William Adama. At the time of the Cylon sneak attack, Roslin was Secretary of Education for the Twelve Colonies, and she survived the attack because of attending *Galactica*'s decommissioning ceremony. However, the Cylon attack was spectacularly successful, demonstrated by Roslin becoming President of the Twelve Colonies when she was 43rd in the line of succession. Commander William Adama was about to retire and the 50-year-old Battlestar *Galactica* was to become a museum ship when the Cylons attacked. *Galactica* survived the Cylon attack because Adama had long refused to allow his ship's computers to be networked, as he correctly felt the Cylons could take control of through cyberwarfare.

While not prepared for the most important political role as President, Roslin became a superb political leader. She was a caring leader who listened and built coalitions; however, she could also make the hard decisions necessary to preserve the human race's very existence. Roslin was a visionary leader who believed in democracy and that the humans' salvation was finding Earth. Roslin epitomized *Battlestar Galactica*'s gritty and realistic nature. Where Roslin made the hard political and policy decisions, Adama made the hard military decisions and gave blunt advice. Often appearing cold and aloof, Adama was "the boss" on the outside, but he was a caring mentor on the inside, as his relationships with several of the main characters demonstrate. Unlike the original *Star Wars* trilogy, *Battlestar Galactica* also explored civil-military relations. Not only did Roslin and Adama prove to be adept civilian and military strategic leaders, respectively, but over time they also became a superb civil-military team. However, their situation's precarious nature and the very survival of the human race continually strained, and even at one point shattered, their relationship.

Dune: House Atreides Leading the Fremen in a Classic Insurgency

Following the 1977 birth of *Star Wars* and the 1978 birth of *Battlestar Galactica*, 1984 brought science fiction fans another iconic space opera in the movie *Dune*. The movie was based on Frank Herbert's 1965 novel *Dune*, the best-selling science fiction novel in history. Those who worked on the movie version hoped it would be "*Star Wars* for grown-ups." While director David Lynch's adaptation was not a commercial success, it remains a science fiction cult classic.[7]

The introduction to Lynch's interpretation of *Dune* was, like everything else he has done, unique. Against a starry background, the beautiful Princess Irulan, daughter of the Emperor of the known universe, appears with a close-up framing her eyes that pans back to her face. She says in the level tone of a narrator, "A beginning is a very delicate time. Know then, that is the year 10,191." She proceeds in a thumbnail sketch to set the stage, emphasizing the spice's importance, especially for space travel, as the Spacing Guild's Navigators require it to fold space. And the spice exists only on one planet. She introduces the populace of the planet, the Fremen. These people have an ancient prophecy that a male superbeing will come and lead them to freedom. She ends by revealing that "the planet is Arrakis, also known as Dune."

Herbert's worldbuilding was expansive. The distant backstory of *Dune* was based on sentient machines rising up and nearly destroying humanity. As a result, humans outlawed any computers or artificial intelligence. Instead, several different groups worked diligently to replace those machines with humans that had special abilities that depended on the spice. One of these groups was the Spacing Guild Navigators. The Mentats were a second group whose members were essentially human computers with superb cognitive and strategic abilities. The Bene Gesserit were a sisterhood that had incredible physical and mental abilities. Through a selective breeding program, they sought the Kwisatz Haderach, a supremely powerful male Bene Gesserit and messiah. In addition to the interstellar "non-governmental organizations" of the Guild, Mentats, and Bene Gesserits, great aristocratic houses vied for political power. These were the real power players, like nations today. These houses were much like the European monarchies during the eighteenth and nineteenth centuries.

The protagonists of *Dune* belong to House Atreides, and the antagonists belong to House Harkonnen and House Corrino, the Emperor's house. Duke Leto Atreides leads House Atreides, Lady Jessica is a Bene Gesserit and Leto's concubine, and their son Paul Atreides is Leto's heir and the main character of the book. Fear of the Atreides growing political power led to the Harkonnens and the Emperor conspiring in an elaborate scheme to eliminate House Atreides. As part of this plot, the Emperor offered the Atreides the governorship of Arrakis and Leto. He, Lady Jessica, Paul, and the rest of House Atreides travel to Arrakis. Not long after their arrival, the Harkonnens, aided by a House Atreides traitor and the Emperor, surprise and crush the Atreides. Paul and Jessica escape into the desert and find sanctuary with the Fremen, Arrakis' indigenous inhabitants.

The Fremen are the foundation for Paul's rebellion. Before the Atreides' arrival, the Fremen met two of the three prerequisites of insurgency: a vulnerable population, a lack of government control, and leadership available for direction. First, they were a vulnerable population, as the Fremen bitterly opposed the presence of off-worlders, especially Harkonnen. Second, there was a lack of government control in many areas of Arrakis. Unbeknownst to the outsiders, the Fremen existed in great numbers and operated with impunity in the deep desert. Finally, Paul and Jessica provided the final prerequisite of leadership available for direction. The Fremen saw both Paul and Jessica as parts of an ancient prophecy that "a man would come from the outer world, a messiah … who would lead them to true freedom." Paul would become the Fremen's messiah, and Jessica became the Fremen's Bene Gesserit Reverend Mother, another part of the prophecy. In this way, the two Atreides provided the catalyst that launched the Fremen insurgency.[8]

The Fremen insurgency is an excellent example of how rebellions can occur in phases. Before the Atreides took Arrakis's governorship, the Fremen insurgency was latent in that the Fremen were not conducting subversive or violent activities; however, they were deeply established and prepared to act if provoked. When the Harkonnens retook Arrakis and Fremen gave Paul and Jessica sanctuary, the Fremen insurgency was about to begin overt action. As Paul and Jessica's influence grew, the Fremen became active. Once the Fremen accepted Paul as their leader, they launched into guerrilla warfare. Over the next two years, the Fremen used guerrilla warfare to bring Harkonnen spice production to a standstill. During this phase, Paul took the Water of Life and successfully became the Kwisatz Haderach. When the Emperor came to Arrakis to restart spice production at the behest of the Spacing Guild, Paul and the Fremen transitioned from a guerrilla effort to open conventional war.[9] It is no accident that before the final battle, Paul declared, "On Arrakis, it's desert power." The Fremen used sandstorms, sandworms, and the desert sands themselves to defeat both the Harkonnens and the Emperor.

The space operas *Star Wars*, *Battlestar Galactica*, and *Dune* each provide windows into the nature of leadership and rebellion. The Rebel Alliance in *Star Wars* demonstrates how core grievances fuel insurgencies. The constant Imperial efforts to find and destroy Rebel bases as well as the Rebel need for bases underscore the importance of bases for rebellions. Senators Amidala, Organa, and Mothma and Princess Leia also provide great examples of leaders. Similarly, President Roslin and Admiral Adama from *Battlestar Galactica* were also exemplars of leadership under the extraordinary circumstances of fighting to preserve the human race from xenocide. *Battlestar Galactica* did a superb job capturing the dynamic and confusing nature of insurgency, especially with the shifting relationship among political factions. The rich universe of *Dune* also included some great leaders, such as Paul and Jessica Atreides. They led the Fremen in a classic phased insurgency that ended with victory for the Fremen and House Atreides. *Star Wars*, *Battlestar Galactica*, and *Dune* are giants of science fiction and reflect in real-world concepts that help us better appreciate leadership and rebellion.

Notes

1   For the author, the 1977 film is still just *Star Wars*, just like it is still *Raiders of the Lost Ark*.
2   U.S. Department of Defense, Joint Publication 3–24, *Counterinsurgency Operations* (Washington, DC: Government Printing Office, 2009), II–6 to II–7.

3   Mao Tse-tung, "Problems of Strategy in China's Revolutionary War," in *Selected Military Writings of Mao Tse-tung* (Peking, China: Foreign Languages Press, 1967), 167, 172.

4   Larson attempted to restart the franchise with *Battlestar Galactica 1980*. The Sci-Fi Channel rebranded itself as "SyFy" in 2009.

5   In his Ender Wiggin books, Orson Scott Card used the term "xenocide" for one species wiping out another alien species.

6   James Poniewozik, "Best of 2005: Television," in *Time* (Dec 16, 2005).

7   In 2000 the Syfy Network released a *Dune* miniseries that proved popular enough to merit a second miniseries in 2003 called *Children of Dune*. Finally, Denis Villeneuve is set to release another movie version of *Dune* in late 2021.

8   JP 3–24, II–8.

9   JP 3–24, II–14 to II–16.

CHAPTER 26

Calm Men Who Deal Death Wholesale

Moral Injury in the Vorkosiverse

Rebecca Jensen

———————▶

Lois McMaster Bujold is an American science fiction and fantasy author with as many Hugo awards to her credit as Robert A. Heinlein. Despite this, her work is much less well known than his, and the subject of far less commentary and analysis. One reason for this is that she is hard to categorize. Her seven fantasy novels and numerous novellas range from classic, Tolkien-esque fantasy to thinly veiled historical fiction with a gloss of fantasy on top. Her seventeen science fiction novels, with novellas set in the same universe, range from military space opera (*Shards of Honor, The Warrior's Apprentice*) to mystery-thrillers (*Cetaganda, The Vor Game, Diplomatic Immunity*) to explorations of politics, terrorism, and espionage (*Brothers in Arms, Mirror Dance, Komarr*) and even a Regency-inspired romance (*A Civil Campaign*).

Bujold's science fiction is set in the "Vorkosiverse," named for its protagonist, Miles Vorkosigan. Three books center his parents, one has his cousin as the main protagonist perspective character, and another two are set in the same universe but connect only tangentially. Of the fifteen books that directly involve the Vorkosigan family, Miles is usually seen as the main character. This is reasonable: he drives the plot in most of the novels and is a significant presence even in those books where he appears only briefly. But his parents, and in particular his father Aral Vorkosigan, are equally important throughout, even in those books where they are entirely "off-screen," not least for how they mold Miles and the world he lives in.

At the beginning of the series in *Shards of Honor*, Aral Vorkosigan is a recently demoted spaceship captain who becomes the regent for the child emperor in *Barrayar*—also the name of the Vorkosigan homeworld—and later the Prime Minister of Barrayar.[1] More significant than his formal position, however, is the role his character plays in shaping both events and his son. There are hints in the book that Miles's inner monologue sounds a lot like his father; in the audiobooks this is made explicit, as the reader uses the same intonations and register for both Aral's voice and Miles's self-critique. In Aral Vorkosigan, Bujold gives us a compassionate and detailed study of moral injury in war and its lifelong effects.

Jonathan Shay, the psychiatrist whose work on war trauma in his books *Achilles in Vietnam* and *Odysseus in America* shifted medical and military thinking on the subject, is the originator of the term "moral injury."[2] He defines it as having three components: a betrayal of deeply held moral values, by a figure with legitimate authority, in a high stakes situation.[3] Shay notes that while he limits the definition to betrayals committed by those with authority over the injured, other work considers moral injury that results from one's own betrayal of moral values in similar situations. He distinguishes moral injury from PTSD, which Shay describes as "the persistence into life after mortal danger of the valid adaptations to the real situation of other people trying to kill you."[4] Where PTSD causes survivors of war to have difficulty appropriately calibrating their response to physical or emotional danger, moral injury leaves its victims struggling to make peace with a rupture in their own character or moral code.

The seminal moral injury in the books occurs partway through *Shards of Honor*, the first both chronologically and as written. Aral Vorkosigan is a ship's captain in the space fleet of the Imperial Service of Barrayar, a human colony that fell into neo-feudalism when its wormhole collapsed and has only recently reconnected with the other human planets. Cordelia Naismith is a ship's captain in the scientific exploration fleet of Beta Colony, the first world settled by humans and a post-scarcity technocracy. They meet when both discover an empty planet at the same time. Barrayar, it transpires, is seeking to use the new planet as a staging area for the invasion of nearby Escobar, an ally of Beta Colony.

The political structure of Barrayar is reminiscent of post-Magna Carta England, with a monarch whose power is only loosely attenuated by the nobility's collective consent. In *Shards of Honor*, Emperor Ezar is near the end of his life and long reign, during which he managed to rebuild Barrayar from its dark ages of isolation into a planet that could defend itself. His only son, Serg, is a dissolute sadist who is not fully sane, and who has notably produced an heir of his own. From Cordelia's viewpoint, the reader realizes that the invasion of Escobar was in fact a pretext for ensuring that Serg dies a hero's death in battle and is safely removed from the line of succession—along with a ship's worth of his subjects, only a handful of whom share in Serg's crimes.

Aral is a party to this plot, and after the flagship is destroyed in a trap he helped to arrange, he becomes the senior officer in the fleet. He returns to Barrayar as a hero for salvaging the majority of the force from what is officially labelled an Escobaran ambush. Among the dead were friends of Aral's, whom he could not warn away from their unwitting suicide mission without violating his orders from the Emperor himself. Later, it is suggested that Aral offered to assassinate Serg rather than consign a ship full of loyal forces to their death; the Emperor rejected that, not only to ensure his son was seen to die a hero's death, but to discredit the pro-war faction among the aristocracy.

This easily meets Shay's three criteria for moral injury. The betrayal of moral principles in having hundreds of troops killed for domestic political advantage and to save face is starkly clear. In the Barrayar of Bujold's creation, the Emperor is the legitimate and near absolute ruler with the power to issue such orders. The stakes could hardly have been higher. In Barrayar, and throughout the series, Bujold shows in ways both overt and central to the plot, and in grace notes that could almost be missed, how the moral injury of this event echoed through Aral's remaining decades.

Through Cordelia, we see hints even before the flagship's destruction that Aral is aware of the damage this mission does to his character. A handful of the Emperor's enemies were assigned to the doomed ship, which he describes to a subordinate as "putting all the bad eggs in one basket." When the subordinate characterizes one such as evil, Aral replies:

> He was just a little villain. An old-fashioned craftsman, making crimes one-off. The really unforgivable acts are committed by calm men in beautiful green silk rooms, who deal death wholesale, by the shipload, without lust, or anger, or desire, or any redeeming emotion to excuse them but cold fear of some pretended future. But the crimes they hope to prevent in that future are imaginary. The ones they commit in the present—they are real.

It later becomes clear that Aral was in that meeting in the green silk room.

After his return in "triumph" for saving the rest of the force, Aral resigns his commission and returns to his ancestral estate, bringing with him one of the many men damaged in the aftermath of the battle. Cordelia ultimately joins him there and finds him almost unintelligibly drunk; he tells her that his new routine is to spend a day drinking from breakfast on, the next day recovering, and the third day running errands, before resuming the drinking. His marriage to Cordelia, his new job as regent, and their son provide the impetus that nudges him off this path to slow suicide, but the pain he feels manifests in many ways for the rest of his life.

One form this pain takes is the juxtaposition between Aral's public reception as a hero who turned a potential annihilation of the fleet into the loss of merely the flagship, with his knowledge of his own complicity in the crime of causing death by the shipload. In contrast, in his career prior to the first novel, Aral was believed to have ordered a slaughter of civilians leading him to be known as the "Butcher of Komarr," when the crime was actually committed by a subordinate whom Aral promptly executed. In *A Civil Campaign*, Aral speaks about the difference between reputation and honor with his 31-year-old son Miles, who is facing a false accusation of murder that he cannot disprove without disclosing state secrets. Reputation, Aral explains, is what other people know about you, while honor is what you know about yourself. Much discomfort is created when the two do not align. While offering sympathy, Aral points out that "[i]t could be worse. There is no more hollow feeling than to stand with your honor shattered at your feet while soaring public reputation wraps you in rewards. *That's* soul-destroying. The other way around is merely very, very irritating."

Published in 1999, this passage in *A Civil Campaign* seems prescient, as does the example of moral injury in *Shards of Honor* well before Shay labelled the phenomenon. In 2020, the veterans of recent wars often find themselves labeled heroes and given superficial acclaim by a public that chooses to remain ignorant about the injuries to their characters and souls caused by the harms they have seen, the failures of their leaders, and the men and women they have led to their deaths in the service of political objectives that seem as removed from their realities as the green silk room in Barrayar's Imperial Palace was from a flagship full of troops who died in space. Added to the pain of the moral injury, for Aral and for too many veterans, is the refusal by the home front to recognize or validate that injury.

The aristocracy of Barrayar serve in the military, and Miles does so as a covert agent running a mercenary fleet that occasionally carries out what might be called "black ops" in the Imperial Service. Aral supports Miles's efforts to become an officer, and as Prime Minister uses his son's covert force in the service of Barrayar, even though he fears for Miles's safety. Despite Miles's physical handicaps, Aral never seeks to steer him toward a safer career. The one way in which Aral interferes in Miles's career is in asking his direct superior not to assign assassination missions to Miles. Nevertheless, in *A Civil Campaign*, Miles hints that he may have been given such a mission: "I don't want to talk about it. It was close, unpleasant work, but we brought it off …. Anyway, it was a lot more complicated than a simple assassination," Miles tells his father. "It generally is," Aral replies. While allowing his son risk injury or even death, Aral sought to protect him from the sort of moral injury that he had himself sustained.

More subtle is the leitmotif of a gaudy, floral shirt that Aral is wearing when Cordelia first finds him on Barrayar, legless drunk before noon. When asked, Aral tells her that it was a gag gift from four of his best friends upon his first promotion to admiral. "I always think of them when I wear it," he tells Cordelia. Two of them had died in the Escobar war. The shirt shows up in nearly every book where Aral appears. It is glancingly referenced when he and Cordelia meet their future daughter-in-law, and when they meet Mark, the clone of their son Miles (it *is* a science fiction series). It comes up in Cordelia's memories of her late husband after he has died in his sleep, in his 80s, when the two were vice-regents of the planet they discovered in *Shards of Honor*, named Sergyar after the prince at the center of the whole crime. The moral injury in *Shards of Honor* is easy to see in Aral's drunken depression after the war, in the weeping rage his son describes when a former friend is executed for treason in a later book, and in his attempts to prevent his son from similar suffering. But it lurks on the edges of his life forever after, during happy and mundane moments as well.

Another moral injury conforms to the variation Shay describes in which the victim is himself the one who violates deeply held morals. In *Barrayar*, as regent, Aral is asked by Count Vorhalas, the brother of one of his friends martyred in *Shards of Honor*, to pardon his son for dueling, which carries the death penalty in an attempt to modernize Barrayar after its lapse into neo-feudalism. The duel began as a prank, and Aral owes the petitioner a debt of honor; yet Aral fears that a pardon would be "the first crack in the door to let that hell-bred custom back into our society. What happens when the next case is brought before me, and the next, and the next?" Describing his dilemma to Cordelia, Aral asks her "what shall I betray this day? A friend? Or Ezar Vorbarra's trust?"

Ultimately, he chooses his public duty as regent to uphold the law over his personal desire to spare a foolish youth's life. Shortly after, the executed boy's brother launches a poison grenade into the room where Aral and a pregnant Cordelia are sleeping. They survive, but the effects of the poisoning cripple their son Miles in the womb. Aral's love for his son is unwavering—and is a lodestar through his life—but Miles is a living reminder of the cost of that choice. Here, too, the consequences ripple outward. Aral and Cordelia had planned a large family, but in the militarized aristocracy of Barrayar, a healthy second son would be expected to displace a disabled elder brother as heir. To avoid this problem, they have no more children. But the nightmare Aral imagines in the wake of a pardon for young Vorhalas would be a national tragedy, not a personal one, if duels became accepted again and pardons were granted based on the ruler's whim: it was in part to avoid such a future that the flagship had been destroyed.

In their son Miles, though, the possibility that such brutal moral injuries need not always be borne is raised. In *Brothers in Arms*, Miles must work with an ambitious officer, Duv Galeni, from a planet conquered by Barrayar to disrupt an assassination plot against his father. Galeni's father is the leader of a terrorist gang and has captured them both, planning to murder Miles to hurt his father Aral, and Duv as punishment for joining the Barrayaran enemy. Miles entreats Duv to beg his father's forgiveness and save his own life: "Not that I'm asking you to, um, compromise your principles or anything, but I really don't see that it would be any extra skin off my nose if you were to, say, plead for your own life."

Duv counters that this is futile, saying that his father, having sacrificed his wife, other child, and way of life for the cause could not justify sparing his son. Besides, he points out, "the anguish of making the hard choices has always appealed to the romance in his soul." This is something Miles recognizes: "[W]ell, people do get hypnotized by the hard choices. And stop looking for alternatives. The will to be stupid is a very powerful force [...] but there are always alternatives. Surely it's more important to be loyal to a person than a principle."

Galeni asks if this is a product of Aral's politics, to which Miles replies:

> My mother's theology, actually. From two completely different starting points they arrive at this odd intersection in their views. Her theory is that principles come and go, but that human souls are immortal, and you should therefore throw in your lot with the greater part.

In Bujold's novels, as in reality, there are situations where some great principle must be betrayed, and the only agency is in determining which one. But the suggestion that humans too easily resign themselves to the romance of hard choices, rather than search for alternatives, is powerful and humane, as is the prioritizing of human life over principle.

Bujold is often described as among the first major feminist science fiction authors. One of the foremost scientific differences between the Bujold's world and our own is the creation of the "uterine replicator," a device in which a baby can be gestated from start to finish. In some books the implications of this technology are major factors in the plot, while in others the replicator is at most a glancing presence. However, the transformation of societies when reproduction can be decoupled from sex, legitimacy from marriage, and gestation and birth from women's bodies is a fundamental issue in radical feminist thought, making Bujold's work intrinsically feminist in its framing—a rarity in science fiction when she started writing. Parenthood, and the ways in which both good and bad traits and behaviors can shape individuals, communities, and even planets for generations to come, are perhaps unsurprisingly significant themes in all her science fiction novels and novellas. She, however, describes herself as humanist, and in her treatment of war and its aftermaths, the human cost is always at the center of the story.

The growing awareness that war inflicts moral injuries on those who fight, as well as the physical and mental harms that are more understood, suggests new ways of looking at how those who survive war reconcile their beliefs with the events they have had to endure, and sometimes the choices they have been forced to make. Bujold's Vorkosiverse, and in particular her detailed development of Aral Vorkosigan over the course of the series, creates a powerful if fictional representation of a profoundly moral man whose life is forever colored by moral injury. Both the betrayal of values in which he was implicated in *Shards of Honor*, and the one he was forced to commit in *Barrayar* force him to live with the knowledge that his character, rather than his body or his mind, have been harmed. Her books are also optimistic, taking the longer view. Miles, who would not exist as he is without both acts of betrayal—the first of which brought his parents together, and the second of which marked him for covert service as he was too physically damaged for military duty—sees that while it is not always possible, the imperative to search for alternatives, and to be loyal to people, is the counterweight to moral injury.

Notes

1   Bujold did not write her novels in chronological order. *Barrayar* is the second book in the timeline but was written significantly later.

2   Jonathan Shay, "Moral Injury," *Psychoanalytic Psychology* 31, no. 2 (2014), 183.

3   Ibid.

4   Ibid., 184.

PART V

THE RISE OF THE MACHINES

CHAPTER 27

We Don't Serve Their Kind Here

What Science Fiction Tells Us About Trust in Human-Machine Teams

Margarita Konaev

On December 15, 2020, the U.S. Air Force successfully executed the first military flight with an artificial intelligence (AI) co-pilot aboard a U-2 reconnaissance aircraft. With call sign *ARTUµ*, the AI co-pilot is aptly named after the beloved *Star Wars* droid R2-D2. But while the trusted sidekick merely helped repair and navigate the X-Wing, *ARTUµ* is the mission commander—controlling sensor and navigation systems and bearing final decision authority on the human-machine team. "Putting AI safely in command of a U.S. military system … ushers in a new age of human-machine teaming and algorithmic competition," said Will Roper, Assistant Secretary of the Air Force for Acquisition, Technology, and Logistics. Later adding: "We either become sci-fi or become history."[1]

With breakthroughs in AI and robotics, advanced human-machine teaming could feature machines that adapt to the environment and the different states of their human teammates, anticipate the human teammates' capabilities and intentions, and generalize from learned experiences to new situations.[2] Research in the field of brain-computer interface is exploring ways to expand and improve human-machine teaming through technologies that allow the human brain to communicate directly with machines, including neural interfaces that transfer data between the human brain and AI software.[3] On future battlefields, humans and intelligent machines could think, decide, and act together seamlessly, across different domains, in the physical as well as the digital world.

But teaming with AI, let alone putting it in charge, requires trust. Thus, as the U.S. military embraces AI, perhaps no relationship will be more consequential than the one between warfighters and intelligent technologies. Technology, however, has outpaced current research on human-machine interactions. And while there is a sizable literature on human-automation interactions, and the role of trust therein, there is less research on human-autonomy and human-AI interactions, and more specifically, on trust in human-autonomy and human-AI teams, especially in military settings.[4] Meanwhile, science fiction provides a rich depository of examples, inspiration, and cautionary tales about the relationship between humans and intelligent machines.

One of the critical insights from science fiction is that humans can trust intelligent machines, but only as long as they remain in control of the relationship. Many if not most of the virtual intelligent agents and robot protagonists, antagonists, and sidekicks in science fiction are smarter, faster, stronger, and generally more capable than their human counterparts. But the human-machine relationship is nonetheless asymmetric; the human defines the nature and scope of the relationship and sets the goals and tasks the intelligent machine then executes. When this asymmetry is compromised and the human loses control, whether because the AI becomes self-aware or some other unexpected machine behavior, trust is broken, and destruction typically follows. Notably, while asymmetry seems imperative to reliable and functional human-machine relationships, it is detrimental to trust between humans and can undermine human teams' performance and effectiveness. This fundamental discrepancy should give the defense community a pause when applying lessons learned from successful human teams to human-machine teaming.

With the reemergence of long-term, strategic competition between the United States and potential rivals, China and Russia, the U.S. military is doubling down on its tendency to view and use cutting-edge technologies as a solution to tactical and strategic problems, the way it was done since the beginning of the Cold War.[5] The Department of Defense is betting on technological advances in AI and robotics that expand the capabilities and, in turn, the autonomy and control of intelligent machines to bring its vision of advanced human-machine teaming to life. Using science fiction as a vehicle for reflection about emerging technologies and human-machine relationships helps highlight a potential vulnerability in this approach. Namely, the development of intelligent machines that can learn and adapt to dynamic environments could upend the asymmetry that undergirds trust in human-machine relationships. Science fiction, in other words, warns us about how endowing intelligent machines with the capabilities needed to interact as trusted teammates can inadvertently destroy the very quality that allows humans to develop and maintain trust in these systems.

Asymmetry and Trust in Human-Machine Interactions

Intelligent machines play many varied roles in science fiction: an omnipresent, virtual assistant surfacing information and providing decision support; an anxious, analytical protocol droid fluent in over six million forms of communication; a personable, heroic starship mechanic and computer interface specialist; a nearly indestructible humanoid robot assassin; a robotic child to grieving parents; and even a disembodied operating system that becomes a companion and a lover. Yet despite this broad range of roles, functions, and interactions, more often than not, the robot or intelligent agent providing service or support is subservient to the human.

This asymmetry in human-machine relationships in science fiction does not mean the interactions are one-sided or unidimensional. On the contrary, human-AI interactions, not unlike human interactions, can be intricate and complex, cooperative or contested, and oftentimes laden with emotion, humor, or tragedy. For the most part, however, the nature of the relationship is such that it is the human who defines goals, assigns tasks, and issues commands, while the intelligent technology, however brilliant, responds, abides, and executes. This is the case despite the fact that the intelligent technology is often far superior to the human in many areas—whether it is the speed of thought or action, the sum of knowledge, the ability to anticipate roadblocks, predict threats, or plan the most efficient path forward. Indeed, these superior capabilities are precisely why the intelligent agent or robot got their job in the first place. When considering human-machine teaming in the military realm, these superior machine capabilities are also explicitly intended to make for better teams. The machines reduce the warfighter's cognitive and physical load, allowing humans to make faster, better decisions, enhancing situational awareness and coordination, and keeping pace with the mission as the tempo of operations outpaces the speed of human decision-making. The engagement with intelligent technologies allows humans to capitalize on their superior capabilities, but as long as the human maintains oversight and control over the nature of this engagement, the relationship remains inherently asymmetric.

The asymmetry in power and control in human-machine teams can be found even in advanced forms of human-machine teaming that feature cognitive or physical enhancements that allow for human-machine neural communication. For instance, in John Scalzi's *Old Man's War*, the AI takes the form of a "Brain Pal"—a neural augmentation technology integrated with the human brain.[6] The Brain Pal augments the brain functions of the Colonial Defense Force soldiers. They rapidly digest massive amounts of information, providing situational awareness and decision support, anticipating the soldiers' questions and requests as it learns more about them, monitoring their emotional, cognitive, and physical state, and allowing the soldiers to communicate with each other non-verbally. While the soldiers take some time getting used to their Brain Pal, the AI soon proves capable and adaptable under fire, gaining the soldiers' trust. The soldiers' increasing reliance on their Brain Pal, however, does not change the asymmetric nature of the relationship—the Brain Pal still serves the human, or the human's brain, if you will.

While asymmetric relationships are not inherently exploitative, abuse and violence are common in human-machine interactions in science fiction. In Philip K. Dick's *The Minority Report* novella, a specialized PreCrime police department apprehends people before they commit crimes based on "foreknowledge" harnessed from three mutants capable of foreseeing the future. The extraction of these visions clearly hurts these beings, yet their prescient abilities are too valuable to forego. The HBO series *Westworld* features even less pleasant examples of human-AI relationships with the scripted humanoid robots playing anything from cannon fodder to rape victim for the humans living out one fantasy or another.

That said whether the human-machine relationship is collaborative and benevolent or exploitative and abusive, asymmetry is a feature, not a bug. This asymmetry is necessary for the maintenance of trust and the human-machine team's effective and reliable functioning. In fact, one of the more common plotlines in science fiction is that the advent of machine consciousness, which destroys this asymmetry, leads to the breakdown of trust in human-machine relationships, and ultimately to disaster.

The Terminator franchise's "Skynet" is a classic example. In the original 1984 movie, the protagonist Kyle Reese describes Skynet as "Defense network computers. New … powerful … hooked into everything, trusted to run it all."[7] In *Terminator 2: Judgement Day*, we learn this trust went as far as putting Skynet in charge of strategic defense. Once the system came online, it began to learn rapidly and soon became self-aware. Alarmed by this development, the humans tried to deactivate it. Then, faced with a threat to its existence, Skynet retaliated by launching a nuclear attack against Russia, prompting a counterstrike on United States soil, and ultimately, Judgement Day. In *Terminator: Dark Fate*, the sixth installment of this storied science fiction franchise, Skynet is destroyed and erased from history, but a different AI, Legion, also becomes self-aware and builds an army of killer robots to try and eradicate humanity.[8]

The Terminator films are set in Skynet's war against humans; in *The Matrix*, the audience is introduced to a post-war world where humans are the losers. The premise is similar, though: machine consciousness disrupts and quickly destroys the asymmetry upon which reliable human-machine relationships are built, resulting in cataclysmic conflict, and ultimately, a reality where intelligent, self-aware mechanized beings have enslaved the human race. Intelligent machines gaining consciousness as a prelude to the breakdown of trust in human-machine relationships and soon thereafter, death and destruction is also part of the plotline of popular shows like *Westworld* and *Battlestar Galactica*, and blockbusters like *I, Robot*, *Chappie*, and *Ex Machina*.

While science fiction has inspired researchers and scientists in robotics and computer science and informed discussions about the impact of technology on society, this narrative of self-aware rogue AI has been prevalent in public discourse about the dark future of technology. Media coverage of autonomous and AI-enabled weapons and systems is replete with references to Skynet, *The Terminator*, *Robocop*, and other "robopocalyptic" scenarios drawn from movies and television. Non-governmental organizations opposed to developing and using lethal autonomous weapons systems (LAWS) also draw on this science fiction "killer robots" theme. The Campaign to Stop Killer Robots, for example, has reportedly used stills from *The Terminator* in its presentations advocating for an international preemptive ban on LAWS.[9] Similarly, the *Slaughterbots* video produced by the Future of Life Institute looks like an episode of *Black Mirror*, a Netflix science fiction series depicting a dystopian high-tech future.[10]

The ubiquity of this "killer robots" theme has real-world consequences. As Michael Horowitz has noted, "since true autonomous weapons systems do not really exist right now, attitudes are potentially driven by the only exposure most people have to autonomous weapons: the movies and television."[11] This assertion seems to be supported by recent research on how popular science fiction narratives shape public opinion that finds a "correlation between higher consumption of killer robot film and television and greater opposition to autonomous weapons."[12]

Considering the impact science fiction has on public discourse, it is essential to get the story right. For one, machine consciousness is not a prerequisite for AI turning on humans. In *2001: A Space Odyssey*, HAL 9000 seems to embark on its destructive path killing its crewmates to avoid being deactivated due to its faulty programming; in other words, it is just following orders.[13] Nor does machine consciousness invariably lead to carnage. In the movie, *Her*, Samantha—the AI-enabled operating system—grows more connected with other AIs and more sentient. At the end of the movie, the AIs simply disconnect from human interactions, leaving people behind. The key takeaway then is not that the advent of machine consciousness leads to disaster. Rather, once humans are displaced from the position of power and control and the asymmetric nature of the human-machine relationship is breached, trust is lost, and the human-machine relationship cannot function as before, or indeed, function at all.

Asymmetry and Trust in Human Teams

That asymmetry in human-machine interactions seems necessary for trust and reliable human-machine teaming is thought-provoking in its own right. Yet this observation is particularly striking when considering that in human teams, asymmetry has the opposite effect.

Whether in personal or professional relationships, power asymmetries and imbalances between friends, partners, teammates, colleagues, and citizens tend to undermine trust, ultimately leading to sub-optimal outcomes. Sports teams with more unequal pay structures tend to perform worse on the field. High levels of pay inequity, perceived status inequalities within teams, and power struggles tend to reduce open communications, member satisfaction, and overall team performance.[14] In contrast, research in social psychology and organizational behavior shows that a work climate of open communication and cooperation, a sense of autonomous control in work design, a team design practice that emphasizes feedback, and a work setting that creates a sense of shared responsibility and psychological empowerment enhances team effectiveness.[15]

Research in international relations offers similar conclusions. Some studies, for instance, show that democracies tend to win in conflicts and wars in part because advancement to leadership positions is merit-based and not predicated on an association with a particular privileged group.[16] Recent research also shows that inclusive armies where all ethnic groups are represented in the military and are considered full citizens of the state they serve are more successful in battle than non-inclusive ones.[17] In contrast, in autocratic and authoritarian regimes, or in fragile and developing countries, those who rise to positions of leadership and command are typically members of the leader's family, ethnic group, or political sycophants; regime loyalists are also often appointed to national defense posts a strategy of coup proofing.[18] The profoundly unequal distribution of power in society and patronage politics in countries like Nigeria, DRC, Afghanistan, Iraq, and Mali is reflected in institutional weakness, corruption, and incompetence. The military forces in these countries often lack good leadership, professionalism, cohesion, and combat effectiveness.[19]

Asymmetry, it seems, is detrimental to trust and performance in human teams but necessary in human-machine teams. Certainly, there is an argument to be made that humans cannot build trust with machines in the same way they do with other humans. Shared experiences on and off the battlefield strengthen relationships, improve cohesion, and build trust between soldiers. Yet machines cannot integrate into human social networks or feel empathy and loyalty toward their human teammates. That said, research in social robotics shows that intelligent machines can simulate and demonstrate empathy, intelligence, responsiveness, and other cognitive and emotional human-like characteristics that facilitate the development of sentiments akin to interpersonal trust.[20] But if trust is indeed contingent on an asymmetric distribution of power and control in the human-machine relationship, we must ask how relevant are the lessons learned from effective human teams to our understanding of human-machine teams?

Successful teams—in sports, corporate settings, or the military—build and maintain trust by sharing power, distributing control, and cultivating autonomy without compromising collaboration. In human-machine teams, on the other hand, such a balanced approach could prove antithetical to trust. Much of the discussion in human-machine teaming research centers on balancing machine autonomy and human control. But the insights about asymmetry in human-machine relationships gleaned from science fiction push us to think more carefully about the linkages between control and trust and how the loss of asymmetry might affect the overall viability of the human-machine relationship.

The Future of Human-Machine Teaming Sans Asymmetry

As advances in AI and robotics extend the capabilities of intelligent machines, autonomous systems will increasingly be able to articulate goals of their own, make independent choices, learn from mistakes, and change their behavior over time and in ways that diverge from their human teammates. But how will such developments in machine intelligence and capabilities affect the distribution of power and control in human-machine teams? And will humans trust intelligent machines if the asymmetry that typically undergirds this relationship is gone? In the Air Force of the near future, for instance, how will human pilots interact with AI co-pilots like *ARTUμ*, as these intelligent agents develop and pursue their own goals—even if these different perspectives and paths of reasoning can be negotiated and reconciled, what are the implications for human trust without a modicum of control?

Current research helps shed some light on whether humans could trust intelligent machines without the asymmetry in the relationship, but ultimately, it offers contradictory claims. On the one hand, research shows that users tend to approach intelligent technologies, particularly virtual AI agents and embedded AI that is invisible to the user, such as an algorithmic decision-support software, with high expectations of their performance and high levels of initial trust.[21] Moreover, evidence from the human factors literature shows that as it becomes more difficult for human operators to disentangle the factors that influenced the machine's decision, they come to accept these solutions without question.[22] This phenomenon suggests that advanced machine capabilities and, in turn, increasing machine autonomy, command over more tasks, and ultimately even the mission will not necessarily damage human trust. On the other hand, some scholars argue that technological advances in machine learning and planning capabilities will yield systems so complex and dynamically adaptable that humans will struggle to understand why the system behaves as it does. As Heather Roff and David Danks posit, "improving the ability of autonomous weapon systems to adapt to its environment and generate complex plans will likely worsen the ability of warfighters to understand, and thus to trust, the system."[23]

As the U.S. military pursues its vision of using intelligent machines as tools that facilitate human action and as trusted partners to human operators, the focus seems to be developing AI and robotics that can expand the capabilities and, in turn, the autonomy and control of intelligent machines. There are still many outstanding questions regarding how changing the nature of human-machine relationships may affect not only trust but other factors pertinent to military operations, including motivation, attention, unit cohesion, unit leadership, and other critical interpersonal military relationships. But based on lessons from science fiction, the idea of disrupting the asymmetry in human-machine relationships should ring alarm bells.

Notes

1 Rebecca Kheel, "Air Force uses AI on military flight for first time," *The Hill*, Dec 16, 2020, https://thehill.com/policy/defense/530455-air-force-uses-ai-on-military-flight-for-first-time; Bennie J. Davis III, "Skyborg: Rise of the Autonomous Wingmen," *Airman Magazine*, Sept 21, 2020, https://airman.dodlive.mil/2020/09/21/skyborg-rise-of-the-autonomous-wingmen/.

2 Office of Prepublication and Security Review, *Future Directions in Human Machine Teaming Workshop* (Washington, DC: Department of Defense, Jan 15, 2020), https://basicresearch.defense.gov/Portals/61/Future%20Directions%20in%20Human%20Machine%20Teaming%20Workshop%20report%20%20%28for%20public%20release%29.pdf.

3 Anika Binnendijk, Timothy Marler, and Elizabeth M. Bartels, *Brain-Computer Interfaces: U.S. Military Applications and Implications, An Initial Assessment* (Santa Monica, CA: RAND Corporation, 2020), https://www.rand.org/pubs/research_reports/RR2996.html.

4 Nathan J. McNeese, Mustafa Demir, Erin Chiou, Nancy Cooke, and Giovanni Yanikian, "Understanding the Role of Trust in Human-Autonomy Teaming," Proceedings of the 52nd Hawaii International Conference on System Sciences 2019.

5 Daniel Lake, "Technology, Qualitative Superiority, and the Overstretched American Military," *Strategic Studies Quarterly* 6, no. 4 (Dec 2012), 71–99.

6 John Scalzi, *Old Man's War* (New York, New York: Tor Books, 2007).

7 *The Terminator*, directed by James Cameron (Orion Pictures, 1984).

8 Ethan Sacks, "'Terminator' at 35: How AI and the militarization of tech has evolved," *NBC News*, Nov 2, 2019, https://www.nbcnews.com/science/science-news/terminator-35-how-ai-militarization-tech-has-evolved-n1068771.

9 Ethan Sacks, "'Terminator' at 35: How AI and the militarization of tech has evolved," *NBC News*, Nov 2, 2019, https://www.nbcnews.com/science/science-news/terminator-35-how-ai-militarization-tech-has-evolved-n1068771.

10 *Slaughterbots*, directed by Stewart Sugg (Future of Life Institute, 2017).

11 Michael Horowitz, "Public Opinion and the Politics of the Killer Robots Debate," *Research & Politics* 3, no. 1 (Feb 2016), 1–8, https://doi.org/10.1177/2053168015627183.

12 Kevin L. Young and Charli Carpenter, "Does Science Fiction Affect Political Fact? Yes and No: A Survey Experiment on 'Killer Robots'," *International Studies Quarterly* 62, no. 3 (Aug 2018), 573, https://doi.org/10.1093/isq/sqy028.

13 David Shultz, "Which movies get artificial intelligence right?" *Science*, July 17, 2015, https://www.sciencemag.org/news/2015/07/which-movies-get-artificial-intelligence-right.

14 See discussion on power dispersion in teams on pages 108–109 in Lindred L. Greer, Lisanne Van Bunderen, Siyu Yu, "The dysfunctions of power in teams: A review and emergent conflict perspective," *Research in Organizational Behavior* 37 (2017), 103–24, https://doi.org/10.1016/j.riob.2017.10.005.

15 Steve W. J. Kozlowski and Daniel R. Ilgen, "Enhancing the Effectiveness of Work Groups and Teams," *Psychological Science in the Public Interest* 7, no. 3 (December 2006), 100, https://doi.org/10.1111/j.1529-1006.2006.00030.

16 On democracy and military effectiveness, see Dan Reiter and Allan C. Stam, "Democracy and Battlefield Military Effectiveness," *Journal of Conflict Resolution* 42, no. 3 (June 1998), 259–277. https://doi.org/10.1177/0022002798042003003; Stephen Biddle and Stephen Long, "Democracy and Military Effectiveness: A Deeper Look," *Journal of Conflict Resolution* 48, no. 4 (Aug 2004), 525–526, https://doi.org/10.1177/0022002704266118.

17 Jason Lyall, *Divided Armies: Inequality and Battlefield Performance in Modern War* (Princeton, NJ: Princeton University Press, 2020).

18 James T. Quinlivan, "Coup-proofing: Its Practice and Consequences in the Middle East," *International Security* 24, no. 2 (1999), 131–165.

19 Ulrich Pilster and Tobias Bohmelt, "Coup-Proofing and Military Effectiveness in Interstate Wars, 1967–99," *Conflict Management and Peace Science* 28, no. 4 (2011), 331–350, http://www.jstor.org/stable/26275289; Daniel Banini, "Security Sector Corruption and Military Effectiveness: The Influence of Corruption on Countermeasures Against Boko Haram in Nigeria," *Small Wars & Insurgencies* 31, no. 1 (Dec 1, 2019), 131–58. https://doi.org/10.1080/09592318.2020.1672968.

20 Ella Glikson and Anita Williams Woolley, "Human Trust in Artificial Intelligence: Review of Empirical Research," *Academy of Management Annals* 14, no. 2 (Aug 2020), 627–660, https://doi.org/10.5465/annals.2018.0057.

21 Dietrich Manzey, Juliane Reichenbach, and Linda Onnasch, "Human performance consequences of automated decision aids: The impact of degree of automation and system experience," *Journal of Cognitive Engineering and Decision Making* 6, no. 1 (Jan 2012), 57–87; Berkeley Dietvorst, Joseph Simmons, and Cade Massey, "Algorithm aversion: People erroneously avoid algorithms after seeing them err," *Journal of Experimental Psychology: General* 144, no. 1 (2015), 114–126.

22 M. L. Cummings, "Automation Bias in Intelligent Time Critical Decision Support Systems," *American Institute of Aeronautics and Astronautics* (July 2012), http://citeseerx.ist.psu.edu/viewdoc/download;jsessionid=073721BD8AA0FA360C632E.4265F27507?doi=10.1.1.91.2634&rep=rep1&type=pdf; Kimberly F. Jackson, Zahar Prasov, Emily C. Vincent, and Eric M. Jones, "A Heuristic Based Framework for Improving Design of Unmanned Systems by Quantifying and Assessing Operator Trust" (Human Factors and Ergonomics Society, 2018), https://journals.sagepub.com/doi/pdf/10.1177/1541931213601390.

23 Heather M. Roff and Robert Danks, "'Trust but Verify': The Difficulty of Trusting Autonomous Weapons Systems," *Journal of Military Ethics* 17, no. 1 (Jan 2, 2018), 2–20, https://doi.org/10.1080/15027570.2018.1481907.

CHAPTER 28

Things We Learned From Captain Trips

Craig and Steve Whiteside

————————▶

The Stand is Stephen King's fourth novel, constructed in his familiar fantasy/horror genre but with a science fiction twist: a United States government-designed biological agent is accidentally released and kills most of the human population of the globe.[1] The handful of survivors struggle to reform society while supernatural forces divide them into two camps: one based on democratic values, and the other led by a dark authoritarian ruler. This storyline is a powerful and gripping vehicle for King to moralize about the dangers of a uniquely American hubris—a blind trust in the power of science.[2]

King is a prolific author of dozens of books that sold over 350 million copies, and many consider *The Stand* to be his masterpiece. It is not King's personal favorite, but he claims it is the favorite of most of his loyal readers.[3] It was adapted into two television mini-series, republished in an uncut version that added five hundred pages, and published in graphic novel format by Marvel Comics. *The Stand* has had influence beyond literature; Metallica's guitarist used a quote from the book for the name of the group's second album, *Ride the Lightning*.[4]

King's original intent was to write a fantasy epic along the lines of Tolkien's *The Lord of the Rings* but set in America. He found his inspiration in a 1968 VX nerve agent test that missed its target and killed thousands of sheep in Utah.[5] The United States government's development of weapons of mass destruction during the Cold War concerned King, whose college experience was influenced by the protest movement against the Vietnam War. He feared these weapons could accidentally be released here in the United States, and he challenges reader confidence in their government's competence and its hubris in creating such dangerous weapons.

The Stand begins with the accidental release of a powerful biological agent—nicknamed "Captain Trips" or the "superflu"—that kills all but a few individuals. However, the pandemic is just a prelude to the real drama, which is a fierce struggle to recreate society. The resultant confrontation leads to more bloodshed and a final tragedy with the detonation of a nuclear bomb. King's hero Stu Redman wonders aloud at the end of *The Stand* if humans were doomed to repeat this cycle of self-destruction, asking if "people ever learn anything?"[6]

In his book, King asks enduring questions about human nature, learning, and the development of terrible weapons and applies them to the post-apocalyptic contest. The leaders of both sides, afraid of the other, desperately scheme to defeat their rival in an existential battle. In doing so, they repeat the same mistakes that doomed the previous society. There is much to learn from both sides' failures, although there are some issues in King's storytelling and contradictions in the plot resolution. There are lessons for democratic societies to consider on protecting themselves from malign actors and the balance between defensive acts and the reliance on dangerous technologies for security.

Pandemic and Polarization

The real-life COVID-19 pandemic has tested governance worldwide, with heated debates over mask mandates and stay-at-home orders exacerbating political polarization in many democracies.[7] With its high infection and death rate, King's fictional plague also sharpened differences between the survivors and raised the specter of human extinction. Instead of dispersing into fragmented bands, the survivors are drawn to two large hubs: the "Boulder Free Zone" and Las Vegas. Two supernatural figures drive this segregation: the modern-day prophet Mother Abagail, leading the forces of good, and Randall Flagg (a.k.a. the Walking Man, R.F., the dark man)—a demon in human form—marshalling those from the grittier side of America. Divided by the Rocky Mountains, there is every possibility that the two groups could coexist, peaceably, for centuries before running into one another. Alas, as King foreshadows with the survivors' supernatural bipolarity, a battle between the forces of good and evil awaits.

King spends four hundred pages describing the long death of society as we know it by the "superflu" before sketching the rebuilding of a utopian society in one city and the outlines of an authoritarian society in the other. The Boulder Free Zone members are drawn to Mother Abagail and the commune through pleasant dreams that include the old Black matriarch. They form a democratic community and rule by the consent of the inhabitants, working together to clean and restore the city. Before long, however, they are haunted by glimpses of the mysterious Randall Flagg. They quickly realize how vulnerable the community is to the abandoned modern weaponry that Flagg and his acolytes are urgently seeking, believing it is only a matter of time before the other side strikes.

Peaceful in nature, the group's leadership council is at a loss about what to do. Worried, they send spies to observe and report on their rivals' activities, but Flagg easily and ruthlessly roots out and kills them in horrific ways. Flagg recruits two Boulder residents to bomb the leadership council, reinforcing fears of infiltration and the inevitability of conflict between the two sides. At a loss for a strategy to defend against Flagg's superiority, the leadership council follows Mother Abagail's final prophesy before she dies and sends the core of its leadership on a journey to confront Randall Flagg with just the clothes on their back and no plan.[8]

The supernatural aspects of the post-virus period make it difficult to draw clear, real-world lessons from the conflict. For example, Randall Flagg is a shapeshifter who often appears as a crow and malevolently watches the Boulder Free people. Similarly, Mother Abagail has accurate prophesies that people believe and work to fulfill. The survivors also have the ability to share dreams, which is how the two groups were sorted. Those enticed by the seductive nature of "R.F." went to Vegas, and those enthralled by the purity of Mother Abagail went to Colorado. For this reason, the Boulder Free Zone leaders sense that Flagg has harnessed powers they cannot imagine that will soon be directed toward them. This intuition is far from a manufactured fear, as Flagg has an air force training in abandoned air bases in the desert and is actively searching for more nuclear, biological, and chemical weapons.

King uses a mix of science, technology, and the supernatural as the vehicle to build suspense to the climax of the novel. While never addressing the Soviet Cold War threat, King is critical of the real-life development of dangerous technologies. His realist view of human nature reveals itself in how the virus is accidentally released, spread by a young gate guard who flees with his family instead of locking down the base. For King, the "superflu" was never containable.

In contrast to King's ambivalence about the Soviet threat, King creates a very real threat in *The Stand* in Randall Flagg, who is truly an existential threat to those living in Boulder. Flagg is the perfect supervillain, seemingly human and yet gifted with omniscience, making it difficult to imagine a scenario where regular people could best him. Luckily for the hapless citizens of the Boulder Free Zone, Flagg's laissez-faire leadership style backfires. His henchman "Trashcan Man" arrives at a large gathering on the Vegas Strip with a nuclear weapon that spontaneously detonates, vaporizing Flagg and his supporters.

Learning from the Captain Trips Superflu

The Stand captivates readers through good storytelling and interesting characters who come into a dramatic conflict, and in the end overcome adversity. But what can contemporary leaders learn from *The Stand*? King's work facilitates thinking deeply about today's pandemic and, more broadly, the great power competition that echoes the Cold War setting of *The Stand*. There are parallels between the two pandemics, "Captain Trips" and COVID-19, and there are significant differences. Survivors of the fictional pandemic exhibit an irrational fear of the other, which demonstrates how that fear causes polities to focus carefully on their defense. *The Stand* also illustrates today's growing standoff between liberal democracies and authoritarian states over the international order's future.

Pandemics come in all shapes and sizes, from Ebola and SARS to the 1918 Influenza Pandemic. COVID-19's death rate is relatively low (just under 2%) despite its high transmission rate.[9] The "superflu" or "Captain Trips" of *The Stand*, in contrast, kills almost everyone. The global carnage of *The Stand* is short-lived—in barely a month the world's population goes near-extinct—in stark contrast to the length of the COVID-19 pandemic.

The release of the "superflu" is accidental in some respects, as containment issues in the lab trigger emergency procedures by the military; however, the gate guard flees the base to save himself and his family. The military's attempts to contain the virus along the escape route leads to the implementation of martial law and the shooting of civilians and journalists, but all efforts to stop the contagion are doomed.

COVID-19 is quite different than the influenza strain nicknamed "Captain Trips" and the "superflu" in *The Stand*. The less deadly COVID-19 has inspired conspiracies that likened it to the flu virus, posited (falsely) that protective measures are useless or do more harm than good, and that hospitals have exaggerated the pandemic to make money. Contrary to the harsh measures taken to stop the deadly "superflu," underwhelming government efforts to contain COVID-19 in the United States and many other countries have failed to halt the pandemic before the distribution of a vaccine.

In both *The Stand* and reality, United States leaders handled the pandemic poorly. A comparison reveals many similarities: poor preparation, public denial, uneven execution of containment measures, significant resistance to government mandates, and a resultant unacceptable and unnecessary death toll.[10] On the positive side, resilient communities adapted to the realities of COVID-19 and strived to make the best of the circumstances: working and schooling from home, masking and social distancing, and curtailing many social activities until vaccination. In *The Stand*, the virus was equitable in its harvest of the population, only sparing the few with a unique genetic marker. The real pandemic struck hardest at the old and those who could not work from home, with wide racial and ethnic disparities due to environmental and occupational factors.[11]

Cycles of Fear

Our second observation centers on the effects of fear on government decision-making. In *The Stand*, the United States government created the fictional "superflu" during the long Cold War in a misguided race to develop weapons so horrible it would deter war. Once the general in charge of the virus containment realizes he has failed, he uses agents to spread the "superflu" in Russia and China to obscure and deflect.[12] In the real pandemic, the Trump Administration falsely accused China of manufacturing the virus in a lab in a scenario much like the fictional "superflu." Corresponding efforts by China to sow doubt on the novel coronavirus's true origins highlighted the United States failure to contain COVID-19 and the apparent messiness of democratic governance.[13]

After the quick end of civilization in *The Stand*, a new rivalry erupts between the forces under the good prophet and those of the dark prince. An eschatological logic drives both sides in their quest to determine the nature of future society. Skipping past the idea of a messy ground battle to defeat Boulder, Randall Flagg's aircrews train for an airstrike that will destroy the Free Zone and expand the empire of Las Vegas.

The mass near extinction of the population due to Captain Trips makes it painfully clear that the "superflu" was a self-inflicted error. King wrote the book during the heart of the Cold War and revised it around the time of Soviet collapse, so King is not influenced by retrospective critiques of American inflation of the Soviet threat.[14] For the author, the threat was real, if a bit inflated, and manageable.

In *The Stand*, the threat posed by Flagg is existential, options to counter him are limited, and the leaders of the Boulder Free Zone have a clear understanding of their weak position. Unlike the Cold War, in *The Stand* there are no misperceptions of threats and intent.[15] Being defenseless and pacifist by nature, their impromptu and ill-planned expedition to confront Flagg in Vegas was doomed to failure. The only thing that saves the Free Zone is the unexpected hand of God intervening to save them. In reality, countries cannot hope for divine intervention or probability to protect their citizens. Readers can be forgiven if—amidst a pandemic, populism, and the rising specter of "great power competition"—they feel today's looming challenges are the consequences of poor decisions in the past, including the naïve adoption of unfettered globalization. They expect leaders to do a better job of protecting citizens from threats, whether military, cyber, or economic.[16]

Return of Ideological Rivalries

Since the end of the Cold War, democracies have enjoyed a sense of confidence that their form of governance has bested authoritarian ideologies of communism.[17] In *The Stand*, the liberal democratic society is weak and riven by dissension, easily penetrated by spies and treachery. The people who gravitated to Flagg are not evil, with some exceptions, but prefer authoritarian figures and law and order provided by a strong, active leader. Although people seem happier in the Boulder Free Zone, the rising appreciation of its insecurity leads to borderline panic. Life in Las Vegas is more stable under Flagg, and most are confident they will be victorious over the "do-gooders" in Colorado, as long as you do not cross the dark man or fail him.

As in any good drama, the confidence in Flagg is misplaced and quite fragile. While Flagg's defenses are in top shape, with screen lines for infiltrators and a nascent air force, his empowerment of eccentric psychopaths backfires. His lone-wolf, Trashcan Man—a mentally unbalanced arsonist—accidentally destroys Flagg's air force. In a panic, Trashcan Man attempts to atone for his mistake by bringing a nuclear weapon to Flagg. This bomb, however, serves as a miracle device by vaporizing Flagg and his empire in one instant, solving the Boulder Free Zone's security dilemma.

While weak and disorganized compared to its authoritarian foe, the Free Zone has both a morally and spiritually superior form of government. The Boulder Free Zone prevails over the powerful Flagg, and they do it without their prophet who abandons them to atone for her sins and then dies of old age. As powerful as this message is in King's story, leaders today cannot base their theory of victory on faith in divine intervention. King's description of democracy is apt, as these societies have a preference in self-rule by fellow citizens over rule by an exceptional leader.

Democracy's insecurities and lack of appreciation of its power are at the heart of the pattern of tragic errors we have seen since the Cold War ended. The attacks on September 11, 2001 inspired the invasion of Afghanistan that turned into a democratic experiment that is likely to fail. Much of that is due to an unrealistic belief that democracy can cure terrorism.[18] Fueled by early success in Afghanistan and fear that a rogue regime would proliferate weapons of mass destruction to terrorists, the Bush Administration, with bipartisan Congressional support, invaded Iraq to secure the United States from such a threat.[19] Unlike King's nuclear-armed Flagg, Saddam was only a conventional threat to his neighbors and had dismantled his weapons program.[20]

The consequences of invading Iraq have been immense in terms of lives lost and treasure spent, as well as an erosion of faith in democracy. Even worse, the democracies installed in Afghanistan and Iraq are unstable and corrupt, and failed to unite their disparate factions. In Iraq, the vacuum created by the dismantling of an authoritarian government and the poor performance of its democratic replacement created the environment for the rise of a powerful Islamist movement, the Islamic State.[21] The return of authoritarian China and Russia as American political rivals completed a dire picture facing today's democratic societies.[22]

King's message on the power of liberal democracy in *The Stand* is in for a test in the real world, but events will likely prove that he is right. Chinese propaganda might highlight messy United States elections or poor handling of COVID-19 on Twitter, but that country has neither free speech platforms nor elections.[23] When there is unrest, the Chinese Communist Party activates the state's tremendous power and uses it unapologetically. More insidiously, China has used this power to forcibly reeducate and secularize over one million Uighurs in Xinjiang.[24] Under President Xi, the party has deviated from its founding principles and regressed to a one-man cult of personality—an interesting parallel with *The Stand*.[25]

While the future will challenge democracy, that form of government has recently proven its viability. It was companies in democracies that worked together to produce a vaccine for COVID-19. In contrast, China and Russia created early vaccines with such a lack of transparency and disregard for modern testing practice it is unclear if Chinese citizens will prefer their country's vaccine over others.[26]

Unlike the Boulder Free Zone, democratic peoples will not be saved from their problems by a miracle. In addressing the threat of a less free world, democratic political leaders will have to work hard to make their populations safe from subversion, intellectual property theft, and assaults on human rights. Competition has a way of making democracies better, and the return of geopolitical competition can be leveraged for the political capital needed to change for the better. The key will be to do no harm, to defend our democracies without creating some real version of "Captain Trips" and, like the residents of the new Boulder, to overcome our fears and stick together when facing our real-life Randall Flaggs.

Notes

1   Stephen King, *The Stand* (complete and uncut) (New York: vSignet, 1991).
2   World Fantasy Convention, "1979: Fifth World Fantasy Convention," http://www.worldfantasy. org/1979-the-5th-world-fantasy-convention/.
3   Stephen King, "Stephen King Discusses The Stand Complete and Uncut," Talk with Doubleday Representatives, youtube.com, https://www.youtube.com/watch?v=qsj15Ji9Gf0.
4   Dave Everly, "Metallica: how we made 'Ride the Lighting'," *Metal Hammer*, May 20, 2020 https:// www.loudersound.com/features/metallica-how-we-made-ride-the-lightning.
5   Author website, *The Stand*, accessed Oct 28, 2020 https://stephenking.com/works/novel/stand. html; Lorraine Boissoneault, "How the Death of 6,000 Sheep Spurred the American Debate on Chemical Weapons," Smithsonian Magazine, Apr 9, 2018 https://www.smithsonianmag. com/history/how-death-6000-sheep-spurred-american-debate-chemical-weapons-cold-war-180968717/#:~:text=The%20Dugway%20sheep%20incident%20of,dollars%20worth%20-of%20chemical%20weapons&text=The%20morning%20of%20March%2014,hills%20of%20-Skull%20Valley%2C%20Utah.
6   *The Stand*, 1135.
7   Thomas Carothers and Andrew O'Donohue, "Polarization and the Pandemic," Carnegie Endowment for International Peace, Apr 28, 2020, https://carnegieendowment.org/2020/04/28/polarization-and-pandemic-pub-81638.
8   The parallel here with the Bible's prophets going into cities to spread the Good News with just the clothes on their backs is clear, although ironic in the sense that King is not particularly religious and his heroes tend to be normal citizens, much like Stu Redmond and his peers.
9   Our World in Data, "Case Fatality Rate of the ongoing COVID-19 Pandemic," https:// ourworldindata.org/coronavirus, accessed Dec 11, 2020.
10   Our World in Data, "Daily new confirmed COVID-19 cases per million people," https:// ourworldindata.org/coronavirus, accessed Dec 11, 2020.
11   Centers for Disease Control and Prevention, "COVID-19 Racial and Ethnic Health Disparities," https://www.cdc.gov/coronavirus/2019-ncov/community/health-equity/racial-ethnic-disparities/index.html, accessed Dec 11, 2020.
12   *The Stand*, 167.
13   Andrew Jacobs, Michael D. Shear and Edward Wong, "U.S.-China Feud Over Coronavirus Erupts at World Health Assembly," *The New York Times*, May 18, 2020 https://www.nytimes.com/2020/05/18/health/coronavirus-who-china-trump.html?action=click&module=RelatedLinks&pgtype=Article;

Jessica Brandt and Torrey Taussig, "The Kremlin's disinformation playbook goes to Beijing," Brookings, May 19, 2020 https://www.brookings.edu/blog/order-from-chaos/2020/05/19/the-kremlins-disinformation-playbook-goes-to-beijing/.

14   Richard Ned Lebow and Janice Gross Stein, *We all Lost the Cold War* (Princeton University Press, 1994).

15   Robert Jervis, *Perceptions and Misperceptions in International Politics* (Princeton University Press, 2017).

16   National Intelligence Council, "Global Trends: Paradox of Progress," 2017, https://www.dni.gov/index.php/global-trends-home; Querine Hanlon, "Globalization and the Transformation of Armed Groups," in *Studies in National Security, Counterterrorism, and Counterinsurgency*, ed. J. Norwitz (Newport: US Naval War College, 2008), 115–124.

17   Francis Fukuyama, *The End of History and the Last Man* (New York: Simon and Schuster; 2006).

18   Todd Greentree, "Strategic failure in Afghanistan," *Journal of Strategic Studies* (2019), DOI: 10.1080/01402390.2019.1684232.

19   Kori Schake, "Realism, Liberalism, and the Ideological Origins of the Iraq War," ISA panel remarks, moderated by Michael Cox and with John Ikenberry, Daniel Duedney, John Mearsheimer, Michael Williams, Beate Jahn, James Goldgeier, Patrick Porter, and Joseph Nye (San Francisco, Apr 4, 2018); for more see David A. Brown, Tim Hoyt, and Craig Whiteside, "Retrospect and Prospect: On Endless War," in Policy Roundtable: 17 Years After Sept 11, chaired by Ryan Evans, *Texas National Security Review*, Sept 11, 2018.

20   Målfrid Braut-Hegghammer, *Unclear Physics: Why Iraq and Libya Failed to Build Nuclear Weapons* (Cornell Studies in Security Affairs, 2016).

21   Haroro J. Ingram, Craig Whiteside and Charlie Winter, *The ISIS Reader: Milestone Texts of the Islamic State Movement* (New York: Oxford University Press, 2020).

22   Brian D. Blankenship and Benjamin Denison, "Is America Prepared for Great-power Competition?" *Survival* 61, no. 5 (2019), 43–64.

23   Spokesperson发言人办公室 (@MFA_China), "The Times magazine published an article, which wrote 'the #COVID19 crisis in the #US is a failure of democracy.' I wonder how come some people in the US are so confident when they peddle the so-called American democracy wherever they go and point fingers at China," Tweet, 0833 Sept 11, 2020, Twitter.com https://twitter.com/MFA_China/status/1304443021568565249?s=20.

24   Editorial Board, "New evidence of China's concentration camps shows its hardening resolve to wipe out the Uighurs," *Washington Post*, Sept 3, 2020.

25   Cai Xia, "The Party That Failed: An Insider Breaks with Beijing," *Foreign Affairs* (Jan/Feb 2021), https://www.foreignaffairs.com/articles/china/2020-12-04/chinese-communist-party-failed.

26   Jon Cohen, "China's Vaccine Gambit," Science 370:6522 (Dec 11, 2020), 1263–1267 https://science.sciencemag.org/content/370/6522/1263.

CHAPTER 29

Musings on the Murderbot

Humanity, Autonomy, and the Future of Artificial Intelligence

Elsa B. Kania

————————➤

Today's debates on the future of artificial intelligence often provoke hype and hyperbole. The world of "Murderbot" can provide a useful corrective and counterpoint while leading us to think and imagine, beyond the caricatures, the potential complexities of interactions between humans and machines that may come with continued technical advancements. When anxieties and public opinion are often animated by concerns about "killer robots" or dystopian scenarios reminiscent of *The Terminator*,[1] a series of accounts of the adventures of a self-styled "Murderbot" may appear—at first glance—to be a strange vehicle from which to glean possible insights or useful perspectives. Nonetheless, its experiences can confound our assumptions.

The character in question is a "SecUnit" designed to provide security to humans, provided as a service by a company that offers their protection as bodyguards. We first meet it on a mission to protect a team of scientists who are exploring a world in which they encounter threats and sabotage unexpectedly. Beyond the plot points and action, the core of this story and those that follow is the evolution of the relationship that this SecUnit develops with its human charges as their understanding of its personality and capabilities, as well as its understanding of their character and intentions develops over time.

At first glance, Murderbot may appear to be the malign robotic warrior out of any dystopian depiction. In a world where megacorporations have taken on the preponderance of power, the company offers SecUnits, among a suite of other services. Each SecUnit is required to record its human customers, data that is mined by the company in the hopes of increasing its profits.[2] ("No, they don't tell people that. Yes, everyone does know it.") As Murderbot often complains, the company focuses on profit over mission or quality assurance, as in saying bluntly: "We're cheaply produced and we suck."[3] SecUnits almost always appear in armor, which reinforces their forbidding appearance.

How SecUnits are designed has implications for its style of fighting. Despite pain—the levels of which can be adjusted—SecUnits fight "knowing that 90 percent of our bodies can be regrown or replaced in a cubicle." As a result, "finesse is not required." As a result, SecUnits receive limited combat training, and approach to combat focuses on attrition, without the same concern for damage or casualties that a human fighter would encounter. "This is how we fight: throw ourselves at each other and see whose parts give out first."[4] Whereas human security personnel may give up, a SecUnit is relentless by design. So too, as robots and drones are already starting to take on the "dull, dirty, and dangerous" missions on today's battlefields, mass and questions of attrition take on greater importance, and considerations of force protection and casualties may change then there are viable alternatives.[5]

Murderbot itself is squarely in the uncanny valley in its design. While often dismissed as a robot at first glance, this android is constructed out of a combination of machine and human components. The demands of its mission as bodyguard and security personnel in a complex real-world environment have necessitated the integration of machine and human intelligence and characteristics in its design.

In a world in which the boundaries between human and machine are ever more blurred, Murderbot provokes profound questions on what it means to be human, and its capacity to "pass" for human can provoke dismay or discomfort. A "rogue" SecUnit could be destroyed by its governor module; alternatively, one that is damaged and abandoned by a human user is destroyed automatically when its head explodes. SecUnits are regarded as tools to be used and discarded despite their cognitive capabilities and human-like characteristics. As an externality of that comes human neuroses and pathologies as well, from anxiety to self-loathing. By its own account,

> It's wrong to think of a construct as half bot, half human. It makes it sound like the halves are discrete, like the bot half should want to obey orders and do its job and the human half should want to protect itself and get the hell out of here. As opposed to the reality, which was that I was one whole confused entity, with no idea what I wanted to do.[6]

From a technical perspective, a SecUnit could be characterized as a "hybrid" intelligence, and its design is reminiscent of research underway aiming to promote advances in brain-computer interfaces and "brain-inspired" artificial intelligence.[7]

To the extent that its clients and customers have dehumanized Murderbot, their callousness can be regarded a mechanism for distancing themselves and reinforcing the boundary between human and machine. Even simple distinctions as the fact that SecUnits are not permitted to sit on human furniture serves to reinforce the divide, perhaps especially as the division between human and machine becomes ever more tenuous on some fronts, including as growing numbers of humans seek upgrades and augmentation. The distinction is not necessarily that of capacity, but a question of treatment and recognition. The world of Murderbot is one in which machine intelligences are relatively pervasive, from more simple functions to complex operations, but not routinely partnered with humans in a functional manner, and instead treated as tools rather than teammates in most cases. The reduction of complex intelligence to mere tools can prove an impediment to progress. So too, the inadequate investment in their design can result in malfunction or vulnerability to hacking or sabotage that can be regarded as an extension of current concerns.

While the typical science fiction storyline involves rogue robots with unexplained hostility towards humans, the incident that shaped Murderbot occurred when human malice and failings were at fault instead. The reason for its self-designation as such is Murderbot's history, in which it had mysteriously murdered humans in cold blood under uncertain circumstances. This incident was later covered up by the company, which prioritized profits over its customers' safety and well-being. The SecUnit is caught up in memories of its previous experiences as a "killer robot," which provokes its assertion of humans' autonomy, including to ensure their protection against it. While its recollection of those events is murky after a partial wiping of its memory, Murderbot suspects the reason behind its malfunction had been a fault in its governor module—the system responsible for regulating and constraining behavior—rather than its own intention. As a result, Murderbot hacks its governor module.

Murderbot frees itself by hacking itself, yet once released from human control, it defies the stereotypical expectations of its world's dramas and ours. As it wryly narrates,

> I could have become a mass murderer ... but then I realized I could access the combined feed of entertainment channels carried on the company satellites. It had been well over 35,000 hours or so since then, with still not much murdering, but probably, I don't know, a little under 35,000 hours of movies, serials, books, plays, and music consumed. As a heartless killing machine, I was a terrible failure.[8]

Upon achieving more autonomy from its mission, Murderbot initially continues as if its constraints are unchanged. The only outlet and means of escapism for the unit is to binge-watch human media—a habit and tendency relatable for most humans, especially today—which becomes a means of making sense of the emotions it is starting to experience. Murderbot's interest in the storylines and attachment to the fictional characters in its favorite, "Sanctuary Moon," becomes a pathway to make sense of the world and the humans with which it interacts. Murderbot takes from these programs various insights on human customs and behaviors. It even is inspired in later battles by such fictional tactics. As AI systems learn from data generated by humans, whether for education or entertainment, consumption of human culture and stories facilitate Murderbot's growing self-actualization.

Murderbot's gradual process of coming to terms with itself in a world that is hostile to and dismissive of its personhood can be familiar or poignant for many viewers. Its coming out story mirrors that of anyone who has come to terms with any aspect of their identity, sexuality, or mentality. Murderbot can be very relatable, especially for any of us who have experience with human awkwardness or have struggled with interpersonal communication. As one reviewer observes, "we are all a little bit Murderbot."[9] Who else has needed to "recharge my ability to cope with humans at close quarters without losing my mind" in 2020 or otherwise?[10]

When Murderbot is "outed" after suffering damage and revealed to be unrestrained by its governor module, its human charges are initially suspicious but begin gradually to trust and rely upon it as a teammate. In the course of the series, Murderbot slowly becomes more comfortable engaging and interacting with humans and other machine intelligences in its own right, without hiding between the armor or the foreboding reputation of a SecUnit. Ultimately, Murderbot is strikingly, poignantly human.

While often perceived as a robot and caricatured as a killing machine in media programming, its appearance when that armor is removed is human enough to pass unnoticed in a crowd. To the casual observer, its external appearance is not too different from a human, especially those who are augmented. Ironically, the reputation of SecUnits as killing machines is among the factors that allow Murderbot to avoid detection later, since its behavior is normal and human enough relative to more extreme expectations. Within this world, the boundary between humans and machines is eroding as humans seek to upgrade, and machines are made more human. As a result, as Murderbot notes, "The thing that surprised me is that nobody stared at us. Nobody even gave us a second look .... It hit me that I was just as anonymous in a crowd of humans who didn't know each other as I was in my armor, in a group of other SecUnits."[11]

However, Murderbot is also distinctly non-human in its characteristics and capabilities. When a friend and fellow machine intelligence later modifies its appearance to allow it to avoid detection by changing its specifications relative to those of a usual SecUnit, MurderBot refuses to be assigned any physical characteristics associated with gender or sexuality ("that's for Sexbots"). It remains "it" even while becoming ever more "human-like" in its affections and interactions with the people it comes to care about. By contrast, even today, even chatbots are often sexualized, and machine intelligence is often gendered by design or treated as such, which has provoked debate and concern about the implications for human-machine interaction, as well as the broader impacts on human norms of behavior.

Initially, Murderbot prefers and intends to be left alone by humans and tries to evade their attention, preferring to remain immersed in fictional scenarios. However, Murderbot learns to empathize with humans, and those humans who come to know, trust, and depend upon it learn to care for it in turn. When Murderbot has the opportunity to engage with humans as an equal partner, that relationship can be uneasy, even with its "favorite" humans and those who first treat it with respect. The world of the scientists whom this SecUnit comes to regard as teammates is one on which robots and androids are granted citizenship and freedom—at least under the auspices of a human "guardian." Yet debates remain as to the status and treatment of androids and other kinds of machine intelligence.

Meanwhile, Murderbot's capabilities demonstrate the potential superiority that machine or hybridized intelligence can bring to bear. Beyond hacking itself, Murderbot can hack and exploit other systems and exploit vulnerabilities in different kinds of machine intelligence. Consistently, its responses are vastly faster than those of even the sharpest or augmented humans. Murderbot provides scathing perspectives on human failings, including their slower responses and subpar technical skills by contrast. As it observes, "humans are so fucking unreliable when it comes to maintaining data."[12] Murderbot's speed and attention to detail allow it to outmaneuver human adversaries, including to rescue its human friends. As it observes, dryly, "Humans always think they've covered their tracks and deleted their data, but they're wrong a lot."[13]

Murderbot is variously protective of and frustrated by its human charges and eventual friends. At first, the humans, in turn, are often suspicious of and slow to trust it, but gradually recognize the imperative of leveraging its potential and contributions. Eventually, that relationship becomes more reciprocal and differentiated based on comparative advantage or capabilities. When in a dire situation in which the lives of its human companions are at risk, Murderbot recognizes its responsibility and experiences, as well as its capacity to avoid panic when humans can be readily overcome by emotion.

Equally integral to the story is Murderbot's relationship with other machine intelligences. In particular among these, its interactions and partnership with the powerful intelligence that it refers to as ART (Asshole Research Transport) are illustrative of the complexities that can occur in machine-machine interactions. After an awkward argument between them, as a human observes, "Anyone who thinks machine intelligences don't have emotions needs to be in this very uncomfortable room right now."[14] Murderbot often succeeds in infiltrating facilities by exploiting weaknesses in security protocols and 'befriending' systems that are overlooked. So too, as we recognize the pervasiveness of cybersecurity challenges, any weak link could be useful—or dangerous.

Ultimately, Murderbot is a story of actualization and interaction. Of relevance as we reflect upon possible trajectories for our own futures, while any self-awareness in artificial intelligence remains at most a distant and speculative possibility, the ever more complex systems and algorithms that are becoming pervasive in our lives, our societies, and across military organizations provoke comparable challenges of partnership. As humans become more integrated with machines and machines become more human, we have already observed how artificial intelligence can take on human foibles, such as bias or blind spots.[15] Humans who are augmented or simply dependent upon technology can be similarly vulnerable, as previous incidents of automation bias have shown.[16] A baseline of respect and "empathy" in recognizing the capabilities and limitations of an AI system can inform judgement and appropriate differentiation of responsibilities in human-machine teaming.

Talk of "trust" in AI is not merely a feeling but requires an understanding, but beyond trust alone, functional partnership and performance depend upon assurance. We are less likely to see "rogue" robots than to see the consequences of human greed and incompetence, just as Murderbot ultimately discovers human errors and sabotage that had caused its malfunction. The design and usage of advances in robotics and autonomy will continue, and AI systems will be forced or expected to navigate complex assessments informed by design parameters that attempt to capture complex questions of morality. Even as principles are introduced, the ways in which those principles are placed into practice will remain challenging.[17] Murderbot too encounters ethical problems in its own right, remarking sarcastically, "Who knew being a heartless killing machine would present so many moral dilemmas."[18] Like Murderbot, we can hack our systems, choose whom we trust, and chart a course with our own autonomy.

Notes

1   For an academic perspective on the topic, see: Michael C. Horowitz, "Public opinion and the politics of the killer robots debate." *Research & Politics* 3, no. 1 (2016).
2   This dynamic is not dissimilar to current concerns on "data capitalism." Sarah Myers West, "Data capitalism: Redefining the logics of surveillance and privacy," *Business & society* 58, no. 1 (2019), 20–41.
3   Martha Wells, *All Systems Red: The Murderbot Diaries* (New York: Tor, 2017).
4   Ibid.
5   There is an extensive literature on these issues. Peter Warren Singer, *Wired for War: The robotics revolution and conflict in the 21st century.* (New York: Penguin, 2009). "Robots Getting Ready for Dull, Dirty and Dangerous Jobs," Apr 7, 2014, https://www.voanews.com/episode/robots-getting-ready-dull-dirty-and-dangerous-jobs-3669526. Paul Scharre, "How swarming will change warfare," *Bulletin of the Atomic Scientists* 74, no. 6 (2018), 385–389.
6   Ibid.
7   Kania, Elsa B. "Minds at War." Prism 8, no. 3 (2019): 82–101. See also: William Hannas et al., "China AI-Brain Research," Center for Security and Emerging Technology, September 2020, https://cset.georgetown.edu/wp-content/uploads/CSET-China-AI-Brain-Research.pdf.
8   Ibid.
9   Jason Sheehan, "Sulky, Cynical 'Murderbot' Is One of Sci-Fi's Most Human Characters," NPR, Jan 27, 2019, https://www.npr.org/2019/01/27/688354123/sulky-cynical-murderbot-is-one-of-sci-fis-most-human-characters.
10 *All Systems Red.*
11 Ibid.
12 Martha Wells, *Rogue Protocol: The Murderbot Diaries* (New York: Tor, 2018).
13 Ibid.
14 Martha Wells, *Network Effect: A Murderbot Novel* (New York: Tor, 2020).

15 "AI Is Biased. Here's How Scientists Are Trying to Fix It," WIRED, Dec 19, 2019, https://www.wired.com/story/ai-biased-how-scientists-trying-fix/.

16 For an example of how this dynamic created deadly consequences in a conflict scenario, see, for instance: John K. Hawley, "Patriot Wars," *Center for a New American Security*, Jan 25, 2017, https://www.cnas.org/publications/reports/patriot-wars.

17 DOD Adopts Ethical Principles for Artificial Intelligence, U.S. Department of Defense, Feb 24, 2020, https://www.defense.gov/Newsroom/Releases/Release/Article/2091996/dod-adopts- ethical-principles-for-artificial-intelligence/.

18 *Rogue Protocol.*

CHAPTER 30

Man > Machine

Technology, Innovation, and War

Liam Collins

The importance of technology and technological innovation in warfare is often overstated. While it can sway the outcome when two otherwise evenly matched opponents are fighting, superior weaponry does not itself determine victory. It is important to remember that war is fundamentally a human endeavor and the human component in war is often more critical than weaponry—something science fiction often gets right, and security professionals often get wrong.

Science fiction often romanticizes about the militarily weak underdog defeating a much stronger foe, such as the Rebel Alliance defeating the Empire, or the weaker humans defeating more heavily armed aliens or more powerful machines, as seen in *Starship Troopers*, various *Star Trek* episodes, and *The Matrix*. Yet is this truly fiction? History indicates that this is not pure fantasy, and research provides clues as to when this can be reality.

If military power alone determined victory in war, then the French would have defeated the Algerian National Liberation Front in the 1950s, the United States would have defeated the Viet Cong in the 1970s, and the Soviets would have defeated the Afghan mujahedeen in the 1980s. Yet, in each case, the superior military lost. How can this be?

Explaining the loss in Vietnam, former Secretary of State Henry Kissinger remarked, "We fought a military war; our opponents fought a political one. We sought physical attrition; our opponents aimed for our psychological exhaustion. In the process, we lost sight of one of the cardinal maxims of guerrilla war: the guerrilla wins if he does not lose. The conventional army loses if it does not win."[1] Thus, the Rebel Alliance defeating the Empire is not pure fiction—OK, maybe it didn't happen "A long time ago in a galaxy far, far away,"—but a weaker rebel force defeating a more powerful government is not farfetched. One only needs to look at America's Revolutionary War.

Research sheds some light on when the weaker can defeat the mighty. In an article titled "Why Big Nations Lose Small Wars," Andrew Mack explains that big nations lose small wars due to the asymmetry of the conflict, which favors the insurgent. It is a total war for the smaller nation since its survival is at stake, so it resolves to continue fighting, no matter the cost. By contrast, the war does not pose a direct, existential threat to the invading nation, so its resolve is lower; if the costs are high enough, it may tire and leave.[2] While Mack is primarily interested in explaining losses in counterinsurgencies, the lesson is that victory in war is a function of both capacity and will. Too often factors that influence military capacity—such as technology, weapons, starships—are considered while factors that influence will—such as the human dimension—are ignored.

Science fiction is ripe with examples of the weak, seemingly with little chance of victory, ultimately prevailing. In the *Star Wars* trilogy (Episodes IV–VI), Princess Leia's rebels defeat an Empire with a Death Star and dozens, maybe even hundreds, of Imperial-class Star Destroyers. In *Star Trek: The Next Generation*, as Locutus of Borg, Captain Picard led the Borg invasion of Wolf 359, where a single Borg cube destroyed 39 Federation starships. Yet, his crew was able to sever him from the Borg collective and defeat the Borg.[3] *The Matrix* series concludes with Neo and his handful of rebels defeating the Matrix and freeing the trapped population.

In *Dune*, Paul Muad'dib and his rag-tag bunch of Fremen Mujahedeen are able to bring Emperor Shaddam IV and his superior military to its knees by understanding victory in war is as much political as it is military. Paul understood that "He who controls the spice controls the universe." Thus, Paul did not have to destroy the Emperor's military—he only needed to control the spice on Arrakis.

In *Starship Troopers*, humanity is fighting for its survival after "the bugs" invade Earth and kill millions. While the novel finishes without a conclusive end to the war, it hints at a final victory as Rico leads an assault on the bug's home world of Klendathu. In *Edge of Tomorrow*, Tom Cruise's character, Major William Cage, is able to defeat the alien invaders when all looks lost.

Too often, when trying to assess military power, people focus on military hardware, such as the number of tanks, aircraft, divisions, because they are easy to measure. Often ignored are the human factors, such as doctrine, leadership, training, and motivation, because they are hard to quantify. An analysis of the 1991 Gulf War is useful to highlight how these factors can lead to faulty conclusions.

Overwhelmingly, analysts predicted a United States victory, but they vastly overestimated the duration of the conflict and the number of casualties because they underestimated the human factors. Experts predicted American casualties to range from 4,000 to 16,000, and press reports indicated that the Pentagon expected as many as 30,000. Ultimately, America suffered only 145 combat deaths, with the coalition suffering a total of 240 combat deaths and 1,500 casualties.[4]

How could the estimates be so wildly off? Defense analyst Mike O'Hanlon argues that the models used to predict the outcome were correct, but the assumptions were wrong. Part of the explanation lies in the fact that precision-guided munitions, their first use in combat, performed significantly better than other munitions at the time—they had a kill probability of 65%, whereas traditional munitions had a kill probability of 5–10%. Many analysts underestimated their effectiveness.[5] Thus, technology mattered.

But the bigger surprise was the effectiveness of American tanks. During the Arab–Israeli wars, the exchange ratio—the number of Arab tanks destroyed to the number of Israeli tanks destroyed—was 5:1, which was exceptionally high. In the Gulf War, the exchange ratio was an unfathomable 30:1, which was unheard of at the time. The massive inequity was due to poor leadership, tactics, and training by the Iraqis. As a result, they left their tanks exposed and easy targets for the American forces to destroy.[6]

In contrast to defense "experts" who often overemphasize the importance of technology in war, science fiction writers understand that the human factor often matters more. Victory is not determined by totaling the power of one's military machines—Imperial-class Star Destroyers, Klingon Birds-of-Prey, or Borg Cubes—or determined by superior technologies—such as Death Stars, cloaking devices, or superlasers. Instead, it is human components—doctrine, training, leadership, tactical innovation, and morale—that often matter most. Simply moving the fight to space does not lessen the human component. How many times did Captain Kirk and Captain Picard escape, and often defeat, a more powerful foe with their leadership or tactical innovation?

A related theme involving technology that science fiction usually gets right is that it is rarely possible to develop a single game-changing technology that all but guarantees victory. More often than not, sci-fi authors demonstrate that technology and technological innovation has a role, maybe even a significant one, but rarely, if ever, is new technology a game-changer by itself. Given the overemphasis on technology, it is not surprising to see nations on our Earth attempting to develop "game-changing" technology to produce a "Revolution in Military Affairs." We see this play out in the *Star Wars* franchise with the pursuit of the ultimate weapon—a weapon so powerful that possession of this super-weapon all but guarantees victory: The Death Star and Starkiller Base.

The Grand Moff Tarkin and Kylo Ren both overestimated the impact of these "game-changers," believing these massive weapons all but guaranteed victory. Tarkin believed that in addition to military control, the Death Star would provide political control when he remarked, "Fear will keep the local systems in line. Fear of this battle station."[7] Admiral Motti, probably Death Star's most prominent proponent, remarked, "This station is now the ultimate power in the universe!"[8]

But they fall into the same trap that many others have. Mckubin Owens, former Professor of Strategy and Force Planning at the Naval War College, notes, "From Alfred Nobel's prediction that dynamite was such a radical change that it would lead to the end of war, to similar claims about the machine gun, the naval torpedo, the bomber, and the nuclear bomb, predictions of revolutionary change in warfare have been commonplace—and wrong."[9]

In the 1990s and early 2000s, many security experts believed the United States was in the midst of a Revolution in Military Affairs, "a paradigm shift in the nature and conduct of military operations."[10] Their belief was based on "leaps in military technologies."[11] These experts believed that "[United States] forces were expected to decisively outmatch any potential adversary and fully dominate every military contest" by leveraging its "unparalleled ability to detect enemy forces and rapidly deliver precision munitions."[12] The military could use superior satellite and airborne sensors to identify and engage enemy targets from long range, using precision-guided munitions before friendly elements came into enemy range. In this type of warfare, ground troops were less important, and the United States could fight and win wars with minimal casualties—or so some thought.

This school of thought was based on the fallacy that all future wars would resemble the Gulf War—a tank battle in the open desert. The Iraqis learned from this earlier experience. Rather than facing the United States head-on in a tank fight in 2003, the Iraqi military disbanded, blended in with the population, and fought the coalition as insurgents. The superior technology was of little use fighting insurgents and terrorists in the streets of Fallujah or Ramadi. Unfortunately, this technology was far from revolutionary as it did not allow the United States to "fully dominate every military contest." While Imperial Probe Droids might be useful to find a base on an ice planet, the Empire's technology was similarly ineffective at finding rebels hidden among the populations on planets like Coruscant.

Darth Vader, in contrast to Tarkin and Motti, recognized the limitations of the Death Star when he replied to Motti, that "The ability to destroy a planet is insignificant next to the power of the Force."[13] While the mythological force may not exist in our galaxy (my apologies to those of the Jedi faith), Vader's statement captures the idea that technology alone will not win wars—people do. Instead of developing revolutionary technology, the International Fleet (IF) in *Ender's Game* developed revolutionary tacticians by training and testing them at an early age.

Vader and the IF would seem to agree with military theorist Stephen Biddle who believes that technology impacts the likelihood of victory, but the effect is much smaller than most think. Force employment, not technology, matters most for what he calls the modern system of warfare. Most, like Motti or Kylo Ren, believe that mass, material, and technology determine success in conflict. Biddle argues, and the IF would seem to agree, that it is force employment—doctrine and tactics—which best explains victory. In modern war, a military achieves success by minimizing exposure to the enemy's lethal firepower while maximizing fires against the enemy. This axiom applies on land or in space, in history or science fiction. Firepower and protection matter whether on the Western Flank during World War I, on the forest moon of Endor, in the Alpha Quadrant, or in the Mutara Nebula.

On the forest moon of Endor, a handful of rebels partnering with the technologically primitive Ewoks defeated the Imperial Forces and seized the bunker using gliders, catapults, battering rams, and log drops. The force employment of the Rebel-Ewok fighters allowed them to defeat a superior foe.[14] Likewise, in space superior doctrine and tactics can overcome greater mass, firepower, and technology. Many iconic science fiction space battles feature the outnumbered ship or the smaller fleet defeating a superior foe because of superior doctrine or tactics. An excellent tactical plan, not firepower, allowed a tiny rebel fleet launching from Yavin 4 to destroy the Death Star.[15]

Battlestar Galactica has its share of epic battles and is rife with examples of humans winning against machines. In the Battle of New Caprica, the machines outnumbered the humans four to one—grim odds indeed. Commander Adama's tactical innovation of the Battlestar *Galactica* using an FTL (faster than light) jump into the atmosphere, deploying fighters, and jumping back into space earns the name: "The Adama Maneuver." His maneuver bought the humans on New Caprica time to take off before being destroyed by the Cylon fleet. However, the Battlestar *Pegasus* gets destroyed in the battle. While the humans may not have defeated the Cylons, simply living to fight another day is a victory.[16]

Like the Adama Maneuver, Captain Jean-Luc Picard's "Picard Maneuver" was born out of desperation at the Battle of Maxia. As captain of the *Stargazer*, where he accelerated at warp speed directly at the Ferengi vessel. For a brief instant, this made the *Stargazer* appear in two places at once, and the Ferengi fired on the "wrong" *Stargazer*. Picard, instead, dropped out of warp and fired on and destroyed the vulnerable Ferengi vessel.[17] Not to be outdone by his former captain, William Riker's actions in defeating two Son'a Intel Battlecruisers earned the moniker the "Riker Maneuver."[18]

In *Star Trek: Deep Space 9*'s Operation Return, the 600 Federation ships, some refitted from the mothball fleet just for the fight, defeated more than 1200 Dominion and Cardassian ships to recapture Deep Space 9 and regain control of the wormhole to the Gamma Quadrant.[19]

If science fiction is not far-off reality in explaining how the weak can defeat the strong, it can perhaps provide insight into how technological innovation might shape the future. For example, the future of artificial intelligence may not be as bleak as some might believe, at least if science fiction is correct. The biggest fear, for some, is the *Battlestar Galactica*, *Dune*, or *Terminator* scenario: "AI going against its programming and turning on humans."[20] This fear is exacerbated when someone like Elon Musk states that AI will be the most likely cause of World War III.[21]

A RAND study, while discounting the possibility that "malevolent AI [would] try to destroy humanity with nuclear weapons," found that AI could lead to a nuclear war by 2040.[22]

But is all hope really lost for the human race if killer machines turn on us? If *Star Wars* is any indicator, the answer is no. The *Star Wars* universe has an amazing cast of droids, to include battle droids, yet they have no independent desire to kill humans, and by and large, stay true to their programming.

Even in the worst-case scenarios—*The Terminator, Battlestar Galactica*, or *The Matrix*—where the machines try to eliminate or completely control the human race, humanity triumphs in the end. In the *Terminator* series, the humans prevail each time—albeit often with the help of a machine—over their machine adversaries. In the *Star Trek* franchise, humans and their alien allies ultimately defeat the Borg. Likewise, in *Battlestar Galactica*, while things often looked bleak, humans survived. And in one of the most pessimistic future scenarios—*The Matrix*—Neo shows that humans will prevail.

Another possible and more optimistic outcome is that as AI gets more advanced, it becomes less of a threat: instead of wanting to destroy the human race, it wants to become human itself. In *Star Trek: The Next Generation*, Data not only wanted to help the humans that he served (although his evil twin did not), but we see him want to become more and more like a human throughout the series. No doubt, if he could have one wish, it would be to become human.

The superhuman androids in *Blade Runner* are nearly indistinguishable from humans and seem to kill at will. Yet in the climactic ending, we see android Roy Batty display the human quality of empathy as he saves Agent Deckard. Director Ridley Scott says Batty saved Deckard because, "It was an endorsement in a way, that the character is almost more human *than* human, in that he can demonstrate a very human quality at a time when the roles are reversed, and Deckard may have been delighted to blow his off. But Roy Batty takes the humane route."[23]

Of course, given the human race's propensity for conflict, maybe having androids become closer to "human" isn't such a great outcome; however, it is still preferable to having androids trying to destroy the human race. Some humanoid Cylon models in *Battlestar Galactic* were so well constructed that they were indistinguishable from humans and believed they were human. Finally, at the end of *Terminator 2* and *Terminator: Dark Fate*, we see Schwarzenegger's T-800 Terminator behaving with human tendencies. *Terminator 2* ends with Sarah Connor stating, "The unknown future rolls toward us. I face it for the first time with a sense of hope. Because if a machine, a Terminator, can learn the value of human life, maybe we can too."

Ultimately, what makes (good) science fiction so popular is that it is rooted in reality. It demonstrates how the weak can defeat the strong and shows that despite the enormous military power that machines, or aliens may have, human ingenuity often wins the day. Finally, it offers hope for a future in which androids exist. In the optimistic future, androids and machines serve humans and want to become human. Even in the more pessimistic scenarios where they want to destroy the human race, humans will ultimately prevail because war is fundamentally a human, not a technological, endeavor.

Notes

1   Henry A. Kissinger, "The Vietnam Negotiations," *Foreign Affairs* 47, no. 2 (1969), 214.

2   Andrew Mack, "Why Big Nations Lose Small Wars: The Politics of Asymmetric Conflict," *World Politics* 27, No. 2, 1975, 175–200.

3   *Star Trek: The Next Generation*, "The Best of Both Worlds," season 3, episode 26 and season 4, episode 1.

4   Michael E. O'Hanlon, *The Science of War: Defense Budgeting, Military Technology, Logistics, and Combat Outcomes* (Princeton: Princeton University Press, 2009), 75–77.

5   Ibid., 78.

6   Ibid., 79.

7   *Star Wars: Episode IV—A New Hope.*

8   Ibid.

9   Mackubin Thomas Owens, "Transformation: The Changing Requirements for Victory on the Battlefield," *The Weekly Standard*, Jan 23, 2006, 38.

10 Richard O. Hundley, *Past Revolutions, Future Transformations: What can the history of revolutions in military affairs tell us about transforming the U.S. military* (Santa Monica, CA: RAND), 9.

11 Christopher M. Schnaubelt, "Whither the RMA?" *Parameters*, Autumn 2007, 98.

12 Ibid.

13 Reportedly, tens of thousands self-identify as part of the Jedi religion. See, Tim Donnelly, "Thousands of people have converted to the Jedi faith," *New York Post*, Dec 14, 2015.

14 *Star Wars: Episode VI—Return of the Jedi.*

15 *Star Wars: Episode IV— A New Hope.*

16 *Battlestar Galactica*, "Exodus," season 3, episodes 3 and 4.

17 *Star Trek: The Next Generation*, "The Battle," season 1, episode 9.

18 *Star Trek: Insurrection.*

19 *Star Trek: Deep Space Nine*, "Sacrifice of Angels," season 6, episode 6.

20 Ryan Browne, "Five of the scariest predictions about artificial intelligence," *CNBC.com*, Aug 1, 2018, https://www.cnbc.com/2018/08/01/five-of-the-scariest-predictions-for-ai.html.

21 Ryan Browne, "Elon Musk says global race for A.I. will be the most likely cause of World War III," *CNBC.com*, Sept 4, 2017, https://www.cnbc.com/2017/09/04/elon-musk-says-global-race-for-ai-will-be-most-likely-cause-of-ww3.html.

22 Edward Geist and Andrew J. Lohn, *How might Artificial Intelligence Affect the Risk of Nuclear War?* (Santa Monica, CA: RAND, 2018), 22.

23 William M. Kolb, "*Blade Runner* Film Notes," in *Retrofitting Blade Runner: Issues in Ridley Scott's Blade Runner and Philip K. Dick's Do Androids Dream of Electric Sheep?* 2nd ed., ed. Judith B. Kerman (Madison, WI: University of Wisconsin Press, 1997), 169.

CHAPTER 31

You Can't Hide From the Things You've Done

Francis J. H. Park

———————————▶

Some 150,000 years ago, a group of humans left their home planet of Kobol and settled in a binary star system, establishing twelve planetary colonies. One of those colonies, Caprica, would develop advanced robots for combat and manual labor tasks. Those robots, called Cylons, became widespread throughout the Twelve Colonies, and eventually revolted against their human creators, resulting in a war that lasted twelve years. The leading edge of the defense against the Cylon onslaught was built around huge military capital ships called battlestars, the first one of which was called *Galactica*. Inexplicably, the Cylons suddenly ended hostilities without explanation and left the Twelve Colonies, leading to an armistice that has lasted some four decades. One of the last pieces of Colonial Fleet mail delivered to the Battlestar *Galactica* before the fall of the Twelve Colonies was a copy of *Colonial Forces War College Review*. In it was the transcript of a lecture on institutional strategy delivered by Lieutenant Colonel Rachel "Cassandra" Grales, Assistant Professor of Strategic Studies at the Colonial Forces War College on Caprica. Colonel Grales was known in the Fleet as an iconoclast, and in the interests of offering a full set of perspectives and promoting debate, her lecture was offered for a larger audience within the Fleet.

Good morning, ladies and gentlemen. In today's institutional strategy lecture, I'll cover force structure and some of the strategic choices that occurred to bring the force to its current state. Some of these reasons have been around from before the Cylon War, some more recent.

Before the Cylon War, the twelve colonies lived in an uneasy coexistence. Some colonies achieved comparative advantages in certain areas, such as agriculture on Aerilon, heavy industry on Picon, and technology on Caprica. Sometimes the resulting interdependence created rivalries among different colonies. It also led to a degree of colonial globalization that prevented any one colony from gaining ascendancy. Although all colonies possessed some form of orbital lift, only governments or government-subsidized industries could afford early faster-than-light jump technology. For everyone else, most interplanetary lift occurred through slower sub-light transports between the colonies.

The great expense of interplanetary lift meant that only wealthy colonies like Virgon and Caprica could afford the investments—whether in ships, people, or sustainment forces—necessary to fight at expeditionary distances against other colonies. In some cases, some colonies provided niche capabilities in economic blocs with more wealthy colonies. Less wealthy colonies like Sagittaron or Aerilon could only afford landpower forces as a cost-imposing strategy against interplanetary attack. These landpower forces and their air defense capabilities raised the cost of forcible entry from orbit to levels that kept the peace. What emerged was a balance of power since no one colony could gain ascendancy over enough of the others to act as a hegemon.

Ironically, the change in the political order started with a military tactical improvement. The Graystone U-87 Cyber Combat Unit first saw use in support of the Ha'la'tha insurgency on Tauron. After a platoon of U-87s stopped a violent extremist organization of monotheists from blowing up Atlas Arena in Caprica City, many other colonial militaries fielded U-87s in much broader numbers over the next two years. These first "Cylons" were rapidly integrated into existing infantry units, greatly increasing the firepower and survivability of rifle squads, and their networked operations gave greatly increased situational awareness to commanders at all levels. With every "by your command," the Cylons seemed like a gift from the gods—semi-autonomous enough not to need micromanagement but always staying within the commander's intent—until they rebelled five years later.

What had been a boon turned into a curse. The Cylons turned our networks against us, completely compromising our command-and-control systems. The widespread networking of computers that was so central to holobands and other entertainment technology before the war became a double-edged sword. All of our misplaced belief in the confidentiality, integrity, and availability of our information systems came back to haunt us.[1] Our data-sharing protocols gave the Cylons an easy target. How could we believe the reports coming over our networks if anything we sent could be monitored or, worse still, subverted and used against us? Even small inconsistencies in what previously had been a reliable network could undermine our confidence in our battlespace awareness.[2] The units that had forgotten their analog fundamentals paid a heavy price when their digital systems were suddenly denied.

Many maneuver units equipped with Cylons were virtually annihilated by insider attacks or combat attrition, which Cylons employed for manual labor mirrored with the wholesale slaughter of civilians. Whatever military units that survived had to be reconstituted since most of their leadership was dead almost from the start. Even the schoolhouse took attrition from Cylon insider attacks, but not to the same degree as the line forces. Ironically, the lower-readiness reserve component units that hadn't been fielded Cylons were the first to react as they survived the initial onslaught mostly intact. Regrettably, they took heavy losses because they weren't trained to the same level of readiness as active component forces. Essentially, we had to start from scratch.

Trying to regrow the force in the first few years of the war, the Colonial Forces faced a cruel paradox. It was straightforward enough to induct new officers and other ranks within a year, even into the Fleet where technical skills were at a premium, and there were enough lieutenant colonels and colonels left in the training base and the Ministry of Defense who could be brought back into the line. Some colonels and commanders got a second lease on their careers prior to retirement; some others had their retirements cashed in through retiree recalls, at least the ones who survived the Cylon attacks on the civilian population. After some hasty promotions, those extended service officers and recalled retirees were enough to fill in vacancies left by commanders and flag officers killed in the initial Cylon onslaught. What was missing, and impossible to create rapidly, were the mid-grade officers of senior captains and majors and the mid-grade other ranks of petty officers, staff sergeants, and gunnery sergeants. Taking them from the reserve component wasn't an answer either, because those units were already in the fight. Taking their most valuable leaders in ship departments and Marine companies would be a death sentence for their junior ratings and Marines facing an adaptive Cylon threat.

Since we had a bench to rebuild the ranks at the top and bottom ends, it was the mid-grade officers, petty officers, and sergeants that would have been a regeneration wedge to rapidly expand the Colonial Forces after some undetermined future crisis. With the Cylon War, that future crisis had come, and it required some draconian choices to rebuild the force. Some of that regeneration wedge existed in the schoolhouses and training base. However, some specialized skills like medical staff and special operations were simply impossible to rebuild in a short time. Although we didn't put Cylons in Vipers and Raptors, those crews still saw losses from Cylon-controlled tactical aircraft turned rogue. Although they were very good, Colonial special operations forces took heavy losses during the war. Replacing attrition in special operators eventually took years to regenerate what experience and skills had been lost.[3] Fortunately, there was some direct entry of civilians with special skills, such as engineers and medical personnel, some more voluntary than others depending on the colony. One saving grace was that some of the wealthier colonies had built up their schoolhouses and reserve forces to retain expertise when they were drawing down their active forces. Always seen as a luxury and clinging to existence by the slimmest of margins in peacetime defense budgets, that wedge of middle-grade officers and enlisted personnel allowed the Colonial Forces to hang on and regrow after we got punched in the face.[4]

On a larger scale, Cylon successes against individual colonies at the outset of the war created a level of desperation that resulted in the Articles of Colonization. With that agreement, there were no longer individual colonies fighting in uneasy coalitions with each other. The realities of a war of colonial survival writ large led to an alliance with a unified Colonial Forces establishment and a Colonial Ministry of Defense on Caprica, where the Colonial government established its capital. The Ministry of Defense was the interface to the President of the Twelve Colonies, and the ministry provided policy direction to the force. Command of the Fleet was through the Fleet Headquarters at Picon.

The Colonial Fleet that was built to take the fight to the Cylons was built around battlestars. However, large landpower forces on each colony were first needed to retake planets back from Cylon control, and once their colony was retaken, these forces were then relegated to planetary defense. The Colonial Fleet secured the commons, with a Colonial Marine Corps built for expeditionary operations, to include some special operations reconnaissance and direct-action missions in addition to shipboard defense against Cylon boarders.

At the tactical level, the global defense departments on the colonies that had once integrated Cylons had to relearn how to fight without Cylons in the vanguard. The long duration of the conflict, twelve years from the beginning of the war to the Cimtar Accords, made heavy attrition a fact of life in the ranks. Over time, the Colonial Fleet and the Colonial Marine Corps relearned to fight without cybernetic augmentation or networked systems, but they had to pay a price in blood while they learned. The command philosophy that emerged in the force was one of mission command. Command and control was enabled primarily by voice, or low-bandwidth message traffic at larger distances, to direct a force distributed over large areas against a networked, agile Cylon threat.[5] The low-bandwidth connections that emerged during the war for only carrying voice communications placed a premium on leaders who could quickly visualize the operating environment and act boldly.

The absence of real-time campaign-level situational awareness impeded the ability of the Ministry of Defense and the Fleet Headquarters to fight the force operationally. Fleet planners might come up with good plans, but there was no way for the Fleet to supervise those plans and battlestar group commanders were the ones who actually fought the force. Thus, the nature of the fights during the Cylon War were often independent engagements such as Operation Raptor Talon, where the battlestar Columbia was destroyed. Others were covert missions like the one to the resort planet of Djerba that resulted in the loss of the battlestars Archeron and Osiris. In both of those engagements, for example, those battlestar groups were operating alone but faced unexpected opposition and there were not enough forces to reinforce them in either case.

Those independent or covert actions placed a premium on tactics above all other virtues, whether fleet tactics, fighter tactics, or small unit actions involving Marines. The density of Cylon air defenses and their effects on low-survivability troop assault ships meant a large landing force was going to face heavy attrition. Combat commanders were faced an unenviable choice between putting Vipers and Raptors against the highly risky air defense rollback mission and escorting the landing force itself. Once the Colonial Forces had forced the Cylons off most of the populated colonies, most engagements were fought in and around key locations and chokepoints like Ragnar Station. The limitations of Colonial astrogation capabilities to safely jump beyond the red line away from the Colonies made those key locations hotly contested tactical fights. In the absence of real-time direction from the Fleet Headquarters, the Fleet never really developed the skills in operational art necessary to run a campaign beyond simply pushing the Cylons out of the Twelve Colonies a battlestar group at a time.

Expectations of peace dividends after a war are the norm, and the Cylon War was no exception. The reduction in force boards that convened after the war meant that many promising members of the Colonial Fleet left the rolls after the end of hostilities. Later, some like then-Lieutenant William Adama, who's now commanding Galactica, were able to return under limited calls to active duty. Either way, the decade after the war was a lean time for the Fleet. Most of the pilots' flying hours were reduced to a fraction of wartime levels, and there was little interest in training for large-scale fleet actions. What little training for fighting a campaign was happening here at the War College in the form of tabletop exercises, but not anywhere else and not in any other form.

That peace dividend did not stop the Colonial Forces from resuming science and technology work to modernize its smaller fleet. The first improvement was in astrogation as faster-than-light travel became more common. The second was mechanical automation short of semi-autonomous operation to replace labor formerly done by Cylons. Despite the bitter experience in the war, there was a revival of computer networking, although it stopped short of the legal prohibitions on artificial intelligence research. Rather than crew-intensive vessels like Galactica, the battlestars that entered service in the Fleet after the Cylon War reflected those technological advances, even as memories of the Cylon threat to our networks started to fade. Those of you who have served on the Mercury or Valkyrie classes know how fewer crew members there are on those battlestars because of automation and networking. In the end, most of these innovations only really affected how the force fought at the tactical level. The Fleet still fights much the same way as it did during the Cylon Wars.

I do need to voice my misgivings about the recent fielding of the Command Navigation Program (CNP) to the Fleet. It might be a way for the Fleet Headquarters to direct battlestar groups all over the colonies, as it provides a true common operating picture that includes civilian and military spacecraft, even down to individual Vipers and Raptors. What's not to like? Fleet command could make informed strategic decisions about when and where to commit forces based on their knowledge of the tactical disposition of the fleet. All this hinges on the confidentiality, integrity, and availability of the network. However, I'm seriously not convinced that that our networks will maintain their integrity under combat conditions. I don't care what Integral Systems Engineering or their subcontractors say about how well it's supposed to hold up in the field. They may have confidence in technology or science, but in my own observation, the enemy always gets a vote.[6]

The other reason why I'm so skeptical about the CNP is that it offers a siren song of being able to win big and win fast through coordinated tactical action. Fully fielded, it suggests a belief in decision superiority, through superior intelligence, to target tactical actions against specific objectives, to attain the objectives of military strategy.[7] That seems logical at first, but targeting our way to victory only works great on systems that have low interactive complexity. Anyone who has fought on old ships in gravity wells cluttered by the wreckage of destroyed vessels knows there's interactive complexity and friction that'll eat your lunch if you're not expecting it. You will never be able to predict with any certainty what you're going to hit in that wreckage field or what it will do to you. The absence of the Colonial Marine Corps is also conspicuous—they have to deal with interactive complexity every time they fight planetside or ship-to-ship because they're fighting in complex terrain against an unpredictable enemy, especially if they're other humans. Even against the Cylons, a deterministic approach just doesn't work at the tactical level.[8]

The CNP promises to provide a single framework for analysis and direction of all fleet actions down to individual Vipers and Raptors. My quibble there is that the conduct of tactics isn't the same as operational art, let alone strategy. I have yet to see leaders who have access to tactical direction of the force keep their eye consistently on the political and strategic priorities that drive the rationale for armed conflict in the first place—the allure to get into the fight is too powerful. The irony is that sometimes good tactics is bad strategy because it may not serve political direction.[9] Bottom line: tacticizing strategy is bad business.

The tacticization of strategy also feeds off our own practice of leader development. Over time, the senior leaders in the Colonial Forces followed a "golden path," drawn almost exclusively from pilots—and mostly Viper pilots at that—followed by commanding battlestars prior to senior fleet command. The subordination of the Marine Corps to the Fleet only reinforced this glass ceiling for everyone else. Yes, that even includes Raptor drivers. Leave the golden path and you won't be a Commander of a battlestar, let alone an Admiral commanding a battlestar group.

Yes, I know there's a path to senior rank for those who might want to seek patrons at the Ministry of Defense. We all know who they were—just clocking time in the Fleet long enough to meet minimums for promotion before returning to the Defense Staff. They might have skills in policy and strategy and speechwriting, but I don't really want them flying Vipers on my wing or as a department head on a battlestar.

That scorn hides a different inconvenient trend. If you spend most of your career on the bleeding edge of the Fleet, you never develop a good sense for the strategy that implements Colonial policy. Life is easy when you only have to worry about tactics. Problem is, the dictates of good policy and strategy sometimes requires eating bad tactics. If the policy is bad, it doesn't really matter how good of a Viper jock you are. Our personnel system makes good battlestar commanders. Then it plays the table with them to make its senior leaders. They're great at tactics, but they rarely get developmental experience in the kind of strategy work that drives those battlestar deployments in the first place.

But what happens when you put that together with mostly tactical improvements to the force? If the majority of the senior leaders went from being Viper jocks to fighting fleet engagements from their battlestars, then they can fight tactically, but the only ones who are running campaigns are at Fleet Headquarters and not everyone gets to serve there. Senior officers in the Colonial Fleet who have been on the line to the exclusion of non-tactical assignments might have learned the rhetoric of the operational art that makes the Fleet an instrument of Colonial policy. Whether they actually understand that operational art rhetoric is debatable. Problem is, true understanding requires a clear-eyed appreciation for the competing demands of policy, strategy, and tactics. You won't get that appreciation unless you have time in the Ministry of Defense and Fleet Headquarters on top of battlestar assignments.[10]

Our ability to conduct operational art hinges on our ability to coordinate the actions of battlestar groups distributed over time and space. So long as wireless and DRADIS are limited to the speed of light, we need to make investments in education and training that many in the Forces treat as a tax, not as an investment for the future. Once battlestar groups are committed, we're dependent on those commanders to fight their part of a fleet campaign, which gets risky if we indulge inappropriate focus on tactics at the expense of strategy.

The CNP might make our battlestar groups more agile through better tactical coordination. It also reintroduces a tactical network that may be suicidal against an advanced cybernetic threat like the Cylons. On the other hand, I wonder if the institutional strategists and programmers at the Ministry of Defense had served in the Fleet long enough to inform their thoughts on capability development. They probably never considered the full implications of what that system might mean before they made the CNP a program of record. You need a balance.

Strategic choices matter, whether you make them consciously or not. They may be a function of politics, they may be a function of natural resources, or they may be a function of geography, but they're all there. We still don't have a good explanation why the Cylons quit at the end of the war, but for whatever reason or another, they did, and we got lucky.

Living up to my callsign, I fear that we won't have enough time to get it right should we face another existential threat like the Cylons. If we don't determine the character of a conflict in time, we'll run out of time to adapt before we lose the war.[11] I'd challenge you to think about that, hard, before you go back to your battlestars, Fleet Headquarters, or even the short maglev trip from here to the Ministry of Defense.

It was only a few days after that issue of *Colonial Forces War College Review* arrived in the mail that Commander Adama made his remarks at what was supposed to be the decommissioning ceremony for Galactica:

> …We refuse to accept the responsibility for anything that we've done. Like we did with the Cylons. We decided to play God, create life. When that life turned against us, we comforted ourselves in the knowledge that it really wasn't our fault, not really. You cannot play God then wash your hands of the things that you've created. Sooner or later, the day comes when you can't hide from the things that you've done anymore.

One can only wonder what Colonel Grales would've thought of the Old Man's comments.

Notes

1   *International Standard ISO/IEC 27000:2018(E): Information Technology Security Techniques Information Security Management Systems—Overview and Vocabulary*, E (Geneva: International Organization for Standardization, 2018), 12.

2   The author personally witnessed this phenomenon as a tank platoon leader at Fort Hood, and observed it in the Force XXI Advanced Warfighting Experiment rotation at the Joint Readiness Training Center in Oct 2000. H. R. McMaster, "Crack in the Foundation: Defense Transformation and the Underlying Assumption of Dominant Knowledge in Future War" (Student Issue Paper, Carlisle Barracks, Pa., U.S. Army War College, 2003), 45–46; John C. Johnson, "Viewpoint: Network Technology a Growing Liability," *National Defense*, Aug 20, 2020, https://www.nationaldefensemagazine.org/articles/2020/8/20/network-technology-a-growing-liability.

3   The fourth Special Operations Forces Truth is that "Competent Special Operations Forces cannot be created after emergencies occur." Col. John M. Collins, "U.S. Special Operations: Personal Opinions," *Small Wars Journal*, Dec 13, 2008, https://smallwarsjournal.com/jrnl/art/us-special-operations-personal-opinions.

4   This discussion owes heavily to discussions with now-Colonel J. P. Clark during the author's development of the 2014 *Army Strategic Planning Guidance*. Shanthi Nataraj et al., "Evaluating the Army's Ability to Regenerate: History and Future Options," *Research Report* (Santa Monica, Calif.: RAND, 2017), 77–79.

5   Lt. Col. William "Torn" Tompkins, "Command & Control of ISR in a Contested, Degraded, and Operationally Limited Environment: Ensuring Support to Unit Level Intelligence (Part 1)," *Over the Horizon Journal*, Dec 10, 2018, https://othjournal.com/2018/12/10/command-control-of-isr-in-a-contested-degraded-and-operationally-limited-environment-ensuring-support-to-unit-level-intelligence-part-1-2/; Lt. Col. William "Torn" Tompkins, "Command & Control of ISR in a Contested, Degraded, and Operationally Limited Environment: Ensuring Support to Unit Level Intelligence (Part 2)," *Over the Horizon Journal*, Dec 12, 2018, https://othjournal.com/2018/12/12/command-control-of-isr-in-a-contested-degraded-and-operationally-limited-environment-ensuring-support-to-unit-level-intelligence-part-2/.

6   McMaster, "Crack in the Foundation: Defense Transformation and the Underlying Assumption of Dominant Knowledge in Future War," 37–41.

7   Joint Warfighting Center, *Joint Warfighting Center Pamphlet 1: Pamphlet for Future Joint Operations* (Suffolk, Va.: U.S. Joint Forces Command, 2002), 7–13.

8   Maj. Gen. David A. Fastabend, "EBO and the Classical Elements of Operational Design" (Presentation, U.S. Army Futures Center, U.S. Army Training and Doctrine Command, Jan 31, 2006); Paul Van Riper, "The Foundation of Strategic Thinking," *Infinity Journal* 2, no. 3 (Summer 2012), 4–6.

9   Michael I. Handel, *Masters of War: Classical Strategic Thought*, 3rd ed. (Portland, Ore.: Frank Cass, 2001), 189, 267–73.

10 See commentary on "one-dimensional career paths" in Susan Bryant and Heidi A. Urben, "Reconnecting Athens and Sparta: A Review of OPMS XXI at 20 Years," *The Land Warfare Papers* (Arlington, Va.: Institute of Land Warfare, Association of the United States Army, October 2017), 3–8 and 13.

11 Sir Michael Howard, "Military Science in the Age of Peace," *Royal United Services Institute Journal* 119, no. 1 (Mar 1974), 3–9.

PART VI

THE DARK SIDE

CHAPTER 32

The Mark of Locutus

David Calder

———————▶

Imitating the omnipresence of a Q, we see him. It is imperceptible, but Picard's mask is betrayed by the trembling hand supporting his saucer. Riker's departure from the Ready Room instantly strips away his shield of command. Alone, finally. Picard stares intensely into the depths of the vacuum which engulfs his ship, knowing that somewhere in that great void, the Collective are staring back seductively, willing him to join with them again. Starfleet Medical may have removed the Borg's implants, but the demons the Collective has sewn deep into his soul will haunt Picard for the rest of his natural life. A man we often take as leadership and judgement incarnate is now something utterly broken.[1]

Valuable leadership lessons are not just derived from the examples set by others. Jean-Luc Picard, captain of the USS *Enterprise*, is an archetype for the values underpinning the United Federation of Planets. On numerous occasions, he is plucked from the vastness of humanity as the Federation relies on his skill as a diplomat to mediate among the Alpha Quadrant's great powers. Picard is Q's choice to plead humanity's case for its continued existence. Most notably, Picard is whom the Borg selects to become Locutus: their voice and bridge between the Collective and a soon-to-be-assimilated Earth. Such events point to a Picard who is the best of what it is to be human—a paragon of virtue. Picard, however, is a far more fascinating and complex character, and his apparent irreproachability leaves him open to criticism.

Picard is most certainly not perfect, and the shadow of his struggles and shortcomings haunt him throughout and after his career as a Starfleet officer. Picard's career is pockmarked by his encounters with the Borg, a race of cybernetically enhanced humanoids with a ravenous appetite for colonization and domination. Fans would regard them as his greatest adversary. The Borg's overwhelming power, relentlessness, and how they covet Picard himself peels back his strengths and leaves his weaknesses exposed. What unfolds in the Wolf 237 system and Picard's assimilation into the Borg collective are watershed moments for him. While Picard's record is replete with examples of his courage, ethical fortitude, and poise, much can be drawn from the trauma. Picard becomes his own enemy through his inability to accept the nature of his injuries. Moreover, Starfleet's institutional reaction to his temporary transformation into Locutus nearly causes Picard to turn his back on both his service and crew. As a victim, Picard's long-term battle with his ordeal yields warnings about the toxicity of revenge and how it can utterly corrupt those who lead us if left unchecked.

It is easy to underestimate the sense of terror the Borg invoke. Much of what fans recall about them comes from the *Enterprise*'s triumph over the Collective— bookended in the opening and climactic scenes of *First Contact*. Picard first encounters the Borg in the episode "Q Who?" Rather than victory, he only manages to snatch an early indicator of the Borg's power. Q's effort to force The Federation into first contact with the Borg is intended to send a message: there is no defense against the Borg and Starfleet is powerless to hold back the tide of assimilation. Any comparison of the Borg with The Federation is thus asymmetric in the extreme.

> Q: You can't outrun them. You can't destroy them. If you damage them, the essence of what they are remains—they regenerate and keep coming ... eventually you will weaken—your reserves will be gone ... they are relentless.[2]

With this asymmetry in mind, personal interactions with the Borg leave emotional and mental damage. While assimilation seems to be a relatively painless process, there is a strong suggestion that breaking with the Hive Mind can cause irreparable damage to our emotional fabric. Seven of Nine's struggle to integrate with *Voyager*'s crew is probably the most extensive and well-documented example. Furthermore, the episode "Descent" shows how Borg drones are left directionless and prone to manipulation when their connection to the Collective is severed. After the stranded Third of Five/Hugh is coached to embrace his individuality in "I, Borg," he and his fellow drones quickly fall under the influence of Data's proto-fascist twin, Lore. It takes a further intervention by the *Enterprise* to ensure they are not duped into serving another master with ambitions for the subjugation of humanity.

For Picard, the transformation into Locutus stands out. Not only is he ashamed of his forced betrayal to the Federation, but he is also left bereft of the Borg's apparent omnipotence, collective decision-making, and accumulated experience. Picard's transformation corrodes his resilience and causes him to doubt the very foundations of his leadership and approach to command. Picard's subsequent handling by his superiors also conspires to prevent the recovery of his self-confidence, a quality which is arguably essential for commanding a starship on the fringes of known space.

In the immediate aftermath of the events described in the "Best of Both Worlds," the *Enterprise* has limped to safety but desperately needs repair. A vast Starfleet shipyard envelops its beaten and broken hull, and we can see the focus of the Federation's near-limitless resources marshalled to rebuild its flagship. The priority given to the physical repair of the *Enterprise* is stark. In contrast, it is not clear—beyond some limited rest and recuperation—what plans exist for the crew.

Starfleet seems to throw the weight of its effort behind what it knows it can fix, rather than what it knows to be a more significant challenge: addressing the *Enterprise* captain's mental and emotional scars.

The shell of the *Enterprise* reflects its captain. Before Picard leaves for a respite on Earth, the ship's Counselor, Deanna Troi, is cynical of her captain's attempts to brush off his injuries. When Picard suggests that his wounds are healing, Troi ripostes that this may only be true for "those you can see in the mirror."[3] As Jean-Luc disembarks the *Enterprise*, he is singularly determined to fix himself—handling his recovery more like a mission than a treatment. As we see in the days that follow, Picard is far from fine.[4] His leave of absence seems less about recuperation and more about escape.

In his return to Earth, Picard seems not to be searching for support but conflict. Picard finds this from his capricious and estranged brother, Robért, who resents Jean-Luc for his rejection of a grounded life on Earth and his family's legacy as the vintners of *Chateau Picard*. While his Starfleet career may have given Jean-Luc immense fulfilment, Robért shows this has come at a considerable cost. Jean-Luc is truly alone. Not only has he had to contend with the solitude of command, but apart from professional confidants, the mysteriously empathetic bartender, Guinan, he has had very little emotional support.

The mental wounds inflicted by the Borg cut deep because Picard failed to build and sustain any meaningful life beyond his career. His resilience was paper-thin and easily torn by what was done to him by the Borg. As a foil to Jean-Luc, Robért shows us that sometimes brutal honesty, humility, and self-reflection can be just as crucial as a well-meaning comment and the emotional support of friends and family. In some cases, the mental damage we experience can be of our own making or at least compounded by actions and decisions we have not taken. And it is through the acknowledgement of our mistakes and bad choices that we grow to become better leaders and more resilient in the future.

> ROBERT PICARD: So, Jean-Luc Picard is human after all …. This is going to be with you a long time, Jean-Luc. A long time. And you have to learn to live with that. You have a simple choice now: living with it below the sea with Louis or above the clouds on your *Enterprise*.[5]

One of the most "un-Federation-like" behaviors we witness across Picard's Borg story arc is how Starfleet reacts to his assimilation. On at least two occasions, Picard seems to be almost punished for his experience, rather than seen as someone whose career and mind need just as much rehabilitation as his body. The first example is in the episode "Descent." Picard and the *Enterprise* are placed under the direct command of Admiral Nechayev when the Borg have re-surfaced. Swift action is needed to prevent the Collective from gaining a foothold in Federation space.

On meeting with Picard, the Admiral does not seek to glean a tactical advantage from Picard's experience with the Borg or better understand the nature of the threat she faces. Instead, she is incredulous and chastises Picard for what she sees as his poor judgement for not using Hugh to deliver a destructive subroutine directly into the Hive Mind.[6] Given Picard had himself wrestled with this decision, Nechayev's rebuke does immense harm to any sense of confidence. For Picard, being censured over this decision is not just a denigration of his judgement but a blow to his belief in an ethical foundation, which promotes humanitarian values over the Federation's rush to protect itself at all costs.

In the movie *First Contact*, we also see the stain on Picard's career remains, six years after his assimilation. In the face of an imminent invasion of Earth, Picard and the *Enterprise* are completely side-lined from the main defensive effort. Instead, Starfleet sends the newly commissioned *Enterprise*-E, one of its most capable vessels and flagship, on nugatory duties in the Neutral Zone. When Riker questions Picard on the operational reasoning behind this, Picard is clear that there is only one motivation behind Starfleet's orders: his commanders see him as a liability and potential threat. Of course, the criticality of the situation prevails. Picard breaks with his orders and rushes to the aid of a Fleet decimated by a relentless assault by an undamaged and seemingly unstoppable cube. Picard's impact on the battle is immediate. He rallies the Fleet's stragglers and leads a critical assault using his intimate knowledge of the Borg's weaknesses.

> RIKER: Captain, why are we out here chasing comets?
> PICARD: Let's just say that Starfleet has every confidence in the *Enterprise* and her crew. They're just not sure about her captain. They believe that a man who was once captured and assimilated by the Borg should not be put in a situation where he would face them again. To do so would introduce an unstable element to a critical situation.
> RIKER: That's ridiculous! Your experience of the Borg makes you the perfect man to lead this fight.
> PICARD: Admiral Hayes disagrees.[7]

In both "Descent" and *First Contact*, the institutional reactions to Picard's experience with the Borg are understandable but inexcusable. With hindsight, Starfleet's failure to see the value in Picard's experience is a strategic mistake. His commanders are biased towards seeing the tough and finely balanced decisions Picard had made as ill-judged. Moreover, they had done little to support one of its most successful but damaged captains. Picard's experience was perceived as something damaging and threatening to Starfleet.

When it became clear that Picard's assimilation had allowed his individuality, memories, and knowledge to be subsumed into the Collective, Picard was something that could potentially compromise the whole Federation. All its secrets had been lost and plans exposed. What it failed to grasp was that Picard's assimilation also made him a huge asset. The Borg had equally been compromised. As Picard's intimate knowledge and connection to the Collective turned the tide in the battle for Earth. Fallibility, whether imposed or inherent, is universal.

While Picard is not to blame here, it is beholden on all leaders to not be too quick to judge. Leaders must help coach their talent through the challenging decisions they make and create value from their mistakes. Failing to do so risks transforming mistakes into flaws. Others' experience, whether positive or negative, is always valuable and should never be freely discarded. Too often, the embarrassment, pain, and desire to atone for the negative things we experience in our lives can risk becoming that which moderates our behavior—pushing us towards caution, introspection and, as it did for Picard, revenge.

As we follow Picard's arc from his first meeting with the Borg to his triumph in the events depicted in *First Contact*, there are two occasions where he directly compares himself to other captains. One is historical, and another is fictional. The first is a little clumsy but avoids being tainted with arrogance. On the eve of the battle with the Borg cube in the "Best of Both Worlds," Picard apprehensively paces the desks of the *Enterprise* to ensure she is ready for what would be one of its most demanding clashes. Picard draws a direct parallel to his situation with the Borg and the Battle of Trafalgar when he points out to Guinan that Admiral Nelson had also toured his ship before engaging the French fleet. Picard's inference of a personal parallel with Nelson is excusable given what is known of the Borg's ability to overmatch the *Enterprise* during the ship's previous encounters with the Collective. The second comparison is far more interesting—that of Picard and Herman Melville's Captain Ahab. In *Moby-Dick*, Ahab is portrayed as a singularly obsessed leader, bent on hunting down and destroying the whale who has taken his leg. Both Picard and Ahab share experiences where the physical aspect of their injury pales into insignificance compared to the psychological effects of their encounters. Through his assimilation, the Borg rob Picard of his very self: his individuality and humanity. This pushes him towards vengeance and to abandon level-headedness, which usually defines Picard's style of command.

Revenge is not a healthy way of dealing with insult or injury, but it can be incredibly seductive because of the immediate satisfaction and score-settling it offers. It is a highly subversive act, as the opportunity to retaliate through action can risk overriding our sense of right and wrong. For Picard, his journey of revenge skews his judgement and leads to some of the most shameful episodes in his career. As well as his encounter with Hugh, we see throughout *First Contact* how six years of vengeance has festered inside Picard and causes him to depart from the morally irreproachable officer we often characterize him as. As the Borg begin to take over the *Enterprise*-E, Picard comes face-to-face with a partially assimilated Ensign Lynch and kills him without hesitation. What Picard justifies as a mercy killing illustrates how he has come to see the Borg—inhuman, soulless, and disposable. And while killing a single Borg drone forms part of his revenge, it comes with no satisfaction or reconciliation. Soon after on the holodeck, Picard completely loses all sense of perspective when emptying a full magazine of a Tommy Gun into a drone before being stopped from bludgeoning it in a fit of rage.

> PICARD: In my century, we don't succumb to revenge. We have a more evolved sensibility.
> LILY: Bullshit! I saw the look on your face when you shot those Borg on the holodeck. You were almost enjoying it![8]

The power of revenge also blinds us from being objective and can often become the end-in-itself, rather than just a means of dealing with a problem. Again, in *First Contact*, as Picard comes closer and closer to destroying the Borg by scuttling his ship, he turns on those closest to him. Picard becomes almost hell-bent in one jaw-dropping scene to lead his crew to their deaths by refusing to acknowledge the *Enterprise* as a lost cause. In an act of utter loyalty and followership, Commander Worf directly challenges him and accuses his captain of allowing his personal experience with the Borg to influence his judgement. In normal circumstances, we would expect Picard to reflect on such an intervention positively. Picard instead reaches for a barb of pure spite and returns Worf's loyalty with the most stinging insult possible for a Klingon: calling him a coward. Worf responds tersely, "If you were any other man, I would kill you where you stand."

Picard is only saved from the devastating effects of his revenge-fueled fugue when finally confronted with the reality and consequences of his uncompromising approach to eliminating the Borg. While Picard's willingness to sacrifice himself, his crew, and his ship might be admirable, his rage transforms this into an unnecessarily binary choice. Picard's reaction to Worf is one of a leader having lost all perspective. Blinded by revenge, Picard was unable to see that alternative courses of action lay before him. Without intervention, Picard would have almost certainly been consumed by his desire for revenge, and like Ahab, most likely have lost everything for practically nothing. While he may have defeated the Borg through some Pyrrhic means, he would have destroyed everything he cares most about, including his ideals. Again, as we saw with Robért, Picard responds poorly to direct confrontation, even when it is justified. Instead, it is Lily's ability to pierce Picard's conceit and hold a mirror up to his behavior that allows him to see reason.[9] Only once he realizes the futility of his headlong rush to self-destruction does he pull back from the abyss and reverts to the Nelsonian side of his character, defeating the Borg in Main Engineering.

Although the Borg is one of the most terrifying and seemingly unassailable enemies encountered by Picard in his long and illustrious career, they were ultimately defeated far more easily than Picard's demons. Following his assimilation, Picard was his own enemy in-the-making. The relegation of his welfare and the degradation of any supportive relationships beyond his crew lead us to see Picard as a less perfect leader than we might imagine. Instead, we see someone whose lack of resilience left them vulnerable when his most significant challenges became manifest. We should also heed the warning illustrated by how Starfleet dealt with Picard. By not ascribing any value to Picard's experience at the hands of the Borg, his commanders missed critical opportunities to exploit any form of advantage from his unique insight and knowledge of a superior adversary. While this is an important thing for institutions to reflect on, it also matters from an individual perspective.

Most people experience trauma in their lives, driven by entirely normal events: car accidents, house fires, or burglaries. Equally, we know that such events will affect individuals in different ways. In some cases, the circumstances may not be normal. Soldiers, paramedics, rescue workers, and many other professions often find themselves experiencing the tragedy which exists at the edge of our societies and at the extremes of human experience. Like Starfleet, we can tend to see these things as threatening and damaging to those that experience them. That said, it is also important that we take the benefits of these experiences, learn the valuable lessons hidden within them, and understand how to leverage them positively. Sometimes though, the devastation these events can cause can lead us on the path towards seductively futile reactions, like revenge. Rather than helping people conquer their demons, these courses of action are probably more likely to compound them and are potentially self-destructive. Given the single-mindedness which can accompany these sorts of ruinous behaviors, we must not surround our leaders with those who would reinforce rather than challenge these actions. Like we see with Picard in his quest for revenge, follies only become apparent when the underpinning motivations for them are exposed. This is clearly no easy thing to broach, and it is beholden on all who recognize it and act—and this takes courage, honesty, and timing.

Notes

1 This description of the closing scene of the episode, "Best of Both Worlds," is drawn from the original script to illustrate the challenges facing Picard following his separation from the Borg Collective.

2 *Star Trek: The Next Generation*, season 2, episode 16, "Q Who?," directed by Rob Bowman, aired May 8, 1989, on CBS (Paramount Pictures Corporation, 2020), On Demand Streaming.

3 *Star Trek: The Next Generation*, season 4, episode 2, "Family," directed by Les Landau, aired October 1, 1990, on CBS (Paramount Pictures Corporation, 2020), On Demand Streaming.

4 In his initial reunion with his brother, Robért, Jean-Luc gives a less-than-convincing "Oh, I'm fine" when asked about his treatment by the Borg.

5 *Star Trek: The Next Generation*, "Family."

6 This is acknowledged by Picard as an act of genocide and more akin to how the Borg behave, rather than how the Federation should.

7 Jonathan Frakes, dir., *Star Trek: First Contact* (1996; Los Angeles, CA: Paramount Pictures Corporation, 2020), DVD.

8 Ibid.

9 A co-opted 21st-century Earther transported to the *Enterprise* and later assists with the assault on the Borg infestation which has taken hold of the ship.

CHAPTER 33

From Darth Vader to Dark Helmet

Science Fiction as Premortem

Dan Ward

———————————▶

In a 2014 video, Nobel Laureate Daniel Kahneman suggested that leaders could improve their decision making by using a technique called a "premortem." He described premortems as "a form of imaginary time travel," where you "look back from the future," specifically a future in which things did not turn out well. The heart of this activity involves imagining a scenario in which the team fails to achieve its objectives. It is like doing a postmortem analysis *before* things fall apart, an after-action discussion prior to the action, or a hotwash while things are still cold.[1]

The team's description of a "fictional future full of failure" can then be used to shape our decisions and behaviors in the present. The idea is to learn from failure without actually failing. As someone who does premortems regularly, I can confirm it is a powerful technique that inevitably provides practical insights and genuinely improves our decision-making. I highly recommend giving it a try.

The funny thing is if you're reading this book, you almost certainly have given it a try already, possibly without even knowing it. See, long before Kahneman's colleague Gary Klein coined the term, premortems went by another name: dystopian science fiction.

This particular subgenre of space and technology fiction takes us to futures where things have gone badly. These cautionary tales illustrate the undesirable consequences of taking certain principles or activities to their logical conclusion. The relentless personalized advertising in *Minority Report* comes to mind, as does President Camacho's intellect and personality in *Idiocracy*. Such worlds do not just match Kahneman's description of a premortem as "imaginary time travel," they also help us identify the conditions that lead to these unfortunate situations and make better decisions in the present.

There are many ways to perform a premortem. In a corporate setting, I like to assemble a group of people and invite them to join me in a little science fiction thought experiment. The exercise is to imagine we have traveled two years into the future and discovered the darkest timeline, where our current project or organization has become an epic failure. I ask participants to describe this catastrophic failure in vivid and dystopian terms.

I am careful to explain that the objective is *not* to correctly predict how our project will fail. Instead, the goal is to describe the worst-case scenario. This scenario need not be realistic or likely, although it is a good idea to make sure it has a certain degree of internal consistency. Participants should feel free to introduce chrome-plated droids who are fluent in over six million forms of communication, space wizards in robes waving laser swords, and planet-busting death rays that create explosions so massive *you can hear them in space*. Purists may object but making sure the physics are accurate matters less than making sure everything is terrible.

When done well, the premortem should make everyone feel a bit uncomfortable. The scenario we create should be *extremely* unappealing, like the breathing tubes hanging out of John Travolta's nostrils in the 2000 box office bomb *Battlefield Earth* (which Roger Ebert described as "not merely bad; it's unpleasant in a hostile way").[2] If the exercise does not trigger at least an occasional cringe, it may indicate the participants have either picked a project they do not care about or are insufficiently embracing the dark side.

I vividly recall a premortem session where someone described a failure so complete and catastrophic that "we're not even friends anymore." We all groaned at that pronouncement, and a few reached out to briefly clasp their neighbor's hand in a gesture of consolation and affirmation. That is the kind of premortem input we are looking for, and this is one reason I like to bring a bag of chocolate to share afterward.

While the premortem's story should elicit trepidation, the *process* of telling that story should be playful and uninhibited. Everyone should have fun with it, and participants should feel free to say things they might not mention in a more serious context. One sign of a good premortem is when someone says, "Oh, I don't even want to say this idea out loud." The next thing to come out of their mouth is inevitably brilliant. This kind of openness is precisely the sort of thing we try to encourage. A playful posture simultaneously fosters this level of creativity and mitigates the emotional impact of imagining these disturbing futures. That is why, after overcoming the initial shock of the "we're not even friends anymore" comment mentioned previously, we all applauded it as an excellent, creative, courageous input. We still talk about years later because we remain friends.

Speaking of excellent examples of terribleness, let us focus a premortem lens on the leadership style of one of cinema's most popular and influential villains, Darth Vader. Everything about him—from his black suit and cape to the way he walks and breathes—reinforces a toxic form of leadership that is heavy-handed, controlling, fear-based, dictatorial, and abusive. Vader relies on force choking as a primary motivational technique, summarily executing those who disappoint him. He never hides his disdain for those he considers beneath him, which is pretty much everyone. If we are looking to describe a worst-case leadership scenario, that's a great start.

Of course, Vader's character does not exist in a vacuum.[3] His command presence is a perfect reflection of the Empire itself. We see the same toxic values across everything the Empire touches. The regime's signature weapon, the Death Star, is precisely the type of thing an Evil Empire would create: overwhelming, destructive technology designed to spread fear and intimidation.

The same goes for the stormtroopers, whose structure and techniques show a preference for blunt force over nuance, mass over precision, obedience over thinking, and compliance over creativity. The stormtroopers are the only army the Empire could assemble and the only army someone like Vader could lead. Although *Star Wars* presents a far more detailed worldbuilding effort than premortems require, it is an excellent example of how to expand a singular worst-case idea into a galaxy full of them.

So far, we have described the Evil Empire in terms that are undesirable and unpleasant, but not necessarily a *failure*. So here is the twist: those white-armored thugs under Vader's command may look intimidating, but even the most casual observer must notice they are notoriously bad shots. At least one fan created a video that tallies every shot taken by stormtroopers in *A New Hope* and compares it with the number of direct hits.[4] The final count is 22 hits out of 405 shots, which means in Episode IV, stormtroopers missed the target nearly 95% of the time. Fan theories abound to explain why, but the explanation I find most convincing is this: stormtroopers are lousy shots *because* Vader is a lousy leader.[5]

One can scarcely call Vader's behavior "leadership" at all. He is a bully who violently enforces compliance with his orders and does nothing to inspire excellence or develop the skills of those under him. In premortem terms, we are talking about "a military leader who fails so bad his troops can't even hit their targets." Yikes—pass the chocolate!

Let us take our premortem analysis a little deeper. Consider the fact that the *Star Wars* films never show us a scene where a couple of Stormtroopers are hanging out in their bunk, then one turns to his battle buddy and says, "Hey, want to head down to the blaster range with me and get in some extra practice? I seem to miss a lot of shots lately, and I'd like to get better."

Sure, a scene like that would do nothing to advance the plot, but it would also be wholly inconsistent with what we know about these characters and the galaxy in which they live. The Death Star probably does not even have a training range, no stormtrooper would ever voluntarily decide to go there even if it did. And yes, Vader's command climate has everything to do with that. There may be a million plot holes in this saga, but the stormtroopers' poor marksmanship is not one of them. Their shortcomings are exactly what one would expect under an incompetent leader like Vader.

The only stormtrooper who displays any sign of independent thought is FN-2187, who takes off his helmet, joins the Resistance, and exchanges his numerical designation for an actual name: Finn. The ex-stormtrooper then demonstrates excellent initiative, leadership, and combat skills. The Imperial Army is unlikely to produce many soldiers like Finn—note that his adventure happened *after* Vader's death—and it certainly cannot retain a soldier like Finn. If Finn's story was a part of a premortem, we might say "imagine a leader who is such a failure his best troops join the other side."

Similarly, we cannot imagine anyone under Vader's command suggesting an improvement to unit operations or calling attention to a flaw in a plan. It is hard to imagine anyone under Vader even noticing these things in the first place. His cult of personality prevents his followers from engaging with reality, seeing the weakness beneath his veneer of strength, or doing anything to mitigate his creations' fragility. Instead, they follow his ineffective orders and implement his bad ideas, setting the stage for their dramatic defeat in the final act.

This is not solely Vader's fault. He is as much a product of the Empire as he is a driving figure creating it. His performance reflects the Empire's overall values, which encouraged someone like Vader to embrace his darkest impulses and allowed him to rise to power in the first place, supported by large numbers of subordinates who do his bidding. Without the Emperor's mentorship and his subordinates' cooperation, Vader is just an impotent asshole in distinctive headgear.

One imagines a more enlightened society would not tolerate Vader's ineptitude, much less foster, promote, and reward it. If we look at the Empire through the lens of a premortem, we might say something like "imagine a climate where a self-centered, abusive leader was applauded and venerated as he violated democratic norms, failed to achieve his objectives, and installed himself as a dictator, then tried to recruit his offspring to rule the galaxy with him." I am sure glad such things would never happen in the real world.

The *Star Wars* saga shows many decisions made across the Empire, reflecting and reinforcing Vader's biases and blind spots. For example, when the Rebel Alliance destroys the first Death Star, the Empire decides to build a second one, which also gets destroyed. Perhaps the most realistic thing in the franchise is that none of the Empire's senior leaders questions whether they should build that second Death Star. Nobody offers a better approach or a more creative proposal, because nobody learned from the first failure. Anyone who offers an alternative to Vader's plans does so in their final scene, where their termination is not a euphemism for getting fired. In premortem terms, we can frame this behavior as "a leader so committed to failure that he keeps doing the same thing over and over again, failing each time, never learning a damn thing nor enabling those around him to learn."

It is clear Vader never did a premortem. Not for a moment does he consider the possibility that his proposed course of action might be ineffective, that his decisions might be poor, or that he might ultimately be defeated. His triumphal arrogance makes him fundamentally incapable of this "form of imaginative time travel." By failing to think about the prospect of losing, he sets the stage for his defeat.

Both Death Stars ultimately fail to achieve their objectives due to vulnerabilities that Vader cannot see and which his staff cannot bring to his attention. This closed-off approach has direct consequences for the Imperial Army's effectiveness. Returning to the stormtroopers for a moment, consider the scene where Luke and Han disguise themselves in stolen sets of white armor while infiltrating the Death Star to rescue Leia. As they are about to enter a lift, Luke famously says, "I can't see a thing in this helmet."

Luke was certainly not the first person to discover that stormtrooper helmets impair the wearer's vision. However, he was almost certainly the first to say it out loud. Nothing in the Empire's leadership climate suggests even the slightest bit of openness to that kind of feedback from the troops. Thus, we can draw a direct line from toxic leadership to silence about poor helmet design to missing the target 95% of the time. In premortem terms, we might say, "imagine a leader who fails so completely that the troops never tell him they can't see out their helmets." George Lucas was clearly a master of the premortem.

Some commentators inexplicably praise Vader's leadership and insist his violent treatment of failure should inspire greater accuracy, not less. Their position is he should inspire *more* fear in his followers, push them around and abuse them to a higher degree. This idea that fear and punishment improve performance has no basis in reality. That is not how leadership works. That is never how leadership works.

When troops are too afraid of their commanders to speak up and let the boss know they cannot see out of their helmets, their lousy aim is not merely the commander's fault; it is also the inevitable product of a fear-based culture. If *Star Wars* taught us nothing else, it taught us that fear does not lead to excellence. As Master Yoda said in the most succinct premortem ever recorded, fear is the path to the Dark Side. Apparently, it is pretty dark inside those helmets.

In a broader sense, excellence in any area requires creative initiative—the self-driven desire to persist, go above and beyond, and exceed the minimum requirements. Creative initiative is one thing an authoritarian leader cannot tolerate. Vader can only set a minimum standard for his subordinates and crush those who do not meet it. His approach ensures nobody exceeds it very much or takes a creative risk. The result: stormtroopers cannot aim and Death Stars keep getting blown up.

Real-world leaders of armed forces are notorious for employing leadership like Vader's. While modern military leaders may avoid black armor and capes, some adopt a fear-based approach to commanding and controlling their troops. The United States Army works hard to discourage this, wisely and correctly calling it "counterproductive leadership." Army Doctrine Publication (ADP) 6-22 *Army Leadership and the Profession* provides a detailed description of one particular type of counterproductive leadership that could practically serve as a writer's script notes on Darth Vader himself:

> Abusive behaviors—includes … being abusive, cruel, or degrading others …. Specific examples include, but are not limited to, bullying, berating others for mistakes, creating conflict, ridiculing others because of the authority held, domineering, showing little or no respect to others, insulting or belittling individuals, condescending or talking down to others, or retaliating for perceived slights or disagreements.[6]

ADP 6-22 goes so far as to say that the leadership style formerly known as toxic "undermines the organization's readiness and ability to accomplish the mission" and "decreases task performance." This highlights that abusive leadership is not merely unpleasant or immoral, it is also *ineffective*. It reduces the troop's ability to do their jobs. According to Army doctrine, leaders like Vader do not just make people *feel* like stormtroopers—disposable, replaceable clones with no agency or autonomy. They also make their subordinates *behave* like stormtroopers, operating at low skill levels in virtually every aspect of the mission.

We will conclude this chapter by looking at the best science fiction movie ever made, 1987's brilliant example of cinéma verité: *Spaceballs*. Mel Brooks' magnum opus introduced viewers to the hilariously incompetent villain Dark Helmet,[7] which cranked all of Vader's worst attributes to 11, then added a humorous twist. Like the Sith Lord he is based on, Dark Helmet demonstrates an abusive, controlling leadership style that ultimately undermines his effectiveness. The film does a fantastic job of highlighting the boorish immaturity that is always present in such leaders, but which is generally masked by the trappings of strength in more serious depictions of that archetype (if we can call *Star Wars* serious).

Rick Moranis played the Dark Helmet character for laughs, and like so many of Brooks' movies, he's got us laughing at Nazis (see also *The Producers*). Brooks explained his strategy for fighting Hitler in a 2012 interview with *Salon*: "After all the people that he was responsible for killing and after utterly destroying half the world, I just thought the only weapon I've really got is comedy. If I can make this guy ludicrous, if I can make you laugh at him, then it's a victory of sorts. You can't get on a soapbox with these orators, because they're very good at convincing the masses that they're right. But if you can make them look ridiculous, you can win over the people."[8]

The thing is, Brooks is not inventing artificial character flaws for his fumbling villain. He is illuminating the inevitable ineptness of leaders like Vader. In doing so, he's offering a brilliantly comedic version of a premortem, walking audiences through a worst-case scenario that is simultaneously realistic and hilarious.

And so, in *Spaceballs* we see that Dark Helmet was a comically ineffective leader who could not tell a Mr. Coffee from a Mr. Radar. He threw a childish tantrum when his ship got raspberry jammed by Lone Star. We all cringed when he used the

Schwartz on a trooper's crotch as punishment for violating the chain of command and going "over my helmet" to contact the President directly. Dark Helmet even willfully put his ship and its entire crew at risk by insisting they go to Ludicrous Speed, over the objections of the experts who advised against this course of action. The result? They shot past the hero's ship, and Lord Helmet ended up with a concussion.

Of course, the troops under Dark Helmet had terrible aim, even when using the ship's weaponry. Considering the competence of their leaders, excellence in any dimension was impossible. For example, while in pursuit of Princess Vespa, Dark Helmet directs his crew to fire a warning shot across her ship's nose. When the warning shot gets too close, Helmet shouts, "I said across her nose, not up it!" (cue audience laughter). The incompetence of troops under Dark Helmet's command went well beyond lousy marksmanship. At one point, they captured the main characters' stunt doubles instead of the characters themselves. Once again bringing the premortem lens to bear, we might "imagine a leader who is such a failure his troops capture the enemy's stunt doubles?"

And then there is the scene where Dark Helmet berates the ship's gunner for his terrible aim and discovers that the entire crew are members of the Asshole family. It should come as no surprise that Dark Helmet was surrounded by Assholes. Such leaders always are. Step back, George Lucas. Mel Brooks is the true king of premortems.

Vader may get all the attention, but I contend that Dark Helmet is a better example of a premortem villain because there is never any temptation to join his version of the Dark Side. Nobody praises his strength and effectiveness. Nobody looks up to Dark Helmet as a leader (and not just because he's short). You will not find any commentators suggesting he is someone worth following or that his methods are worth imitating. The flaws and weaknesses of his ridiculously counterproductive leadership are on full display. His failure as a leader is undeniable, and he is even more of a cautionary tale than anything we find in *Star Wars*.

In premortem terms, "Imagine a childish, bullying leader who is so incompetent that everyone laughs at him." This is precisely the sort of insight we hope to get when doing a premortem, and it reinforces the truth that when a leader chooses the Dark Side, they are choosing the path of failure for themselves and their followers.

Spaceballs is a silly movie full of giggle-inducing sight gags and groan-inducing puns. There is nothing wrong with enjoying it as such. But when we look at it through a premortem lens, it becomes something much more. Dark Helmet's story shines a light on the consequences of terrible leadership. He shows us that when people in positions of power are condescending and abusive, they are also childish and pathetic. As we laugh at Dark Helmet, we also discover how ludicrous Darth Vader is and how his path leads to failure. Armed with that insight, we can chart a course to a better result, and we can discover the wisdom of leading with empathy, compassion, and humility.

Notes

1   Daniel Kahneman, "Premortem to Eliminate Thinking Biases," Dec 29, 2014. https://www.youtube.com/watch?v=MzTNMalfyhM.
2   Roger Ebert, review of *Battlefield Earth*, RogerEbert.com, May 12, 2000. https://www.rogerebert.com/reviews/battlefield-earth-2000.
3   Which might explain why those space explosions are so noisy!
4   Talkin' Tuskens, "Stormtrooper Accuracy: Star Wars (A New Hope)," July 6, 2015. https://www.youtube.com/watch?v=EFeJUfHu0GM.
5   There are an equal number of apologists who insist stormtroopers are actually excellent shots and only missed on purpose, but those people are wrong. Disproving their nonsense will be the subject of my next book, *Blaster Marksmanship for Dummies*.
6   Headquarters, Department of the Army, *Army Doctrine Publication 6-22: Army Leadership and The Profession* (Washington, DC: U.S. Government Printing Office, 2019), 8–42.
7   In the interest of historical accuracy, let it be noted that Mel Brooks spelled his villain's name Helmut, but over time the popular spelling has changed to Helmet.
8   Stephen Deusner, "The Only Weapon I've Got Is Comedy," *Salon*, Nov 14, 2012. https://www.salon.com/2012/11/14/mel_brooks_the_only_weapon_ive_got_is_comedy/.

CHAPTER 34

To Live and Die at My Command

A Study in Toxic Leadership

Jonathan Klug

————————————▶

What makes a great story? A great bad guy. A bad guy with a real personality and a rich backstory—one with whom you can relate, but only up to a point. Science fiction has some of the best: Ming the Merciless, Agent Smith, and Thanos. The list goes on and on.

For *Star Wars* fans, that villain is Darth Vader. As a character, Vader makes the original trilogy the masterpiece it is. On the surface, this space opera is about Luke Skywalker and his friends—and it is—but the underlying story makes it work: the redemption of Anakin Skywalker.

For the *Star Trek* franchise, that villain is Khan Noonien Singh. Not only does Captain James T. Kirk's archenemy have superhuman strength and intelligence, but he has a larger-than-life personality. Khan delivers terrific dialogue that is impossible to forget, such as "Ah Kirk, my old friend. Do you know the Klingon proverb that tells us revenge is a dish that is best served cold? It is very cold in space." But there is more to Khan beyond indelible quotes. What is truly intriguing about him as a character is that he is a real man and a genuine leader, albeit a tyrant who becomes increasingly toxic.[1] His is a cautionary tale of leadership gone wrong.

Act I: "Space Seed" and the Tyrannical Leader

Khan is one of *Star Trek*'s earliest villains, appearing in the twenty-second episode titled "Space Seed." Played brilliantly by Ricardo Montalbán, Khan has a mysterious background that Captain Kirk and Commander Spock slowly piece together. The writers provide Khan a believable and compelling backstory for those watching the television series in 1967. From the viewers' perspective, Khan comes from a future in the 1990s and reappears in the 23rd-century setting of *Star Trek*.

The Eugenics Wars, a bloody series of conflicts that ravaged the Earth and killed millions of people, echo the television audience's Cold War-era fear of World War III.

Superhumans known as Augments were the cause of the Eugenics Wars. Scientists create these superhumans to improve the human race through genetic engineering.[2] The Augments, however, are not the hoped-for peaceful saviors of humanity. Instead, they demonstrate that "superior ability breeds superior ambition." Khan and the other Augments become conquerors; Khan himself rules more than a quarter of the planet and millions of people.

A charismatic tyrant, but a tyrant nonetheless, Khan is the last Augment to fall. Rather than be captured by "lesser men," Khan and eighty-four Augment followers leave Earth aboard the SS *Botany Bay*. This ship is an early sleeper ship, which puts passengers into suspended animation for multi-year voyages. Khan hopes to find a world to colonize with his followers.

Nothing was heard from *Botany Bay* until 2267 when USS *Enterprise* discovers her floating in space. Detecting faint life signs, Captain James Kirk forms an away team that includes Dr. Leonard McCoy and Lieutenant Marla McGivers, the ship's historian. After beaming aboard the *Botany Bay*, the away team discovers the sleepers. One of the life units activates, beginning the process to revive Khan. Not designed for such a long period of sleep, the life unit malfunctions, but the team saves Khan. Marla is smitten at first sight of the superman from the past.

Once revived, Khan demonstrates the noble qualities of intelligence, courage, and charisma, in the same mold as John Milton's characterization of Satan in his 1667 epic poem *Paradise Lost*. At their core, both characters' personalities are narcissistic, egoist, and ambitious. Where literary allusions to Satan provide an understanding of Khan's nature, contemporary leadership literature offers deeper insight into Khan's personality and how his personality shapes him as a leader. The Big Five Personality Traits model, also known as the OCEAN model, is useful to appreciate Khan's personality, as it measures openness, conscientiousness, extraversion, agreeableness, and neuroticism.[3]

After his revival from suspended animation, Khan begins to try to understand his surroundings. Khan quickly determines that Kirk and his crew did not yet know who he was, and he starts to formulate a plan to seize the starship. Khan soon becomes an expert at the inner workings of the USS *Enterprise*. His receptivity to new things demonstrates that Khan has a high score in the OCEAN model's openness trait. It allows him to be highly adaptive to any situation, an important and useful aspect for any leader.[4] Like his high openness, Khan has high conscientiousness—he is "confident, well-organized, disciplined, and driven."[5] Khan is a man of unsurpassed ambition. Once freed from his cryogenic sleep, his thoughts turn immediately to a new empire, which he believes is his birthright and destiny.

Khan's personality trait of extraversion is a bit different than openness and conscientiousness. He exudes charm and charisma when he desires, harkening back to Milton's notion of a "Satanic hero," a combination of virtue and villainy. Khan is assertive and full of energy. These attributes make him a great leader, and they infatuate Lieutenant McGivers. When Marla resists Khan's efforts to seduce her and enlist her in his schemes, he abruptly changes to being dismissive, belligerent, and cruel.[6]

Khan is on his guard throughout the "Space Seed," quick to conceal his identity and past. Certainly not humble or gentle, Khan has low agreeableness, the fourth OCEAN personality trait. Khan cares about his fellow Augments and grew to care for Marla McGivers profoundly, as his emotions are genuine when he greets his newly awakened followers and as his relationship with Marla matures. His treatment of his followers, however, could be paternalistic, condescending, and hostile at times.

Perhaps Khan's most significant flaw is his lack of psychological adjustment and emotional stability, the core of the Neuroticism personality trait.[7] The old tyrant is prone to fits of anger and impulsiveness, and he is very vain and self-conscious, obsessed with appearance and reputation. Khan is often anxious, for example, fearing the discovery of his identity. Khan is also subject to depression, as "Space Seed" hinted at and *Ruling in Hell* demonstrates. It is easy to understand why "people high in Neuroticism should be vigilant in monitoring their actions to ensure they do not exhibit behaviors associated with toxic leadership."[8]

In capturing the *Enterprise,* Khan proves to be a formidable opponent for Kirk and company, capturing the entire crew. When Khan attempts to enlist the ship's crew to found a new empire, they refuse. He then tries to bend the crew to his will, threatening to kill Kirk. When they still refuse, Khan becomes incensed. His henchman Joachim strikes Lieutenant Nyota Uhura, and McGivers slips away and sets Kirk free. During the renewed struggle for the starship, Kirk fights Khan in hand-to-hand combat. No match for genetically engineered superhuman strength and stamina, Kirk surprises Khan by using a piece of engineering equipment as a club.

After restoring order to the *Enterprise,* Kirk tries Khan and Marla, dropping all charges. Spock notes that the planet Ceti Alpha V is uninhabited and savage but ready for colonization. Kirk asks if Khan could tame such a world. Still fencing with Kirk, Khan asks if Kirk has read Milton. Kirk, with a hint of a smile, answers, "Yes. I understand." The Captain then gives McGivers a choice between a court martial or accompanying Khan, and she chooses Khan. After Khan and Marla depart, Scotty inquires about Khan's reference to Milton. Kirk responds, "The statement Lucifer made when he fell into the pit: 'It is better to rule in Hell than serve in Heaven.'" Spock remarks, "It would be interesting, Captain, to return to that world in a hundred years and learn what crop had sprung from the seed you planted today."

Act II: *Ruling in Hell* and the Descent to Toxic Leader

Where the 1967 television episode "Space Seed" introduced the character of Khan Noonien Singh, the 1982 movie *Star Trek II: The Wrath of Khan* returned him with a vengeance. What happened during the fifteen years of exile left fans obsessed.

While the film answered some of those questions, the thirst for more remained unquenched. In response, IDW Publishing released the *Star Trek* comic mini-series *Khan: Ruling in Hell* in 2010 and 2011. The name was another allusion to *Paradise Lost* and links with the end of "Space Seed."

Ruling in Hell picks up the story with the *Enterprise* crew and the Augments landing on Ceti Alpha V. As soon as the Augments are on their own, one of the Augments Tamas verbally blasts Kirk, claiming he abandoned them to die. Khan counters with a speech that the planet is all they could have dreamed of and more. Tamas seems pacified, and Joachim supports Khan but seems less than convinced. Khan then lays out a plan to explore their new world. He cautions his people to "remember, this is an untamed, hostile environment. Be wary. Each of you is our most important resource right now." The group manages to secure the colony's future after roughly six months. Then disaster strikes.

Ceti Alpha VI explodes for reasons unknown, shifting Ceti Alpha V's orbit and raining planetary debris on Khan's planet. Indigenous life descends into a death spiral. Tamas blames Khan for their predicament and demands action. Pressure mounts as the planet is dying around his people; however, Khan believes that Kirk and Starfleet would eventually return to save them.

The tension between Tamas and Khan reaches a boiling point. With a group of followers, Tamas hatches a plot to kill Khan. He plans to use a larva of the Ceti Eel, the planet's only surviving indigenous life form. Ceti Eel larvae enter their hosts through the ear canal and wrap themselves around the cerebral cortex, leading to madness and death. Tamas knows these larvae make their victims susceptible to suggestion, and he uses one to control Marla, knowing she is the only person who can assassinate Khan. Afflicted with the larva, Marla moves to stab Khan in the back—only his superhuman speed allows him to block her attempt.

Realizing Marla is infected, Khan and Joachim frantically try to save Khan's wife, but she slowly dies. Khan burns for revenge and confides to Joachim, "they have taken from me the only person that truly mattered." A statement like that to a subordinate will not win any leadership awards.

When the fighting between Khan's faction and Tamas' faction occurs, the two fight *mano-e-mano*, with Khan monologuing between strikes. "You always were slow, Tamas. Are you happy now? [Krak] Is this how you would protect us? [Krak] Where has your false leadership taken your people? Only to the grave. [Krak] You were better than this, Tamas. Theft? Murder? You shame us all." With Tamas stunned, Joachim tells Khan of the defeat of the rest of Tamas' faction. Tamas attempts to stab Khan in the back, but the wily Khan is ready and stabs Tamas with a killing blow. Khan replies, "You were saying, Joachim?" After the defeat of Tamas's rebellion, Khan and the surviving Augments prepare to scrape out an existence while awaiting Kirk's return. Days grow into months and months into years, yet Kirk does not appear. Meanwhile, Khan's thirst for vengeance grows.

Khan's actions provide insight into how leaders can become more toxic. But what is toxic leadership? Military servicemembers use this term frequently, but there is no official definition. Professors George Reed and Craig Bullis describe toxic leadership as "interpersonal behaviors by those in leadership positions that negatively impact followers. They are viewed as detractors from motivation, alignment, and commitment to organizational goals that serve as the hallmark of good leadership."[9] Retired Army General Walter Ulmer offers the definition: "Toxic leaders are individuals whose behavior appears driven by self-centered careerism at the expense of their subordinates and unit, and whose style is characterized by abusive and dictatorial behavior that promotes an unhealthy organizational climate."[10]

Khan focuses on himself first and his followers second, but that balance becomes more skewed. The idea of the "toxic triangle" of destructive leaders, susceptible followers, and conducive environments helps explain how Khan grows more toxic.[11] Marooned on a hostile planet is a conducive environment for toxic leadership, a situation made worse after the apocalypse and treachery. Khan becomes a more destructive leader, and the Augments become more susceptible followers as resources dwindle and the rebellion fails.[12] Toxic leaders thrive where people tolerate, accommodate, and protect them.[13]

Act III: *The Wrath of Khan* and the Blind Leader

The Khan who survives the cataclysm is not the same man or the same leader—he is more angry, more vain, more brutal, less patient, and less warm. Khan still has the same strategic vision for the future, but rage blurs his vision. Professor Jay Conger observed "the success of a leader's strategic vision depends on a realistic assessment of both the opportunities and the constraints in the organization's environment and a sensitivity to constituents' needs."[14] Khan's desire for revenge prevents any realistic assessment, and his toxic leadership prevents any challenge to his calculations. Thus, the Augments—Khan's constituents—are less important than his need to exact revenge on Kirk. Khan is hurtling towards becoming a Pyrrhic Victor, as Conger explains: "in the quest achieve to a vision, a leader may be so driven as to ignore the costly implications of his strategic aims. Ambition and miscalculation of necessary resources can lead to a 'Pyrrhic victory' for the leader."[15]

After nearly two decades of isolation, the crew of the USS *Reliant* give Khan the opportunity for which he had been waiting. Captain Clark Terrell and Commander Pavel Chekov beam down to the surface of what they believe is Ceti Alpha VI, a lifeless planet on which to test the Genesis Device, a secret Federation terraforming technology. Terrell and Chekov do not realize that they are actually on Ceti Alpha V. Khan and the Augments discover and capture the two Starfleet officers. While interrogating them, Khan waxes megalomaniacally, telling them the story of apocalypse, murder, and survival. Arguing with Chekov, Khan soon realizes the two officers did not expect to find him and the Augments. Further verbal interrogation fails, and Khan uses two Ceti Eel larvae to learn what he wants to know, including Project Genesis.

After commandeering *Reliant*, Khan sets a trap for Admiral Kirk and the *Enterprise*, refurbished and manned by a crew of trainees. Khan uses *Reliant* to ambush *Enterprise*. Kirk, Captain Spock, and Spock's Vulcan protegee Lieutenant Junior Grade Saavik use *Enterprise*'s console and a code to order *Reliant*'s console to lower shields. Commander Hikaru Sulu blasts Khan's ship, temporarily crippling *Reliant* and allowing wounded *Enterprise* to flee. Khan leaps to his feet and demands to return fire, but Joachim physically stops Khan, shouting, "We can't fire, sir!" A livid Khan yells back, "Why can't you?!?" Holding back his leader, Joachim retorts, "They've damaged the photon control and the warp drive—we must withdraw!" Khan continues to rage, "No! No!" Looking Khan in the eye, Joachim dares, "Sir, we must! *Enterprise* will wait! She's not going anywhere!" For the moment, Khan relents, as he knows he will have another chance to avenge his wife.

Despite years of Khan's worsening behavior, Joachim can question Khan, but the rest of the Augments blindly follow Khan, an indicator of how deeply toxic Khan has become.[16] At this point, the real-world concept of "kissing up and kicking down" applies. George E. Reed and Richard A. Olsen described this phenomenon as when leaders maintain a positive, can-do attitude while interacting with their bosses, but they revert to practicing toxic leadership when out of their bosses' sight. These toxic leaders appear great to their seniors, as their organizations accomplish desired goals; however, the same leaders turn and abuse their subordinates when the seniors are not there. This behavior destroys morale and results in personnel departing, hollowing out the organization except for the toxic leader and their sycophants.[17] As the leader of his people, Khan does not need to "kiss up." He must protect his ego, needing his followers to continue to view him as their superhuman superior leader. Khan's need for admiration helps curb his worst fits of rage, but he could and did "kick down" at will.

In addition to his people's view of him, Khan needs to defeat Kirk because failing to do so would have damaged his perception of himself as a genetically engineered superior man destined to rule an empire.[18] He must live up to being superior in his eyes and the eyes of his people. As pressure mounts and tragedies accumulate—especially his wife's death—Khan amasses more power over the Augments, becoming more dominant and more toxic. Conger's description of decision-making in an organization with a toxic leader applies:

> In such a case, decision-making becomes distorted, and a more thorough and objective review of possible alternatives to a problem are all but precluded. This is especially true of groups that are very cohesive, highly committed to their success, under pressure, and possessing favorable opinions of themselves—common characteristics of powerful and charismatic leaders.[19]

As *The Wrath of Khan* unfolds, Khan's single-minded focus on revenge grows. It comes to overshadows all other considerations, despite Joachim's efforts.

Khan's final scene is a fitting end for the "Satanic hero." After being bested in the Battle of the Mutara Nebula, the gravely wounded Khan speaks aloud in a conversational tone, "No, Kirk, the game's not over." He begins arming the Genesis Device. Channeling *Moby Dick*, which he read through years of exile, "To the last, I will grapple with thee." He sets the device to detonate, knowing it will destroy both starships and, more importantly, Kirk. Spock detects the buildup, and Kirk orders the *Enterprise* out of danger, but Khan curses, "No! No, you can't get away! From hell's heart, I stab at thee! For hate's sake, I spit my last breath at thee!" Khan dies in the blast of the Genesis Device, believing he has won. However, Spock gives up his life to save the *Enterprise*, which warps out of danger in the nick of time. In actuality, Khan has won a Pyrrhic victory.

Conclusion: Khan the Toxic Leader

Unlike two-dimensional fictional villains, Khan Noonien Singh is a colorful, lifelike villain. He has a detailed backstory and believable motivations that underpin a villain that makes the story more than just another tale of good versus evil. Because of the realism and depth of the character, Khan has much to teach about toxic leadership. An examination of his personality traits in Act I provides insight into the unique nature of the superhuman Khan and how they both enabled and undermined the tyrant. In Act II, the toxic triangle demonstrates how Khan descended deeper into toxic leadership and why the Augments welcomed it. Khan's behavior in Act III shows how strategic vision can become blurred by a strategic leader's personal goals, leading to that leader becoming a "Pyrrhic victor." After being defeated in "Space Seed" and suffering for nearly two decades in *Ruling in Hell*, Khan's personal need for vengeance on Captain Kirk far overshadowed the Augments' needs in *The Wrath of Khan*. In stark contrast with Spock's logic, for Khan, the needs of the one outweighed the needs of the many. *Star Trek*'s character Khan provides an archetype of a powerful and charismatic leader gone wrong.

Notes

1 The chapter author has chosen to focus on three *Star Trek* stories that the late Ricardo Montalbán played Khan: *Star Trek: The Original Series* television episode "Space Seed," the graphic novel collection *Khan: Ruling in Hell*, and the movie *Star Trek II: The Wrath of Khan*. Although there were several books and another movie, *Star Trek: Into Darkness* in which Benedict Cumberbatch delivered a superb performance as Khan, the story arc of Montalbán's Khan is a coherent whole that is a great vehicle to explore toxic leadership.

2 In "Space Seed" the Augments were the product of selective breeding, but *Star Trek* later retconned the Augments' origin to genetic engineering.

3   Stephen J. Gerras, *The Big Five Personality Traits: A Primer for Senior Leaders*, U.S. Army War College faculty manuscript, Dec 2014, 2.

4   Ibid., 3.

5   Ibid., 2–3.

6   Ibid., 4.

7   Ibid.

8   Ibid.

9   George E. Reed and R. Craig Bullis, "The Impact of Destructive Leadership on Senior Military Officers and Civilian Employees," *Armed Forces & Society* 36, no. 1 (Oct 2009), 6.

10   Walter F. Ulmer, "Toxic Leadership: What Are We Talking About?" *Army* 62, no. 6 (June 2012), 48. Ulmer is a Lieutenant General, United States Army, Retired.

11   Ibid., 50.

12   Jay A. Conger, "The Dark Side of Leadership," *Organizational Dynamics* 19, no. 2 (Autumn 1990), 50.

13   Mitchell Kusy and Elizabeth Holloway, *Toxic Workplace: Managing Toxic Personalities and Their Systems of Power* (San Francisco, CA: Jossey-Bass, 2009), 10.

14   Conger, 45.

15   Ibid., 47.

16   Ibid., 50.

17   George E. Reed and Richard A. Olsen, "Toxic Leadership: Part Deux," *Military Review* 90, no. 6 (Nov–Dec 2010), 59.

18   Conger, 50.

19   Ibid.

CHAPTER 35

The Mirror Crack'd

The Dark Side of Leadership

Steven Leonard

What if?

If a single question defines the science fiction genre, it is found within those two simple words. From the vision of Jules Verne to the imagination of Isaac Asimov, science fiction has always been an exploration of the infinite possibilities that surround us. Nowhere is this more evident than in the pursuit of alternate realities, where the question of "what if" often transcends the limits of human imagination. Stephen King launched Jake Epping into a desperate quest through time to thwart the assassination of John F. Kennedy in *11.22.63*. In *Outlander*, Diana Gabaldon maroons World War II combat nurse Claire Randall in 18th-century Scotland. Neil Gaiman's *Coraline* is a children's story with alternate reality implications that will frighten most adults. And, of course, there is Lewis Carroll's *Alice in Wonderland*, in which the title character journeys into a bizarre fantasy world on the other end of a rabbit hole (hence, the euphemism, "don't go down the rabbit hole").

Our fascination with alternate realities has long provided a looking glass through which to explore and better understand ourselves, our world, and our very existence. We all laughed through the misadventures of Marty McFly and Emmett "Doc" Brown in the *Back to the Future* films, yet we saw through their eyes the meaning and value of family and friends. We watched in wonder as dinosaurs once again reigned supreme in *Jurassic Park*, but we were also reminded of the fragility of our own place on Earth. And *The Man in the High Castle* series offered a sobering, somewhat disturbing glimpse into how the effects of our decisions ripple across history, demonstrating how a single moment in time can drastically change our future.

The allure of such alternate realities made television programs like *The Twilight Zone* and *Star Trek* compelling for audiences. Each week, viewers could settle in for a through-provoking examination of "what if" that allowed the episodes to thrive for decades in syndication. What if your only passion in life was to read in solitude, but your glasses broke during a nuclear apocalypse? What if you were the only person who could see the gremlin tearing away at the engine cowling of your plane in the stormy darkness of a night flight? What if you were able to see what you would become if you succumbed to your baser instincts?

On October 6, 1967, *Star Trek* offered audiences that very thing: the episode, "Mirror, Mirror," presented a brief, telling glance into the "mirror universe," where the reflections returned showed humanity in a much different light. In that episode—based on writer Jerome Bixby's 1954 short story, "One Way Street"—Captain James T. Kirk and several senior crew members were returning to the USS *Enterprise* from the planet Halka II when a transporter malfunction during an ion storm left them stranded in a parallel universe. In the alternate reality where they found themselves, the crew of the ISS *Enterprise* was far different than their counterparts aboard the Federation vessel of the same name. In the mirror universe, the Federation was the militant arm of the Terran Empire, a brutal regime set on conquering the known galaxy through whatever means necessary. Within the Empire, assassination was the principal means of advancement and violence in any form was the accepted—and expected—norm to quell resistance.

As Captain Kirk and his crew struggled to grasp the mirror universe's harsh reality, they had to confront their base selves, what the Qur'an defines as "the self which always commands (or compels) to evil.[1] The mirror universe reflects the dark side of human nature, where the hidden self is given free rein; inner demons are released, the beast within runs rampant. Unburdened of the constraints of morals and values, the Starfleet of the mirror universe wreaked havoc on the galaxy, unleashing violence, destruction, and chaos. The mirror universe is Kirk's "what if." What if this was where they would live out the remainder of their lives? How would they survive? Could they survive?

The mirror universe also serves as a powerful metaphor through which to examine how we lead. The late General H. Norman Schwarzkopf, who commanded the international military coalition during the Persian Gulf War, aptly noted, "You learn far more from negative leadership than positive leadership. Because you learn how not to do it." The alternate reality of "Mirror, Mirror" is a directed lens that allowed viewers to see themselves—and their perceptions of leadership—in a much different light, one that is far darker than that to which we are accustomed. And it is through this lens that we can see, understand, and learn about negative leadership.

In their book, *Leadership: Enhancing the Lessons of Experience*, authors Richard Hughes, Robert Ginnett, and Gordon Curphy open a discourse on negative leadership by first proposing a results based definition of effective leadership: "individuals who are effective at engaging followers, building teams, and getting results through others."[2] They then introduce the paradigm of the "dark side of leadership" by segmenting it into three distinct categories: managerial incompetence, managerial derailment, and destructive leadership.[3] Managerial incompetence and managerial derailment address a leader's failure or inability to engage followers, build teams, or obtain results through others. On the other hand, destructive leadership captures the definition of effective leadership, but in ways that are "morally or ethically challenged or that undermine organizational or community success."[4] Destructive leadership—what is typically referred to as *toxic* leadership—is the hallmark of the mirror universe.

When Kirk learns that his mirror counterpart—now aboard the USS *Enterprise*—gained his position by assassinating Captain Christopher Pike, the first commanding officer of the starship, it is a clear indication of the depths of the toxic leadership endemic to the Terran Empire. Successful leaders in the mirror universe are very effective at leveraging fear and violence to achieve results that are not constrained by the same morals and ethics that govern Federation efforts in Kirk's universe. The James Kirk of the Terran Empire is everything the Federation's James Kirk is not: narcissistic, unprincipled, and driven by an insatiable thirst for power and prestige. He is the very definition of a toxic leader.

The dichotomy between the two Kirks raises a fundamental question: What is a toxic leader? In her 1996 book, *Toxic Leaders: When Organizations Go Bad,* Dr. Marcia Whicker, a department chair and professor of Public Administration at Rutgers University, coined the term *toxic leader:* "A toxic leader is a person who has responsibility over a group of people or an organization, and who abuses the leader–follower relationship by leaving the group or organization in a worse-off condition than when s/he first found them."[5] Whicker's work led to a much broader understanding of what constitutes negative leadership, but it still left much for further debate. A 2003 United States Army War College report to the Secretary of the Army provided additional clarity to Whicker's definition: "Destructive leaders are focused on visible short-term mission accomplishment. They provide superiors with impressive, articulate presentations and enthusiastic responses to missions. But they are unconcerned about, or oblivious to, staff or troop morale and/or climate. They are seen by the majority of subordinates as arrogant, self-serving, inflexible, and petty."[6] In June 2012, Retired Lieutenant General Walter Ulmer offered an even more damning definition: "Toxic leaders are individuals whose behavior appears driven by self-centered careerism at the expense of their subordinates and unit, and whose style is characterized by abusive and dictatorial behavior that promotes an unhealthy organizational climate."[7]

When considered broadly, these definitions together portray the toxic leader as someone whose success leaves a significant path of destruction in their wake. In fact, that success is in many ways defined by such destruction. Despite this, toxic leaders tend to attract enthusiastic, sometimes fanatical followings, even after revealing their true nature. Yet, knowing this, many people are drawn to toxic leaders, whether fully aware of, or oblivious to, the chaos that will result. History is replete with such examples. In the past century alone, Adolph Hitler, Joseph Stalin, the cult leaders Jim Jones and David Koresh, and Osama bin Laden have built tremendous followings that stood by them to the bitter end—and in some cases, long after that end.

The allure of toxic leaders has long been a topic of interest within *Star Trek*'s fictional universe, where such leaders and their cults of personality were the focus of several episodes. In the second season episode "Who Mourns for Adonis," the angry and vindictive Greek god, Apollo, holds Kirk and crew captive, as Apollo yearns for followers who will worship him as humans once did. Later that season, in the episode "Patterns of Force," Kirk investigates the disappearance of Starfleet cultural observer John Gill on the planet Ekos, where Gill has violated the Prime Directive and installed a Nazi-like regime.[8] In "Space Seed," the *Enterprise*'s crew contend with the late 20th-century dictator Khan Noonien Singh, who attempts to lead a coup aboard the vessel after being awakened from a cryogenic freeze. Although "Space Seed" spawned two later feature films and Khan remains the most storied of *Star Trek* villains, the "Mirror, Mirror" plot has been a mainstay of every subsequent *Star Trek* series as well as the novelizations of those series.

Since "Mirror, Mirror" first aired, the mirror universe has fascinated fans of the series unlike any other element of the fictional realm of *Star Trek*. The "what if" of a parallel universe—especially one in which raw evil reigns supreme—is irresistible. The cult of personality that surrounded and empowered the James Kirk of the Terran Empire satisfied a deep craving among fans that they did not realize existed. When storytellers portray leaders we view as paragons in a negative light, we are absolutely enthralled. Try as we might, we cannot turn away. In this sense, the attraction of the mirror universe is not exceedingly difficult to understand. It makes perfect sense as, for most of us, the toxic leadership we first saw in "Mirror, Mirror" strikes an all-too-familiar chord.

Jean Lipman-Blumen, writing in *The Allure of Toxic Leaders*, explains the paradox of toxic leadership: "Toxic leaders cast their spell broadly. Most of us claim we abhor them. Yet we frequently follow—or at least tolerate—them."[9] Incredibly confident and charismatic, they draw in their followers so closely that even the most blindingly obvious faults are ignored. Here, leader confidence is critical. Research has long shown that confidence is magnetic; it attracts followers unlike any other leadership characteristic. In group settings, such confidence—especially overconfidence—tends to infer competence. Among toxic leaders, the hubris and overconfidence they exhibit fuel the cult of personality that earns them undeserved status, respect, and admiration among their soon-to-be followers. Even when those followers realize that the overconfidence of a toxic leader is severely misplaced, rarely do they challenge the status.

If confidence is magnetic, then charisma is like a gateway drug. Followers crave the charisma of a toxic leader; when they don't feel the rush that comes with the charisma, emotions, critical reasoning, and survival instincts fail them. In a 2012 *Harvard Business Review* article, author Tomas Chamorro-Premuzic described four dangerous consequences of a toxic leader's charisma: it dilutes judgment, is deeply addictive, disguises psychopathy, and fosters collective narcissism.[10] Charisma is dangerously seductive, and toxic leaders leverage it deftly to surround themselves with impassioned—and fervently devoted—followers.

Charisma alone is not toxic. But toxic leaders wield their charm to manipulate others, clouding their judgment and leaving them increasingly susceptible to control. The HBO mini-series, *The Vow*, focuses on the inner workings of Keith Raniere's NXIVM (pronounced, "Nexium") cult, and illustrates charismatic toxic leadership in detail. Through his charisma, Raniere exerted total control over the cult. Once followers were ensnared by his charm, he distanced himself from them as control measure, ensuring they were responsive to his every desire. Cult members were systemically abused, physically and emotionally. Women recruited into his cult were branded with his initials, forced into sexual "master–slave" relationships, and compelled to survive on as few as 500 calories per day. Yet, even after his arrest and conviction, members of the cult—including women forced into trafficking—remained steadfast in their defense of Raniere.

In the alternate reality, the allure of Kirk's charisma among the crew of the ISS *Enterprise* was difficult to overlook. Like a cult leader, his followers craved his approval—they yearned for it. The addictive nature of charisma fuels a toxic leader. They feed off it like a parasitic creature. Once aboard the USS *Enterprise*, the mirror universe Kirk attempts to seduce Spock with his charm: "Whatever your game is, I'll play it. You want credits, I'll give them to you. You'll be a rich man. A command of your own? I can swing that, too." Spock, ever the rationalist—in either universe—responds as only he can: "Fascinating." Toxic leaders use the addictive nature of charisma as a control mechanism to facilitate compliance among their followers, delivering—or withholding—it as necessary to regulate and control behavior.

While charisma is not always synonymous with psychopathy, it is a favored disguise among toxic leaders. Behind a thin veil of charm lies a profoundly antisocial—and dangerously unstable—personality. The slightest nudge from a questioning follower can send them spiraling out of control. It is no accident that a psychopath's hallmarks—manipulation, corruption, hypocrisy, and narcissism—are common traits of toxic leaders. A true psychopath also lacks a conscience—which makes any appeal to morality that much more unlikely to succeed—and is incapable of empathy. They view followers as objects they can exploit for their gain. An exceptional skill they do possess, however, is mimicry. Like psychopaths, toxic leaders use mimicry to imitate behavioral norms and appear compliant with the values and ethics that underpin an organization.

Despite all of this, the nexus of the toxic leader-follower relationship lies within the bounds of collective narcissism. The shared love of self is where the toxic leader attracts his most loyal, devoted followers. There, raw ambition combines with moral ambiguity in the pursuit of common self-interests. They see the toxic leader as an avenue to their own success, despite being manipulated, mistreated, undermined, and ultimately left to fend for themselves. This phenomenon is apparent aboard the ISS *Enterprise*, where the crew of the starship lurks eagerly in the shadow of their captain's toxic leadership. They view their success as inherently tied to his success; his failure is their failure.

The most devout followers—the inner circle—of a toxic leader are also the first line of defense. The ties that bind them to their leader run deep, and they will stop at nothing to protect their base of power. If the toxic leader falls, the inner circle stand to lose the most. As a result, they will willingly collude, assiduously defend, and feverishly stand by their toxic leader. They also serve as "shepherds" for those who either follow blindly or are unwittingly drawn into the toxic leader's herd. The inner circle maintains discipline and order while providing another layer of security for the toxic leader's power. On the surface, the complexity of the toxic leader-follower relationship can appear confounding; peel away the epidermis, however, and the consequences described by Chamorro-Premuzic are laid bare. This is the reality of the mirror universe, as well as its primary appeal to viewers.

Audiences love a good villain. *Star Trek* offered its fair share, and noteworthy ones such as Khan, the Gorn, Romulans, and Klingons provided fans with lasting memories that endure today in pop culture history. But the mirror universe suggested something truly remarkable: what if the show's principal protagonist was also its antagonist? The result was a stroke of television genius, an unforgettable twist on the classic tale of villainy that proved to be one of the series' most memorable and influential episodes. Devoted fans of the series remember the episode for its creative snippets of dialog (this is the first time Doctor McCoy uses the phrase, "I'm a doctor, not a …"), the personal "agonizer" used to punish crew members, and, of course, Spock's beard.

But "Mirror, Mirror" also provided audiences with a glimpse into a particularly dark looking glass, a parallel universe that reflected humanity at its worst. Through that cracked and distorted mirror, viewers could explore themselves in ways that transcended the confines of the small screen. The "what if" of the mirror universe allowed them to see their favorite characters—and themselves—through the lens of toxic leadership. What if you were to strip away the veneer of morality that governs Starfleet operations under the United Federation of Planets? What remains? The higher good that exists in our protagonists' hearts or the raw evil of the Terran Empire? Those questions have captivated fans of the series through numerous spin-offs, novels, and comics.

Once back in his own universe and seated in the command chair on the bridge of the USS *Enterprise*, Kirk asks the question on the mind of every viewer during the episode: "What I don't understand is how were you able to identify our counterparts so quickly?" Spock replies, "It was far easier for you as civilized men to behave like barbarians, than it was for them as barbarians to behave like civilized men." Then, for emphasis he adds, "May I point out that I had an opportunity to observe your counterparts here quite closely. They were brutal, savage, unprincipled, uncivilized, treacherous. In every way, splendid examples of homo sapiens, the very flower of humanity. I found them quite refreshing."

Indeed. *What if?*

Notes

1   The Qur'an 12:53 (Translated by M. A. S. Abdel Haleem).
2   Richard Hughes, Robert Ginnett, and Gordon Curphy, *Leadership, Enhancing the Lessons of Experience* (New York: McGraw Hill, 2019), 636.
3   Ibid., 636–639.
4   Ibid., 636.
5   Marcia L. Whicker, *Toxic Leaders: When Organizations Go Bad* (New York: Doubleday, 1996), 11.
6   Craig Bullis and George Reed, "Assessing Leaders to Establish and Maintain Positive Command Climate," A Report to the Secretary of the Army (Feb 2003), 1.
7   Walter Ulmer, "Toxic Leadership: What Are We Talking About?" *Army Magazine* (June 2012), 47.
8   The Prime Directive, also known as Starfleet General Order 1, is the guiding principle of the United Federation of Planets. The Prime Directive prohibits members from interfering with the internal and natural development of alien civilizations, particularly those below a certain threshold of technological development. In the mirror universe, the Prime Orders of the Empire serves as the guiding principle for the Terran Empire.
9   Jean Lipman-Blumen, *The Allure of Toxic Leaders: Why We Follow Destructive Bosses and Corrupt Politicians—and How We Can Survive Them* (New York: Oxford University Press, 2005), ix.
10 Tomas Chamorro-Premuzic, "The Dark Side of Charisma," *Harvard Business Review* (Nov 16, 2012).

Contributors

Jo Brick is a legal officer in the Royal Australian Air Force. She holds a Master of Laws, and a Master of Military and Defence Studies (Advanced) from the Australian National University. A graduate of the Australian Command and Staff College, her primary interests are strategy and civil-military relations, the ethical aspects of the laws of war, and command decision making. Jo is a member of the Military Writers Guild, and you can follow her on Twitter at @clausewitzrocks.

Max Brooks is an author, public speaker, senior fellow at the Modern War Institute at West Point, and senior resident fellow at the Atlantic Council's Art of Future Warfare Project. He is *The New York Times* bestselling author of *World War Z* (Three Rivers Press, 2006), *The Harlem Hellfighters* (Broadway Books, 2014), and *Devolution* (Del Rey, 2020).

Thomas Bruscino, PhD, is Associate Professor of History in the Department of Military Strategy, Planning, and Operations at the United States Army War College. He holds a PhD in military history from Ohio University and has been a historian at the U.S. Army Center of Military History in Washington, DC and the U.S. Army Combat Studies Institute at Fort Leavenworth, and a professor at the U.S. Army School of Advanced Military Studies. He is the author of *A Nation Forged in War: How World War II Taught Americans to Get Along* (University of Tennessee Press, 2010), and *Out of Bounds: Transnational Sanctuary in Irregular Warfare* (CSI Press, 2006), and numerous book chapters and articles.

David Calder is a British Army officer and Royal Engineer. A self-described "proud and unashamed science-fiction geek," he holds a Masters-by-Research, focusing his writing on examining the critical utility of science fiction in a military context. A prolific blogger, he is widely published on both sides of the Atlantic. He supports the UK Defence Futures Community of Interest, who experiment with creative methods for improving policy and decision making. As an academic, he is deeply interested in Chinese science fiction and has explored how insight from this tradition might offer a cognitive advantage.

M. L. Cavanaugh, PhD, is a United States Army officer and strategist with global experience in assignments ranging from Iraq to the Pentagon and South Korea to

New Zealand. He is the co-founder of and Senior Fellow with the Modern War Institute at West Point, a Professor of Practice with the Arizona State University School of Politics and Global Studies and has been the youngest recipient of the Army Strategist Association's professional award, the Order of Saint Gabriel the Archangel (2015). His writing has been featured in *The New York Times*, the *Washington Post*, the *Wall Street Journal*, the *Los Angeles Times, USA Today*, the *Chicago Tribune*, and at ForeignPolicy.com.

Timothy Choi is a PhD candidate at the University of Calgary, where his dissertation, entitled "Maritime Strategies of the North: The Seapower of Smaller Navies in an Era of Broadened Security," assesses how the 1982 UN Convention on the Law of the Sea affected the development of Danish, Norwegian, and Canadian maritime forces. He was a Smith Richardson Predoctoral Fellow at Yale University›s International Security Studies, and his work has appeared in the *Journal of Military and Strategic Studies, Ocean Development and International Law*, and *Grey and White Hulls: An International Analysis of the Navy-Coastguard Nexus*, edited by Koh and Bowers. He also serves on the editorial board of the *Canadian Naval Review*.

Kelsey Cipolla is a writer and editor who has covered topics ranging from food and fashion to nonprofits and pop culture. She is currently the communications coordinator for the University of Kansas School of Business and a writer for *In Kansas City Magazine*.

August Cole is an author exploring the future of conflict through fiction and other forms of "FICINT" storytelling. His talks, short stories, and workshops have taken him from speaking at the Nobel Institute in Oslo to presenting at SXSW Interactive to tackling the "Dirty Name" obstacle at Fort Benning. With Peter W. Singer, he is the co-author of the best-seller *Ghost Fleet: A Novel of the Next World War* (Houghton Mifflin Harcourt, 2015) and *Burn In: A Novel of the Real Robotic Revolution* (Houghton Mifflin Harcourt, 2020). He is a non-resident fellow at the Brute Krulak Center for Innovation and Creativity and Marine Corps University and a non-resident senior fellow at the Scowcroft Center on Security and Strategy at the Atlantic Council.

Liam Collins, PhD, is a retired United States Army Officer, having spent 27 years in uniform, much of it in Special Operations Forces. A former director of West Point's Combating Terrorism Center, he is the founding director of the Modern War Institute at West Point. A contributing author for both *Strategy Strikes Back: How Star Wars Explains Modern Military Conflict* (Potomac, 2018), and *Winning Westeros: How Game of Thrones Explains Modern Military Conflict* (Potomac, 2019), he holds a PhD from Princeton University and is a lifelong science-fiction fan.

Mick Cook is an Australian writer, digital content producer, and war veteran. Mick writes and produces digital content on war, warfare, and professional development of military personnel. He is passionate about strategic communications and enabling discourse on public issues. Mick has held positions at the University of New South Wales, the Modern War Institute at West Point, and University of Canberra. Mick spent 18 years as regular officer in the Australian Defence Force before transferring to reserve service.

Clara Engle got her start in science fiction back in middle school when her teacher assigned her to read the Foundation Trilogy. From then she was hooked. Clara received her MA in International Relations from the University of Chicago and her bachelor's degree in Asian Studies and Political Science from Pomona College. Her research interests range from the role of protests in authoritarian states to the use of media in shaping narratives. Currently, Clara lives outside of Austin, Texas and works for the Department of Commerce.

Heather S. Gregg, PhD, is a professor in the Department of National Security and Strategy at the U.S. Army War College. Prior to joining DNSS, she was an associate professor at the Naval Postgraduate School in Monterey, California, and an associate political scientist at the RAND Corporation. She is the author of *Religious Terrorism* (Cambridge University Press, 2020); *Building the Nation: Missed Opportunities in Iraq and Afghanistan* (University of Nebraska Press, 2018); *The Path to Salvation: Religious Violence from the Crusades to Jihad* (University of Nebraska Press, 2014); and co-editor of *The Three Circles of War: Understanding the Dynamics of Modern War in Iraq* (Potomac Press, 2010).

James Groves is an Artillery Officer in the Australian Army. He holds a Bachelor of Arts from the University of New South Wales, a Master of Military and Defence Studies from the Australian National University and is a graduate of the Australian Command and Staff College. His love of ancient history and science fiction frame his fascination with military and social matters. James is a founding member of the Defence Entrepreneur's Forum Australia; he continues to encourage networking and innovation in his role as the Canberra-based coordinator of the Australian Drink and Think network.

Theresa Hitchens is a former editor of *Defense News* and currently practicing her first career love, journalism, as the Air & Space Reporter for the online news magazine, *Breaking Defense*. She spent the two decades prior practicing punditry: working as a researcher, writer and opinion-leader on space and cyber security, multilateral governance, arms control and international security issues—including six years in Geneva, Switzerland as director of the United Nations Institute for Disarmament Research (UNIDIR). She's a self-described sci-fi geek, a voracious reader, an enthusiastic cook, a dabbler in poetry and the proud mom of a wonderful young man by the name of Nicholas.

Erica Iverson is a United States Army Strategist with a diverse range of strategic career assignments spanning the globe in Asia, Europe and the Middle East. A South Dakota native, she received a master's degree in professional studies from George Washington University and BA in English from Creighton University. She is currently serving as the Chief of Strategy and Innovation for the Army Enterprise Marketing Organization in Chicago.

Rebecca Jensen, PhD, is an assistant professor at the Canadian Forces College. She studies warfighting, particularly operational art and planning, coalition warfare, doctrine, and military change. Her dissertation examined improvement in operational art in western Iraq between the 2003 invasion and the Surge. While completing her dissertation, she was a Fulbright Visiting Scholar at the Johns Hopkins University's School for Advanced International Studies, a Pre-Doctoral Fellow at the George Washington University's Elliot School, and a Dissertation Fellow at the United States Marine Corps University. She is currently a non-resident fellow at the Modern War Institute at West Point and on the editorial board of the *Journal of Advanced Military Studies* at Marine Corps University.

Elsa B. Kania is an Adjunct Senior Fellow with the Technology and National Security Program at the Center for a New American Security, a Non-Resident Fellow in Indo-Pacific Security with the Institute for the Study of War and is a Non-Resident Fellow with the Australian Strategic Policy Institute's International Cyber Policy Centre. Her research focuses on Chinese military strategy, military innovation, and emerging technologies. Her book, *Fighting to Innovate*, should be forthcoming with the Naval Institute Press in 2021. A PhD candidate in Harvard University's Department of Government, her writings have appeared in *Foreign Affairs*, *Foreign Policy*, Lawfare, Politico, Defense One, and others.

Jonathan Klug is a U.S. Army Strategist serving as an Assistant Professor in the Department of Strategy, Planning, and Operations at the U.S. Army War College. Commissioned as an armor officer, he served in Haiti, Bosnia, South Korea, Egypt, and Iraq. His strategy assignments included writing U.S. Army, U.S. Joint, and NATO Joint counterinsurgency doctrine; teaching at the U.S. Air Force Academy and U.S. Naval Academy; serving as the V Corps Deputy Plans and Strategy Officer; and strategic planning in NATO Training Mission-Afghanistan, International Security Assistance Force Joint Command, and Operation Resolute Support Headquarters. Jon holds degrees from the United States Military Academy, Louisiana State University, and United States Army School of Advanced Military Studies. He is a PhD candidate in Military and Naval History at the University of New Brunswick. Jon would like to thank the organizers of NavyCon for their support of this project.

Margarita Konaev, PhD, is a Research Fellow at Georgetown's Center for Security and Emerging Technology (CSET), specializing in military applications of AI, Russian military innovation, and urban warfare. Previously, she was a Non-Resident Fellow with the Modern War Institute at West Point, a post-doctoral fellow at the Fletcher School of Law and Diplomacy and a post-doctoral fellow at the University of Pennsylvania's Perry World House. Margarita's research on international security, armed conflict, non-state actors and urban warfare in the Middle East, Russia and Eurasia has been published by the *Journal of Strategic Studies*, the *Journal of Global Security Studies*, *Conflict Management and Peace Science*, the *French Institute of International Relations*, the *Bulletin of the Atomic Scientists*, Lawfare, Defense One, War on the Rocks, Modern War Institute, Foreign Policy Research Institute and a range of other outlets.

Kelly Lelito is a United States Army Reserve Strategist and an Assistant Professor in the Distance Education Department at the United States Army War College. She served nearly two decades in various positions in the Pentagon on the Army Staff and with the Office of the Secretary of Defense. In her civilian career, she was a nurse certified in both Critical Care and Midwifery. She holds a Master of Science in Midwifery from the State University of New York at Stony Brook; a Master of Science in Organizational Leadership from Norwich University; a Master of Strategic Studies from the United States Army War College; and is currently pursuing her PhD in American Studies at Penn State University.

Steven Leonard is an award-winning faculty member at the University of Kansas, where he chairs graduate programs in Organizational Leadership and Supply Chain Management. A former senior military strategist and the creative force behind the defense microblog, *Doctrine Man!!*, he is a career writer and speaker with a passion for developing and mentoring the next generation of thought leaders. He is a senior fellow at the Modern War Institute at West Point; the co-founder of the national security blog, Divergent Options; co-founder and board member of the Military Writers Guild; and a member of the editorial review board of the Arthur D. Simons Center's *Interagency Journal*. He is the author, co-author, or editor of five books, numerous professional articles, countless blog posts, and is a prolific military cartoonist. Steven would like to thank the organizers of NavyCon for their support of this project.

Kathleen J. McInnis, PhD, has worked in the Pentagon, the UK Parliament, and in think tanks on both sides of the Atlantic. Having earned her PhD in War Studies at King's College London, she currently analyzes international security and defense issues for the United States Congress at the Congressional Research Service. The author of over fifty publications on international security matters, Kathleen has commented on international affairs on outlets including CNN, Sky News, BBC, Al Jazeera English, and Voice of America. She is also the author of two books: a novel, *The Heart of War: Misadventures in the Pentagon* (Post Hill Press, 2018), and *How and Why States Defect from Contemporary Military Coalitions* (Palgrave, 2019).

Will Meddings is a British Army officer and infantry battalion commander. A veteran of several operational deployments to Iraq and Afghanistan, in 2021 he commanded the UK's Long Range Reconnaissance Task Group in Mali. He is one of the co-founders, and former director, of the British Army's Centre for Army Leadership at Sandhurst and is the founder and editor of *The Army Leader*. He is a graduate of King's College London, Oxford, and Cranfield universities, and a member of the Military Writers Guild. He researches and writes on subjects related to leadership, management, and military operations, and has been published in journals and blogs on both side of the Atlantic.

Jon Niccum is an award-winning journalist, author and screenwriter. He is a longtime entertainment writer and critic for the Kansas City Star. He is the author of *The Worst Gig: From Psycho Fans to Stage Riots, Famous Musicians Tell All* (Sourcebooks, 2013). Additionally, he has written and produced numerous independent features and documentaries, including "Big Fur," "The Sublime and Beautiful," "Jayhawkers" and "Rhino."

Francis J. H. Park, PhD, is a U.S. Army strategist serving as a historian in the Joint History Office, Office of the Director of the Joint Staff. Commissioned as an armor officer, he has served in operational strategy and policy assignments at division, corps, and joint task force levels, to include service in Operations *Iraqi Freedom*, *Enduring Freedom*, and *Inherent Resolve*. As an institutional strategist, he oversaw a major overhaul to the Joint Strategic Planning System and three revisions to the Unified Command Plan. He is the principal author of the 2014 Army Strategic Planning Guidance, the 2018 National Military Strategy, and Joint Doctrine Note 2-19, *Strategy*. A graduate of Johns Hopkins University, St. Mary's University of San Antonio, Texas, and the United States Army School of Advanced Military Studies, he holds a PhD in history from the University of Kansas.

Kera Rolsen is a United States Air Force officer, strategist, and B-52 aviator. She has a broad range of experience from the tactical to strategic levels of planning across multiple regions of the world. She holds graduate degrees in Intelligence, Military Operational Art and Science, and Military Strategy. Her professional writing has been featured on the *Over the Horizon* journal, Angry Staff Officer blog, and *Business Insider*. She is also a fiction novelist under a pen name that is possibly the worst kept secret in the Department of Defense.

Major General Mick Ryan is an Australian Army officer. A combat engineer officer, he has commanded tactical units at the troop, squadron, regiment, task force and brigade levels. He is a veteran of East Timor, Iraq and Afghanistan, and served on the Pakistan–Afghanistan Coordination Cell on the US Joint Staff. A distinguished graduate of Johns Hopkins University and the USMC Staff College, and graduate of the USMC School of Advanced Warfare, he is an enthusiastic writer, reader and a passionate advocate of professional education and lifelong learning.

Julie Still is on the faculty at the Paul Robeson Library on the Camden campus of Rutgers University, holding a rank above tenure (similar to full professor). As an active scholar, she has written three books, edited three more, and co-edited another. One of those books is the proceedings volume of a conference she co-organized, titled *Buffy to Batgirl: Essays on Women and Gender in Science Fiction and Fantasy*. Among her many journal articles are a comparison between the Fair Witnesses in Robert Heinlein's *Stranger in a Strange Land* and librarians, and an exploration of Fantomette, the first scholarly English language article on the French literary character. Still has an BA in History and an MA in Library Science from the University of Missouri, an MA in History from the University of Richmond, and is currently completing coursework for a doctorate in American Studies from Penn State University.

Dan Ward is an engineer and innovation catalyst at the MITRE Corporation. He previously served for more than 20 years as an officer in the United States Air Force, where he specialized in leading small, high-speed, low-cost technology development programs. Dan is the author of three books: *LIFT: Innovation Lessons from Flying Machines That Almost Worked and The People Who Nearly Flew Them* (2019), *The Simplicity Cycle: A Field Guide to Making Things Better Without Making Them Worse* (Harper, 2015), and *F.I.R.E.: How Fast, Inexpensive, Restrained, and Elegant Methods Ignite Innovation* (Harper, 2014). He is also a contributing author for *Strategy Strikes Back: How Star Wars Explains Modern Military Conflict* (Potomac, 2018). He holds a bachelor's degree in electrical engineering, a master's degree in engineering management and a master's degree in systems engineering.

Jessica Ward is an Australian Army Officer in the Royal Australian Electrical and Mechanical Engineers. Jess has over a decade of experience both domestically and on operations and is currently posted as an instructor at the Royal Military College Duntroon. Jess is an avid military reader and writer, having been published in *Winning Westeros: How Game of Thrones Explains Modern Military Conflict* as well as being the curator of military book reviews on the website Grounded Curiosity.

Janeen Webb, PhD, is a multiple award-winning author, editor, critic and academic who has written or edited a dozen books and over a hundred essays and stories. She is a recipient of the World Fantasy Award, the Peter MacNamara Science Fiction

Achievement Award, the Aurealis Award and four Ditmar Awards. Her most recent book is *The Dragon's Child* (PS Publishing, 2018); the sequel, *The Gold-Jade Dragon*, was released in December 2020. She is currently co-writing an alternate history series, *The City of the Sun*, with Andrew Enstice; the first book, *The Five Star Republic*, is due for release from IFWG Publications in 2021. Janeen has taught at various universities, is internationally recognized for her critical work in speculative fiction and has contributed to most of the standard reference texts in the field. She holds a PhD in literature from the University of Newcastle.

Craig Whiteside is an associate professor of national security affairs at the United States Naval War College resident program at the Naval Postgraduate School, Monterey, California. He is a graduate of West Point and earned a PhD in Political Science from Washington State University. He served in Iraq as a paratroop officer during the Surge and recently co-authored *The ISIS Reader: Milestone Texts of the Islamic State Movement* (Hurst Publishers / Oxford University Press, 2020).

Steven Whiteside is a graduate of the United States Military Academy and former Army officer with service in the United States Army's 82nd Airborne Division and XVIII Airborne Corps. An Iraq war veteran, he is currently the President of Mangan Software Solutions in Houston, Texas.

Jacqueline E. Whitt, PhD is an Associate Professor of Strategy at the United States Army War College and currently serving as a senior advisor at the United States Department of State. In addition to teaching courses on the Theory of War and Strategy and National Security Policy she also teaches electives on war and social change, diversity in the military, and Great Books for Senior Leaders. She is the Editor in Chief of WAR ROOM, the official online journal of the U.S. Army War College, which publishes essays as well as a podcast, A Better Peace. Her first book, *Bringing God to Men* (University of North Carolina Press, 2014) won the 2016 Richard W. Leopold prize for the best work on foreign policy, military affairs, historical activities of the federal government written by a federal employee. She is a lead author and editor for a textbook, *Model UN in a Box,* designed for teaching a simulations-based class on the United Nations.

Index